GHOSTS FOR CHRISTMAS

GHOSTS FOR CHRISTMAS

EDITED BY RICHARD DALBY

Castle Books

Published by Castle Books,
a division of Book Sales, Inc.
110 Enterprise Avenue
Secaucus, NJ 07094

Manufactured in the United States of America
ISBN 1-55521-805-9

CONTENTS

FOREWORD

Ghost stories have been associated with Christmas for hundreds of years. The winter prospect of long dark nights, howling winds, low-lying mist and snowed-up roads all contributed to the appropriate setting for the recital of supernatural tales around the Christmas fireside. In the days before television, when people were far more dependent upon their own resources and imagination to keep themselves amused, it was only natural that storytelling should be a quintessential part of Christmas. According to Dickens: 'There is probably a smell of roasted chestnuts and other good comfortable things all the time, for we are telling Winter Stores—Ghost Stories, or more shame for us—round the Christmas fire . . .'

It was Charles Dickens, just 150 years ago, who ensured that Christmas would be the only holiday season specifically associated with a fictional genre. He began with a segment of *The Pickwick Papers*, 'The Story of the Goblins who Stole a Sexton' (told by Pickwick's friend Mr. Wardle of Dingley Dell), a prototype of the later full-length story *A Christmas Carol* with the immortal and repentant Scrooge based on the sexton Gabriel Grub.

The immensely popular Christmas Numbers of *Household Words* and *All the Year Round*, both edited by Dickens, really popularized 'Ghosts at Christmas' as an annual event in the minds of the reading public.

Over half a century later M.R. James, the greatest practitioner of the English ghost story, composed his superb Christmas productions annually, read aloud to a select band of devotees, little realising that his hair-raising tales would pass into literary folklore, and kept permanently in print.

Comparatively few ghost stories by M.R. James were actually set in the Christmas season (the best example, 'The Story of a Disappearance and an Appearance', is included in this volume); and modern writers have generally shied away from the more old-fashioned and traditional setting.

Several of the stories in the present anthology were originally published in magazine Christmas Numbers of the late nineteenth and early twentieth century. Some have become major classics in the genre, whereas others have been unjustly forgotten like Algernon Blackwood's 'The Kit-Bag' which is reprinted here for the first time in eighty years. Great names like Barrie, Stevenson, Le Fanu, and Priestley, rub shoulders with less familiar (though once popular) authors including Mrs. B.M. Croker, Bernard Capes, and Mrs. Alfred Baldwin—the mother of prime minister Stanley Baldwin.

A selection of more recent tales are also included to demonstrate that this particular genre is far from 'antiquated' and continues to thrive.

Jerome K. Jerome's tongue-in-cheek essay, 'Our Ghost Party', written nearly a hundred years ago, serves as a witty taster to the delights that follow.

R.D.

GHOSTS FOR CHRISTMAS

OUR GHOST PARTY

by Jerome K. Jerome

This witty essay on Christmas Ghosts served as
Jerome's introduction to his collection of humorous
tales *Told After Supper* (1891), written shortly after
his classic work *Three Men In A Boat*.

I t was Christmas Eve.

I begin this way, because it is the proper, orthodox, respectable way to begin, and I have been brought up in a proper, orthodox, respectable way, and taught to always do the proper, orthodox, respectable thing; and the habit clings to me.

Of course, as a mere matter of information it is quite unnecessary to mention the date at all. The experienced reader knows it was Christmas Eve, without my telling him. It always is Christmas Eve, in a ghost story.

Christmas Eve is the ghosts' great gala night. On Christmas Eve they hold their annual fête. On Christmas Eve everybody in Ghostland who *is* anybody—or rather, speaking of ghosts, one should say, I suppose, every nobody who *is* any nobody—comes out to show himself or herself, to see and to be seen, to promenade about and display their winding-sheets and grave-clothes to each other, to criticise one another's style, and sneer at one another's complexion.

'Christmas Eve parade,' as I expect they themselves term it, is a function, doubtless, eagerly prepared for and looked forward to throughout Ghostland, especially by the swagger set, such as the murdered Barons, the crime-stained Countesses, and the Earls who

[1]

came over with the Conqueror, and assassinated their relatives, and died raving mad.

Hollow moans and fiendish grins are, one may be sure, energetically practised up. Blood-curdling shrieks and marrow-freezing gestures are probably rehearsed for weeks beforehand. Rusty chains and gory daggers are overhauled, and put into good working order; and sheets and shrouds, laid carefully by from the previous year's show, are taken down and shaken out, and mended, and aired.

Oh, it is a stirring night in Ghostland, the night of December the twenty-fourth!

Ghosts never come out on Christmas night itself, you may have noticed. Christmas Eve, we suspect, has been too much for them; they are not used to excitement. For about a week after Christmas Eve, the gentlemen ghosts, no doubt, feel as if they were all head, and go about making solemn resolutions to themselves that they will stop in next Christmas Eve; while the lady spectres are contradictory and snappish, and liable to burst into tears and leave the room hurriedly on being spoken to, for no perceptible cause whatever.

Ghosts with no position to maintain—mere middle-class ghosts— occasionally, I believe, do a little haunting on off-nights: on All-hallows Eve, and at Midsummer; and some will even run up for a mere local event—to celebrate, for instance, the anniversary of the hanging of somebody's grandfather, or to prophesy a misfortune.

He does love prophesying a misfortune, does the average British ghost. Send him out to prognosticate trouble to somebody, and he is happy. Let him force his way into a peaceful home, and turn the whole house upside down by foretelling a funeral, or predicting a bankruptcy, or hinting at a coming disgrace, or some other terrible disaster, about which nobody in their senses would want to know sooner than they could possibly help, and the prior knowledge of which can serve no useful purpose whatsoever, and he feels that he is combining duty with pleasure. He would never forgive himself if anybody in his family had a trouble and he had not been there for a couple of months beforehand, doing silly tricks on the lawn, or balancing himself on somebody's bedrail.

Then there are, besides, the very young, or very conscientious ghosts with a lost will or an undiscovered number weighing heavy on their minds, who will haunt steadily all the year round; and also the fussy ghost, who is indignant at having been buried in the dust-bin or in the village pond, and who never gives the parish a

[2]

single night's quiet until somebody has paid for a first-class funeral for him.

But these are the exceptions. As I have said, the average orthodox ghost does his one turn a year, on Christmas Eve, and is satisfied.

Why on Christmas Eve, of all nights in the year, I never could myself understand. It is invariably one of the most dismal of nights to be out in—cold, muddy, and wet. And besides, at Christmas time, everybody has quite enough to put up with in the way of a houseful of living relations, without wanting the ghosts of any dead ones mooning about the place, I am sure.

There must be something ghostly in the air of Christmas— something about the close, muggy atmosphere that draws up the ghosts, like the dampness of the summer rains brings out the frogs and snails.

And not only do the ghosts themselves always walk on Christmas Eve, but live people always sit and talk about them on Christmas Eve. Whenever five or six English-speaking people meet round a fire on Christmas Eve, they start telling each other ghost stories. Nothing satisfies us on Christmas Eve but to hear each other tell authentic anecdotes about spectres. It is a genial, festive season, and we love to muse upon graves, and dead bodies, and murders, and blood.

There is a good deal of similarity about our ghostly experiences; but this of course is not our fault but the fault of the ghosts, who never will try any new performances, but always will keep steadily to the old, safe business. The consequence is that, when you have been at one Christmas Eve party, and heard six people relate their adventures with spirits, you do not require to hear any more ghost stories. To listen to any further ghost stories after that would be like sitting out two farcical comedies, or taking in two comic journals; the repetition would become wearisome.

There is always the young man who was, one year, spending the Christmas at a country house, and, on Christmas Eve, they put him to sleep in the west wing. Then in the middle of the night, the room door quietly opens and somebody—generally a lady in her night-dress —walks slowly in, and comes and sits on the bed. The young man thinks it must be one of the visitors, or some relative of the family, though he does not remember having previously seen her, who, unable to go to sleep, and feeling lonesome, all by herself, has come into his room for a chat. He has no idea it is a ghost: he is so unsuspicious. She does not speak, however; and, when he looks again, she is gone!

[3]

The young man relates the circumstance at the breakfast-table next morning, and asks each of the ladies present if it were she who was his visitor. But they all assure him that it was not, and the host, who has grown deadly pale, begs him to say no more about the matter, which strikes the young man as a singularly strange request.

After breakfast the host takes the young man into a corner, and explains to him that what he saw was the ghost of a lady who had been murdered in that very bed, or who had murdered somebody else there—it does not really matter which: you can be a ghost by murdering somebody else or by being murdered yourself, whichever you prefer. The murdered ghost is, perhaps, the more popular; but, on the other hand, you can frighten people better if you are the murdered one, because then you can show your wounds and do groans.

Then there is the sceptical guest—it is always 'the guest' who gets let in for this sort of thing, by-the-bye. A ghost never thinks much of his own family: it is 'the guest' he likes to haunt who after listening to the host's ghost story, on Christmas Eve, laughs at it, and says that he does not believe there are such things as ghosts at all; and that he will sleep in the haunted chamber that very night, if they will let him.

Everybody urges him not to be reckless, but he persists in his foolhardiness, and goes up to the Yellow Chamber (or whatever colour the haunted room may be) with a light heart and a candle, and wishes them all goodnight, and shuts the door.

Next morning he has got snow-white hair.

He does not tell anybody what he has seen: it is too awful.

There is also the plucky guest, who sees a ghost, and knows it is a ghost, and watches it, as it comes into the room and disappears through the wainscot, after which, as the ghost does not seem to be coming back, and there is nothing, consequently, to be gained by stopping awake, he goes to sleep.

He does not mention having seen the ghost to anybody, for fear of frightening them—some people are so nervous about ghosts,—but determines to wait for the next night, and see if the apparition appears again.

It does appear again, and, this time, he gets out of bed, dresses himself and does his hair, and follows it; and then discovers a secret passage leading from the bedroom down into the beer-cellar,—a passage which, no doubt, was not unfrequently made use of in the bad old days of yore.

After him comes the young man who woke up with a strange sensation in the middle of the night, and found his rich bachelor uncle

[4]

standing by his bedside. The rich uncle smiled a weird sort of smile and vanished. The young man immediately got up and looked at his watch. It had stopped at half-past four, he having forgotten to wind it.

He made inquiries the next day, and found that, strangely enough, his rich uncle, whose only nephew he was, had married a widow with eleven children at exactly a quarter to twelve, only two days ago.

The young man does not attempt to explain the extraordinary circumstance. All he does is to vouch for the truth of his narrative.

And, to mention another case, there is the gentleman who is returning home late at night, from a Freemasons' dinner, and who, noticing a light issuing from a ruined abbey, creeps up, and looks through the keyhole. He sees the ghost of a 'grey sister' kissing the ghost of a brown monk, and is so inexpressibly shocked and frightened that he faints on the spot, and is discovered there the next morning, lying in a heap against the door, still speechless, and with his faithful latch-key clasped tightly in his hand.

All these things happen on Christmas Eve, they are all told of on Christmas Eve. For ghost stories to be told on any other evening than the evening of the twenty-fourth of December would be impossible in English society as at present regulated.

THE STORY OF THE GOBLINS WHO STOLE A SEXTON

by Charles Dickens

Several of the most famous books by Charles
Dickens contain short individual tales (often told
around the evening fireside), which have become
popular classics in their own right. This story
originally appeared as Chapter 28 in *The
Posthumous Papers of the Pickwick Club* (1836–7),
and is an obvious prototype of *A Christmas Carol*,
with the curmudgeonly sexton, Gabriel Grub, a
forerunner of Scrooge.

I n an old abbey town, down in this part of the country, a long,
long while ago—so long, that the story must be a true one,
because our great grandfathers implicitly believed it—there offi-
ciated as sexton and grave-digger in the church-yard, one Gabriel
Grub. It by no means follows that because a man is a sexton, and
constantly surrounded by emblems of mortality, therefore he should be
a morose and melancholy man; your undertakers are the merriest
fellows in the world, and I once had the honour of being on intimate
terms with a mute, who in private life, and off duty, was as comical
and jocose a little fellow as ever chirped out a devil-may-care song,
without a hitch in his memory, or drained off a good stiff glass of grog
without stopping for breath. But notwithstanding these precedents to
the contrary, Gabriel Grub was an ill-conditioned, cross-grained, surly

fellow—a morose and lonely man, who consorted with nobody but himself, and an old wicker bottle which fitted into his large deep waistcoat pocket; and who eyed each merry face as it passed him by, with such a deep scowl of malice and ill-humour, as it was difficult to meet without feeling something the worse for.

A little before twilight one Christmas Eve, Gabriel shouldered his spade, lighted his lantern, and betook himself towards the old church-yard, for he had got a grave to finish by next morning, and feeling very low he thought it might raise his spirits perhaps, if he went on with his work at once. As he wended his way, up the ancient street, he saw the cheerful light of the blazing fires gleam through the old casements, and heard the loud laugh and the cheerful shouts of those who were assembled around them; he marked the bustling preparations for the next day's good cheer, and smelt the numerous savoury odours consequent thereupon, as they steamed up from the kitchen windows in clouds. All this was gall and wormwood to the heart of Gabriel Grub; and as groups of children, bounded out of the houses, tripped across the road, and were met, before they could knock at the opposite door, by half a dozen curly-headed little rascals who crowded round them as they flocked up stairs to spend the evening in their Christmas games, Gabriel smiled grimly, and clutched the handle of his spade with a firmer grasp, as he thought of measles, scarlet-fever, thrush, hooping-cough, and a good many other sources of consolation beside.

In this happy frame of mind, Gabriel strode along, returning a short, sullen growl to the good-humoured greetings of such of his neighbours as now and then passed him, until he turned into the dark lane which led to the church-yard. Now Gabriel had been looking forward to reaching the dark lane, because it was, generally speaking, a nice gloomy mournful place, into which the towns-people did not care much to go, except in broad day-light, and when the sun was shining; consequently he was not a little indignant to hear a young urchin roaring out some jolly song about a merry Christmas, in this very sanctuary, which had been called Coffin Lane ever since the days of the old abbey, and the time of the shaven-headed monks. As Gabriel walked on, and the voice drew nearer, he found it proceeded from a small boy, who was hurrying along, to join one of the little parties in the old street, and who, partly to keep himself company, and partly to prepare himself for the occasion, was shouting out the song at the highest pitch of his lungs. So Gabriel waited till the boy came up, and then dodged him into a corner, and rapped him over the head with his

[7]

lantern five or six times, just to teach him to modulate his voice. And as the boy hurried away with his hand to his head, singing quite a different sort of tune, Gabriel Grub chuckled very heartily to himself, and entered the church-yard, locking the gate behind him.

He took off his coat, set down his lantern, and getting into the unfinished grave, worked at it for an hour or so, with right good will. But the earth was hardened with the frost, and it was no very easy matter to break it up, and shovel it out; and although there was a moon, it was a very young one, and shed little light upon the grave, which was in the shadow of the church. At any other time, these obstacles would have made Gabriel Grub very moody and miserable, but he was so well pleased with having stopped the small boy's singing, that he took little heed of the scanty progress he had made, and looked down into the grave when he had finished work for the night, with grim satisfaction, murmuring as he gathered up his things—

> Brave lodgings for one, brave lodgings for one,
> A few feet of cold earth, when life is done;
> A stone at the head, a stone at the feet,
> A rich, juicy meal for the worms to eat;
> Rank grass over-head, and damp clay around,
> Brave lodgings for one, these, in holy ground!

'Ho! Ho!' laughed Gabriel Grub, as he sat himself down on a flat tombstone which was a favourite resting place of his; and drew forth his wicker bottle. 'A coffin at Christmas—a Christmas Box. Ho! Ho! Ho!'

'Ho! ho! ho!' repeated a voice which sounded close behind him.

Gabriel paused in some alarm, in the act of raising the wicker bottle to his lips, and looked round. The bottom of the oldest grave about him, was not more still and quiet, than the church-yard in the pale moonlight. The cold hoar frost glistened on the tombstones, and sparkled like rows of gems among the stone carvings of the old church. The snow lay hard and crisp upon the ground, and spread over the thickly-strewn mounds of earth, so white and smooth a cover, that it seemed as if corpses lay there, hidden only by their winding sheets. Not the faintest rustle broke the profound tranquillity of the solemn scene. Sound itself appeared to be frozen up, all was so cold and still.

'It was the echoes,' said Gabriel Grub, raising the bottle to his lips again.

'It was *not*,' said a deep voice.

[8]

Gabriel started up, and stood rooted to the spot with astonishment and terror; for his eyes rested on a form which made his blood run cold.

Seated on an upright tombstone, close to him, was a strange unearthly figure, whom Gabriel felt at once, was no being of this world. His long fantastic legs which might have reached the ground, were cocked up, and crossed after a quaint, fantastic fashion; his sinewy arms were bare, and his hands rested on his knees. On his short round body he wore a close covering, ornamented with small slashes; and a short cloak dangled at his back; the collar was cut into curious peaks, which served the goblin in lieu of ruff or neckerchief; and his shoes curled up at the toes into long points. On his head he wore a broad-brimmed sugar loaf hat, garnished with a single feather. The hat was covered with the white frost, and the goblin looked as if he had sat on the same tombstone very comfortably, for two or three hundred years. He was sitting perfectly still; his tongue was put out, as if in derision; and he was grinning at Gabriel Grub with such a grin as only a goblin could call up.

'It was *not* the echoes,' said the goblin.

Gabriel Grub was paralysed, and could make no reply.

'What do you do here on Christmas Eve?' said the goblin sternly.

'I came to dig a grave Sir,' stammered Gabriel Grub.

'What man wanders among graves and church-yards on such a night as this?' said the goblin.

'Gabriel Grub! Gabriel Grub!' screamed a wild chorus of voices that seemed to fill the church-yard. Gabriel looked fearfully round— nothing was to be seen.

'What have you got in that bottle?' said the goblin.

'Hollands, Sir,' replied the sexton, trembling more than ever; for he had bought it off the smugglers, and he thought that perhaps his questioner might be in the excise department of the goblins.

'Who drinks Hollands alone, and in a church-yard, on such a night as this?' said the goblin.

'Gabriel Grub! Gabriel Grub!' exclaimed the wild voices again.

The goblin leered maliciously at the terrified sexton, and then raising his voice, exclaimed—

'And who, then, is our fair and lawful prize?'

To this enquiry the invisible chorus replied, in a strain that sounded like the voices of many choristers singing to the mighty swell of the old church organ—a strain that seemed borne to the sexton's ears upon a gentle wind, and to die away as its soft breath passed onward—but the burden of the reply was still the same, 'Gabriel Grub! Gabriel Grub!'

The goblin grinned a broader grin than before, as he said, 'Well, Gabriel, what do you say to this?'

The sexton gasped for breath.

'What do you think of this, Gabriel?' said the goblin, kicking up his feet in the air on either side of the tombstone, and looking at the turned-up points with as much complacency as if he had been contemplating the most fashionable pair of Wellingtons in all Bond Street.

'It's—it's—very curious, Sir,' replied the sexton, half dead with fright, 'very curious, and very pretty, but I think I'll go back and finish my work, Sir, if you please.'

'Work!' said the goblin, 'what work?'

'The grave, Sir, making the grave,' stammered the sexton.

'Oh, the grave, eh?' said the goblin, 'who makes graves at a time when all other men are merry, and takes a pleasure in it?'

Again the mysterious voices replied, 'Gabriel Grub! Gabriel Grub!'

'I'm afraid my friends want you, Gabriel,' said the goblin, thrusting his tongue further into his cheek than ever—and a most astonishing tongue it was—'I'm afraid my friends want you, Gabriel,' said the goblin.

'Under favour, Sir,' replied the horror-struck sexton, 'I don't think they can, Sir; they don't know me, Sir; I don't think the gentlemen have ever seen me, Sir.'

'Oh yes they have,' replied the goblin; 'we know the man with the sulky face and the grim scowl, that came down the street to-night, throwing his evil looks at the children, and grasping his burying spade the tighter. We know the man that struck the boy in the envious malice of his heart, because the boy could be merry, and he could not. We know him, we know him.'

Here the goblin gave a loud shrill laugh, that the echoes returned twenty-fold, and throwing his legs up in the air, stood upon his head, or rather upon the very point of his sugar-loaf hat, on the narrow edge of the tombstone, from whence he threw a summerset with extraordinary agility, right to the sexton's feet, at which he planted himself in the attitude in which tailors generally sit upon the shop-board.

'I—I—am afraid I must leave you, Sir,' said the sexton, making an effort to move.

'Leave us!' said the goblin, 'Gabriel Grub going to leave us. Ho! ho! ho!'

As the goblin laughed, the sexton observed for one instant a brilliant illumination within the windows of the church, as if the whole building were lighted up; it disappeared, the organ peeled forth a lively air, and whole troops of goblins, the very counterpart of the first one, poured into the church-yard, and began playing at leap-frog with the tombstones, never stopping for an instant to take breath, but overing the highest among them, one after the other, with the most marvellous dexterity. The first goblin was a most astonishing leaper, and none of the others could come near him; even in the extremity of his terror the sexton could not help observing, that while his friends were content to leap over the common-sized gravestones, the first one took the family vaults, iron railings and all, with as much ease as if they had been so many street posts.

At last the game reached to a most exciting pitch; the organ played quicker and quicker, and the goblins leaped faster and faster, coiling themselves up, rolling head over heels upon the ground, and bounding over the tombstones like foot-balls. The sexton's brain whirled round with the rapidity of the motion he beheld, and his legs reeled beneath him, as the spirits flew before his eyes, when the goblin king suddenly darting towards him, laid his hand upon his collar, and sank with him through the earth.

When Gabriel Grub had had time to fetch his breath, which the rapidity of his descent had for the moment taken away, he found himself in what appeared to be a large cavern, surrounded on all sides by crowds of goblins, ugly and grim; in the centre of the room, on an elevated seat, was stationed his friend of the church-yard; and close beside him stood Gabriel Grub himself, without the power of motion.

'Cold to-night,' said the king of the goblins, 'very cold. A glass of something warm, here.'

At this command, half a dozen officious goblins, with a perpetual smile upon their faces, whom Gabriel Grub imagined to be courtiers on that account, hastily disappeared, and presently returned with a goblet of liquid fire, which they presented to the king.

'Ah!' said the goblin, whose cheeks and throat were quite transparent, as he tossed down the flame, 'this warms one, indeed: bring a bumper of the same, for Mr. Grub.'

It was in vain for the unfortunate sexton to protest that he was not

[11]

in the habit of taking anything warm at night; for one of the goblins held him while another poured the blazing liquid down his throat, and the whole assembly screeched with laughter as he coughed and choked, and wiped away the tears which gushed plentifully from his eyes, after swallowing the burning draught.

'And now,' said the king, fantastically poking the taper corner of his sugar-loaf hat into the sexton's eye, and thereby occasioning him the most exquisite pain—'And now, show the man of misery and gloom a few of the pictures from our own great storehouse.'

As the goblin said this, a thick cloud which obscured the further end of the cavern, rolled gradually away, and disclosed, apparently at a great distance, a small and scantily furnished, but neat and clean apartment. A crowd of little children were gathered round a bright fire, clinging to their mother's gown, and gambolling round her chair. The mother occasionally rose, and drew aside the window-curtain as if to look for some expected object; a frugal meal was ready spread upon the table, and an elbow chair was placed near the fire. A knock was heard at the door: the mother opened it, and the children crowded round her, and clapped their hands for joy, as their father entered. He was wet and weary, and shook the snow from his garments, as the children crowded round him, and seizing his cloak, hat, stick, and gloves, with busy zeal, ran with them from the room. Then as he sat down to his meal before the fire, the children climbed about his knee, and the mother sat by his side, and all seemed happiness and comfort.

But a change came upon the view, almost imperceptibly. The scene was altered to a small bed-room, where the fairest and youngest child lay dying; the roses had fled from his cheek, and the light from his eye; and even as the sexton looked upon him with an interest he had never felt or known before, he died. His young brothers and sisters crowded round his little bed, and seized his tiny hand, so cold and heavy; but they shrank back from its touch, and looked with awe on his infant face; for calm and tranquil as it was, and sleeping in rest and peace as the beautiful child seemed to be, they saw that he was dead, and they knew that he was an angel looking down upon, and blessing them, from a bright and happy Heaven.

Again the light cloud passed across the picture, and again the subject changed. The father and mother were old and helpless now, and the number of those about them was diminished more than half; but content and cheerfulness sat on every face, and beamed in every eye, as they crowded round the fireside, and told and listened to old stories of earlier and bygone days. Slowly and peacefully the father sank into the grave, and, soon after, the sharer of all his cares and troubles followed him to a place of rest and peace. The few, who yet survived them, knelt by their tomb, and watered the green turf which covered it with their tears; then rose and turned away, sadly and mournfully, but not with bitter cries, or despairing lamentations, for they knew that they should one day meet again; and once more they mixed with the busy world, and their content and cheerfulness was restored. The cloud settled upon the picture, and concealed it from the sexton's view.

'What do you think of *that*?' said the goblin, turning his large face towards Gabriel Grub.

Gabriel murmured out something about its being very pretty, and looked somewhat ashamed, as the goblin bent his fiery eyes upon him.

'*You* a miserable man!' said the goblin, in a tone of excessive contempt. 'You!' He appeared disposed to add more, but indignation choked his utterance, so he lifted up one of his very pliable legs, and flourishing it above his head a little, to insure his aim, administered a good sound kick to Gabriel Grub; immediately after which, all the goblins in waiting crowded round the wretched sexton, and kicked him without mercy, according to the established and invariable custom of courtiers upon earth, who kick whom royalty kicks, and hug whom royalty hugs.

'Show him some more,' said the king of the goblins.

At these words the cloud was again dispelled, and a rich and beautiful landscape was disclosed to view—there is just such another to this day, within half a mile of the old abbey town. The sun shone from out the clear blue sky, the water sparkled beneath his rays, and the trees looked greener, and the flowers more gay, beneath his cheering influence. The water rippled on, with a pleasant sound, the trees rustled in the light wind that murmured among their leaves, the birds sang upon the boughs, and the lark carolled on high, her welcome to the morning. Yes, it was morning, the bright, balmy morning of summer; the minutest leaf, the smallest blade of grass, was instinct with life. The ant crept forth to her daily toil, the butterfly fluttered and basked in the warm rays of the sun; myriads of insects spread their transparent wings, and revelled in their brief but happy existence. Man walked forth, elated with the scene; and all was brightness and splendour.

'*You* a miserable man!' said the king of goblins, in a more contemptuous tone than before. And again the king of the goblins gave his leg a flourish; again it descended on the shoulders of the sexton; and again the attendant goblins imitated the example of their chief.

Many a time the cloud went and came, and many a lesson it taught to Gabriel Grub, who although his shoulders smarted with pain from the frequent applications of the goblin's feet thereunto, looked on with an interest which nothing could diminish. He saw that men who worked hard, and earned their scanty bread with lives of labour, were cheerful and happy; and that to the most ignorant, the sweet face of nature was a never-failing source of cheerfulness and joy. He saw those who had been delicately nurtured, and tenderly brought up, cheerful under privations, and superior to suffering, that would have crushed many of a rougher grain, because they bore within their own bosoms the materials of happiness, contentment, and peace. He saw that women, the tenderest and most fragile of all God's creatures, were the oftenest superior to sorrow, adversity, and distress; and he saw that it was because they bore in their own hearts an inexhaustible well-spring of affection and devotedness. Above all, he saw that men like himself, who snarled at the mirth and cheerfulness of others, were the foulest weeds on the fair surface of the earth; and setting all the good of the world against the evil, he came to the conclusion that it was a very decent and respectable sort of world after all. No sooner had he formed it, than the cloud which had closed over the last picture, seemed to settle on his senses, and lull him to repose. One by one, the goblins faded from his sight, and as the last one disappeared, he sunk to sleep.

The day had broken when Gabriel Grub awoke, and found himself lying at full length on the flat gravestone in the church-yard, with the wicker bottle lying empty by his side, and his coat, spade, and lantern, all well whitened by the last night's frost, scattered on the ground. The stone on which he had first seen the goblin seated, stood bolt upright before him, and the grave at which he had worked, the night before, was not far off. At first he began to doubt the reality of his adventures, but the acute pain in his shoulders when he attempted to rise, assured him that the kicking of the goblins was certainly not ideal. He was staggered again, by observing no traces of footsteps in the snow on which the goblins had played at leap-frog with the gravestones, but he speedily accounted for this circumstance when he remembered that being spirits, they would leave no visible impression behind them. So Gabriel Grub got to his feet as well as he could, for the pain in his back; and brushing the frost off his coat, put it on, and turned his face towards the town.

But he was an altered man, and he could not bear the thought of returning to a place where his repentance would be scoffed at, and his reformation disbelieved. He hesitated for a few moments; and then turned away to wander where he might, and seek his bread elsewhere.

The lantern, the spade, and the wicker bottle, were found that day in the church-yard. There were a great many speculations about the sexton's fate at first, but it was speedily determined that he had been carried away by the goblins; and there were not wanting some very credible witnesses who had distinctly seen him whisked through the air on the back of a chestnut horse blind of one eye, with the hind quarters of a lion, and the tail of a bear. At length all this was devoutly believed; and the new sexton used to exhibit to the curious for a trifling emolument, a good-sized piece of the church weathercock which had been accidentally kicked of by the aforesaid horse in his aërial flight, and picked up by himself in the church-yard, a year or two afterwards.

Unfortunately these stories were somewhat disturbed by the unlooked-for reappearance of Gabriel Grub himself, some ten years afterwards, a ragged, contented, rheumatic old man. He told his story to the clergyman, and also to the mayor; and in course of time it began to be received as a matter of history, in which form it has continued down to this very day. The believers in the weathercock tale, having misplaced their confidence once, were not easily prevailed upon to part with it again, so they looked as wise as they could, shrugged their shoulders, touched their foreheads, and murmured something about Gabriel Grub's having drunk all the Hollands, and then fallen asleep on the flat tombstone; and they affected to explain what he supposed he had witnessed in the goblin's cavern, by saying that he had seen the world, and grown wiser. But this opinion, which was by no means a popular one at any time, gradually died off, and be the matter how it may, as Gabriel Grub was afflicted with rheumatism to the end of his days, this story has at least one moral, if it teach no better one—and that is, that if a man turns sulky and drinks by himself at Christmas time, he may make up his mind to be not a bit the better for it, let the spirits be ever so good, or let them be even as many degrees beyond proof, as those which Gabriel Grub saw, in the goblin's cavern.

THE GHOST DETECTIVE

by Mark Lemon

Mark Lemon (1809-1870) was celebrated as one of
the founders and the first editor of *Punch* (from
1841 until his death). He also edited the *London
Journal*, for which he wrote many Christmas
stories and later established and edited the *Field*.
The first Christmas supplement of the *Illustrated
London News* came from his pen. 'The Ghost
Detective' was first published in 1866, and features
an apparition rarely found in 19th century ghost
stories: the phantom of a living person.

'You take an interest in Christmas legends, I believe?' said my
friend Carraway, passing the claret.
'Yes, I think they are as good as any other,' I replied.
'And have faith in ghosts?'
'Well, I must answer that question with an equivocation. Yes—no.'
'Then if you care to listen, I can, I fancy, remove your scepticism,'
said Carraway.
I professed my willingness to be converted, provided I might smoke
whilst my friend talked, and the conditions being agreed to, Carraway
commenced:
'When I first came into the City—now some thirty years ago—I
formed an intimacy with a young man in the wine trade, and we
passed most of our leisure time together. He was much liked by his
employers, whose principal business was with publicans and tavern-

keepers, and after a time my friend became their town traveller—a position of trust and fair emolument. This advancement enabled my friend, James Loxley, to carry out a long-cherished desire, and that was to marry a fair cousin to whom he had been attached from his boyhood. The girl was one of those pretty *blondes* that are so attractive to young fellows with a turn for the sentimental, and a tendency to sing about violet eyes and golden hair and all that. I was never given that way myself, and I confess Loxley's cousin would not have been the woman I should have chosen for a wife had I ever thought of taking to myself an incumbrance. I had had a step-mother, and she cured me of any matrimonial inclinations which I might have had at one time. Well, Loxley thought differently to me, and his marriage with his cousin, Martha Lovett, was settled, and I was appointed best man upon the occasion.

'The bride certainly looked very pretty in her plain white dress— very pretty, though somewhat paler than usual, and that perhaps made me think more than ever that Martha was not the wife my friend James should have selected, knowing as I did that they would only have his salary to live upon, and that much would depend upon her to make his means sufficient for decent comfort. However, they were sincerely attached to each other, and that, I was told, was worth one or two hundred a year, which I did not believe. Martha was greatly agitated at the altar, and at one time I thought she would have fainted before the ceremony, as they call it, had finished. As it was, she had a slight attack of hysteria in the vestry, but the pew-opener told me that was nothing unusual with brides, especially with those who had been widows.

'The wedding-breakfast was a quiet affair—nothing like the sacrificial feasts of the present day—and we were all merry enough until the happy pair were to leave for their own home, and then poor little Martha hung about her mother's neck and sobbed—much more than I thought was complimentary to her new husband—but then I was not a fair judge of the sex, having been worried all my life by a step-mother.

'When Loxley and his wife were fairly settled in their new home I used frequently to pop in for a game at cribbage or a chat with my old friend, and a more loving couple I never saw in my life. Not being by any means rich, they had babies, of course, and in less than three years there were two most charming creatures—when they didn't cry or poke out their eyes with the tea-spoons, or perform any other of those antics which are the delight of parents, but can only be designated as inflictions to unattached spectators.

'I have thought it only fair to mention these little matters; you will see wherefore by and by.

'Loxley had invited me to take my Christmas dinner with him, and a pleasant day we had! He was partial to keeping Christmas with all the honours, and his little dining-room—it was his drawing-room also—was sprigged about with holly, even to the picture frames. He had only two oil paintings—portraits of his father and mother, both long deceased, but the likenesses, he said, were so good, that he could always fancy his parents were present.

'Well, as I have mentioned, we passed a happy day and night; Loxley had arranged to go with me for a couple of days into the country, on a visit to a good old uncle of mine, as an atonement for keeping me away from the family dinner.

'The visit was paid; but I was rather annoyed at the effort which Loxley evidently made to appear entertained, and I thought he was home-sick, or vexed that I had not invited his wife to join us, as there were lady visitors at my uncle's. Whatever was the cause of his frequent abstractions, I could only regret it, as I had given him such a good character for cheerfulness and pleasant companionship, that one of my cousins twitted me, with rural delicacy, for having brought a thorough wet blanket from London.

'During our journey back to town Loxley was silent and thoughtful, and I longed to ask if anything troubled him. But we had passed such a jovial Christmas Day together that I could not suppose he had any other anxiety than what the restoration to the arms of his Martha would remove. We parted, however, without any explanation being asked or volunteered.

'On the second day after our return, I was astounded at receiving a message from Loxley to come to him at the Mansion House. The officer who brought the note told me that Loxley was in custody, charged, he believed, by his employer with no less an offence than embezzlement.

'Such an accusation seemed at first to me, who had known Loxley so long, so intimately, preposterous—impossible. As I walked to the Mansion House a cold sweat seized me, and for a moment I thought I should have fallen, as the strange conduct of my friend during the past two days came to my recollection. Had he found his means too small for his home requirements? Had he been tempted, and yielded as good men had done before him? No, no!—a thousand times, no!—if I knew James Loxley rightly.

'He was standing at the prisoners' bar when I reached the Mansion House, and I was not permitted to speak to him. He saw me, however, and knew his friend was with him.

'The junior principal, who had recently joined the firm of X. and Co.—by the bye, he had for some reason never taken kindly to Loxley—was giving his evidence. He said: "That John Rogers, a customer of the house, had caused a great deal of trouble with his over-due account, and that it was thought he would prove a defaulter. Mr. X. (the prosecutor) had heard accidentally that Rogers had received a large sum of money, and as Mr. Loxley was away from business Mr. X. had called upon the debtor to demand payment of his debt. Mr. X. was received with much insolence by Rogers; and his conduct was accounted for subsequently by the production of Loxley's receipt for the money, dated the 24th of December. The man had paid £40 by a cheque to Loxley, and no such amount was credited in the books of X. and Co. Rogers produced his banker's book, and the cheque with Loxley's signature on the back. It was found, also, that a person answering by description to Loxley had received two notes of £20 each, one of which had been paid at the Bank of England in gold early on the morning after Christmas Day."

'This evidence was confirmed by John Rogers, who had given the cheque; by the banker's cashier, who had paid it; and by the Bank of England clerk, who had given gold for the note.

'Loxley was asked—having received the usual caution—if he wished to say anything.'

'He answered:

' "Yes; and he thought he had been hardly used by his employers, that an explanation of the matter had not been required from him by them before he had been taken into custody as a thief. He had also heard of Rogers' accession to money; and having the interests of his employers in view, went at once to the man and with great difficulty succeeded in obtaining payment of the debt. He received the cheque, but, fearing that Rogers might stop the payment of it at his banker's he, Loxley, cashed it immediately, placing the notes he received, as he believed, in his pocket-book.

' "As it was Christmas Eve, he did not return to X. and Co.'s, the house being closed, but walked home with a friend he had met in the banking house when he received the money for Roger's cheque. On the morning of the 26th he had intended calling at X. and Co.'s on his way to his appointment with me; but, finding he was late, he attached no consquence to the omission, having a holiday. When he was at his journey's end and in his bedroom, he was looking in his pocket-book for some matter or other, and for the first time missed the banknotes he had received for the cheque. He was completely perplexed, being certain that he had placed the notes in the case, and that he had never lost possession of them. He had employed the morning of his return to town in searching—vainly, he knew—all conceivable places at home for the missing notes, and of course without success. Before he could go to X. and Co.'s offices he was taken into custody." '

' "One of the notes was cashed at the Bank of England early on the morning of the 26th, was it not?" ' asked the Lord Mayor.

'The bank clerk who cashed the note said, "Yes, it appeared so, but he could not remember exactly whether it was presented by a man or a woman. He thought it was not paid to the prisoner." '

' "But it was paid, and in gold," said the Lord Mayor. "The embezzlement of employers' money is one of the gravest offences against the law, and must be severely punished and put a stop to. The statement of the prisoner is very plausible—very feasible, perhaps I should say—but I cannot feel it my duty to decide upon its truth or falsehood. He must be committed for trial." '

'Loxley bowed his head and remained immovable, until a shriek in the passage of the court reached him, and he started as from a dream. He instantly looked to where I had been standing, and I understood his meaning. He was right. He had recognized the voice of his wife, who, having heard where they had taken her husband, had followed after. I found her as I had seen her on her wedding day—hysterical, but the attack was very violent; it was with great difficulty I conveyed her to her mother's, and thence to her own home.'

'I said all I could to comfort her. I told her my own conviction of Loxley's innocence, my full belief in the explanation which he had given, and the certainty of his speedy liberation. But I spoke to a stricken woman, to a distracted wife, a half mad mother. She sat for some time with her children in her lap, rocking to and fro, and sobbing as though her heart would burst. She cried to me to succour her husband, to bring him home, if not for her sake, for that of her innocent children. She would not let her mother speak, but continued to appeal to me until—yes, I own it—until I fairly broke down and could not answer her. And all this while the green holly garnishing the room, and the faces of the father and mother looking on placidly from the walls.'

The recollection of the painful scene he had been describing made Carraway silent for a time, and I remarked that he had the satisfaction of knowing he had done his duty to his friend, whether he proved guilty or innocent.

'Yes,' continued Carraway, 'I had that satisfaction, though I did not desire to blow my own trumpet in what I have said. Well, when the elder X., who had been away from town, heard of the matter he was inclined to believe Loxley's statement, and blamed his son for his precipitancy. The matter, however, was beyond his control now, and the law had to vindicate its supremacy.

'The trial came on, and the gentleman whose professional business it was to prove Loxley guilty necessarily did all that was possible to show the weakness of the defence. He asked why Loxley had not instantly returned to town when he had discovered the loss of the notes? Why had he not written to his employers? Why had he not mentioned his loss to me—the friend whom he had called to speak to his character? No satisfactory answer could be given for such omissions. What had become of the other note? If a dishonest person had found the notes—supposing them to have been lost—would they not have changed both of them for gold? The most favourable construction which could be placed upon the case was the supposition that the prisoner had need of twenty pounds and had taken his employer's money, intending, very likely, to replace it. That was no uncommon case. The pressure of what seemed to be only a temporary difficulty had often led well-meaning men into such unpardonable breaches of trust. And now, having placed the case as fairly as he could before the jury, his duty was done, and it rested with the twelve intelligent men in the box to pronounce their verdict.

' "Embezzlement," the judge said, very properly, "was a serious crime, and must be repressed by the punishment of offenders. The jury had heard the prosecutor's statement—proved by highly respectable witnesses; and the prisoner's defence—unsupported by any corroborative evidence. The jury had to judge between them." '

'Without leaving their box the jury, after a brief consultation, pronounced a verdict of 'Guilty,' and my friend—my dear friend, James Loxley—was sentenced to transportation.

'This terrible sentence was almost fatal to Mrs. Loxley. Her delicate constitution would have given way under her excess of grief had not—well, had not I set before her the duty she owed to her children, who had a right to a share in her affection. Poor thing! She struggled bravely

[21]

to overcome her great sorrow, but I doubt much if she would have succeeded but for what I am now about to relate to you. Stay—I must mention one or two matters before I tell you that portion of my story.'

'The Loxleys occupied only part of the house in which they lived. They had their own furniture, but the landlady of the house provided servants, excepting a little girl who acted as nurse.'

'The general servant who waited upon the Loxleys was one of those patient drudges often found in lodging-houses. Her name was Susan, but Loxley had given her the sobriquet of 'Dormouse,' as she was a drowsy, stupid—perhaps sullen is the better word—girl, who moved about more like a piece of machinery than a living being. She never showed any feeling, either of displeasure or gratification, excepting in her strong attachment to Loxley's children. That arose, perhaps, from her womanly instinct. But when Mrs. Loxley's great trouble came, when the girl had come to understand what had befallen Mr. Loxley, and that misery and ruin had overtaken them and their children, Susan's whole nature appeared to undergo a change. She seemed to watch every want, every movement of Mrs. Loxley. More than once she was found sitting on the stairs near Mrs. Loxley's door, when that poor lady was in her paroxysms of grief, as though desirous to lend what aid she could in subduing them. I was so struck by the devotion and sympathy of this poor, stupid creature that I could not help noticing her, and on one occasion offered her money. She refused to take it.'

' "No, thank'ee, sir," she said; "that's not what I want; but I should like to be of use to poor missus, if I could, sir."

'I told her she had been of great use, great comfort, to Mrs. Loxley, who had seen, as I had, how much she felt for her misfortunes.'

' "Yes, sir, that's true enough. And what will they do to Mr. Loxley, sir?" ' she asked.

' "He will have to suffer a great deal, Susan—great misery; but neither you nor I can help him." '

'The girl burst into tears, and cried so bitterly that Mrs. Loxley overheard her, and I have no doubt questioned her when I was gone.'

'Mrs. Loxley's mother was staying with her, the elder Mr. X. having insisted upon making a temporary provision for the unhappy wife of the man he still believed to be innocent—I say Mrs. Loxley's mother was staying with her daughter. She had gone to bed in an adjoining room, as Mrs. Loxley frequently begged to be allowed to sit alone, as she found it difficult to sleep. I have reason to believe that after her mother had gone to rest, Mrs. Loxley had an interview with Susan; but, for reasons which will appear, I never questioned her on that point. It was past midnight, according to Mrs. Loxley's statement, when, sitting with her head resting on her hands, she saw the door of her room open, and her husband enter; saw him as plainly and like himself as she had ever seen him. She rose up; but the figure motioned her to remain where she was. She complied; now conscious that it was not her husband in the flesh upon which she looked. The figure sat down in his accustomed place, and then appeared to gaze steadfastly on the portrait of his father, still ornamented with the faded holly twigs which had been placed there at Christmas-time. This continued for some minutes. The figure then rose up and, looking towards Mrs. Loxley with a most loving expression on its face, walked from the room, opening and closing the door after it.'

'Mrs. Loxley tried to follow, but could not. She was not asleep, she had not been even dozing—she was sure of that, but had seen with her waking senses the apparition of her husband, then lying in Newgate prison.'

'What followed seemed equally inexplicable to me, who had more than once witnessed her tendency to hysteria and fainting. She said she had felt no alarm at what she had seen. She was stupefied for a few moments, but not alarmed. She went to her mother; but finding her quietly sleeping Mrs. Loxley lay down beside her without disturbing her. In the morning she narrated to her mother what she had witnessed during the past night, and subsequently repeated her story— word for word, her mother said—to me, in the presence of her landlady and the maid Susan.'

'The effect upon the poor, dull-witted servant was very remarkable. She fixed her eyes on the portrait which had attracted the notice of the apparition as though she were fascinated by it. She then asked Mrs. Loxley, with a voice and look of terror, "Did you speak to the ghost, missus?" And when Mrs. Loxley replied "No," Susan enquired, "And didn't the ghost speak to you?" '

'Mrs. Loxley answered that she had told all that had occurred, adding nothing, keeping back nothing; and this assurance seemed to have a consolatory effect upon the girl, who then busied herself with her work. I had made inquiries at the prison, as Mrs. Loxley foreboded illness or death to her husband, and learned that my unfortunate friend was in health, and had become more resigned to the cruel future which awaited him. Mrs. Loxley appeared to be satisfied with this account of her husband.

'The night which succeeded Mrs. Loxley proposed to pass in the same manner; but her mother insisted upon remaining with her, and that night no apparition came.'

'Mrs. Loxley was disappointed, and attributed the absence of the spirit to the presence of her mother, and it was now her turn to insist. Mrs. Lovett went to her room, having promised to go to bed and not seek to watch or return to her daughter. It was impossible, however, for the old lady to sleep, and she listened to every noise in the street, and to those unaccountable sounds which we have all heard in our lonely rooms.'

'It was again past midnight, and Mrs. Loxley had, she admitted, worked herself into a high state of expectancy, when, without the opening of the door, the figure of her husband stood in the room. Again it regarded her most tenderly for a few seconds, and then fixed its gaze on the portrait of Loxley's father. It had not seated itself, as on the former visitation, but stood, with its hands folded, as though in supplication. It then turned its face to Mrs. Loxley and opened its arms, as if inviting her to its embrace. Without a moment's hesitation she rose, and almost rushed to the bosom of the shadow. But the impalpable figure offering no resistance, she dashed herself against the panelling of the room, and the withered holly sprigs in the frame of the picture above her fell rustling to the ground. The shade was gone!'

'Mrs. Lovett, hearing the noise against the panel and the scratching of the falling holly, immediately went to her daughter. Mrs. Loxley had not borne the second visitation so bravely as she had done the former one, and it was necessary to call for assistance, as a violent attack of hysteria succeeded the vision.'

'The "Dormouse," usually most difficult to arouse, was the first to hear the calling of Mrs. Lovett and to go to her assistance.'

' "Has she seen it again?" asked Susan, almost directly she had entered.

' "Yes."

' "And did he speak to her this time, missus?" asked Susan. Mrs Lovett could not satisfy the girl's curiosity, but when Mrs. Loxley revived sufficiently to tell what she had seen, Susan repeated her enquiries and appeared to be relieved when she heard that the ghost had been silent.'

"I was sent for early in the morning, and, having dispatched what pressing business matters I had, I went to Mrs. Loxley. She was, as before, perfectly circumstantial in her account of what she had seen, not varying in the least from her first statement; and she and her mother believed that she had seen with her corporeal eyes the spirit of her living husband. I could not bring myself quite to this conclusion. I therefore suggested that it was possibly the association of the portrait with her husband, acting upon her over-taxed brain, that had conjured up these shadows. Mrs. Loxley admitted the possibility of such a solution and readily acceded to my proposal to take down the portrait which had attracted, as it seemed, the attention of the figure, and then to abide the result of another night, if Mrs. Loxley felt equal to courting the return of the vision.'

'I rang the bell for the maid, and requested her to bring the steps.

' "What for?" she asked quickly.'

' "To take down one of the pictures," ' I replied.

' "There ain't no steps," ' she said firmly.

'I could have sworn I had seen a pair in the passage as I entered, but I might have been mistaken, and I did not press the request. The picture was easily removed by my standing on a chair.'

'As I turned to place the picture on the floor I was perfectly thunderstruck to see the change which had come over Susan. She stood transfixed as it were, her mouth and eyes distended to the full, her hands stretched out, as though she were looking upon the ghost which had disturbed us all.'

' "What is the matter with the girl?" I exclaimed, and all eyes were directed to her.'

'Susan fell upon her knees and hid her face almost on the ground and screamed out, "I'm guilty, missus! I'm found out! I knowed why the ghost come! I'm guilty!" '

'We were all astounded! After a few moments, as I stood on the chair with the face of the portrait towards me, Mrs. Loxley uttered a shrill cry and rushed to the picture. From the inside of the frame to which the canvas was attached she took out a note for £20—the note which had formed part of the forty which Loxley had received and had lost so mysteriously!'

'There had been no doubt who had been the thief. Susan had already confessed herself guilty, and I did not hesitate to obtain what other confession I could from her. It seemed that Loxley had been mistaken in supposing he had placed the notes in his pocket-book. Owing to his suprise at meeting the friend he had spoken to at the banker's he had placed the notes in his trousers-pocket, and the force of habit had induced him to think he had otherwise disposed of

[25]

them. These notes, so carelessly placed, he had drawn forth with his hand whilst ascending his own stairs, and Susan had found them. The half-witted creature showed her prize to an old man employed to clean shoes and knives, and he counselled the changing of one of the notes, with what success we know. Susan received none of the money, as the old scoundel declared himself a partner in the waif, and told Susan she might keep the other note. But what Susan saw and heard subsequently had so terrified her and filled her with remorse, that she dared not dispose of her ill-gotten money, but strangely enough, concealed it behind the portrait of Loxley's father.'

'My friend, by the exertions of X., sen., was soon liberated, and by the honourable conduct of the same gentleman, who did all he could to repair the wrong unwittingly done to Loxley, an excellent appointment was found in Australia. There James and Martha and their progeny are now, and thriving, I am glad to say.'

'I'll trouble you for the claret,' added Carraway. 'And now do you believe in ghosts?'

'I must make the answer I did before,' I replied. 'Yes—no. I think the apparition was provoked by the cause you at first suggested—namely, the association of Loxley's with his father's portrait and Mrs. Loxley's over-taxed brain. You have heard, no doubt, of the well-known case of M. Nicolai, the Berlin banker, who, according to his own account, having experienced several unpleasant circumstances, saw phantasms of the living and the dead by dozens, and was yet convinced they were not ghosts. Mrs. Loxley might have also been dreaming, without being aware of it, as others have done; and it is rather against the ghost, if he appeared only to discover the lost note, that he came not when Mrs. Lovett was present.'

'But the note was found behind the portrait at which the ghost looked so earnestly. How can you account for that?' asked Carraway.

'Well, I am so much a doubter of spiritual manifestation that I can satisfy myself, though not you, perhaps, on that particular. Suppose this stupid Dormouse had taken it into her silly head that Mr. Loxley's ghost had come for Mr. Loxley's money, and under that impression had placed the note behind the picture after she had heard Mrs. Loxley's account of the first visitation, in order to get rid of the money which the ghost wanted?'

'I don't believe that!' said Carraway. 'I believe it was a real, actual ghost!'

'I don't,' I replied, 'and so we end as we began. I'll thank you for the cigars.'

THE DEAD SEXTON

by J. Sheridan Le Fanu

Joseph Sheridan Le Fanu (1814-73) is now
regarded, by general consent, as the greatest 19th
century writer of ghost stories. 'The Dead Sexton',
set in 'the beautiful little town of Golden Friars'
(a favourite locale of Le Fanu), first appeared in the
Christmas Number (entitled 'Across the Bridge') of
Once a Week, 1871, with a full-page illustration by
C.O. Murray. It is one of Le Fanu's most powerful
and eerie tales.

The sunsets were red, the nights were long, and the weather pleasantly frosty; and Christmas, the glorious herald of the New Year, was at hand, when an event—still recounted by winter firesides, with a horror made delightful by the mellowing influence of years—occurred in the beautiful little town of Golden Friars, and signalized, as the scene of its catastophe, the old inn known throughout a wide region of the Northumbrian counties as the George and Dragon.

Toby Crooke, the sexton, was lying dead in the old coach-house in the inn yard. The body had been discovered, only half an hour before this story begins, under strange circumstances, and in a place where it might have lain the better part of a week undisturbed; and a dreadful suspicion astounded the village of Golden Friars.

A wintry sunset was glaring through a gorge of the western mountains, turning into fire the twigs of the leafless elms, and all the tiny blades of grass on the green by which the quaint little town is

[27]

surrounded. It is built of light, grey stone, with steep gables and slender chimneys rising with airy lightness from the level sward by the margin of the beautiful lake, and backed by the grand amphitheatre of the fells at the other side, whose snowy peaks show faintly against the sky, tinged with the vaporous red of the western light. As you descend towards the margin of the lake, and see Golden Friars, its' taper chimneys and slender gables, its' curious old inn and gorgeous sign, and over all the graceful tower and spire of the ancient church, at this hour or by moonlight, in the solemn grandeur and stillness of the natural scenery that surrounds it, it stands before you like a fairy town.

Toby Crooke, the lank sexton, now fifty or upwards, had passed an hour or two with some village cronies, over a solemn pot of purl, in the kitchen of that cosy hostelry, the night before. He generally turned in there about seven o'clock, and heard the news. This contented him: for he talked little, and looked always surly.

Many things are now raked up and talked over about him.

In early youth, he had been a bit of a scamp. He broke his indentures, and ran away from his master, the tanner of Bryemere; he had got into fifty bad scrapes and out again; and, just as the little world of Golden Friars had come to the conclusion that it would be well for all parties—except, perhaps, himself—and a happy riddance for his afflicted mother, if he were sunk, with a gross of quart pots about his neck, in the bottom of the lake in which the grey gables, the elms, and the towering fells of Golden Friars are mirrored, he suddenly returned, a reformed man at the ripe age of forty.

For twelve years he had disappeared, and no one knew what had become of him. Then, suddenly, as I say, he reappeared at Golden Friars—a very black and silent man, sedate and orderly. His mother was dead and buried; but the 'prodigal son' was received good-naturedly. The good Vicar, Doctor Jenner, reported to his wife:

'His hard heart has been softened, dear Dolly. I saw him dry his eyes, poor fellow, at the sermon yesterday.'

'I don't wonder, Hugh darling. I know the part—"There is joy in Heaven." I am sure it was—wasn't it? It was quite beautiful. I almost cried myself.'

The Vicar laughed gently, and stooped over her chair and kissed her, and patted her cheek fondly.

'You think too well of your old man's sermons,' he said. 'I preach, you see, Dolly, very much to the *poor*. If *they* understand me, I am

[28]

pretty sure everyone else must; and I think that my simple style goes more home to both feelings and conscience—'

'You ought to have told me of his crying before. You *are* so eloquent,' exclaimed Dolly Jenner. 'No one preaches like my man. I have never heard such sermons.'

Not many, we may be sure; for the good lady had not heard more than six from any other divine for the last twenty years.

The personages of Golden Friars talked Toby Crooke over on his return. Doctor Lincote said:

'He must have led a hard life; he had *dried in* so, and a good deal of hard muscle; and he rather fancied he had been soldiering—he stood like a soldier; and the mark over his right eye looked like a gunshot.'

People might wonder how he could have survived a gunshot over the eye; but was not Lincote a Doctor—and an army Doctor to boot—when he was young; and who, in Golden Friars, could dispute with him on points of surgery? And I believe the truth is, that this mark had been really made by a pistol bullet.

Mr. Jarlcot, the attorney, would 'go bail' he had picked up some sense in his travels; and honest Turnbull, the host of the George and Dragon, said heartily:

'We must look out something for him to put his hand to. *Now's* the time to make a man of him.'

The end of it was that he became, among other things, the sexton of Golden Friars.

He was a punctual sexton. He meddled with no other person's business; but he was a silent man, and by no means popular. He was reserved in company; and he used to walk alone by the shore of the lake, while other fellows played at fives or skittles; and when he visited the kitchen of the George, he had his liquor to himself, and in the midst of the general talk was a saturnine listener. There was something sinister in this man's face; and when things went wrong with him, he could look dangerous enough.

There were whispered stories in Golden Friars about Toby Crooke. Nobody could say how they got there. Nothing is more mysterious than the spread of rumour. It is like a vial poured on the air. It travels, like an epidemic, on the sightless currents of the atmosphere, or by the laws of a telluric influence equally intangible. These stories treated, though darkly, of the long period of his absence from his native village; but they took no well-defined shape, and no one could refer them to any authentic source.

[29]

The Vicar's charity was of the kind that thinketh no evil; and in such cases he always insisted on proof. Crooke was, of course, undisturbed in his office.

On the evening before the tragedy came to light—trifles are always remembered after the catastophe—a boy, returning along the margin of the mere, passed him by seated on a prostrate trunk of a tree, under the 'bield' of a rock, counting silver money. His lean body and limbs were bent together, his knees were up to his chin, and his long fingers were turning the coins over hurriedly in the hollow of his other hand. He glanced at the boy, as the old English saying is, like 'the devil looking over Lincoln.' But a black and sour look from Mr. Crooke, who never had a smile for a child nor a greeting for a wayfarer, was nothing strange.

Toby Crooke lived in the grey stone house, cold and narrow, that stands near the church porch, with the window of its staircase looking out into the church-yard, where so much of his labour, for many a day, had been expended. The greater part of this house was untenanted.

The old woman who was in charge of it slept in a settle-bed, among broken stools, old sacks, rotten chests and other rattle-traps, in the small room at the rear of the house, floored with tiles.

At what time of the night she could not tell, she awoke, and saw a man, with his hat on, in her room. He had a candle in his hand, which he shaded with his coat from her eye; his back was towards her, and he was rummaging in the drawer in which she usually kept her money.

Having got her quarter's pension of two pounds that day, however, she had placed it, folded in a rag, in the corner of her tea caddy, and locked it up in the 'eat-malison' or cupboard.

She was frightened when she saw the figure in her room, and she could not tell whether her visitor might not have made his entrance from the contiguous church-yard. So, sitting bolt upright in her bed, her grey hair almost lifting her kerchief off her head, and all over in 'a fit o' t' creepins,' as she expressed it, she demanded:

'In God's name, what want ye thar?'

'Whar's the peppermint ye used to hev by ye, woman? I'm bad wi' an inward pain.'

'It's all gane a month sin',' she answered; and offered to make him a 'het' drink if he'd get to his room.

But he said:

'Never mind, I'll try a mouthful o' gin.'

And, turning on his heel, he left her.

[30]

In the morning the sexton was gone. Not only in his lodging was there no account of him, but, when inquiry began to be extended, nowhere in the village of Golden Friars could he be found.

Still he might have gone off, on business of his own, to some distant village, before the town was stirring; and the sexton had no near kindred to trouble their heads about him. People, therefore, were willing to wait, and take his return ultimately for granted.

At three o'clock the good Vicar, standing at his hall door, looking across the lake towards the noble fells that rise, steep and furrowed, from that beautiful mere, saw two men approaching across the green, in a straight line, from a boat that was moored at the water's edge. They were carrying between them something which, though not very large, seemed ponderous.

'Ye'll ken this, sir,' said one of the boatmen as they set down, almost at his feet, a small church bell, such as in old-fasioned chimes yields the treble notes.

'This won't be less nor five stean. I ween it's fra' the church steeple yon.'

'What! one of our church bells?' ejaculated the Vicar—for a moment lost in horrible amazement. 'Oh, no!—no, that can't possibly be! Where did you find it?'

He had found the boat, in the morning, moored about fifty yards from her moorings where he had left it the night before, and could not think how that came to pass; and now, as he and his partner were about to take their oars, they discovered this bell in the bottom of the boat, under a bit of canvas, also the sexton's pick and spade—'tom-spey'ad,' they termed that peculiar, broad-bladed implement.

'Very extraordinary! We must try whether there is a bell missing from the tower,' said the Vicar, getting into a fuss. 'Has Crooke come back yet? Does anyone know where he is?'

The sexton had not yet turned up.

'That's odd—that's provoking,' said the Vicar. 'However, my key will let us in. Place the bell in the hall while I get it; and then we can see what all this means.'

To the church, accordingly, they went, the Vicar leading the way, with his own key in his hand. He turned it in the lock, and stood in the shadow of the ground porch, and shut the door.

A sack, half full, lay on the ground, with open mouth, a piece of cord lying beside it. Something clanked within it as one of the men shoved it aside with his clumsy shoe.

[31]

The Vicar opened the church door and peeped in. The dusky glow from the western sky, entering through a narrow window, illuminated the shafts and arches, the old oak carvings, and the discoloured monuments, with the melancholy glare of a dying fire.

The Vicar withdrew his head and closed the door. The gloom of the porch was deeper than ever as, stooping, he entered the narrow door that opened at the foot of the winding stair that leads to the first loft; from which a rude ladder-stair of wood, some five and twenty feet in height, mounts through a trap to the ringers' loft.

Up the narrow stairs the Vicar climbed, followed by his attendants, to the first loft. It was very dark: a narrow bow-slit in the thick wall admitted the only light they had to guide them. The ivy leaves, seen from the deep shadow, flashed and flickered redly, and the sparrows twittered among them.

'Will one of you be so good as to go up and count the bells, and see if they are all right?' said the Vicar. 'There should be—'

'Agoy! what's that?' exclaimed one of the men, recoiling from the foot of the ladder.

'By Jen!' ejaculated the other, in equal suprise.

'Good gracious!' gasped the Vicar, who, seeing indistinctly a dark mass lying on the floor, had stooped to examine it, and placed his hand upon a cold, dead face.

The men drew the body into the streak of light that traversed the floor.

It was the corpse of Toby Crooke! There was a frightful scar across his forehead.

The alarm was given. Doctor Lincote, and Mr. Jarlcot, and Turnbull, of the George and Dragon, were on the spot immediately; and many curious and horrified spectators of minor importance.

The first thing ascertained was that the man must have been many hours dead. The next was that his skull was fractured, across the forehead, by an awful blow. The next was that his neck was broken.

His hat was found on the floor, where he had probably laid it, with his handkerchief in it.

The mystery now began to clear a little; for a bell—one of the chime hung in the tower—was found where it had rolled to, against the wall, with blood and hair on the rim of it, which corresponded with the grizzly fracture across the front of his head.

The sack that lay in the vestibule was examined, and found to contain all the church plate; a silver salver that had disappeared, about a month before, from Dr. Lincote's store of valuables; the Vicar's gold pencil-case, which he thought he had forgotten in the vestry book; silver spoons, and various other contributions, levied from time to time off a dozen different households, the mysterious disappearance of which spoils had, of late years, begun to make the honest little community uncomfortable. Two bells had been taken down from the chime; and now the shrewd part of the assemblage, putting things together, began to comprehend the nefarious plans of the sexton, who lay mangled and dead on the floor of the tower, where only two days ago he had tolled the holy bell to call the good Christians of Golden Friars to worship.

The body was carried into the yard of the George and Dragon and laid in the old coach-house; and the townsfolk came grouping in to have a peep at the corpse, and stood round, looking darkly, and talking as low as if they were in a church.

The Vicar, in gaiters and slightly shovel hat, stood erect, as one in a little circle of notables—the Doctor, the attorney, Sir Geoffrey Mardykes, who happened to be in the town, and Turnbull, the host— in the centre of the paved yard, they having made an inspection of the body, at which troops of the village stragglers, to-ing and fro-ing, were gaping and frowning as they whispered their horrible conjectures.

'What d'ye think o' that?' said Tom Scales, the old hostler of the George, looking pale, with a stern, faint smile on his lips, as he and Dick Linklin sauntered out of the coach-house together.

'The deaul will hev his ain noo,' answered Dick, in his friend's ear. 'T' sexton's got a craigthraw like he gav' the lass over the clints of Scarsdale; ye mind what the ald soger telt us when he hid his face in the kitchen of the George here? By Jen! I'll ne'er forget that story.'

'I ween 'twas all true enough,' replied the hostler; 'and the sizzup he gav' the sleepin' man wi' t' poker across the forehead. See whar the edge o' t' bell took him, and smashed his ain, the self same lids. By ma sang, I wonder the deaul did na carry awa' his corpse i' the night, as he did wi' Tam Lunder's at Mooltern Mill.'

'Hout, man, who ever sid t' deaul inside o' a church?'

'The corpse is ill-faur'd enew to scare Satan himsel', for that matter; though it's true what you say. Ay, ye're reet tul a trippet, thar; for Beelzebub dar'n't show his snout inside the church, not the length o' the black o' my nail.'

While this discussion was going on, the gentlefolk who were talking the matter over in the centre of the yard had dispatched a message for the coroner all the way to the town of Hextan.

The last tint of sunset was fading from the sky by this time; so, of course, there was no thought of an inquest earlier than the next day.

In the meantime it was horribly clear that the sexton had intended to rob the church of its plate, and had lost his life in the attempt to carry the second bell, as we have seen, down the worn ladder of the tower. He had tumbled backwards and broken his neck upon the floor of the loft; and the heavy bell, in its fall, descended with its edge across his forehead.

Never was a man more completely killed by a double catastrophe, in a moment.

The bells and the contents of the sack, it was surmised, he meant to have conveyed across the lake that night, and with the help of his spade and pick to have buried them in Clousted Forest, and returned, after an absence of but a few hours—as he easily might—before morning, unmissed and unobserved. He would no doubt, having secured his booty, have made such arrangements as would have made it appear that the church had been broken into. He would, of course, have taken all measures to divert suspicion from himself, and have watched a suitable opportunity to repossess himself of the buried treasure and dispose of it in safety.

And now came out, into sharp relief, all the stories that had, one way or other, stolen after him into the town. Old Mrs. Pullen fainted when she saw him, and told Doctor Lincote, after, that she thought he was the highwayman who fired the shot that killed the coachman the night they were robbed on Hounslow Heath. There were the stories also told by the wayfaring old soldier with the wooden leg, and fifty others, up to this more than half disregarded, but which now seized on the popular belief with a startling grasp.

The fleeting light soon expired, and twilight was succeeded by the early night.

The inn yard gradually became quiet; and the dead sexton lay alone, in the dark, on his back, locked up in the old coach-house, the key of which was safe in the pocket of Tom Scales, the trusty old hostler of the George.

It was about eight o'clock, and the hostler, standing alone on the road in the front of the open door of the George and Dragon, had just smoked his pipe out. A bright moon hung in the frosty sky. The fells rose from the opposite edge of the lake like phantom mountains. The air was stirless. Through the boughs and sprays of the leafless elms no sigh or motion, however hushed, was audible. Not a ripple glimmered on the lake, which at one point only reflected the brilliant moon from its dark blue expanse like burnished steel. The road that runs by the inn door, along the margin of the lake, shone dazzlingly white.

White as ghosts, among the dark holly and juniper, stood the tall piers of the Vicar's gate, and their great stone balls, like heads, overlooking the same road, a few hundred yards up the lake, to the left. The early little town of Golden Friars was quiet by this time. Except for the townsfolk who were now collected in the kitchen of the inn itself, no inhabitant was now outside his own threshold.

Tom Scales was thinking of turning in. He was beginning to feel a little queer. He was thinking of the sexton, and could not get the fixed features of the dead man out of his head, when he heard the sharp though distant ring of a horse's hoof upon the frozen road. Tom's instinct apprized him of the approach of a guest to the George and Dragon. His experienced ear told him that the horseman was approaching by the Dardale road, which, after crossing that wide and dismal moss, passes the southern fells by Dunner Cleugh and finally enters the town of Golden Friars by joining the Mardykes-road, at the edge of the lake, close to the gate of the Vicar's house.

A clump of tall trees stood at this point; but the moon shone full upon the road and cast their shadow backward.

The hoofs were plainly coming at a gallop, with a hollow rattle. The horseman was a long time in appearing. Tom wondered how he had heard the sound—so sharply frosty as the air was—so very far away.

He was right in his guess. The visitor was coming over the mountainous road from Dardale Moss; and he now saw a horseman, who must have turned the corner of the Vicar's house at the moment when his eye was wearied; for when he saw him for the first time he was advancing, in the hazy moonlight, like the shadow of a cavalier, at a gallop, upon the level strip of road that skirts the margin of the mere, between the George and the Vicar's piers.

The hostler had not long to wonder why the rider pushed his beast at so furious a pace, and how he came to have heard him, as he now calculated, at least three miles away. A very few moments sufficed to bring horse and rider to the inn door.

It was a powerful black horse, something like the great Irish hunter that figured a hundred years ago, and would carry sixteen stone with ease across country. It would have made a grand charger. Not a hair turned. It snorted, it pawed, it arched its neck; then threw back its ears and down its head, and looked ready to lash, and then to rear; and seemed impatient to be off again, and incapable of standing quiet for a moment.

The rider got down

'As light as shadow falls.'

But he was a tall, sinewy figure. He wore a cape or short mantle, a cocked hat, and a pair of jack-boots, such as held their ground in some primitive corners of England almost to the close of the last century.

'Take him, lad,' said he to old Scales. 'You need not walk or wisp him—he never sweats or tires. Give him his oats, and let him take his own time to eat them. House!' cried the stranger—in the old-fashioned form of summons which still lingered, at that time, in out-of-the-way places—in a deep and piercing voice.

As Tom Scales led the horse away to the stables it turned its head towards its master with a short, shrill neigh.

'About *your* business, old gentleman—we must not go too fast,' the stranger cried back again to his horse, with a laugh as harsh and piercing; and he strode into the house.

The hostler led this horse into the inn yard. In passing, it sidled up to the coach-house gate, within which lay the dead sexton—snorted, pawed and lowered its head suddenly, with ear close to the plank, as if listening for a sound from within; then uttered again the same short, piercing neigh.

The hostler was chilled at this mysterious coquetry with the dead. He liked the brute less and less every minute.

In the meantime, its master had proceeded.

'I'll go to the inn kitchen,' he said, in his startling bass, to the drawer who met him in the passage.

And on he went, as if he had known the place all his days: not seeming to hurry himself—stepping leisurely, the servant thought—but gliding on at such a rate, nevertheless, that he had passed his guide and was in the kitchen of the George before he had got much more than half-way to it.

A roaring fire of dry wood, peat and coal lighted up this snug but spacious apartment—flashing on pots and pans, and dressers high-piled with pewter plates and dishes; and making the uncertain

[36]

shadows of the long 'hanks' of onions and many a flitch and ham, depending from the ceiling, dance on its glowing surface.

The doctor and the attorney, even Sir Geoffrey Mardykes, did not disdain on this occasion to take chairs and smoke their pipes by the kitchen fire, where they were in the thick of the gossip and discussion excited by the terrible event.

The tall stranger entered uninvited.

He looked like a gaunt, athletic Spaniard of forty, burned half black in the sun, with a bony, flattened nose. A pair of fierce black eyes were just visible under the edge of his hat; and his mouth seemed divided, beneath the moustache, by the deep scar of a hare-lip.

Sir Geoffrey Mardykes and the host of the George, aided by the doctor and the attorney, were discussing and arranging, for the third or fourth time, their theories about the death and the probable plans of Toby Crooke, when the stranger entered.

The new-comer lifted his hat, with a sort of smile, for a moment from his black head.

'What do you call this place, gentlemen?' asked the stranger.

'The town of Golden Friars, sir,' answered the doctor politely.

'The George and Dragon, sir: Anthony Turnbull, at your service,' answered mine host, with a solemn bow, at the same moment—so that the two voices went together, as if the doctor and the innkeeper were singing a catch.

'The George and the Dragon,' repeated the horseman, expanding his long hands over the fire which he had approached. 'Saint George, King George, the Dragon, The Devil: it is a very grand idol, that outside your door, sir. You catch all sorts of worshippers—courtiers, fanatics, scamps: all's fish, eh? Everybody welcome, provided he drinks like one. Suppose you brew a bowl or two of punch. I'll stand it. How many are we? Here—count, and let us have enough. Gentlemen, I mean to spend the night here, and my horse is in the stable. What holiday, fun, or fair has got so many pleasant faces together? When I last called here—for, now I bethink me, I have seen the place before—you all looked sad. It was on a Sunday, that dismalest of holidays; and it would have been positively melancholy only that your sexton—that saint upon earth—Mr. Crooke, was here.' He was looking round, over his shoulder, and added: 'Ha! don't I see him there?'

Frightened a good deal were some of the company. All gaped in the direction in which, with a nod, he turned his eyes.

[37]

'He's *not* thar—he *can't* be thar—we *see* he's not thar,' said Turnbull, as dogmatically as old Joe Willet might have delivered himself—for he did not care that the George should earn the reputation of a haunted house. 'He's met an accident, sir: he's dead—he's elsewhere—and therefore can't be here.'

Upon this the company entertained the stranger with the narrative —which they made easy by a division of labour, two or three generally speaking at a time, and no one being permitted to finish a second sentence without finding himself corrected and supplanted.

'The man's in Heaven, so sure as you're not,' said the traveller so soon as the story was ended. 'What! he was fiddling with the church bell, was he, and damned for that—eh? Landlord, get us some drink. A sexton damned for pulling down a church bell he has been pulling at for ten years!'

'You came, sir, by the Dardale-road, I believe?' said the doctor (village folk are curious). 'A dismal moss is Dardale Moss, sir; and a bleak clim' up the fells on t'other side.'

'I say "Yes" to all—from Dardale Moss, as black as pitch and as rotten as the grave, up that zigzag wall you call a road, that looks like chalk in the moonlight, through Dunner Cleugh, as dark as a coal-pit, and down here to the George and the Dragon, where you have a roaring fire, wise men, good punch—here it is—and a corpse in your coach-house. Where the carcass is, there will the eagles be gathered together. Come, landlord, ladle out the nectar. Drink, gentlemen— drink, all. Brew another bowl at the bar. How divinely it stinks of alcohol! I hope you like it, gentlemen: it smells all over of spices, like a mummy. Drink, friends. Ladle, landlord. Drink all. Serve it out.'

The guest fumbled in his pocket, and produced three guineas, which he slipped into Turnbull's fat palm.

'Let punch flow till that's out. I'm an old friend of the house. I call here, back and forward. I know you well, Turnbull, though you don't recognise me.'

'You have the advantage of me, sir,' said Mr. Turnbull, looking hard on that dark and sinister countenance—which, or the like of which, he could have sworn he had never seen before in his life. But he liked the weight and colour of his guineas, as he dropped them into his pocket. 'I hope you will find yourself comfortable while you stay.'

'You have given me a bedroom?'

'Yes, sir—the cedar chamber.'

'I know it—the very thing. No—no punch for me. By and by, perhaps.'

The talk went on, but the stranger had grown silent. He had seated himself on an oak bench by the fire, towards which he extended his feet and hands with seeming enjoyment; his cocked hat being, however, a little over his face.

Gradually the company began to thin. Sir Geoffrey Mardykes was the first to go; then some of the humbler townsfolk. The last bowl of punch was on its last legs. The stranger walked into the passage and said to the drawer:

'Fetch me a lantern. I must see my nag. Light it—hey! That will do. No—you need not come.'

The gaunt traveller took it from the man's hand and strode along the passage to the door of the stable-yard, which he opened and passed out.

Tom Scales, standing on the pavement, was looking through the stable window at the horses when the stranger plucked his shirt-sleeve. With an inward shock the hostler found himself alone in presence of the very person he had been thinking of.

'I say—they tell me you have something to look at in there'—he pointed with his thumb at the old coach-house door. 'Let us have a peep.'

Tom Scales happened to be at that moment in a state of mind highly favourable to anyone in search of a submissive instrument. He was in great perplexity, and even perturbation. He suffered the stranger to lead him to the coach-house gate.

'You must come in and hold the lantern,' said he. 'I'll pay you handsomely.'

The old hostler applied his key and removed the padlock.

'What are you afraid of? Step in and throw the light on his face,' said the stranger grimly. 'Throw open the lantern: stand there. Stoop over him a little—he won't bite you. Steady, or you may pass the night with him!'

In the meantime the company at the George had dispersed; and, shortly after, Anthony Turnbull—who, like a good landlord, was always last in bed, and first up, in his house—was taking, alone, his last look round the kitchen before making his final visit to the stable-yard, when Tom Scales tottered into the kitchen, looking like death, his hair standing upright; and he sat down on an oak chair, all in a tremble, wiped his forehead with his hand, and, instead of speaking, heaved a great sigh or two.

[39]

It was not till after he had swallowed a dram of brandy that he found his voice, and said:

'We'ev the deaul himsel' in t' house! By Jen! ye'd best send fo t' sir' (the clergyman). 'Happen he'll tak him in hand wi' holy writ, and send him elsewhidder deftly. Lord atween us and harm! I'm a sinfu' man. I tell ye, Mr. Turnbull, I dar'n't stop in t' George to-night under the same roof wi' him.'

'Ye mean the ra-beyoned, black-feyaced lad, wi' the brocken neb? Why, that's a gentleman wi' a pocket ful o' guineas, man, and a horse worth fifty pounds!'

'That horse is no better nor his rider. The nags that were in the stable wi' him, they all tuk the creepins, and sweated like rain down a thack. I tuk them all out o' that, away from him, into the hack-stable, and I thocht I cud never get them past him. But that's not all. When I was keekin inta t' window at the nags, he comes behint me and claps his claw on ma shouther, and he gars me gang wi' him, and open the aad coach-house door, and haad the cannle for him, till he pearked into the deed man's feyace; and, as God's my judge, I sid the corpse open its eyes and wark its mouth, like a man smoorin' and strivin' to talk. I cudna move or say a word, though I felt my hair rising on my heed; but at lang-last I gev a yelloch, and say I 'La! what is that?' and he himsel' looked round on me, like the devil he is; and, wi' a skirl o' a laugh, he strikes the lantern out o' my hand. When I cum to myself we were outside the coach-house door. The moon was shinin' in, and I cud see the corpse stretched out on the table whar we left it; and he kicked the door to wi' a purr o' his foot. "Lock it," says he; and so I did. And here's the key for ye—tak it yoursel', sir. He offer'd me money: he said he'd mak me a rich man if I'd sell him the corpse, and help him awa' wi' it.'

'Hout, man! What cud he want o' t' corpse? He's not doctor, to do a' that lids. He was takin' a rise out o' ye lad,' said Turnbull.

'Na, na—he wants the corpse. There's summat you a' me can't tell he wants to do wi' 't; and he'd liefer get it wi' sin and thievin', and the damage of my soul. He's one of them freytens a boo or a dobbies off Dardale Moss, that's always astir wi' the like after nightfall; unless—Lord save us!—he be the deaul himsel'.'

'Whar is he noo?' asked the landlord, who was growing uncomfortable.

'He spang'd up the back stair to his room. I wonder you didn't hear him trampin' like a wild horse; and he clapt his door that the house shook again—but Lord knows whar he is noo. Let us gang awa' up to the Vicar's, and gan *him* come down, and talk wi' him,'

'Hoity toity, man—you're too easy scared,' said the landlord, pale enough by this time. ' 'Twould be a fine thing, truly, to send abroad that the house was haunted by the deaul himsel'! Why, 'twould be the ruin o' the George. You're sure ye locked the door on the corpse?'

'Aye, sir—sartain.'

'Come wi' me, Tom—we'll gi' a last look round the yard.'

So, side by side, with many a jealous look right and left, and over their shoulders, they went in silence. On entering the old-fashioned quadrangle, surrounded by stables and other offices—built in the antique cage-work fashion—they stopped for a while under the shadow of the inn gable, and looked round the yard, and listened. All was silent—nothing stirring.

The stable lantern was lighted; and with it in his hand Tony Turnbull, holding Tom Scales by the shoulder, advanced. He hauled Tom after him for a step or two; then stood still and shoved him before him for a step or two more; and thus cautiously—as a pair of skirmishers under fire—they approached the coach-house door.

'There, ye see—all safe,' whispered Tom, pointing to the lock, which hung—distinct in the moonlight—in its place. 'Cum back, I say!'

'Cum on, say I!' retorted the landlord valorously. 'It would never do to allow any tricks to be played with the chap in there'—he pointed to the coach-house door.

'The coroner here in the morning, and never a corpse to sit on!' He unlocked the padlock with these words, having handed the lantern to Tom. 'Here, keck in, Tom,' he continued; 'ye hev the lantern—and see if all's as ye left it.'

'Not me—na, not for the George and a' that's in it!' said Tom, with a shudder, sternly, as he took a step backward.

What the—what are ye afraid on? Gi' me the lantern—it is all one: I will.'

And cautiously, little by little, he opened the door; and, holding the lantern over his head in the narrow slit, he peeped in—frowning and pale—with one eye, as if he expected something to fly in his face. He closed the door without speaking, and locked it again.

'As safe as a thief in a mill,' he whispered with a nod to his companion. And at that moment a harsh laugh overhead broke the silence startlingly, and set all the poultry in the yard gabbling.

[41]

'Thar he be!' said Tom, clutching the landlord's arm—'in the winda—see!'

The window of the cedar-room, up two pair of stairs, was open; and in the shadow a darker outline was visible of a man, with his elbows on the window-stone, looking down upon them.

'Look at his eyes—like two live coals!' gasped Tom.

The landlord could not see all this so sharply, being confused, and not so long-sighted as Tom.

'Time, sir,' called Tony Turnbull, turning cold as he thought he saw a pair of eyes shining down redly at him—'time for honest folk to be in their beds, and asleep!'

'As sound as your sexton!' said the jeering voice from above.

'Come out of this,' whispered the landlord fiercely to his hostler, plucking him hard by the sleeve.

They got into the house, and shut the door.

'I wish we were shot of him,' said the landlord, with something like a groan, as he leaned against the wall of the passage. 'I'll sit up, anyhow—and, Tom, you'll sit wi' me. Cum into the gun-room. No one shall steal the dead man out of my yard while I can draw a trigger.'

The gun-room in the George is about twelve feet square. It projects into the stable-yard and commands a full view of the old coach-house; and, through a narrow side window, a flanking view of the back door of the inn, through which the yard is reached.

Tony Turnbull took down the blunderbuss—which was the great ordnance of the house—and loaded it with a stiff charge of pistol bullets.

He put on a great-coat which hung there, and was his covering when he went out at night, to shoot wild ducks. Tom made himself comfortable likewise. They then sat down at the window, which was open, looking into the yard, the opposite side of which was white in the brilliant moonlight.

The landlord laid the blunderbuss across his knees, and stared into the yard. His comrade stared also. The door of the gun-room was locked; so they felt tolerably secure.

An hour passed; nothing had occurred. Another. The clock struck one. The shadows had shifted a little; but still the moon shone full on the old coach-house, and the stable where the guest's horse stood.

Turnbull thought he heard a step on the back-stair. Tom was watching the back-door through the side window, with eyes glazing

[42]

with the intensity of his stare. Anthony Turnbull, holding his breath, listened at the room door. It was a false alarm.

When he came back to the window looking into the yard:

'Hish! Look thar!' said he in a vehement whisper.

From the shadow at the left they saw the figure of the gaunt horseman, in short cloak and jack-boots, emerge. He pushed open the stable door, and led out his powerful black horse. He walked it across the front of the building till he reached the old coach-house door; and there, with its bridle on its neck, he left it standing, while he stalked to the yard gate; and, dealing it a kick with his heel, it sprang back with the rebound, shaking from top to bottom, and stood open. The stranger returned to the side of his horse; and the door which secured the corpse of the dead sexton seemed to swing slowly open of itself as he entered, and returned with the corpse in his arms, and swung it across the shoulders of the horse, and instantly sprang into the saddle.

'Fire!' shouted Tom, and bang went the blunderbuss with a stunning crack. A thousand sparrows' wings winnowed through the air from the thick ivy. The watch-dog yelled a furious bark. There was a strange ring and whistle in the air. The blunderbuss had burst into shivers right down to the very breech. The recoil rolled the inn-keeper upon his back on the floor, and Tom Scales was flung against the side of the recess of the window, which had saved him from a tumble as violent. In this position they heard the scaring laugh of the departing horseman, and saw him ride out of the gate with his ghastly burden.

Perhaps some of my readers, like myself, have heard this story told by Roger Turnbull, now host of the George and Dragon, the grandson of the very Tony who then swayed the spigot and keys of that inn, in the identical kitchen of which the fiend treated so many of the neighbours to punch.

What infernal object was subserved by the possession of the dead villain's body, I have not learned. But a very curious story, in which a vampire resuscitation of Crooke the sexton figures, may throw a light upon this part of the tale.

The result of Turnbull's shot at the disappearing fiend certainly justifies old Andrew Moretons's dictum, which is thus expressed in his curious 'History of Apparitions': 'I warn rash brands who, pretending not to fear the devil, are for using the ordinary violences with him, which affect one man from another—or with an apparition, in which they may be sure to receive some mischief. I knew one fired a gun at an apparition and the gun burst in a hundred pieces in his hand; another struck at an apparition with a sword, and broke his sword in pieces and wounded his hand grievously; and 'tis next to madness for anyone to go that way to work with any spirit, be it angel or be it devil.'

MARKHEIM

by Robert Louis Stevenson

Robert Louis Stevenson (1850–94) wrote some of
the most enduring and memorable Christmas tales
of the 1880s including 'Olalla' and the shorter
'Markheim'. The latter, written in 1884, was
inspired by an article on the subconscious which
Stevenson had read in a French scientific journal.
It was published in *The Merry Men and other Tales
and Fables*, 1887.

'Yes,' said the dealer, 'our windfalls are of various kinds. Some
customers are ignorant, and then I touch a dividend on my
superior knowledge. Some are dishonest,' and here he held
up the candle so that the light fell strongly on his visitor, 'and in that
case,' he continued, 'I profit by my virtue.'

Markheim had but just entered from the daylight streets, and his
eyes had not yet grown familiar with the mingled shine and darkness
in the shop. At these pointed words, and before the near presence of
the flame, he blinked painfully and looked aside.

The dealer chuckled. 'You come to me on Christmas Day,' he
resumed, 'when you know that I am alone in my house, put up my
shutters, and make a point of refusing business. Well, you will have to
pay for that; you will have to pay for my loss of time, when I should be
balancing my books; you will have to pay, besides, for a kind of
manner that I remark in you to-day very strongly. I am the essence of
discretion, and ask no awkward questions; but when a customer
cannot look me in the eye, he has to pay for it.' The dealer once more
chuckled; and then, changing to his usual business voice, though still

with a note of irony, 'You can give, as usual, a clear account of how you came in to the possession of the object?' he continued. 'Still your uncle's cabinet? A remarkable collector, sir!'

And the little pale, round-shouldered dealer stood almost on tiptoe, looking over the top of his gold spectacles, and nodding his head with every mark of disbelief. Markheim returned his gaze with one of infinite pity, and a touch of horror.

'This time,' said he, 'you are in error. I have not come to sell, but to buy. I have no curios to dispose of; my uncle's cabinet is bare to the wainscot; even were it still intact, I have done well on the Stock Exchange, and should more likely add to it than otherwise, and my errand to-day is simplicity itself. I seek a Christmas present for a lady,' he continued, waxing more fluent as he struck into the speech he had prepared; 'and certainly I owe you every excuse for thus disturbing you upon so small a matter. But the thing was neglected yesterday; I must produce my little compliment at dinner; and, as you very well know, a rich marriage is not a thing to be neglected.'

There followed a pause, during which the dealer seemed to weigh this statement incredulously. The ticking of many clocks among the curious lumber of the shop, and the faint rushing of the cabs in a near thoroughfare, filled up the interval of silence.

'Well, sir,' said the dealer, 'be it so. You are an old customer after all; and if, as you say, you have the chance of a good marriage, far be it from me to be an obstacle. Here is a nice thing for a lady now,' he went on, 'this hand glass—fifteenth century, warranted; comes from a good collection, too; but I reserve the name, in the interests of my customer, who was just like yourself, my dear sir, the nephew and sole heir of a remarkable collector.'

The dealer, while he thus ran on in his dry and biting voice, had stooped to take the object from its place; and, as he had done so, a shock had passed through Markheim, a start both of hand and foot, a sudden leap of many tumultuous passions to the face. It passed as swiftly as it came, and left no trace beyond a certain trembling of the hand that now received the glass.

'A glass,' he said hoarsely, and then paused, and repeated it more clearly. 'A glass? For Christmas? Surely not?'

'And why not?' cried the dealer. Why not a glass?'

Markheim was looking upon him with an indefinable expression.

'You ask me why not?' he said. 'Why, look here—look in it—look at yourself! Do you like to see it? No! nor I—nor any man.'

The little man had jumped back when Markheim had so suddenly confronted him with the mirror; but now, perceiving there was nothing worse on hand, he chuckled. 'Your future lady, sir, must be pretty hard favoured,' said he.

'I ask you,' said Markheim, 'for a Christmas present, and you give me this—this damned reminder of years, and sins, and follies—this hand-conscience! Did you mean it? Had you a thought in your mind? Tell me. It will be better for you if you do. Come, tell me about yourself. I hazard a guess now, that you are in secret a very charitable man?'

The dealer looked closely at his companion. It was very odd, Markheim did not appear to be laughing; there was something in his face like an eager sparkle of hope, but nothing of mirth.

'What are you driving at?' the dealer asked.

'Not charitable?' returned the other gloomily. 'Not charitable; not pious; not scrupulous; unloving, unbeloved; a hand to get money, a safe to keep it. Is that all? Dear God, man, is that all?'

'I will tell you what it is,' began the dealer, with some sharpness, and then broke off again into a chuckle. 'But I see this is a love match of yours, and you have been drinking the lady's health.'

'Ah!' cried Markheim, with a strange curiosity. 'Ah, have you been in love? Tell me about that.'

'I,' cried the dealer. 'I in love! I never had the time, nor have I the time to-day for all this nonsense. Will you take the glass?'

'Where is the hurry?' returned Markheim. 'It is very pleasant to stand here talking; and life is so short and insecure that I would not hurry away from any pleasure—no, not even from so mild a one as this. We should rather cling, cling to what little we can get, like a man at a cliff's edge. Every second is a cliff, if you think upon it—a cliff a mile high—high enough, if we fall, to dash us out of every feature of humanity. Hence it is best to talk pleasantly. Let us talk of each other: why should we wear this mask? Let us be confidential. Who knows, we might become friends?'

'I have just one word to say to you,' said the dealer. 'Either make your purchase, or walk out of my shop!'

'True, true,' said Markheim. 'Enough fooling. To business. Show me something else.'

The dealer stooped once more, this time to replace the glass upon the shelf, his thin blond hair falling over his eyes as he did so. Markheim moved a little nearer, with one hand in the pocket of his great-coat; he drew himself up and filled his lungs; at the same time many different emotions were depicted together on his face—terror, horror, and resolve, fascination and a physical repulsion; and through a haggard lift of his upper lip, his teeth looked out.

'This, perhaps, may suit,' observed the dealer: and then, as he began to re-arise, Markheim bounded from behind upon his victim. The long, skewer-like dagger flashed and fell. The dealer struggled like a hen, striking his temple on the shelf, and then tumbled on the floor in a heap.

Time had some score of small voices in that shop, some stately and slow as was becoming to their great age; others garrulous and hurried. All these told out the seconds in an intricate chorus of tickings. Then the passage of a lad's feet, heavily running on the pavement, broke in upon these smaller voices and startled Markheim into the consciousness of his surroundings. He looked about him awfully. The candle stood on the counter, its flame solemnly wagging in a draught; and by that in considerable movement, the whole room was filled with noiseless bustle and kept heaving like a sea: the tall shadows nodding, the gross blots of darkness swelling and dwindling as with respiration, the faces of the portraits and the china gods changing and wavering like images in water. The inner door stood ajar, and peered into that leaguer of shadows with a long slit of daylight like a pointing finger.

From these fear-stricken rovings, Markheim's eyes returned to the body of his victim, where it lay both humped and sprawling, incredibly small and strangely meaner than in life. In these poor, miserly clothes, in that ungainly attitude, the dealer lay like so much sawdust. Markheim had feared to see it, and, lo! it was nothing. And yet, as he gazed, this bundle of old clothes and pool of blood began to find eloquent voices. There it must lie; there was none to work the cunning hinges or direct the miracle of locomotion—there it must lie till it was found. Found! aye, and then? Then would this dead flesh lift up a cry that would ring over England, and fill the world with the echoes of pursuit. Aye, dead or not, this was still the enemy.

'Time was that when the brains were out,' he thought; and the first word struck into his mind. Time, now that the deed was accomplished—time, which had closed for the victim, had become instant and momentous for the slayer.

The thought was yet in his mind, when, first one and then another, with every variety of pace and voice—one deep as the bell from a cathedral turret, another ringing on its treble notes the prelude of a waltz—the clocks began to strike the hour of three in the afternoon.

The sudden outbreak of so many tongues in that dumb chamber staggered him. He began to bestir himself, going to and fro with the candle, beleaguered by moving shadows, and startled to the soul by chance reflections. In many rich mirrors, some of home design, some from Venice or Amsterdam, he saw his face repeated and repeated as it were an army of spies; his own eyes met and detected him; and the sound of his own steps, lightly as they fell, vexed the surrounding quiet. And still, as he continued to fill his pockets, his mind accused him with a sickening iteration, of the thousand faults of his design. He should have chosen a more quiet hour; he should have prepared an alibi; he should not have used a knife; he should have been more cautious, and only bound and gagged the dealer, and not killed him; he should have been more bold, and killed the servant also; he should have done all things otherwise: poignant regrets, weary, incessant toiling of the mind to change what was unchangeable, to plan what was now useless, to be the architect of the irrevocable past. Meanwhile, and behind all this activity, brute terrors, like the scurrying of rats in a deserted attic, filled the more remote chambers of his brain with riot; the hand of the constable would fall heavy on his shoulder, and his nerves would jerk like a hooked fish; or he beheld, in galloping defile, the dock, the prison, the gallows, and the black coffin.

Terror of the people in the street sat down before his mind like a besieging army. It was impossible, he thought, but that some rumour of the struggle must have reached their ears and set on edge their curiosity; and now, in all the neighbouring houses, he divined them sitting motionless and with uplifted ear—solitary people, condemned to spend Christmas dwelling alone on memories of the past, and now startlingly recalled from that tender exercise; happy family parties, struck into the silence round the table, the mother still with raised finger: every degree and age and humour, but all, by their own hearths, prying and hearkening and weaving the rope that was to hang him. Sometimes it seemed to him he could not move too softly; the clink of the tall Bohemian goblets rang out loudly like a bell; and alarmed by the bigness of the ticking, he was tempted to stop the clocks. And then, again, with a swift transition of his terrors, the very silence of the place appeared a source of peril, and a thing to strike and freeze the passer-by; and he would step more boldly, and bustle aloud among the contents of the shop, and imitate, with elaborate bravado, the movements of a busy man at ease in his own house.

But he was now so pulled about by different alarms that, while one portion of his mind was still alert and cunning, another trembled on the brink of lunacy. One hallucination in particular took a strong hold on his credulity. The neighbour hearkening with white face beside his window, the passer-by arrested by a horrible surmise on the pavement—these could at worst suspect, they could not know; through the brick walls and shuttered windows only sounds could penetrate. But here, within the house, was he alone? He knew he was; he had watched the servant set forth sweethearting, in her poor best, 'out for the day' written in every ribbon and smile. Yes, he was alone, of course; and yet, in the bulk of empty house above him, he could surely hear a stir of delicate footing—he was surely conscious, inexplicably conscious of some presence. Aye, surely; to every room and corner of the house his imagination followed it; and now it was a faceless thing, and yet had eyes to see with; and again it was a shadow of himself; and yet again behold the image of the dead dealer, reinspired with cunning and hatred.

At times, with a strong effort, he would glance at the open door which still seemed to repel his eyes. The house was tall, the skylight small and dirty, the day blind with fog; and the light that filtered down to the ground story was exceedingly faint, and showed dimly on the threshold of the shop. And yet, in that strip of doubtful brightness, did there not hang wavering a shadow?

Suddenly, from the street outside, a very jovial gentleman began to beat with a staff on the shop-door, accompanying his blows with shouts and railleries in which the dealer was continually called upon by name. Markheim, smitten into ice, glanced at the dead man. But no! he lay quite still; he was fled away far beyond earshot of these blows and shoutings; he was sunk beneath seas of silence; and his name, which would once have caught his notice above the howling of a storm, had become an empty sound. And presently the jovial gentleman desisted from his knocking and departed.

Here was a broad hint to hurry what remained to be done, to get forth from this accusing neighbourhood, to plunge into a bath of London multitudes, and to reach, on the other side of the day, that haven of safety and apparent innocence—his bed. One visitor had come: at any moment another might follow and be more obstinate. To have done the deed, and yet not to reap the profit, would be too abhorrent a failure. The money, that was now Markheim's concern; and as a means to that, the keys.

He glanced over his shoulder at the open door, where the shadow was still lingering and shivering; with no conscious repugnance of the mind, yet with a tremor of the belly, he drew near the body of his victim. The human character had quite departed. Like a suit half-stuffed with bran, the limbs lay scattered, the trunk doubled, on the floor; and yet the thing repelled him. Although so dingy and inconsiderable to the eye, he feared it might have more significance to the touch. He took the body by the shoulders, and turned it on its back. It was strangely light and supple, and the limbs, as if they had been broken, fell into the oddest postures. The face was robbed of all expression; but it was as pale as wax, and shockingly smeared with blood about one temple. That was, for Markheim, the one displeasing circumstance It carried him back, upon the instant, to a certain fairday in a fishers' village: a grey day, a piping wind, a crowd upon the street, the blare of brasses, the booming of drums, the nasal voice of a ballad singer; and a boy going to and fro, buried over head in the crowd and divided between interest and fear, until, coming out upon the chief place of concourse, he beheld a booth and a great screen with pictures, dismally designed, garishly coloured: Brownrigg with her apprentice; the Mannings with their murdered guest; Weare in the death-grip of Thurtell; and a score besides of famous crimes. The thing was as clear as an illusion; he was once again that little boy; he was looking once again, and with the same sense of physical revolt, at these vile pictures; he was still stunned by the thumping of the drums. A bar of that day's music returned upon his memory; and at that, a qualm came over him, a breath of nausea, a sudden weakness of the joints, which he must instantly resist and conquer.

He judged it more prudent to confront than to flee from these considerations; looking the more hardily in the dead face, bending his mind to realize the nature and greatness of his crime. So little a while ago that face had moved with every change of sentiment, that pale mouth had spoken, that body had been all on fire with governable energies; and now, by this act, that piece of life had been arrested, as the horologist, with interjected finger, arrests the beating of the clock. So he reasoned in vain; he could rise to no more remorseful consciousness; the same heart which had shuddered before the painted effigies of crime, looked on its reality unmoved. At best, he felt a gleam of pity for one who had been endowed in vain with all those faculties that can make the world a garden of enchantment, one who had never lived and who was now dead. But of penitence, no, not a tremor.

With that, shaking himself clear of these considerations, he found

[51]

the keys and advanced towards the open door of the shop. Outside, it had begun to rain smartly; and the sound of the shower upon the roof had banished silence. Like some dripping cavern, the chambers of the house were haunted by an incessant echoing, which filled the ear and mingled with the ticking of the clocks. And, as Markheim approached the door, he seemed to hear, in answer to his own cautious tread, the steps of another foot withdrawing up the stair. The shadow still palpitated loosely on the threshold. He threw a ton's weight of resolve upon his muscles, and drew back the door.

The faint, foggy daylight glimmered dimly on the bare floor and stairs; on the bright suit of armour posted, halbert in hand, upon the landing; and on the dark wood-carvings, and framed pictures that hung against the yellow panels of the wainscot. So loud was the beating of the rain through all the house that, in Markheim's ears, it began to be distinguished into many different sounds. Footsteps and sighs, the tread of regiments marching in the distance, the chink of money in the counting, and the creaking of doors held stealthily ajar, appeared to mingle with the patter of the drops upon the cupola and the gushing of the water in the pipes. The sense that he was not alone grew upon him to the verge of madness. On every side he was haunted and begirt by presences. He heard them moving in the upper chambers; from the shop, he heard the dead man getting to his legs; and as he began with a great effort to mount the stairs, feet fled quietly before him and followed stealthily behind. If he were but deaf, he thought, how tranquilly he would possess his soul! And then again, and hearkening with ever fresh attention, he blessed himself for that unresting sense which held the outposts and stood a trusty sentinel upon his life. His head turned continually on his neck; his eyes, which seemed starting from their orbits, scouted on every side, and on every side were half-rewarded as with the tail of something nameless vanishing. The four-and-twenty steps to the first floor were four-and-twenty agonies.

On that first storey, the doors stood ajar, three of them like three ambushes, shaking his nerves like the throats of cannon. He could never again, he felt, be sufficiently immured and fortified from men's observing eyes; he longed to be home, girt in by walls, buried among bedclothes, and invisible to all but God. And at that thought he wondered a little, recollecting tales of other murderers and the fear they were said to entertain of heavenly avengers. It was not so, at least, with him. He feared the laws of nature, lest, in their callous and immutable procedure, they should preserve some damning evidence of his crime. He feared tenfold more, with a slavish, superstitious terror, some scission in the community of man's experience, some wilful illegality of nature. He played a game of skill, depending on the rules, calculating consequence from cause; and what if nature, as the defeated tyrant overthrew the chess-board, should break the mould of their succession? The like had befallen Napoleon (so writers said) when the winter changed the time of its appearance. The like might befall Markheim: the solid walls might become transparent and reveal his doings like those of bees in a glass hive; the stout planks might yield under his foot like quicksands and detain him in their clutch; aye, and there were soberer accidents that might destroy him: if, for instance, the house should fall and imprison him beside the body of his victim; or the house next door should fly on fire, and the firemen invade him from all sides. These things he feared; and, in a sense, these things might be called the hands of God reached forth against sin. But about God Himself he was at ease; his act was doubtless exceptional, but so were his excuses, which God knew; it was there, and not among men, that he felt sure of justice.

When he had got safe into the drawing-room, and shut the door behind him, he was aware of a respite from alarms. The room was quite dismantled, uncarpeted besides, and strewn with packing cases and incongruous furniture; several great pier-glasses, in which he beheld himself at various angles, like an actor on a stage; many pictures, framed and unframed, standing, with their faces to the wall; a fine Sheraton sideboard, a cabinet of marquetry, and a great old bed, with tapestry hangings. The windows opened to the floor; but by great good fortune the lower part of the shutters had been closed, and this concealed him from the neighbours. Here, then, Markheim drew in a packing case before the cabinet, and began to search among the keys. It was a long business, for there were many; and it was irksome, besides; for, after all, there might be nothing in the cabinet, and time was on the wing. But the closeness of the occupation sobered him. With the tail of his eye he saw the door—even glanced at it from time to time directly, like a besieged commander pleased to verify the good estate of his defences. But in truth he was at peace. The rain falling in the street sounded natural and pleasant. Presently, on the other side, the notes of a piano were wakened to the music of a hymn, and the voices of many children took up the air and words. How stately, how comfortable was the melody! How fresh the youthful voices! Markheim gave ear to it smilingly, as he sorted out the keys; and his mind was thronged with answerable ideas and images; church-going children and the pealing of the high organ; children afield, bathers by the brookside, ramblers on the brambly common, kite-flyers in the windy and cloud-navigated sky; and then, at another cadence of the hymn, back again to church, and the somnolence of summer Sundays, and the high genteel voices of the parson (which he smiled a little to recall) and the painted Jacobean tombs, and the dim lettering of the Ten Commandments in the chancel.

And as he sat thus, at once busy and absent, he was startled to his feet. A flash of ice, a flash of fire, a bursting gush of blood, went over him, and then he stood transfixed and thrilling. A step mounted the stair slowly and steadily, and presently a hand was laid upon the knob, and the lock clicked, and the door opened.

Fear held Markheim in a vice. What to expect he knew not, whether the dead man walking, or the official ministers of human justice, or some chance witness blindly stumbling in to consign him to the gallows. But when a face was thrust into the aperture, glanced round the room, looked at him, nodded and smiled as if in friendly recognition, and then withdrew again, and the door closed behind it, his fear broke loose from his control in a hoarse cry. At the sound of this the visitant returned.

'Did you call me?' he asked pleasantly, and with that he entered the room and closed the door behind him.

Markheim stood and gazed at him with all his eyes. Perhaps there was a film upon his sight, but the outlines of the newcomer seemed to change and waver like those of the idols in the wavering candlelight of the shop; and at times he thought he knew him; and at times he thought he bore a likeness to himself; and always, like a lump of living terror, there lay in his bosom the conviction that this thing was not of the earth and not of God.

And yet the creature had a strange air of the commonplace, as he stood looking on Markheim with a smile; and when he added: 'You are looking for the money, I believe?' it was the tones of everyday politeness.

Markheim made no answer.

'I should warn you,' resumed the other, 'that the maid has left her sweetheart earlier than usual and will soon be here. If Mr. Markheim be found in this house, I need not describe to him the consequences.'

'You know me?' cried the murderer.

The visitor smiled. 'You have long been a favourite of mine,' he said; 'and I have long observed and often sought to help you.'

[54]

'What are you?' cried Markheim: 'the devil?'

'What I may be,' returned the other, 'cannot affect the service I propose to render you.'

'It can,' cried Markheim; 'it does! Be helped by you? No, never; not by you! You do not know me yet; thank God, you do not know me!'

'I know you,' replied the visitant, with a sort of kind severity or rather firmness. 'I know you to the soul.'

'Know me!' cried Markheim. 'Who can do so? My life is but a travesty and slander on myself. I have lived to belie my nature. All men do; all men are better than this disguise that grows about and stifles them. You see each dragged away by life, like one whom bravos have seized and muffled in a cloak. If they had their own control—if you could see their faces, they would be altogether different, they would shine out for heroes and saints! I am worse than most; myself is more overlaid; my excuse is known to me and God. But, had I the time, I could disclose myself.'

'To me?' inquired the visitant.

'To you before all,' returned the murderer. 'I supposed you were intelligent. I thought—since you exist—you would prove a reader of the heart. And yet you would propose to judge me by my acts! Think of it; my acts! I was born and I have lived in a land of giants; giants have dragged me by the wrists since I was born out of my mother—the giants of circumstance. And you would judge me by my acts! But can you not look within? Can you not understand that evil is hateful to me? Can you not see within me the clear writing of conscience, never blurred by any wilful sophistry, although too often disregarded? Can you not read me for a thing that surely must be common as humanity—the unwilling sinner?'

'All this is very feelingly expressed,' was the reply, 'but it regards me not. These points of consistency are beyond my province, and I care not in the least by what compulsion you may have been dragged away, so as you are but carried in the right direction. But time flies; the servant delays, looking in the faces of the crowd and at the pictures on the hoardings, but still she keeps moving nearer; and remember, it is as if the gallows itself was striding towards you through the Christmas streets! Shall I help you; I, who know all? Shall I tell you where to find the money?'

'For what price?' asked Markheim.

'I offer you the service for a Christmas gift,' returned the other.

Markheim could not refrain from smiling with a kind of bitter

[55]

triumph. 'No,' said he, 'I will take nothing at your hands; if I were dying of thirst, and it was your hand that put the pitcher to my lips, I should find the courage to refuse. It may be credulous, but I will do nothing to commit myself to evil.'

'I have no objection to a deathbed repentance,' observed the visitant.

'Because you disbelieve their efficacy!' Markheim cried.

'I do not say so,' returned the other; 'but I look on these things from a different side, and when the life is done my interest falls. The man has lived to serve me, to spread black looks under colour of religion, or to sow tares in the wheat-field, as you do, in a course of weak compliance with desire. Now that he draw so near to his deliverance, he can add but one act of service — to repent, to die smiling, and thus to build up in confidence and hope the more timorous of my surviving followers. I am not so hard a master. Try me. Accept my help. Please yourself in life as you have done hitherto; please yourself more amply, spread your elbows at the board; and when the night begins to fall and the curtains to be drawn, I tell you, for your greater comfort, that you will find it even easy to compound your quarrel with your conscience, and to make a truckling peace with God. I came but now from such a deathbed, and the room was full of sincere mourners, listening to the man's last words: and when I looked into that face, which had been set as a flint against mercy, I found it smiling with hope.'

'And do you, then, suppose me such a creature?' asked Markheim. 'Do you think I have no more generous aspirations than to sin, and sin, and sin, and, at the last, sneak into heaven? My heart rises at the thought. Is this, then, your experience of mankind? or is it because you find me with red hands that you presume such baseness? and is this crime of murder indeed so impious as to dry up the very springs of good?'

'Murder is to me no special category,' replied the other. 'All sins are murder, even as all life is war. I behold your race, like starving mariners on a raft, plucking crusts out of the hands of famine and feeding on each others' lives. I follow sins beyond the moment of their acting; I find in all that the last consequence is death; and to my eyes, the pretty maid who thwarts her mother with such taking graces on a question of a ball, drips no less visibly with human gore than such a murderer as yourself. Do I say that I follow sins? I follow virtues also; they differ not by the thickness of a nail, they are both scythes for the reaping angel of Death. Evil, for which I live, consists not in action

[56]

but in character. The bad man is dear to me; not the bad act, whose fruits, if we could follow them far enough down the hurtling cataract of the ages, might yet be found more blessed than those of the rarest virtues. And it is not because you have killed a dealer, but because you are Markheim, that I offer to forward your escape.'

'I will lay my heart open to you,' answered Markheim. 'This crime on which you find me is my last. On my way to it I have learned my lessons; itself is a lesson, a momentous lesson. Hitherto I have been driven with revolt to what I would not; I was a bond-slave to poverty, driven and scourged. There are robust virtues that can stand in these temptations; mine was not so: I had a thirst of pleasure. But to-day, and out of this deed, I pluck both warning and riches—both the power and a fresh resolve to be myself. I become in all things a free actor in the world; I begin to see myself all changed, these hands the agents of good, this heart at peace. Something comes over me out of the past; something of what I have dreamed on Sabbath evenings to the sound of the church organ, of what I forecast when I shed tears over noble books, or talked, an innocent child, with my mother. There lies my life; I have wandered a few years, but now I see once more my city of destination.'

'You are to use this money on the Stock Exchange, I think?' remarked the visitor; 'and there, if I mistake not, you have already lost some thousands?'

'Ah,' said Markheim, 'but this time I have a sure thing.'

'This time again, you will lose,' replied the visitor quietly.

'Ah, but I keep back the half!' cried Markheim.

'That also you will lose,' said the other.

The sweat started upon Markheim's brow. 'Well, then, what matter?' he exclaimed. 'Say it be lost, say I am plunged again in poverty, shall one part of me, and that the worse, continue until the end to override the better? Evil and good run strong in me, haling me both ways. I do not love the one thing, I love all. I can conceive great deeds, renunciations, martyrdoms; and though I be fallen to such a crime as murder, pity is no stranger to my thoughts. I pity the poor; who knows their trials better than myself? I pity and help them; I prize love, I love honest laughter; there is no good thing nor true thing on earth but I love it from my heart. And are my vices only to direct my life, and my virtues to lie without effect, like some passive limber of the mind? Not so; good, also is a spring of acts.'

But the visitor raised his finger. 'For the six-and-thirty years that you have been in this world,' said he, 'through many changes of fortune and varieties of humour, I have watched you steadily fall. aifteen years ago you would have started at a theft. Three years back you would have blenched at the name of murder. Is there any crime, is there any cruelty or meanness, from which you still recoil?—five years from now I shall detect you in the fact! Downward, downward, lies your way; nor can anything but death avail to stop you.'

'It is true,' Markheim said huskily, 'I have in some degree complied with evil. But it is so with all: the very saints, in the mere exercise of living, grow less dainty, and take on the tone of their surroundings.'

'I will propound to you one simple question,' said the other; 'and as you answer, I shall read to you your moral horoscope. You have grown in many things more lax; possibly you do right to be so; and at any account, it is the same with all men. But granting that, are you in any one particular, however trifling, more difficult to please with your own conduct, or do you go in all things with a looser rein?'

'In any one?' repeated Markheim, with an anguish of consideration. 'No,' he added, with despair, 'in none! I have gone down in all.'

'Then,' said the visitor, 'content yourself with what you are, for you will never change; and the words of your part on this stage are irrevocably written down.'

Markheim stood for a long while silent, and indeed it was the visitor who first broke the silence. 'That being so,' he said, 'shall I show you the money?'

'And grace?' cried Markheim.

'Have you not tried it?' returned the other. 'Two or three years ago, did I not see you on the platform of revival meetings, and was not your voice the loudest in the hymn?'

'It is true,' said Markheim; 'and I see clearly what remains for me by way of duty. I thank you for these lessons from my soul; my eyes are opened, and I behold myself at last for what I am.'

At this moment, the sharp note of the door-bell rang through the house; and the visitor, as though this were some concerted signal for which he had been waiting, changed at once in his demeanour.

'The maid!' he cried. 'She has returned, as I forewarned you, and there is now before you one more difficult passage. Her master, you must say, is ill; you must let her in, with an assured but rather serious countenance—no smiles, no overacting, and I promise you success! Once the girl within, and the door closed, the same dexterity that has already rid you of the dealer will relieve you of this last danger in your path. Thenceforward you have the whole evening—the whole night, if needed—to ransack the treasures of the house and to make good your safety. This is help that comes to you with the mask of danger. Up!' he cried; 'up, friend; your life hangs trembling in the scales: up, and act!'

Markheim steadily regarded his counsellor. 'If I be condemned to evil acts,' he said, 'there is still one door of freedom open—I can cease from action. If my life be an ill thing, I can lay it down. Though I be, as you say truly, at the beck of every small temptation, I can yet, by one decisive gesture, place myself beyond the reach of all. My love of good is damned to barrenness; it may, and let it be! But I have still my hatred of evil; and from that, to your galling disappointment, you shall see that I can draw both energy and courage.'

The features of the visitor began to undergo a wonderful and lovely change: they brightened and softened with a tender triumph, and, even as they brightened, faded and dislimned. But Markheim did not pause to watch or understand the transformation. He opened the door and went downstairs very slowly, thinking to himself. His past went soberly before him; he beheld it as it was, ugly and strenuous like a dream, random as chance-medley—a scene of defeat. Life, as he thus reviewed it, tempted him no longer; but on the farther side he perceived a quiet haven for his bark. He paused in the passage, and looked into the shop, where the candle still burned by the dead body. It was strangely silent. Thoughts of the dealer swarmed into his mind, as he stood gazing. And then the bell once more broke out into impatient clamour.

He confronted the maid upon the threshold with something like a smile.

'You had better go for the police,' said he: 'I have killed your master.'

THE GHOST OF CHRISTMAS EVE

by J. M. Barrie

The name of James Matthew Barrie (1860–1937)
has been part of Christmas for eighty years, ever
since his creation of 'Peter Pan', one of the most
timeless and popular of all pantomimes.
Always interested in the fantastic and the
supernatural, Barrie's short tale of 'The Ghost of
Christmas Eve' appeared in his collection My *Lady
Nicotine* in 1890.

A few years ago, as some may remember, a startling ghost paper
appeared in the monthly organ of the Society for Haunting
Houses. The writer guaranteed the truth of his statement,
and even gave the name of the Yorkshire manor-house in which the
affair took place. The article and the discussion to which it gave rise
agitated me a good deal, and I consulted Pettigrew about the
advisability of clearing up the mystery. The writer wrote that he
'distinctly saw his arm pass through the apparition and come out at the
other side,' and indeed I still remember his saying so next morning.
He had a scared face, but I had presence of mind to continue eating
my rolls and marmalade as if my briar had nothing to do with the
miraculous affair.

Seeing that he made a 'paper' of it, I suppose he is justified in
touching up the incidental details. He says, for instance, that we were
told the story of the ghost which is said to haunt the house, just before
going to bed. As far as I remember, it was only mentioned at

luncheon, and then sceptically. Instead of there being snow falling outside and an eerie wind wailing through the skeleton trees, the night was still and muggy. Lastly, I did not know, until the journal reached my hands, that he was put into the room known as the Haunted Chamber, nor that in that room the fire is noted for casting weird shadows upon the walls. This, however, may be so. The legend of the manor-house ghost he tells precisely as it is known to me.

The tragedy dates back to the time of Charles I, and is led up to by a pathetic love-story, which I need not give. Suffice it that for seven days and nights the old steward had been anxiously awaiting the return of his young master and mistress from their honeymoon. On Christmas Eve, after he had gone to bed, there was a great clanging of the door-bell. Flinging on a dressing-gown, he hastened downstairs. According to the story, a number of servants watched him, and saw by the light of his candle that his face was an ashy white. He took off the chains of the door, unbolted it, and pulled it open. What he saw no human being knows; but it must have been something awful, for without a cry the old steward fell dead in the hall. Perhaps the strangest part of the story is this: that the shadow of a burly man, holding a pistol in his hand, entered by the open door, stepped over the steward's body, and, gliding up the stairs, disappeared, no one , could say where.

Such is the legend. I shall not tell the many ingenious explanations of it that have been offered. Every Christmas Eve, however, the silent scene is said to be gone through again; and tradition declares that no person lives for twelve months at whom the ghostly intruder points his pistol.

On Christmas Day the gentleman who tells the tale in the scientific journal created some sensation at the breakfast-table by solemnly asserting that he had seen the ghost. Most of the men present scouted his story, which may be condensed into a few words. He had retired to his bedroom at a fairly early hour, and as he opened the door his candle-light was blown out. He tried to get a light from the fire, but it was too low, and eventually he went to bed in the semi-darkness. He was wakened—he did not know at what hour—by the clanging of a bell. He sat up in bed, and the ghost-story came in a rush to his mind. His fire was dead, and the room was consequently dark; yet by and by he knew, though he heard no sound, that his door had opened. He cried out, 'Who is that?' but got no answer. By an effort he jumped up and went to the door, which was ajar. His bedroom was on the first floor, and looking up the stairs he could see nothing. He felt a cold sensation at his heart, however, when he looked the other way.

Going slowly and without a sound down the stairs, was an old man in a dressing-gown. He carried a candle. From the top of the stairs only part of the hall is visible, but as the apparition disappeared the watcher had the courage to go down a few steps after him. At first nothing was to be seen, for the candlelight had vanished. A dim light, however, entered by the long narrow windows which flank the hall-door, and after a moment the onlooker could see that the hall was empty. He was marvelling at this sudden disappearance of the steward, when, to his horror, he saw a body fall upon the hall-floor within a few feet of the door.

The watcher cannot say whether he cried out, nor how long he stood there trembling. He came to himself with a start as he realized that something was coming up the stairs. Fear prevented his taking flight, and in a moment the thing was at his side. Then he saw indistinctly that it was not the figure he had seen descend. He saw a younger man in a heavy overcoat, but with no hat on his head. He wore on his face a look of extravagant triumph. The guest boldly put out his hand towards the figure. To his amazement his arm went through it. The ghost paused for a moment and looked behind it. It was then the watcher realized that it carried a pistol in its right hand. He was by this time in a highly-strung condition, and he stood trembling lest the pistol should be pointed at him. The apparition, however, rapidly glided up the stairs and was soon lost to sight. Such are the main facts of the story; none of which I contradicted at the time.

I cannot say absolutely that I can clear up this mystery; but my suspicions are confirmed by a good deal of circumstantial evidence. This will not be understood unless I explain my strange infirmity. Wherever I went I used to be troubled with a presentiment that I had left my pipe behind. Often even at the dinner-table, I paused in the middle of a sentence as if stricken with sudden pain. Then my hand went down to my pocket. Sometimes, even after I felt my pipe, I had a conviction that it was stopped, and only by a desperate effort did I keep myself from producing it and blowing down it. I distinctly remember once dreaming three nights in succession that I was on the Scotch express without it. More than once, I know, I have wandered in my sleep, looking for it in all sorts of places, and after I went to bed I generally jumped out, just to make sure of it.

[62]

My strong belief, then, is that I was the ghost seen by the writer of the paper. I fancy that I rose in my sleep, lighted a candle and wandered down the hall to feel if my pipe was safe in my coat, which was hanging there. The light had gone out when I was in the hall. Probably the body seen to fall on the hall floor was some other coat which I had flung there to get more easily at my own. I cannot account for the bell; but perhaps the gentleman in the Haunted Chamber dreamt that part of the affair. I had put on the overcoat before reascending; indeed, I may say that next morning I was surprised to find it on a chair in my bedroom, also to notice that there were several long streaks of candle-grease on my dressing-gown. I conclude that the pistol, which gave my face such a look of triumph, was my briar, which I found in the morning beneath my pillow. The strangest thing of all, perhaps, is that when I awoke there was a smell of tobacco-smoke in the bedroom.

THE REAL AND
THE COUNTERFEIT

by Mrs. Alfred Baldwin

Some of the best and most prolific writers of ghost
stories, and contributors to the popular Christmas
numbers, were women—notably Mrs. Henry
Wood, Mrs. J.H. Riddell, Mrs. Margaret
Oliphant, and Amelia B. Edwards. One of the
lesser known today is Louisa Baldwin (née
Macdonald) (1845–1925), who married the
ironmaster and MP Alfred Baldwin, and lived long
enough to see her only son Stanley become Prime
Minister. She penned several excellent ghost
stories for the *Argosy, Cornhill,* and other
magazines. The best were collected into a volume
entitled *The Shadow on the Blind* (1895), and
dedicated to her nephew Rudyard Kipling.

W ill Musgrave determined that he would neither keep
Christmas alone, nor spend it again with his parents and
sisters in the south of France. The Musgrave family
annually migrated southward from their home in Northumberland,
and Will as regularly followed them to spend a month with them in
the Riviera, till he had almost forgotten what Christmas was like in
England. He rebelled at having to leave the country at a time when, if
the weather was mild, he should be hunting, or if it was severe,
skating, and he had no real or imaginary need to winter in the south.
His chest was of iron and his lungs of brass. A raking east wind that
drove his parents into their thickest furs, and taught them the number

of their teeth by enabling them to count a separate and well-defined ache for each, only brought a deeper colour into the cheek, and a brighter light into the eye of the weather-proof youth. Decidedly he would not go to Cannes, though it was no use annoying his father and mother, and disappointing his sisters, by telling them beforehand of his determination.

Will knew very well how to write a letter to his mother in which his defection should appear as an event brought about by the over-mastering power of circumstances, to which the sons of Adam must submit. No doubt that a prospect of hunting or skating, as the fates might decree, influenced his decision. But he had also long promised himself the pleasure of a visit from two of his college friends, Hugh Armitage and Horace Lawley, and he asked that they might spend a fortnight with him at Stonecroft, as a little relaxation had been positively ordered for him by his tutor.

'Bless him,' said his mother fondly, when she had read his letter, 'I will write to the dear boy and tell him how pleased I am with his firmness and determination.' But Mr. Musgrave muttered inarticulate sounds as he listened to his wife, expressive of incredulity rather than of acquiescence, and when he spoke it was to say, 'Devil of a row three young fellows will kick up alone at Stonecroft! We shall find the stables full of broken-kneed horses when we go home again.'

Will Musgrave spent Christmas Day with the Armitages at their place near Ripon. And the following night they gave a dance at which he enjoyed himself as only a very young man can do, who has not yet had his fill of dancing, and who would like nothing better than to waltz through life with his arm round his pretty partner's waist. The following day, Musgrave and Armitage left for Stonecroft, picking up Lawley on the way, and arriving at their destination late in the evening, in the highest spirits and with the keenest appetites. Stonecroft was a delightful haven of refuge at the end of a long journey across country in bitter weather, when the east wind was driving the light dry snow into every nook and cranny. The wide, hospitable front door opened into an oak panelled hall with a great open fire burning cheerily, and lighted by lamps from overhead that effectually dispelled all gloomy shadows. As soon as Musgrave had entered the house he seized his friends, and before they had time to shake the snow from their coats, kissed them both under the misletoe bough and set the servants tittering in the background.

'You're miserable substitutes for your betters,' he said, laughing and pushing them from him, 'but it's awfully unlucky not to use the mistletoe. Barker, I hope supper's ready, and that it is something very hot and plenty of it, for we've travelled on empty stomachs and brought them with us,' and he led his guests upstairs to their rooms.

'What a jolly gallery!' said Lawley enthusiastically as they entered a long wide corridor, with many doors and several windows in it, and hung with pictures and trophies of arms.

'Yes, it's our one distinguishing feature at Stonecroft,' said Musgrave. 'It runs the whole length of the house, from the modern end of it to the back which is very old, and built on the foundations of a Cistercian monastery which once stood on this spot. The gallery's wide enough to drive a carriage and pair down it, and it's the main thoroughfare of the house. My mother takes a constitutional here in bad weather, as though it were the open air, and does it with her bonnet on to aid the delusion.'

Armitage's attention was attracted by the pictures on the walls, and especially by the life-size portrait of a young man in a blue coat, with powdered hair, sitting under a tree with a staghound lying at his feet.

'An ancestor of yours?' he said, pointing at the picture.

'Oh, they're all one's ancestors, and a motley crew they are, I must say for them. It may amuse you and Lawley to find from which of them I derive my good looks. That pretty youth whom you seem to admire is my great-great-grandfather. He died at twenty-two, a preposterous age for an ancestor. But come along Armitage, you'll have plenty of time to do justice to the pictures by daylight, and I want to show you your rooms. I see everything is arranged comfortably, we are close together. Our pleasantest rooms are on the gallery, and here we are nearly at the end of it. Your rooms are opposite to mine, and open into Lawley's in case you should be nervous in the night and feel lonely so far from home, my dear children.'

And Musgrave bade his friends make haste, and hurried away whistling cheerfully to his own room.

The following morning the friends rose to a white world. Six inches of fine snow, dry as salt, lay everywhere, the sky overhead a leaden lid, and all the signs of a deep fall yet to come.

'Cheerful this, very,' said Lawley, as he stood with his hands in his pockets, looking out of the window after breakfast. 'The snow will have spoilt the ice for skating.'

'But it won't prevent wild duck shooting,' said Armitage, 'and I say, Musgrave, we'll rig up a toboggan out there. I see a slope that might

[66]

have been made on purpose for it. If we get some tobogganing, it may snow day and night for all I care, we shall be masters of the situation anyway.'

'Well thought of, Armitage,' said Musgrave, jumping at the idea.

'Yes, but you need two slopes and a little valley between for a real good tobogganing,' objected Lawley, 'Otherwise you only rush down the hillock like you do from the Mount Church to Funchal, and then have to retrace your steps as you do there, carrying your car on your back. Which lessens the fun considerably.'

'Well, we can only work with the material at hand,' said Armitage; 'let's go and see if we can't find a better place for our toboggan, and something that will do for a car to slide in.'

'That's easily found—empty wine cases are the thing, and stout sticks to steer with,' and away rushed the young men into the open air, followed by half a dozen dogs barking joyfully.

'By Jove! if the snow keeps firm, we'll put runners on strong chairs and walk over to see the Harradines at Garthside, and ask the girls to come out sledging, and we'll push them,' shouted Musgrave to Lawley and Armitage, who had outrun him in the vain attempt to keep up with a deer-hound that headed the party. After a long and careful search they found a piece of land exactly suited to their purpose, and it would have amused their friends to see how hard the young men worked under the beguiling name of pleasure. For four hours they worked like navvies making a toboggan slide. They shovelled away the snow, then with pickaxe and spade, levelled the ground, so that when a carpet of fresh snow was spread over it, their improvised car would run down a steep incline and be carried by the impetus up another, till it came to a standstill in a snow drift.

'If we can only get this bit of engineering done to-day,' said Lawley, chucking a spadeful of earth aside as he spoke, 'the slide will be in perfect order for to-morrow.'

'Yes, and when once it's done, it's done for ever,' said Armitage, working away cheerfully with his pick where the ground was frozen hard and full of stones, and cleverly keeping his balance on the slope as he did so. 'Good work lasts no end of a time, and posterity will bless us for leaving them this magnificent slide.'

'Posterity may, my dear fellow, but hardly our progenitors if my father should happen to slip down it,' said Musgrave.

When their task was finished, and the friends were transformed in appearance from navvies into gentlemen, they set out through thick

[67]

falling snow to walk to Garthside to call on their neighbours the Harradines. They had earned their pleasant tea and lively talk, their blood was still aglow from their exhilarating work, and their spirits at the highest point. They did not return to Stonecroft till they had compelled the girls to name a time when they would come with their brothers and be launched down the scientifically prepared slide, in wine cases well padded with cushions for the occasion.

Late that night the young men sat smoking and chatting together in the library. They had played billiards till they were tired, and Lawley had sung sentimental songs, accompanying himself on the banjo, till even he was weary, to say nothing of what his listeners might be. Armitage sat leaning his light curly head back in the chair, gently puffing out a cloud of tobacco smoke. And he was the first to break the silence that had fallen on the little company.

'Musgrave,' he said suddenly, 'an old house is not complete unless it is haunted. You ought to have a ghost of your own at Stonecroft.'

Musgrave threw down the yellow-backed novel he had just picked up, and became all attention.

'So we have, my dear fellow. Only it has not been seen by any of us since my grandfather's time. It is the desire of my life to become personally acquainted with our family ghost.'

Armitage laughed. But Lawley said, 'You would not say that if you really believed in ghosts.'

'I believe in them most devoutly, but I natually wish to have my faith confirmed by sight. You believe in them too, I can see.'

'Then you see what does not exist, and so far you are in a fair way to see ghosts. No, my state of mind is this,' continued Lawley, 'I neither believe, nor entirely disbelieve in ghosts. I am open to conviction on the subject. Many men of sound judgment believe in them, and others of equally good mental capacity don't believe in them. I merely regard the case of the bogies as not proven. They may, or may not exist, but till their existence is plainly demonstrated, I decline to add such an uncomfortable article to my creed as a belief in bogies.'

Musgrave did not reply, but Armitage laughed a strident laugh.

'I'm one against two, I'm in an overwhelming minority,' he said. 'Musgrave frankly confesses his belief in ghosts, and you are neutral, neither believing nor disbelieving, but open to conviction. Now I'm a complete unbeliever in the supernatural, root and branch. People's nerves no doubt play them queer tricks, and will continue to do so to the end of the chapter, and if I were so fortunate as to see Musgrave's family ghost to-night, I should no more believe in it than I do now. By the way, Musgrave, is the ghost a lady or a gentleman?' he asked flippantly.

'I don't think you deserve to be told,'

'Don't you know that a ghost is neither he nor she?' said Lawley. 'Like a corpse, it is always *it*.'

'That is a piece of very definite information from a man who neither believes nor disbelieves in ghosts. How do you come by it, Lawley?' asked Armitage.

'Mayn't a man be well informed on a subject although he suspends his judgment about it? I think I have the only logical mind among us. Musgrave believes in ghosts though he has never seen one, you don't believe in them, and say that you would not be convinced if you saw one, which is not wise, it seems to me.'

'It is not necessary to my peace of mind to have a definite opinion on the subject. After all, it is only a matter of patience, for if ghosts really exist we shall each be one in the course of time, and then, if we've nothing better to do, and are allowed to play such unworthy pranks, we may appear again on the scene, and impartially scare our credulous and incredulous surviving friends.'

'Then I shall try to be beforehand with you, Lawley, and turn bogie first; it would suit me better to scare than to be scared. But, Musgrave, do tell me about your family ghost; I'm really interested in it, and quite respectful now.'

'Well, mind you are, and I shall have no objection to tell you what I know about it, which is briefly this:—Stonecroft, as I told you, is built on the site of an old Cistercian Monastery destroyed at the time of the Reformation. The back part of the house rests on the old foundations, and its walls are built with the stones that were once part and parcel of the monastery. The ghost that has been seen by members of the Musgrave family for three centuries past, is that of a Cistercian monk, dressed in the white habit of his order. Who he was, or why he has haunted the scenes of his earthly life so long, there is no tradition to enlighten us. The ghost has usually been seen once or twice in each generation. But as I said, it has not visited us since my grandfather's time, so, like a comet, it should be due again presently.'

'How you must regret that was before your time,' said Armitage.

'Of course I do, but I don't despair of seeing it yet. At least I know where to look for it. It has always made its appearance in the gallery, and I have my bedroom close to the spot where it was last seen, in the hope that if I open my door suddenly some moonlight night I may find the monk standing there.'

'Standing where?' asked the incredulous Armitage.

'In the gallery, to be sure, midway between your two doors and mine. That is where my grandfather last saw it. He was waked in the dead of night by the sound of a heavy door shutting. He ran into the gallery where the noise came from, and, standing opposite the door of the room I occupy, was the white figure of the Cistercian monk. As he looked, it glided the length of the gallery and melted like mist into the wall. The spot where he disappeared is on the old foundations of the monastery, so that he was evidently returning to his own quarters.'

'And your grandfather believed that he saw a ghost?' asked Armitage disdainfully.

'Could he doubt the evidence of his senses? He saw the thing as clearly as we see each other now, and it disappeared like a thin vapour against the wall.'

'My dear fellow, don't you think that it sounds more like an anecdote of your grandmother than of your grandfather?' remarked Armitage. He did not intend to be rude, though he succeeded in being so, as he was instantly aware by the expression of cold reserve that came over Musgrave's frank face.

'Forgive me, but I never can take a ghost story seriously,' he said. 'But this much I will concede—they may have existed long ago in what were literally the dark ages, when rushlights and sputtering dip candles could not keep the shadows at bay. But in this latter part of the nineteenth century, when gas and the electric light have turned night into day, you have destroyed the very conditions that produced the ghost—or rather the belief in it, which is the same thing. Darkness has always been bad for human nerves. I can't explain why, but so it is. My mother was in advance of the age on the subject, and always insisted on having a good light burning in the night nursery, so that when as a child I woke from a bad dream I was never frightened by the darkness. And in consequence I have grown up a complete unbeliever in ghosts, spectres, wraiths, apparitions, dopplegängers, and the whole bogie crew of them,' and Armitage looked round calmly and complacently.

'Perhaps I might have felt as you do if I had not begun life with the knowledge that our house was haunted,' replied Musgrave with visible pride in the ancestral ghost. 'I only wish that I could convince you of the existence of the supernatural from my own personal experience.

I always feel it to be the weak point in a ghost-story, that it is never told in the first person. It is a friend, or a friend of one's-friend, who was the lucky man, and actually saw the ghost.' And Armitage registered a vow to himself, that within a week from that time Musgrave should see his family ghost with his own eyes, and ever after be able to speak with his enemy in the gate.

Several ingenious schemes occurred to his inventive mind for producing the desired apparition. But he had to keep them burning in his breast. Lawley was the last man to aid and abet him in playing a practical joke on their host, and he feared he should have to work without an ally. And though he would have enjoyed his help and sympathy, it struck him that it would be a double triumph achieved, if both his friends should see the Cistercian monk. Musgrave already believed in ghosts, and was prepared to meet one more than half way, and Lawley, though he pretended to a judicial and impartial mind concerning them, was not unwilling to be convinced of their exist- ence, if it could be visibly demonstrated to him.

Armitage became more cheerful than usual as circumstances favoured his impious plot. The weather was propitious for the attempt he meditated, as the moon rose late and was approaching the full. On consulting the almanac he saw with delight that three nights hence she would rise at 2 A.M., and an hour later the end of the gallery nearest Musgrave's room would be flooded with her light. Though Armitage could not have an accomplice under the roof, he needed one within reach, who could use needle and thread, to run up a specious imitation of the white robe and hood of a Cistercian monk. And the next day, when they went to the Harradines to take the girls out in their improvised sledges, it fell to his lot to take charge of the youngest Miss Harradine. As he pushed the low chair on runners over the hard snow, nothing was easier than to bend forward and whisper to Kate, 'I am going to take you as fast as I can, so that no one can hear what we are saying. I want you to be very kind, and help me play a perfectly harmless practical joke on Musgrave. Will you promise to keep my secret for a couple of days, when we shall all enjoy a laugh over it together?'

'O yes, I'll help you with pleasure, but make haste and tell me what your practical joke is to be.'

'I want to play ancestral ghost to Musgrave, and make him believe that he has seen the Cistercian monk in his white robe and cowl, that was last seen by his respected credulous grandpapa.'

[71]

'What a good idea! I know he is always longing to see the ghost, and takes it as a personal affront that it has never appeared to him. But might it not startle him more than you intend?' and Kate turned her glowing face towards him, and Armitage involuntarily stopped the little sledge, 'for it is one thing to wish to see a ghost, you know, and quite another to think that you see it.'

'O, you need not fear for Musgrave! We shall be conferring a positive favour on him, in helping him to see what he's so wishful to see. I'm arranging it so that Lawley shall have the benefit of the show as well, and see the ghost at the same time with him. And if two strong men are not a match for one bogie, leave alone a home-made counterfeit one, it's a pity.'

'Well, if you think it's a safe trick to play, no doubt you are right. But how can I help you? With the monk's habit, I suppose?'

'Exactly. I shall be so grateful to you if you will run up some sort of garment, that will look passably like a white Cistercian habit to a couple of men, who I don't think will be in a critical frame of mind during the short time they are allowed to see it. I really wouldn't trouble you if I were anything of a sempster (is that the masculine of sempstress?) myself, but I'm not. A thimble bothers me very much, and at college, when I have to sew on a button, I push the needle through on one side with a threepenny bit, and pull it out the other with my teeth, and it's a laborious process.'

Kate laughed merrily. 'Oh, I can easily make something or other out of a white dressing gown, fit for a ghost to wear, and fasten a hood to it.'

Armitage then told her the details of his deeply-laid scheme, how he would go to his room when Musgrave and Lawley went to theirs on the eventful night, and sit up till he was sure that they were fast asleep. Then when the moon had risen, and if her light was obscured by clouds he would be obliged to postpone the entertainment till he could be sure of her aid, he would dress himself as the ghostly monk, put out the candles, softly open the door and look into the gallery to see if all was ready. 'Then I shall slam the door with an awful bang, for that was the noise that heralded the ghost's last appearance, and it will take Musgrave and Lawley, and bring them both out of their rooms like a shot. Lawley's door is next to mine, and Musgrave's opposite, so that each will command a magnificent view of the monk at the same instant, and they can compare notes afterwards at their leisure.'

'But what shall you do if they find you out at once?'

'Oh, they won't do that! The cowl will be drawn over my face, and I shall stand with my back to the moonlight. My private belief is, that in spite of Musgrave's yearning after a ghost, he won't like it when he thinks he sees it. Nor will Lawley, and I expect they'll dart back into their rooms and lock themselves in as soon as they catch sight of the monk. That would give me time to whip back into my room, turn the key, strip off my finery, hide it, and be roused with difficulty from a deep sleep when they come knocking at my door to tell me what a horrible thing has happened. And one more ghost story will be added to those already in circulation,' and Armitage laughed aloud in anticipation of the fun.

'It is to be hoped that everything will happen just as you have planned it, and then we shall all be pleased. And now will you turn the sledge round and let us join the others, we have done conspiring for the present. If we are seen talking so exclusively to each other, they will suspect that we are brewing some mischief together. Oh, how cold the wind is! I like to hear it whistle in my hair!' said Kate as Armitage deftly swung the little sledge round and drove it quickly before him, facing the keen north wind, as she buried her chin in her warm furs.

Armitage found an opportunity to arrange with Kate, that he would meet her half way between Stonecroft and her home, on the afternoon of the next day but one, when she would give him a parcel containing the monk's habit. The Harradines and their house party were coming on Thursday afternoon to try the toboggan slide at Stonecroft. But Kate and Armitage were willing to sacrifice their pleasure to the business they had in hand.

There was no other way but for the conspirators to give their friends the slip for a couple of hours, when the important parcel would be safely given to Armitage, secretly conveyed by him to his own room, and locked up till he should want it in the small hours of the morning.

When the young people arrived at Stonecroft Miss Harradine apologised for her younger sister's absence, occasioned, she said, by a severe headache. Armitage's heart beat rapidly when he heard the excuse, and he thought how convenient it was for the inscrutable sex to be able to turn on a headache at will, as one turns on hot or cold water from a tap.

After luncheon, as there were more gentlemen than ladies, and Armitage's services were not necessary at the toboggan slide, he elected to take the dogs for a walk, and set off in the gayest spirits to keep his appointment with Kate. Much as he enjoyed maturing his ghost plot, he enjoyed still more the confidential talks with Kate that had sprung out of it, and he was sorry that this was to be the last of them. But the moon in heaven could not be stayed for the performance of his little comedy, and her light was necessary to its due performance. The ghost must be seen at three o'clock next morning, at the time and place arranged, when the proper illumination for its display would be forthcoming.

As Armitage walked swiftly over the hard snow, he caught sight of Kate at a distance. She waved her hand gaily and pointed smiling to the rather large parcel she was carrying. The red glow of the winter sun shone full upon her, bringing out the warm tints in her chestnut hair, and filling her brown eyes with soft lustre, and Armitage looked at her with undisguised admiration.

'It's awfully good of you to help me so kindly,' he said as he took the parcel from her, 'and I shall come round to-morrow to tell you the result of our practical joke. But how is the headache?' he asked smiling, 'you look so unlike aches or pains of any kind, I was forgetting to enquire about it.'

'Thank you, it is better. It is not altogether a made-up headache, though it happened opportunely. I was awake in the night, not in the least repenting that I was helping you, of course, but wishing it was all well over. One has heard of this kind of trick sometimes proving too successful, of people being frightened out if their wits by a make-believe ghost, and I should never forgive myself if Mr Musgrave or Mr Lawley were seriously alarmed.'

'Really Miss Harradine, I don't think that you need give yourself a moment's anxiety about the nerves of a couple of burly young men. If you are afraid for anyone, let it be for me. If they find me out, they will fall upon me and rend me limb from limb on the spot. I can assure you I am the only one for whom there is anything to fear,' and the transient gravity passed like a cloud from Kate's bright face. And she admitted that it was rather absurd to be uneasy about two stalwart young men compounded more of muscle than of nerves. And they parted, Kate hastening home as the early twilight fell, and Armitage, after watching her out of sight, retracing his steps with the precious parcel under his arm.

He entered the house unobserved, and reaching the gallery by a back staircase, felt his way in the dark to his room. He deposited his treasure in the wardrobe, locked it up, and, attracted by the sound of laughter, ran downstairs to the drawing-room. Will Musgrave and his friends, after a couple of hours of glowing exercise, had been driven indoors by the darkness, nothing loath to partake of tea and hot cakes, while they talked and laughed over the adventures of the afternoon.

'Wherever have you been, old fellow?' said Musgrave as Armitage entered the room. 'I believe you've a private toboggan of your own somewhere that you keep quiet. If only the moon rose at a decent time, instead of at some unearthly hour in the night, when it's not of the slightest use to anyone, we would have gone out looking for you.'

'You wouldn't have had far to seek, you'd have met me on the turnpike road.'

'But why this subdued and chastened taste? Imagine preferring a constitutional on the high road when you might have been tobogganning with us! My poor friend, I'm afraid you are not feeling well!' said Musgrave with an affectation of sympathy that ended in boyish laughter and a wrestling match between the two young men, in the course of which Lawley more than once saved the tea table from being violently overthrown.

Presently, when the cakes and toast had disappeared before the youthful appetites, lanterns were lighted, and Musgrave and his friends, and the Harradine brothers, set out as a bodyguard to take the young ladies home. Armitage was in riotous spirits, and finding that Musgrave and Lawley had appropriated the two prettiest girls in the company, waltzed untrammelled along the road before them with lantern in hand, like a very will-o'-the-Wisp.

The young people did not part till they had planned fresh pleasures for the morrow, and Musgrave, Lawley, and Armitage returned to Stonecroft to dinner, making the thin air ring to the jovial songs with which they beguiled the homeward journey.

Late in the evening, when the young men were sitting in the library, Musgrave suddenly exclaimed, as he reached down a book from an upper shelf, 'Hallo! I've come on my grandfather's diary! Here's his own account of how he saw the white monk in the gallery. Lawley, you may read it if you like, but it shan't be wasted on an unbeliever like Armitage. By Jove! what an odd coincidence! It's forty years this very night, the thirtieth of December, since he saw the ghost,' and he handed the book to Lawley, who read Mr Musgrave's narrative with close attention.

'Is it a case of "almost thou persuadest me"?' asked Armitage, looking at his intent and knitted brow.

'I hardly know what I think. Nothing positive either way at any rate,' and he dropped the subject, for he saw Musgrave did not wish to discuss the family ghost in Armitage's unsympathetic presence.

They retired late, and the hour that Armitage had so gleefully anticipated drew near. 'Good-night both of you,' said Musgrave as he entered his room, I shall be asleep in five minutes. All this exercise in the open air makes a man absurdly sleepy at night,' and the young men closed their doors, and silence settled down upon Stonecroft Hall. Armitage and Lawley's rooms were next to each other, and in less than a quarter of an hour Lawley shouted a cheery good-night, which was loudly returned by his friend. Then Armitage felt somewhat mean and stealthy. Musgrave and Lawley were both confidingly asleep, while he sat up alert and vigilant maturing a mischievous plot that had for its object the awakening and scaring of both the innocent sleepers. He dared not smoke to pass the tedious time, lest the tell-tale fumes should penetrate into the next room through the keyhole, and inform Lawley if he woke for an instant that his friend was awake too, and behaving as though it were high noon.

Armitage spread the monk's white habit on the bed, and smiled as he touched it to think that Kate's pretty fingers had been so recently at work upon it. He need not put it on for a couple of hours yet, and to occupy the time he sat down to write. He would have liked to take a nap. But he knew that if he once yielded to sleep, nothing would wake him till he was called at eight o'clock in the morning. As he bent over his desk the big clock in the hall struck one, so suddenly and sharply it was like a blow on the head, and he started violently. 'What a swinish sleep Lawley must be in that he can't hear a noise like that!' he thought, as snoring became audible from the next room. Then he drew the candles nearer to him, and settled once more to his writing, and a pile of letters testified to his industry, when again the clock struck. But this time he expected it, and it did not startle him, only the cold made him shiver. 'If I hadn't made up my mind to go through with this confounded piece of folly, I'd go to bed now,' he thought, 'but I can't break faith with Kate. She's made the robe and I've got to wear it, worse luck,' and with a great yawn he threw down his pen, and rose to look out of the window. It was a clear frosty night. At the edge of the dark sky, sprinkled with stars, a faint band of cold light heralded the rising moon. How different from the grey light of dawn, that ushers in the cheerful day, is the solemn rising of the moon in the depth of a winter night. Her light is not to rouse the sleeping world and lead men forth to their labour, it falls on the closed eyes of the weary, and silvers the graves of those whose rest shall be broken no more. Armitage was not easily impressed by the sombre aspect of nature, though he was quick to feel her gay and cheerful influence, but he would be glad when the farce was over, and he no longer obliged to watch the rise and spread of the pale light, solemn as the dawn of the last day.

He turned from the window, and proceeded to make himself into the best imitation of a Cistercian monk that he could contrive. He slipped the white habit over all his clothing, that he might seem of portly size, and marked dark circles round his eyes, and thickly powdered his face a ghastly white.

Armitage silently laughed at his reflection in the glass, and wished that Kate could see him now. Then he softly opened the door and looked into the gallery. The moonlight was shimmering duskily on the end window to the right of his door and Lawley's. It would soon be where he wanted it, and neither too light nor too dark for the success of his plan. He stepped silently back again to wait, and a feeling as much akin to nervousness as he had ever known came over him. His heart beat rapidly, he started like a timid girl when the silence was suddenly broken by the hooting of an owl. He no longer cared to look at himself in the glass. He had taken fright of the mortal pallor of his powdered face. 'Hang it all! I wish Lawley hadn't left off snoring. It was quite companionable to hear him.' And again he looked into the gallery, and now the moon shed her cold beams where he intended to stand.

He put out the light and opened the door wide, and stepping into the gallery threw it to with an echoing slam that only caused Musgrave and Lawley to start and turn on their pilllows. Armitage stood dressed as the ghostly monk of Stonecroft, in the pale moonlight in the middle of the gallery, waiting for the door on either side to fly open and reveal the terrified faces of his friends.

He had time to curse the ill-luck that made them sleep so heavily that night of all nights, and to fear lest the servants had heard the noise their master had been deaf to, and would come hurrying to the spot and spoil the sport. But no one came, and as Armitage stood, the objects in the long gallery became clearer every moment, as his sight accommodated itself to the dim light. 'I never noticed before that there was a mirror at the end of the gallery! I should not have believed the moonlight was bright enough for me to see my own reflection so far off, only white stands out so in the dark. But is it my own reflection? Confound it all, the thing's moving and I'm standing still! I know what it is! It's Musgrave dressed up to try to give me a fright, and Lawley's helping him. They've forestalled me, that's why they didn't come out of their rooms when I made a noise fit to wake the dead. Odd we're both playing the same practical joke at the same moment! Come on, my counterfeit bogie, and we'll see which one of us turns white-livered first!'

But to Armitage's surprise, that rapidly became terror, the white figure that he believed to be Musgrave disguised, and like himself playing ghost, advanced towards him, slowly gliding over the floor which its feet did not touch. Armitage's courage was high, and he determined to hold his ground against the something ingeniously contrived by Musgrave and Lawley to terrify him into belief in the supernatural. But a feeling was creeping over the strong young man that he had never known before. He opened his dry mouth as the thing floated towards him, and there issued a hoarse inarticulate cry, that woke Musgrave and Lawley and brought them to their doors in a moment, not knowing by what strange fright they had been startled out of their sleep. Do not think them cowards that they shrank back appalled from the ghostly forms the moonlight revealed to them in the gallery. But as Armitage vehemently repelled the horror that drifted nearer and nearer to him, the cowl slipped from his head, and his friends recognised his white face, distorted by fear, and, springing towards him as he staggered, supported him in their arms. The Cistercian monk passed them like a white mist that sank into the wall, and Musgrave and Lawley were alone with the dead body of their friend, whose masquerading dress had become his shroud.

'NUMBER NINETY'

by Mrs. B.M. Croker

Bithia Mary Croker (1849–1920) was one of a
number of Irish-born novelists who became very
successful and popular in the late Victorian period
(others including Mrs. J.H. Riddell and
L.T. Meade). This story is taken from the
Christmas Number of *Chapman's Magazine of
Fiction*, December 1895 (which also contained
atmospheric horror stories by Arthur Machen,
M.P. Shiel, and Violet Hunt).

'To let furnished, for a term of years, at a very low rental, a large old-
fashioned family residence, comprising eleven bed-rooms, four reception-
rooms, dressing-rooms, two staircases, complete servants' offices, ample
accommodation for a Gentleman's establishment, including six-stall stable,
coach-house, etc.'

The above advertisement referred to number ninety. For a
period extending over some years this notice appeared spas-
modically in various daily papers. Occasionally you saw it
running for a week or a fortnight at a stretch, as if it were resolved to
force itself into consideration by sheer persistency. Sometimes for
months I looked for it in vain. Other ignorant folk might possibly
fancy that the effort of the house agent had been crowned at last with
success—that it was let, and no longer in the market.

I knew better. I knew that would never, never find a tenant as long as oak and ash endured. I knew that it was passed on as a hopeless case, from house-agent to house-agent. I knew that it would never be occupied, save by rats—and, more than this, I knew the reason why!

I will not say in what square, street, or road number ninety may be found, nor will I divulge to human being its precise and exact locality, but this I'm prepared to state, that it is positively in existence, is in London, and is still empty.

Twenty years ago, this very Christmas, my friend John Hollyoak (civil engineer) and I were guests at a bachelor's party; partaking, in company with eight other celibates, of a very *recherché* little dinner, in the neighbourhood of Piccadilly. Conversation became very brisk as the champagne circulated, and many topics were started, discussed, and dismissed.

They (I say *they* advisedly, as I myself am a man of few words) talked on an extraordinary variety of subjects.

I distinctly recollect a long argument on mushrooms—mushrooms, murders, racing, cholera; from cholera we came to sudden death, from sudden death to churchyards, and from churchyards, it was naturally but a step to ghosts.

On this last topic the arguments became fast and furious, for the company was divided into two camps. The larger, 'the opposition,' who scoffed, sneered, and snapped their fingers, and laughed with irritating contempt at the very name of ghosts, was headed by John Hollyoak; the smaller party, who were dogged, angry, and prepared to back their opinions to any extent, had for their leader our host, a bald-headed man of business, whom I certainly would have credited (as I mentally remarked) with more sense.

The believers in the supernatural obtained a hearing, so far as to relate one or two blood-curdling, first or second-hand experiences, which, when concluded, instead of being received with an awe-struck and respectful silence, were pooh-poohed, with shouts of laughter, and taunting suggestions that were by no means complimentary to the intelligence, or sobriety, of the victims of superstition. Argument and counter-argument waxed louder and hotter, and there was every prospect of a very stormy conclusion to the evening's entertainment.

John Hollyoak, who was the most vehement, the most incredulous, the most jocular, and the most derisive of the anti-ghost faction, brought matters to a climax by declaring that nothing would give him

[80]

greater pleasure than to pass a night in a haunted house—and the worse its character, the better he would be pleased!

His challenge was instantly taken up by our somewhat ruffled host, who warmly assured him that his wishes could be easily satisfied, and that he would be accommodated with a night's lodging in a haunted house within twenty-four hours—in fact, in a house of such a desperate reputation, that even the adjoining mansions stood vacant.

He then proceeded to give a brief outline of the history of number ninety. It had once been the residence of a well-known county family, but what evil events had happened therein tradition did not relate.

On the death of the last owner—a diabolical-looking aged person, much resembling the typical wizard—it had passed into the hands of a kinsman, resident abroad, who had no wish to return to England, and who desired his agents to let it, if they could—a most significant proviso!

Year by year went by, and still this 'Highly desirable family mansion' could find no tenant, although the rent was reduced, and reduced, and again reduced, to almost zero!

The most ghastly whispers were afloat—the most terrible experiences were actually proclaimed on the housetops!

No tenant would remain, even *gratis*; and for the last ten years, this, 'handsome, desirable town family residence' had been the abode of rats by day, and something else by night—so said the neighbours.

Of course it was the very thing for John, and he snatched up the gauntlet on the spot. He scoffed at its evil repute, and solemnly promised to rehabilitate its character within a week.

It was in vain that he was solemnly warned—that one of his fellow guests gravely assured him 'that he would not pass a night in number ninety for ninety thousand pounds—it would be the price of his reason.'

'You value your reason at a very high figure,' replied John, with an indulgent smile. 'I will venture mine for nothing,'

'Those laugh who win,' put in our host sharply. 'You have not been through the wood yet though your name is Hollyoak! I invite all present to dine with me in three days from this; and then, if our friend here has proved that he has got the better of the spirits, we will all laugh together. Is that a bargain?'

This invitation was promptly accepted by the whole company; and then they fell to making practical arrangements for John's lodgings for the next night.

I had no actual hand—or, more properly speaking, tongue—in this discussion, which carried us on till a late hour; but nevertheless, the next night at ten o'clock—for no ghost with any self respect would think of appearing before that time—I found myself standing, as John's second, on the steps of the notorious abode; but I was not going to remain; the hansom that brought us was to take me back to my respectable chambers.

This ill-fated house was large, solemn-looking, and gloomy. A heavy portico frowned down on neighbouring bare-faced hall-doors. The caretaker (an army pensioner, bravest of the brave in daylight) was prudently awaiting us outside with a key, which said key he turned in the lock, and admitted us into a great echoing hall, black as Erebus, saying as he did so: 'My missus has haired the bed, and made up a good fire in the first front, sir. Your things is all laid hout, and (dubiously to John) I hope you'll have a comfortable night, sir.'

'No, sir! Thank you, sir! Excuse me, I'll not come in! Good-night!' and with the words still on his lips, he clattered down the steps with most indecent haste, and—vanished.

'And of course you will not come in either?' said John. 'It is not in the bond, and I prefer to face them alone!' and he laughed contemptuously, a laugh that had a curious echo, it struck me at the time. A laugh strangely repeated, with an unpleasant mocking emphasis. 'Call for me, alive or dead, at eight o'clock to-morrow morning!' he added, pushing me forcibly out into the porch, and closing the door with a heavy, reverberating clang, that sounded half-way down the street.

I did call for him the next morning as desired, with the army pensioner, who stared at his common-place, self-possessed appearance, with an expression of respectful astonishment.

'So it was all humbug, of course,' I said, as he took my arm, and we set off for our club.

'You shall have the whole story whenever we have had something to eat,' he replied somewhat impatiently. 'It will keep till after breakfast—I'm famishing!'

I remarked that he looked unusually grave as we chatted over our broiled fish and omelette, and that occasionally his attention seemed wandering, to say the least of it. The moment he had brought out his cigar-case and lit up he turned to me and said:

'I see you are just quivering to know my experience, and I won't keep you on tenter-hooks any longer. In four words—I have seen them!'

I am (as before hinted) a silent man. I merely looked at him with widely-parted mouth and staring interrogative eyes.

I believe I had best endeavour to give the narrative without comment, and in John Hollyoak's own way. This is, as well as I can recollect, his experience word for word:—

'I proceeded upstairs, after I had shut you out, lighting my way by a match, and found the front room easily, as the door was ajar, and it was lit up by a roaring and most cheerful-looking fire, and two wax candles. It was a comfortable apartment, furnished with old-fashioned chairs and tables, and the traditional four-poster. There were numerous doors, which proved to be cupboards; and when I had executed a rigorous search in each of these closets and locked them, and investigated the bed above and beneath, sounded the walls, and bolted the door, I sat down before the fire, lit a cigar, opened a book, and felt that I was going to be master of the situation, and most thoroughly and comfortably 'at home.' My novel proved absorbing. I read on greedily, chapter after chapter, and so interested was I, and amused—for it was a lively book—that I positively lost sight of my whereabouts, and fancied myself reading in my own chamber! There was not a sound—not even a mouse in wainscot. The coals dropping from the grate occasionally broke the silence, till a neighbouring church-clock slowly boomed twelve! *"The hour!"* I said to myself, with a laugh, as I gave the fire a rousing poke, and commenced a fresh chapter; but ere I had read three pages I had occasion to pause and listen. What was that distinct sound now coming nearer and nearer? "Rats, of course," said Common-sense—"it was just the house for vermin." Then a longish silence. Again a stir, sounds approaching, as if apparently caused by many feet passing down the corridor—high heeled shoes, the sweeping switch of silken trains! Of course it was all imagination, I assured myself—or rats! Rats were capable of making such curious improbable noises!

'Then another silence. No sound but cinders and the ticking of my watch, which I had laid upon the table.

'I resumed my book, rather ashamed, and a little indignant with myself for having neglected it, and calmly dismissed my late interruption as 'rats—nothing but rats.'

'I had been reading and smoking for some time in a placid and highly incredulous frame of mind, when I was somewhat rudely startled by a loud single knock at my room door. I took no notice of it, but merely laid down my novel and sat tight. Another knock more imperious this time. After a moment's mental deliberation I arose, armed myself with the poker, prepared to brain any number of rats, and threw the door open with a violent swing that strained its very hinges, and beheld, to my amazement, a tall powdered footman in a laced scarlet livery, who, making a formal inclination of his head, astonished me still further by saying:

' "Dinner is ready!" '

' "I'm not coming!" I replied, without a moment's hesitation, and thereupon I slammed the door in his face, locked it, and resumed my seat, also my book; but reading was a farce; my ears were aching for the next sound.

'It came soon—rapid steps running up the stairs, and again a single knock. I went over to the door, and once more discovered the tall footman, who repeated, with a studied courtesy:

' "Dinner is ready, and the company are waiting," '

' "I told you I was not coming. Be off, and be hanged to you!" I cried again, shutting the door violently.

'This time I did not make even a pretence at reading, I merely sat and waited for the next move.

'I had not long to sit. In ten minutes I heard a third loud summons. I rose, went to the door, and tore it open. There, as I expected, was the servant again, with his parrot speech:

' "Dinner is ready, the company are waiting, and the master says you must come!" '

' "All right, then, I'll come," ' I replied, wearied by reason of his importunity, and feeling suddenly fired with a desire to see the end of the adventure.

'He accordingly led the way downstairs, and I followed him, noting as I went the gilt buttons on his coat, and his splendidly turned calves, also that the hall and passages were now brilliantly illuminated, and that several liveried servants were passing to and fro, and that from— presumably—the dining room, there issued a buzz of tongues, loud volleys of laughter, many hilarious voices, and a clatter of knives and forks. I was not left much time for speculation, as in another second I found myself inside the door, and my escort announced me in a stentorian voice as "Mr. Hollyoak."

'I could hardly credit my senses, as I looked round and saw about two dozen people, dressed in a fashion of the last century, seated at the table, which was loaded with gold and silver plate, and lighted up by a blaze of wax candles in massive candelabra.

'A swarthy elderly gentleman, who presided at the head of the board, rose deliberately as I entered. He was dressed in a crimson coat, braided with silver. He wore a peruke, had the most piercing black eyes I ever encountered, made me the finest bow I ever received in all my life, and with a polite wave of a taper hand, indicated my seat—a vacant chair between two powdered and patched beauties, with overflowing white shoulders and necks sparkling with diamonds.

'At first I was fully convinced that the whole affair was a superbly-matured practical joke. Everything looked so real, so truly flesh and blood, so complete in every detail; but I gazed around in vain for one familiar face.

'I saw young, old, and elderly; handsome and the reverse. On all faces there was a similar expression—reckless, hardened defiance, and something else that made me shudder, but that I could not classify or define.

'Were they a secret community? Burglars or coiners? But no; in one rapid glance I noticed that they belonged exclusively to the upper stratum of society—bygone society. The jabber of talking had momentarily ceased, and the host, imperiously hammering the table with a knife-handle, said in a singularly harsh grating voice:

' "Ladies and gentlemen, permit me to give you a toast! 'Our guest!' " looking straight at me with his glittering coal-black eyes.

'Every glass was immediately raised. Twenty faces were turned towards mine, when, happily, a sudden impulse seized me. I sprang to my feet and said:

' "Ladies and gentlemen, I beg to thank you for your kind hospitality, but before I accept it, allow me to say grace!"

'I did not wait for permission, but hurriedly repeated a Latin benediction. Ere the last syllable was uttered, in an instant there was a violent crash, an uproar, a sound of running, of screams, groans and curses, and then utter darkness.

'I found myself standing alone by a big mahogany table which I could just dimly discern by the aid of a street-lamp that threw its meagre rays into the great empty dining-room from the other side of the area.

'I must confess that I felt my nerves a little shaken by this instantaneous change from light to darkness—from a crowd of gay and noisy companions, to utter solitude and silence. I stood for a moment trying to recover my mental balance. I rubbed my eyes hard to assure myself that I was wide awake, and then I placed this very cigar-case in

[85]

the middle of the table, as a sign and token that I had been downstairs—which cigar-case I found exactly where I left it this morning—and then went and groped my way into the hall and regained my room.

'I met with no obstacle *en route*. I saw no one, but as I closed and double-locked my door I distinctly heard a low laugh outside the keyhole—a sort of suppressed, malicious titter, that made me furious.

'I opened the door at once. There was nothing to be seen. I waited and listened—dead silence. I then undressed and went to bed, resolved that a whole army of footmen would fail to allure me once more to that festive board. I was determined not to lose my night's rest—ghosts or no ghosts.

'Just as I was dozing off I remember hearing the neighbouring clock chime two. It was the last sound I was aware of; the house was now as silent as a vault. My fire burnt away cheerfully. I was no longer in the least degree inclined for reading, and I fell fast asleep and slept soundly till I heard the cabs and milk-carts beginning their morning career.

'I then rose, dressed at my leisure, and found you, my good, faithful friend, awaiting me, rather anxiously, on the hall-door steps.

'I have not done with that house yet. I'm determined to find out who these people are, and where they come from. I shall sleep there again to-night, and so shall "Crib," my bulldog; and you will see that I shall have news for you to-morrow morning—if I am still alive to tell the tale,' he added with a laugh.

In vain I would have dissuaded him. I protested, argued, and implored. I declared that rashness was not courage; that he had seen enough; that I, who had seen nothing, and only listened to his experiences, was convinced that number ninety was a house to be avoided.

I might just as well have talked to my umbrella! So, once more, I reluctantly accompanied him to his previous night's lodging. Once more I saw him swallowed up inside the gloomy, forbidding-looking, re-echoing hall.

I then went home in an unusually anxious, semi-excited, nervous state of mind; and I, who generally outrival the Seven Sleepers, lay wide awake, tumbling and tossing hour after hour, a prey to the most foolish ideas—ideas I would have laughed to scorn in daylight.

More than once I was certain that I heard John Hollyoak distractedly calling me; and I sat up in bed and listened intently. Of course it was fancy, for the instant I did so, there was no sound.

At the first gleam of winter dawn, I rose, dressed, and swallowed a cup of good strong coffee to clear my brain from the misty notions it had harboured during the night. And then I invested myself in my warmest topcoat and comforter, and set off for number ninety. Early as it was—it was but half-past seven—I found the army pensioner was before me, pacing the pavement with a countenance that would have made a first-rate frontispiece for 'Burton's Anatomy of Melancholy'—a countenance the reverse of cheerful.

I was not disposed to wait for eight o'clock. I was too uneasy, and too impatient for further particulars of the dinner-party. So I rang with all my might, and knocked with all my main.

No sound within—no answer! But John was always a heavy sleeper. I was resolved to arouse him all the same, and knocked and rang, and rang and knocked, incesssantly for fully ten minutes.

I then stooped down and applied my eye to the keyhole; I looked steadily into the aperture, till I became accustomed to the darkness, and then it seemed to me that another eye—a very strange, fiery eye— was glaring into mine from the other side of the door!

I removed my eye and applied my mouth instead, and shouted with all the power of my lungs (I did not care a straw if passers-by took me for an escaped lunatic):

'John! John! Hollyoak!'

How his name echoed and re-echoed up through that great empty house! 'He must hear *that*,' I said to myself as I pressed my ear closely against the lock, and listened with throbbing suspense.

The echo of 'Hollyoak' had hardly died away when I swear that I distinctly heard a low, sniggering, mocking laugh—*that* was my only answer—that; and a vast unresponsive silence.

I was now quite desperate. I shook the door frantically, with all my strength. I broke the bell; in short, my behaviour was such that it excited the curiosity of a policeman, who crossed the road to know 'What was up?'

'I want to get in!' I panted, breathless with my exertions.

'You'd better stay where you are!' said Bobby; 'the outside of this house is the best of it! There are terrible stories—'

'But there is a gentleman inside it!' I interrupted impatiently. 'He slept there last night, and I can't wake him. He has the key!'

'Oh, you can't *wake* him!' returned the policeman gravely. 'Then we must get a locksmith!'

But already the thoughtful pensioner had procured one; and already

[87]

a considerable and curious crowd surrounded the steps.

After five minutes of (to me) maddening delay, the great heavy door was opened and swung slowly back, and I instantly rushed in, followed less precipitately by the policeman and pensioner.

I had not far to seek John Hollyoak! He and his dog were lying at the foot of the stairs, both stone dead!

THURLOW'S
CHRISTMAS STORY

by J. K. Bangs

John Kendrick Bangs (1862–1922) was an
American humorist, on the staff of *Harper's
Monthly* for many years, and best known for the
books *Coffee and Repartee* and *A House Boat on the
Styx*. Late in life, Bangs became on of the most
humorous lecturers of his generation. 'Thurlow's
Christmas Story' is a unique and wonderful tale on
the struggles of an author trying to write a Ghost
Story for Christmas! It appeared, with five
illustrations by A.B. Frost, in his collection *Ghosts
I Have Met* in 1898.

I

*(Being the Statement of Henry Thurlow, Author, to George Currier,
Editor of the 'Idler,' a Weekly Journal of Human Interest.)*

I have always maintained, my dear Currier, that if a man wishes to
be considered sane, and has any particular regard for his reputation as a truth-teller, he would better keep silent as to the singular
experiences that enter into his life. I have had many such experiences
myself; but I have rarely confided them in detail, or otherwise, to
those about me, because I know that even the most trustful of my
friends would regard them merely as the outcome of an imagination
unrestrained by conscience, or of a gradually weakening mind subject

to hallucinations. I know them to be true, but until Mr. Edison or some other modern wizard has invented a search-light strong enough to lay bare the secrets of the mind and conscience of man, I cannot prove to others that they are not pure fabrications, or at least the conjurings of a diseased fancy.

For instance, no man would believe me if I were to state to him the plain and indisputable fact that one night last month, on my way up to bed shortly after midnight, having been neither smoking nor drinking, I saw confronting me upon the stairs, with the moonlight streaming through the windows back of me, lighting up its face, a figure in which I recognized my very self in every form and feature. I might describe the chill of terror that struck to the very marrow of my bones, and wellnigh forced me to stagger backward down the stairs, as I noticed in the face of this confronting figure every indication of all the bad qualities which I know myself to possess, of every evil instinct which by no easy effort I have repressed heretofore, and realized that that *thing* was, as far as I knew, entirely independent of my true self, in which I hope at least the moral has made an honest fight against the immoral always.

I might describe this chill, I say, as vividly as I felt it at that moment, but it would be of no use to do so, because, however realistic it might prove as a bit of description, no man would believe that the incident really happened; and yet it did happen as truly as I write, and it has happened a dozen times since, and I am certain that it will happen many times again, though I would give all that I possess to be assured that never again should that disquieting creation of mind or matter, whichever it may be, cross my path. The experience has made me afraid almost to be alone, and I have found myself unconsciously and uneasily glancing at my face in mirrors, in the plate-glass of shop-windows on the shopping streets of the city, fearful lest I should find some of those evil traits which I have struggled to keep under, and have kept under so far, cropping out there where all the world, all *my* world, can see and wonder at, having known me always as a man of right doing and right feeling. Many a time in the night the thought has come to me with prostrating force, what if that thing were to be seen and recognized by others, myself and yet not my whole self, my unworthy self unrestrained and yet recognizable as Henry Thurlow.

I have also kept silent as to that strange condition of affairs which has tortured me in my sleep for the past year and a half; no one but myself has until this writing known that for that period of time I have had a continuous, logical dream-life; a life so vivid and so dreadfully real to me that I have found myself at times wondering which of the two lives I was living and which I was dreaming; a life in which that other wicked self has dominated, and forced me to a career of shame and horror; a life which, being taken up every time I sleep where it ceased with the awakening from a previous sleep, has made me fear to close my eyes in forgetfulness when others are near at hand, lest, sleeping, I shall let fall some speech that, striking on their ears, shall lead them to believe that in secret there is some wicked mystery connected with my life. It would be of no use for me to tell these things. It would merely serve to make my family and my friends uneasy about me if they were told in their awful detail, and so I have kept silent about them. To you alone, and now for the first time, have I hinted as to the troubles which have oppressed me for many days, and to you they are confided only because of the demand you have made that I explain to you the extraordinary complication in which the Christmas story sent you last week has involved me.

You know that I am a man of dignity; that I am not a school-boy and a lover of childish tricks; and knowing that, your friendship, at least, should have restrained your tongue and pen when, through the former, on Wednesday, you accused me of perpetrating a trifling, and to you excessively embarrassing, practical joke—a charge which, at the moment, I was too overcome to refute; and through the latter, on Thursday, you reiterated the accusation, coupled with a demand for an explanation of my conduct satisfactory to yourself, or my immediate resignation from the staff of the *Idler*. To explain is difficult, for I am certain that you will find the explanation too improbable for credence, but explain I must. The alternative, that of resigning from your staff, affects not only my own welfare, but that of my children, who must be provided for; and if my post with you is taken from me, then are all resources gone. I have not the courage to face dismissal, for I have not sufficient confidence in my powers to please elsewhere to make me easy in my mind, or, if I could please elsewhere, the certainty of finding the immediate employment of my talents which is necessary to me, in view of the at present over-crowded condition of the literary field.

To explain, then, my seeming jest at your expense, hopeless as it appears to be, is my task; and to do so as completely as I can, let me go back to the very beginning.

In August you informed me that you would expect me to provide, as I have been in the habit of doing, a story for the Christmas issue of the *Idler*; that a certain position in the make-up was reserved for me, and that you had already taken steps to advertise the fact that the story would appear. I undertook the commission, and upon seven different occasions set about putting the narrative into shape. I found great difficulty, however, in doing so. For some reason or other I could not concentrate my mind upon the work. No sooner would I start in on one story than a better one, in my estimation, would suggest itself to me; and all the labour expended on the story already begun would be cast aside, and the new story set in motion. Ideas were plenty enough, but to put them properly upon paper seemed beyond my powers. One story, however, I did finish; but after it had come back to me from my typewriter I read it, and was filled with consternation to discover that it was nothing more nor less than a mass of jumbled sentences, conveying no idea to the mind—a story which had seemed to me in the writing to be coherent had returned to me as a mere bit of incoherence—formless, without ideas—a bit of raving. It was then that I went to you and told you, as you remember, that I was worn out, and needed a month of absolute rest, which you granted. I left my work wholly, and went into the wilderness, where I could be entirely free from everything suggesting labour, and where no summons back to town could reach me. I fished and hunted. I slept; and although, as I have already said, in my sleep I found myself leading a life that was not only not to my taste, but horrible to me in many particulars, I was able at the end of my vacation to come back to town greatly refreshed, and, as far as my feelings went, ready to undertake any amount of work.

For two or three days after my return I was busy with other things. On the fourth day after my arrival you came to me, and said that the story must be finished at the very latest by October 15th, and I assured you that you should have it by that time. That night I set about it. I mapped it out, incident by incident, and before starting up to bed had actually written some twelve or fifteen hundred words of the opening chapter—it was to be told in four chapters. When I had gone thus far I experienced a slight return of one of my nervous chills, and, on consulting my watch, discovered that it was after midnight, which was a sufficient explanation of my nervousness: I was merely tired. I arranged my manuscripts on my table so that I might easily take up the work the following morning. I locked up the windows and doors, turned out the lights, and proceeded upstairs to my room.

It was then that I first came face to face with myself—that other self, in which I recognized, developed to the full, every bit of my capacity for an evil life.

Conceive of the situation if you can. Imagine the horror of it, and then ask yourself if it was likely that when next morning came I could by any possibility bring myself to my work-table in fit condition to prepare for you anything at all worthy of publication in the *Idler*. I tried. I implore you to believe that I did not hold lightly the responsibilities of the commission you had intrusted to my hands. You must know that if any of your writers has a full appreciation of the difficulties which are strewn along the path of an editor, I, who have myself had an editorial experience, have it, and so would not, in the nature of things, do anything to add to your troubles. You cannot but believe that I have made an honest effort to fulfil my promise to you. But it was useless, and for a week after that visitation was it useless for me to attempt the work. At the end of the week I felt better, and again I started in, and the story developed satisfactorily until—*it* came again. That figure which was my own figure, that face which was the evil counterpart of my own countenance, again rose up before me, and once more was I plunged into hopelessness.

Thus matters went on until the 14th day of October, when I received your peremptory message that the story must be forthcoming the following day. Needless to tell you that it was not forthcoming; but what I must tell you, since you do not know it, is that on the evening of the 15th day of October a strange thing happened to me, and in the narration of that incident, which I almost despair of your believing, lies my explanation of the discovery of October 16th, which has placed my position with you in peril.

At half-past seven o'clock on the evening of October 15th I was sitting in my library trying to write. I was alone. My wife and children had gone away on a visit to Massachusetts for a week. I had just finished my cigar, and had taken my pen in hand, when my front-door bell rang. Our maid, who is usually prompt in answering summonses of this nature, apparently did not hear the bell, for she did not respond to its clanging. Again the bell rang, and still did it remain unanswered, until finally, at the third ringing, I went to the door myself. On opening it I saw standing before me a man of, I should say, fifty odd years of age, tall, slender, pale-faced, and clad in sombre black. He was entirely unknown to me. I had never seen him before, but he had about him such an air of pleasantness and wholesomeness that I instinctively felt glad to see him, without knowing why or whence he had come.

'Does Mr. Thurlow live here?' he asked.

You must excuse me for going into what may seem to you to be petty details, but only by a perfectly circumstantial account of all that happened that evening can I hope to give a semblance of truth to my story, and that it must be truthful I realize as painfully as you do.

'I am Mr. Thurlow,' I replied.

'Henry Thurlow, the author?' he said, with a surprised look upon his face.

'Yes,' said I; and then, impelled by the strange appearance of surprise on the man's countenance, I added, 'don't I look like an author?'

He laughed, and candidly admitted that I was not the kind of man he had expected to find from reading my books, and then he entered the house in response to my invitation that he do so. I ushered him into my library, and, after asking him to be seated, inquired as to his business with me.

His answer was gratifying at least. He replied that he had been a reader of my writings for a number of years, and that for some time past he had had a great desire, not to say curiosity, to meet me and tell me how much he had enjoyed certain of my stories.

'I'm a great devourer of books, Mr. Thurlow,' he said, 'and I have taken the keenest delight in reading your verses and humorous sketches. I may go further, and say to you that you have helped me over many a hard place in my life by your work. At times when I have felt myself worn out with my business, or face to face with some knotty problem in my career, I have found much relief in picking up and reading your books at random. They have helped me to forget my weariness or my knotty problems for the time being; and to-day, finding myself in this town, I resolved to call upon you this evening and thank you for all that you have done for me.'

Thereupon we became involved in a general discussion of literary men and their works, and I found that my visitor certainly did have a pretty thorough knowledge of what has been produced by the writers of to-day. I was quite won over to him by his simplicity, as well as attracted to him by his kindly opinion of my own efforts, and I did my best to entertain him, showing him a few of my little literary treasures in the way of autograph letters, photographs, and presentation copies of well-known books from the authors themselves. From this we drifted naturally and easily into a talk on the methods of work adopted by literary men. He asked me many questions as to my own methods; and when I had in a measure outlined to him the manner of life which I had adopted, telling him of my days at home, how little detail office-work I had, he seemed much interested with the picture—indeed, I painted the picture of my daily routine in almost too perfect colours for, when I had finished, he observed quietly that I appeared to him to lead the ideal life, and added that he supposed I knew very little unhappiness.

The remark recalled to me the dreadful reality, that through some perversity of fate I was doomed to visitations of an uncanny order which were practically destroying my usefulness in my profession and my sole financial resource.

'Well,' I replied, as my mind reverted to the unpleasant predicament in which I found myself, 'I can't say that I know little unhappiness. As a matter of fact, I know a great deal of that undesirable thing. At the present moment I am very much embarrassed through my absolute inability to fulfil a contract into which I have entered, and which should have been filled this morning. I was due to-day with a Christmas story. The presses are waiting for it, and I am utterly unable to write it.'

He appeared deeply concerned at the confession. I had hoped, indeed, that he might be sufficiently concerned to take his departure, that I might make one more effort to write the promised story. His solicitude, however, showed itself in another way. Instead of leaving me, he ventured the hope that he might aid me.

'What kind of a story is it to be?' he asked.

'Oh, the usual ghostly tale,' I said, 'with a dash of the Christmas flavour thrown in here and there to make it suitable to the season.'

'Ah,' he observed. 'And you find your vein worked out?'

It was a direct and perhaps an impertinent question; but I thought it best to answer it, and to answer it as well without giving him any clue as to the real facts. I could not very well take an entire stranger into my confidence, and describe to him the extraordinary encounters I was having with an uncanny other self. He would not have believed the truth, hence I told him an untruth, and assented to his proposition.

'Yes,' I replied, 'the vein is worked out. I have written ghost stories

[95]

for years now, serious and comic, and I am to-day at the end of my tether—compelled to move forward and yet held back.'

'That accounts for it,' he said, simply. 'When I first saw you to-night at the door I could not believe that the author who had provided me with so much merriment could be so pale and worn and seemingly mirthless. Pardon me, Mr. Thurlow, for my lack of consideration when I told you that you did not appear as I had expected to find you.'

I smiled my forgiveness, and he continued:

'It may be,' he said, with a show of hesitation—'it may be that I have come not altogether inopportunely. Perhaps I can help you.'

I smiled again. 'I should be most grateful if you could,' I said.

'But you doubt my ability to do so?' he put in. 'Oh—well—yes—of course you do; and why shouldn't you? Nevertheless, I have noticed this: At times when I have been baffled in my work a mere hint from another, from one who knew nothing of my work, has carried me on to a solution of my problem. I have read most of your writings, and I have thought over some of them many a time, and I have even had ideas for stories, which, in my own conceit, I have imagined were good enough for you, and I have wished that I possessed your facility with the pen that I might make of them myself what I thought you would make of them had they been ideas of your own.'

The old gentleman's pallid face reddened as he said this, and while I was hopeless as to anything of value resulting from his ideas, I could not resist the temptation to hear what he had to say further, his manner was so deliciously simple, and his desire to aid me so manifest. He rattled on with suggestions for a half-hour. Some of them were good, but none were new. Some were irresistibly funny, and did me good because they made me laugh, and I hadn't laughed naturally for a period so long that it made me shudder to think of it, fearing lest I should forget how to be mirthful. Finally I grew tired of his persistence, and, with a very ill-concealed impatience, told him plainly that I could do nothing with his suggestions, thanking him, however, for the spirit of kindliness which had prompted him to offer them. He appeared somewhat hurt, but immediately desisted, and when nine o'clock came he rose up to go. As he walked to the door he seemed to be undergoing some mental struggle, to which, with a sudden resolve, he finally succumbed, for, after having picked up his hat and stick and donned his overcoat, he turned to me and said:

'Mr. Thurlow, I don't want to offend you. On the contrary, it is my dearest wish to assist you. You have helped me, as I have told you. Why may I not help you?'

'I assure you, sir—' I began, when he interrupted me.

'One moment, please,' he said, putting his hand into the inside pocket of his black coat and, extracting from it an envelope addressed to me. 'Let me finish: it is the whim of one who has an affection for you. For ten years I have secretly been at work myself on a story. It is a short one, but it has seemed good to me. I had a double object in seeking you out to-night. I wanted not only to see you, but to read my story to you. No one knows that I have written it; I had intended it as a surprise to my—to my friends. I had hoped to have it published somewhere, and I had come here to seek your advice in the matter. It is a story which I have written and rewritten and rewritten time and time again in my leisure moments during the ten years past, as I have told you. It is not likely that I shall ever write another. I am proud of having done it, but I should be prouder yet if it—if it could in some way help you. I leave it with you, sir, to print or to destroy; and if you print it, to see it in type will be enough for me; to see your name signed to it will be a matter of pride to me. No one will ever be the wiser, for, as I say, no one knows I have written it, and I promise you that no one shall know of it if you decide to do as I not only suggest but ask you to do. No one would believe me after it has appeared as *yours*, even if I should forget my promise and claim it as my own. Take it. It is yours. You are entitled to it as a slight measure of repayment for the debt of gratitude I owe you.'

He pressed the manuscript into my hands, and before I could reply had opened the door and disappeared into the darkness of the street. I rushed to the sidewalk and shouted out to him to return, but I might as well have saved my breath and spared the neighbourhood, for there was no answer. Holding his story in my hand, I re-entered the house and walked back into my library, where, sitting and reflecting upon the curious interview, I realized for the first time that I was in entire ignorance as to my visitor's name and address.

I opened the envelope hoping to find them, but they were not there. The envelope contained merely a finely written manuscript of thirty odd pages, unsigned.

And then I read the story. When I began it was with a half-smile upon my lips, and with a feeling that I was wasting my time. The smile soon faded, however; after reading the first paragraph there was no question of wasted time. The story was a masterpiece. It is needless to say to you that I am not a man of enthusiasms. It is difficult to arouse that emotion in my breast, but upon this occasion I yielded to a force too great for me to resist. I have read the tales of Hoffmann and of Poe, the wonderous romances of De La Motte Fouque, the unfortunately little-known tales of the lamented Fitz-James O'Brien, the weird tales of writers of all tongues have been thoroughly sifted by me in the course of my reading, and I say to you now that in the whole of my life I never read one story, one paragraph, one line, that could approach in vivid delineation, in weirdness of conception, in anything, in any quality which goes to make up the truly great story, that story which came into my hands as I have told you. I read it once and was amazed. I read it a second time and was—tempted. It was mine. The writer himself had authorized me to treat it as if it were my own; had voluntarily sacrificed his own claim to its authorship that he might relieve me of my very pressing embarrassment. Not only this; he had almost intimated that in putting my name to his work I should be doing him a favour. Why not do so, then, I asked myself; and immediately my better self rejected the idea as impossible. How could I put out as my own another man's work and retain my self-respect? I resolved on another and better course—to send you the story in lieu of my own with a full statement of the circumstances under which it had come into my possession—when, suddenly, that demon rose up out of the floor at my side, this time more evil of aspect than before, more commanding in its manner. With a groan I shrank back into the cushions of my chair, and by passing my hands over my eyes tried to obliterate forever the offending sight; but it was useless. The uncanny thing approached me, and as truly as I write sat upon the edge of my couch, where for the first time it addressed me.

'Fool!' it said, 'how can you hesitate? Here is your position: you have made a contract which must be filled; you are already behind, and in a hopeless mental state. Even granting that between this and to-morrow morning you could put together the necessary number of words to fill the space allotted to you, what kind of a thing do you think that story would make? It would be a mere raving like that other precious effort of August. The public, if by some odd chance it ever reached them, would think your mind was utterly gone; your reputation would go with that verdict. On the other hand, if you do not have the story ready by to-morrow, your hold on the *Idler* will be destroyed. They have their announcements printed, and your name and portrait appear among those of the prominent contributors. Do you suppose the editor and publisher will look leniently upon your failure?'

'Considering my past record, yes,' I replied. 'I have never yet broken a promise to them.'

'Which is precisely the reason why they will be severe with you. You, who have been regarded as one of the few men who can do almost any kind of literary work at will—you, of whom it is said that your 'brains are on tap'—will they be lenient with *you*? Bah! Can't you see that the very fact of your invariable readiness heretofore is going to make your present unreadiness a thing incomprehensible?'

'Then what shall I do?' I asked. 'If I can't, I can't, that is all.'

'You can. There is the story in your hands. Think what it will do for you. It is one of the immortal stories—'

'You have read it, then?' I asked.

Haven't you?'

'Yes—but—'

'It is the same,' it said, with a leer and a contemptuous shrug. 'You and I are inseparable. Aren't you glad?' it added, with a laugh that grated on every fibre of my being. I was too overwhelmed to reply, and it resumed: 'It is one of the immortal stories. We agree to that. Published over your name, your name will live. The stuff you write yourself will give you present glory; but when you have been dead ten years people won't remember your name even—unless I get control of you, and in that case there is a very pretty though hardly a literary record in store for you.'

Again it laughed harshly, and I buried my face in the pillows of my couch, hoping to find relief there from this dreadful vision.

'Curious,' it said. 'What you call your decent self doesn't dare look me in the eye! What a mistake people make who say that the man who won't look you in the eye is not to be trusted! As if mere brazenness were a sign of honesty; really, the theory of decency is the most amusing thing in the world. But come, time is growing short. Take that story. The writer gave it to you. Begged you to use it as your own. It is yours. It will make your reputation, and save you with your publishers. How can you hesitate?'

'I shall not use it!' I cried, desperately.

'You must—consider your children. Suppose you lose your connection with these publishers of yours?'

'But it would be a crime.'

'Not a bit of it. Whom do you rob? A man who voluntarily came to you, and gave you that of which you rob him. Think of it as it is—and act, only act quickly. It is now midnight.'

The tempter rose up and walked to the other end of the room, whence, while he pretended to be looking over a few of my books and pictures, I was aware he was eyeing me closely, and gradually compelling me by sheer force of will to do a thing which I abhorred. And I—I struggled weakly against the temptation, but gradually, little by little, I yielded, and finally succumbed altogether. Springing to my feet, I rushed to the table, seized my pen, and signed my name to the story.

'There!' I said. 'It is done. I have saved my position and made my reputation, and am now a thief!'

'As well as a fool,' said the other, calmly. 'You don't mean to say you are going to send that manuscript in as it is?'

'Good Lord!' I cried. 'What under heaven have you been trying to make me do for the last half hour?'

'Act like a sane being,' said the demon.

'If you send that manuscript to Currier he'll know in a minute it isn't yours. He knows you haven't an amanuensis, and that handwriting isn't yours. Copy it.'

'True!' I answered. 'I haven't much of a mind for details to-night. I will do as you say.'

I did so. I got out my pad and pen and ink, and for three hours diligently applied myself to the task of copying the story. When it was finished I went over it carefully, made a few minor corrections, signed it, put it in an envelope, addressed it to you, stamped it, and went out to the mail-box on the corner, where I dropped it into the slot, and returned home. When I had returned to my library my visitor was still there.

'Well,' it said, 'I wish you'd hurry and complete this affair. I am tired, and wish to go.'

'You can't go too soon to please me,' said I, gathering up the original manuscripts of the story and preparing to put them away in my desk.

'Probably not,' it sneered. 'I'll be glad to go too, but I can't go until that manuscript is destroyed. As long as it exists there is evidence of you having appropriated the work of another. Why, can't you see that? Burn it!'

'I can't see my way clear in crime!' I retorted. 'It is not in my line.'

Nevertheless, realizing the value of his advice, I thrust the pages one by one into the blazing log fire, and watched them as they flared and flamed and grew to ashes. As the last page disappeared in the embers the demon vanished. I was alone, and throwing myself down for a moment's reflection upon my couch, was soon lost in sleep.

It was noon when I again opened my eyes, and, ten minutes after I awakened, your telegraphic summons reached me.

'Come down at once,' was what you said, and I went; and then came the terrible *dénouement*, and yet a *dénouement* which was pleasing to me since it relieved my conscience. You handed me the envelope containing the story.

'Did you send that?' was your question.

'I did—last night, or rather early this morning. I mailed it about three o'clock,' I replied.

'I demand an explanation of your conduct,' you said.

'Of what?' I asked.

'Look at your so-called story and see. If this is a practical joke, Thurlow, it's a damned poor one.'

I opened the envelope and took from it the sheets I had sent you—twenty-four of them.

They were every one of them as blank as when they left the paper-mill!

You know the rest. You know that I tried to speak; that my utterance failed me; and that, finding myself unable at the time to control my emotions, I turned and rushed madly from the office, leaving the mystery unexplained. You know that you wrote demanding a satisfactory explanation of the situation or my resignation from your staff.

This, Currier, is my explanation. It is all I have. It is absolute truth. I beg you to believe it, for if you do not, then my condition is a hopeless one. You will ask me perhaps for a *résumé* of the story which I thought I had sent you.

It is my crowning misfortune that upon that point my mind is an absolute blank. I cannot remember it in form or in substance. I have racked my brains for some recollection of some small portion of it to help make my explanation more credible, but alas! it will not come back to me. If I were dishonest I might fake up a story to suit the purpose, but I am not dishonest. I came near to doing an unworthy act; I did do an unworthy thing, but by some mysterious provision of fate my conscience is cleared of that.

Be sympathetic, Currier, or, if you cannot, be lenient with me this time. *Believe, believe, believe*, I implore you. Pray let me hear from you at once.

(Signed)   HENRY THURLOW.

II

(Being a note from George Currier, Editor of the 'Idler,' to Henry Thurlow, Author.)

Your explanation has come to hand. As an explanation it isn't worth the paper it is written on, but we are all agreed here that it is probably the best bit of fiction you ever wrote. It is accepted for the Christmas issue. Enclosed please find a cheque for one hundred dollars.

Dawson suggests that you take another month up in the Adirondacks. You might put in your time writing up some account of that dream-life you are leading while you are there. It seems to me there are possibilities in the idea. The concern will pay all expenses. What do you say?

(Signed)   Yours ever,   G.C.

THEIR DEAR
LITTLE GHOST

by Elia W. Peattie

Mrs. Elia Wilkinson Peattie (1862–1935) was an
American journalist who wrote many supernatural
stories. The best of them, including 'Their Dear
Little Ghost', were collected in 1898 as *The Shape
of Fear and other ghostly tales*.

The first time one looked at Elsbeth, one was not prepossessed.
She was thin and brown, her nose turned slightly upward, her
toes went in just a perceptible degree, and her hair was
perfectly straight. But when one looked longer, one perceived that she
was a charming little creature. The straight hair was as fine as silk, and
hung in funny little braids down her back; there was not a flaw in her
soft brown skin; and her mouth was tender and shapely. But her
particular charm lay in a look which she habitually had, of seeming to
know curious things—such as it is not allotted to ordinary persons to
know. One felt tempted to say to her:

'What are these beautiful things which you know, and of which
others are ignorant? What is it you see with those wise and pellucid
eyes? Why is it that everybody loves you?'

Elsbeth was my little godchild, and I knew her better than I knew
any other child in the world. But still I could not truthfully say that I
was familiar with her, for to me her spirit was like a fair and fragrant
road in the midst of which I might walk in peace and joy, but where I
was continually to discover something new. The last time I saw her

[103]

quite well and strong was over in the woods where she had gone with her two little brothers and her nurse to pass the hottest weeks of summer. I followed her, foolish old creature that I was, just to be near her, for I needed to dwell where the sweet aroma of her life could reach me.

One morning when I came from my room, limping a little, because I am not so young as I used to be, and the lake wind works havoc with me, my little godchild came dancing to me singing:

'Come with me and I'll show you my places, my places, my places!'

Miriam, when she chanted by the Red Sea might have been more exultant, but she could not have been more bewitching. Of course I knew what 'places' were, because I had once been a little girl myself, but unless you are acquainted with the real meaning of 'places,' it would be useless to try to explain. Either you know 'places' or you do not—just as you understand the meaning of poetry or you do not. There are things in the world which cannot be taught.

Elsbeth's two tiny brothers were present, and I took one by each hand and followed her. No sooner had we got out of doors in the woods than a sort of mystery fell upon the world and upon us. We were cautioned to move silently; and we did so, avoiding the crunching of dry twigs.

'The fairies hate noise,' whispered my little godchild, her eyes narrowing like a cat's.

'I must get my wand first thing I do,' she said in an awed undertone. 'It is useless to try to do anything without a wand.'

The tiny boys were profoundly impressed, and, indeed, so was I. I felt that at last, I should, if I behaved properly, see the fairies, which had hitherto avoided my materialistic gaze. It was an enchanting moment, for there appeared, just then, to be nothing commonplace about life.

There was a swale near by, and into this the little girl plunged. I could see her red straw hat bobbing about among the tall rushes, and I wondered if there were snakes.

'Do you think there are snakes?' I asked one of the tiny boys.

'If there are,' he said with conviction, 'they won't dare hurt her.'

He convinced me. I feared no more. Presently Elsbeth came out of the swale. In her hand was a brown 'cattail,' perfectly full and round. She carried it as queens carry their sceptres—the beautiful queens we dream of in our youth.

'Come,' she commanded, and waved the sceptre in a fine manner.

[104]

So we followed, each tiny boy gripping my hand tight. We were all three a trifle awed. Elsbeth led us into a dark underbrush. The branches, as they flew back in our faces, left them wet with dew. A wee path, made by the girl's dear feet, guided our footsteps. Perfumes of elderberry and wild cucumber scented the air. A bird, frightened from its nest, made frantic cries above our heads. The underbrush thickened. Presently the gloom of the hemlocks was over us, and in the midst of the shadowy green a tulip tree flaunted its leaves. Waves boomed and broke upon the shore below. There was a growing dampness as we went on, treading very lightly. A little green snake ran coquettishly from us. A fat and glossy squirrel chattered at us from a safe height, stroking his whiskers with a complaisant air.

At length we reached the 'place.' It was a circle of velvet grass, bright as the first blades of spring, delicate as fine sea-ferns. The sunlight, falling down the shaft between the hemlocks, flooded it with a softened light and made the forest round about look like deep purple velvet. My little godchild stood in the midst and raised her wand impressively.

'This is my place,' she said, with a sort of wonderful gladness in her tone. 'This is where I come to the fairy balls. Do you see them?'

'See what?' whispered one tiny boy.

'The fairies.'

There was a silence. The older boy pulled at my skirt.

'Do you see them?' he asked, his voice trembling with expectancy.

'Indeed,' I said, 'I fear I am too old and wicked to see fairies, and yet—are their hats red?'

'They are,' laughed my little girl. 'Their hats are red, and as small— as small!' She held up the pearly nail of her wee finger to give us the correct idea.

'And their shoes are very pointed at the toes?'

'Oh, very pointed!'

'And their garments are green?'

'As green as grass.'

'And they blow little horns?'

'The sweetest little horns!'

'I think I see them,' I cried.

'We think we see them too,' said the tiny boys, laughing in perfect glee.

'And you hear their horns, don't you?' my little godchild asked somewhat anxiously.

[105]

'Don't we hear their horns?' I asked the tiny boys.

'We think we hear their horns,' they cried. 'Don't you think we do?'

'It must be we do,' I said. 'Aren't we very, very happy?'

We all laughed softly. Then we kissed each other and Elsbeth led us out, her wand high in the air.

And so my feet found the lost path to Arcady.

The next day I was called to the Pacific coast, and duty kept me there till well into December. A few days before the date set for my return to my home, a letter came from Elsbeth's mother.

'Our little girl is gone into the Unknown,' she wrote—'that Unknown in which she seemed to be forever trying to pry. We knew she was going, and we told her. She was quite brave, but she begged us to try some way to keep her till after Christmas. "My presents are not finished yet," she made moan. "And I did so want to see what I was going to have. You can't have a very happy Christmas without me, I should think. Can you arrange to keep me somehow till after then?" We could not "arrange" either with God in heaven or science upon earth, and she is gone.'

She was only my little godchild, and I am an old maid, with no business fretting over children, but it seemed as if the medium of light and beauty had been taken from me. Through this crystal soul I had perceived whatever was loveliest. However, what was, was! I returned to my home and took up a course of Egyptian history, and determined to concern myself with nothing this side of the Ptolemies.

Her mother has told me how, on Christmas eve, as usual, she and Elsbeth's father filled the stockings of the little ones, and hung them, where they had always hung, by the fireplace. They had little heart for the task, but they had been prodigal that year in their expenditures, and had heaped upon the two tiny boys all the treasures they thought would appeal to them. They asked themselves how they could have been so insane previously as to exercise economy at Christmas time, and what they meant by not getting Elsbeth the autoharp she had asked for the year before.

'And now—' began her father, thinking of harps. But he could not complete this sentence, of course, and the two went on passionately and almost angrily with their task. There were two stockings and two piles of toys. Two stockings only, and only two piles of toys! Two is very little!

They went away and left the darkened room, and after a time they slept—after a long time. Perhaps that was about the time the tiny boys

[106]

awoke, and, putting on their little dressing gowns and bed slippers, made a dash for the room where the Christmas things were always placed. The older one carried a candle which gave out a feeble light. The other followed behind through the silent house. They were very impatient and eager, but when they reached the door of the sitting-room they stopped, for they saw that another child was before them.

It was a delicate little creature, sitting in her white night gown, with two rumpled funny braids falling down her back, and she seemed to be weeping. As they watched, she arose, and putting out one slender finger as a child does when she counts, she made sure over and over again—three sad times—that there were only two stockings and two piles of toys! Only those and no more.

The little figure looked so familiar that the boys started toward it, but just then, putting up her arm and bowing her face in it, as Elsbeth had been used to do when she wept or was offended, the little thing glided away and went out. That's what the boys said. It went out as a candle goes out.

They ran and woke their parents with the tale, and all the house was searched in a wonderment, and disbelief, and hope, and tumult! But nothing was found. For nights they watched. But there was only the silent house. Only the empty rooms. They told the boys they must have been mistaken. But the boys shook their heads.

'We know our Elsbeth,' said they. 'It was our Elsbeth, cryin' 'cause she hadn't no stockin' an' no toys, and we would have given her all ours, only she went out—jus' went out!'

Alack!

The next Christmas I helped with the little festival. It was none of my affair, but I asked to help, and they let me, and when we were all through there were three stockings and three piles of toys, and in the largest one was all the things that I could think of that my dear child would love. I locked the boys' chamber that night, and I slept on the divan in the parlour off the sitting-room. I slept but little, and the night was very still—so windless and white and still that I think I must have heard the slightest noise. Yet I heard none. Had I been in my grave I think my ears would not have remained more unsaluted.

Yet when daylight came and I went to unlock the boys' bedchamber door, I saw that the stocking and all the treasures which I had bought for my little godchild were gone. There was not a vestige of them remaining!

Of course we told the boys nothing. As for me, after dinner I went home and buried myself once more in my history, and so interested was I that midnight came without my knowing it. I should not have looked up at all, I suppose, to become aware of the time, had it not been for a faint, sweet sound as of a child striking a stringed instrument. It was so delicate and remote that I hardly heard it, but so joyous and tender that I could not but listen, and when I heard it a second time it seemed as if I caught the echo of a child's laugh. At first I was puzzled. Then I remembered the little autoharp I had placed among the other things in that pile of vanished toys. I said aloud:

'Farewell, dear little ghost. Go rest. Rest in joy, dear little ghost. Farewell, farewell.'

That was years ago, but there has been silence since. Elsbeth was always an obedient little thing.

WOLVERDEN TOWER

by Grant Allen

Grant Allen (1848–1899) was a Canadian-born
writer who spent most of his career in Britain.
He became one of the most prolific and famous
authors of the 1890's, his most controversial works
being *The Evolution of the Idea of God* (1897) and
The Woman Who Did (1895), a novel (in the
Keynotes series) in which the title-figure decided
that free love was less degrading than the bondage
of marriage.
'Wolverden Tower', one of the best of his
supernatural tales, appeared in his collection
Twelve Tales (1899).

I

M aisie Llewelyn had never been asked to Wolverden before;
therefore, she was not a little elated at Mrs. West's invitation. For Wolverden Hall, one of the loveliest Elizabethan
manor-houses in the Weald of Kent, had been bought and fitted up in
appropriate style (the phrase is the upholsterer's) by Colonel West,
the famous millionaire from South Australia. The Colonel had
lavished upon it untold wealth, fleeced from the backs of ten thousand
sheep and an equal number of his fellow-countrymen; and Wolverden
was now, if not the most beautiful, at least the most opulent country-
house within easy reach of London.

Mrs. West was waiting at the station to meet Maisie. The house was full of Christmas guests already, it is true; but Mrs. West was a model of stately, old-fashioned courtesy: she would not have omitted meeting one among the number on any less excuse than a royal command to appear at Windsor. She kissed Maisie on both cheeks—she had always been fond of Maisie—and, leaving two haughty young aristocrats (in powdered hair and blue-and-gold livery) to hunt up her luggage by the light of nature, sailed forth with her through the door to the obsequious carriage.

The drive up the avenue to Wolverden Hall Maisie found quite delicious. Even in their leafless winter condition the great limes looked so noble; and the ivy-covered hall at the end, with its mullioned windows, its Inigo Jones porch, and its creeper-clad gables, was as picturesque a building as the ideals one sees in Mr. Abbey's sketches. If only Arthur Hume had been one of the party now, Maisie's joy would have been complete. But what was the use of thinking so much about Arthur Hume, when she didn't even know whether Arthur Hume cared for her?

A tall, slim girl, Maisie Llewelyn, with rich black hair, and ethereal features, as became a descendant of Llewelyn ap Iorwerth—the sort of girl we none of us would have called anything more than 'interesting' till Rossetti and Burne-Jones found eyes for us to see that the type is beautiful with a deeper beauty than that of your obvious pink-and-white prettiness. Her eyes, in particular, had a lustrous depth that was almost superhuman, and her fingers and nails were strangely transparent in their waxen softness.

'You won't mind my having put you in a ground-floor room in the new wing, my dear, will you?' Mrs. West inquired, as she led Maisie personally to the quarters chosen for her. 'You see, we're so unusually full, because of these tableaux!'

Maisie gazed round the ground-floor room in the new wing with eyes of mute wonder. If *this* was the kind of lodging for which Mrs. West thought it necessary to apologise, Maisie wondered of what sort were those better rooms which she gave to the guests she delighted to honour. It was a large and exquisitely decorated chamber, with the softest and deepest Oriental carpet Maisie's feet had ever felt, and the daintiest curtains her eyes had ever lighted upon. True, it opened by French windows on to what was nominally the ground in front; but as the Italian terrace, with its formal balustrade and its great stone balls, was raised several feet above the level of the sloping garden below, the room was really on the first floor for all practical purposes. Indeed, Maisie rather liked the unwonted sense of space and freedom which was given by this easy access to the world without; and, as the windows were secured by great shutters and fasteners, she had no counterbalancing fear lest a nightly burglar should attempt to carry off her little pearl necklet or her amethyst brooch, instead of directing his whole attention to Mrs. West's famous diamond tiara.

She moved naturally to the window. She was fond of nature. The view it disclosed over the Weald at her feet was wide and varied. Misty range lay behind misty range, in a faint December haze, receding and receding, till away to the south, half hidden by vapour, the Sussex downs loomed vague in the distance. The village church, as happens so often in the case of old lordly manors, stood within the grounds of the Hall, and close by the house. It had been built, her hostess said, in the days of the Edwards, but had portions of an older Saxon edifice still enclosed in the chancel. The one eyesore in the view was its new white tower, recently restored (or rather, rebuilt), which contrasted most painfully with the mellow grey stone and mouldering corbels of the nave and transept.

'What a pity it's been so spoiled!' Maisie exclaimed, looking across at the tower. Coming straight as she did from a Merioneth rectory, she took an ancestral interest in all that concerned churches.

'Oh, my dear!' Mrs. West cried, '*please* don't say that, I beg of you, to the Colonel. If you were to murmur "spoiled" to him you'd wreck his digestion. He's spent ever so much money over securing the foundations and reproducing the sculpture on the old tower we took down, and it breaks his dear heart when anybody disapproves of it. For *some* people, you know, are so absurdly opposed to reasonable restoration.'

'Oh, but this isn't even restoration, you know,' Maisie said, with the frankness of twenty, and the specialist interest of an antiquary's daughter. 'This is pure reconstruction.'

'Perhaps so,' Mrs. West answered. 'But if you think so, my dear, don't breathe it at Wolverden.'

A fire, of ostentatiously wealthy dimensions, and of the best glowing coal, burned bright on the hearth; but the day was mild, and hardly more than autumnal. Maisie found the room quite unpleasantly hot. She opened the windows and stepped out on the terrace. Mrs. West followed her. They paced up and down the broad gravelled platform for a while—Maisie had not yet taken off her travelling-cloak and hat—and then strolled half unconsciously towards the gate of the church. The churchyard, to hide the tombstones of which the parapet had been erected, was full of quaint old monuments, with broken-nosed cherubs, some of them dating from a comparatively early period. The porch, with its sculptured niches deprived of their saints by puritan hands, was still rich and beautiful in its carved detail. On the seat inside an old woman was sitting. She did not rise as the lady of the manor approached, but went on mumbling and muttering inarticulately to herself in a sulky undertone. Still, Maisie was aware, none the less, that the moment she came near a strange light gleamed suddenly in the old woman's eyes, and that her glance was fixed upon her. A faint thrill of recognition seemed to pass like a flash through her palsied body. Maisie knew not why, but she was dimly afraid of the old woman's gaze upon her.

'It's a lovely old church!' Maisie said, looking up at the trefoil finials on the porch—'all, except the tower.'

'We *had* to reconstruct it,' Mrs. West answered apologetically—Mrs. West's general attitude in life was apologetic, as though she felt she had no right to so much more money than her fellow-creatures. 'It would have fallen if we hadn't done something to buttress it up. It was really in a most dangerous and critical condition.'

'Lies! lies! lies!' the old woman burst out suddenly, though in a strange, low tone, as if speaking to herself. 'It would *not* have fallen—they knew it would not. It could not have fallen. It would never have fallen if they had not destroyed it. And even then—I was there when they pulled it down—each stone clung to each, with arms and legs and hands and claws, till they burst them asunder by main force with their new-fangled stuff—I don't know what they call it—dynamite, or something. It was all of it done for one man's vainglory!'

'Come away, dear,' Mrs. West whispered. But Maisie loitered.

'Wolverden Tower was fasted thrice,' the old woman continued, in a sing-song quaver. 'It was fasted thrice with souls of maids against every assault of man or devil. It was fasted at the foundation against earthquake and ruin. It was fasted at the top against thunder and lightning. It was fasted in the middle against storm and battle. And there it would have stood for a thousand years if a wicked man had not raised a vainglorious hand against it. For that's what the rhyme says—

'Fasted thrice with souls of men,
Stands the tower of Wolverden;

[112]

Fasted thrice with maidens' blood,
A thousand years of fire and flood
Shall see it stand as erst it stood.'

She paused a moment, then, raising one skinny hand towards the brand-new stone, she went on in the same voice, but with malignant fervour—

'A thousand years the tower shall stand
Till ill assailed by evil hand;
By evil hand in evil hour,
Fasted thrice with warlock's power,
Shall fall the stanes of Wulfhere's tower.'

She tottered off as she ended, and took her seat on the edge of a depressed vault in the churchyard close by, still eyeing Maisie Llewelyn with a weird and curious glance, almost like the look which a famishing man casts upon the food in a shop-window.

'Who is she?' Maisie asked, shrinking away in undefined terror.

'Oh, old Bessie,' Mrs. West answered, looking more apologetic (for the parish) than ever. 'She's always hanging about here. She has nothing else to do, and she's an outdoor pauper. You see, that's the worst of having the church in one's grounds, which is otherwise picturesque and romantic and baronial; the road to it's public; you must admit all the world; and old Bessie will come here. The servants are afraid of her. They say she's a witch. She has the evil eye, and she drives girls to suicide. But they cross her hand with silver all the same, and she tells them their fortunes—gives them each a butler. She's full of dreadful stories about Wolverden Church—stories to make your blood run cold, my dear, compact with old superstitions and murders, and so forth. And they're true, too, that's the worst of them. She's quite a character. Mr. Blaydes, the antiquary, is really attached to her; he says she's now the sole living repository of the traditional folklore and history of the parish. But I don't care for it myself. It 'gars one greet,' as we say in Scotland. Too much burying alive in it, don't you know, my dear, to quite suit my fancy.'

They turned back as she spoke towards the carved wooden lych-gate, one of the oldest and most exquisite of its class in England. When they reached the vault by whose doors old Bessie was seated, Maisie turned once more to gaze at the pointed lancet windows of the

Early English choir, and the still more ancient dog-tooth ornament of the ruined Norman Lady Chapel.

'How solidly it's built!' she exclaimed, looking up at the arches which alone survived the fury of the Puritan. 'It really looks as if it would last for ever.'

Old Bessie had bent her head, and seemed to be whispering something at the door of the vault. But at the sound she raised her eyes, and, turning her wizened face towards the lady of the manor, mumbled through her few remaining fang-like teeth an old local saying, 'Bradbury for length, Wolverden for strength, and Church Hatton for beauty!

'Three brothers builded churches three;
And fasted thrice each church shall be:
Fasted thrice with maidens' blood,
To make them safe from fire and flood;
Fasted thrice with souls of men,
Hatton, Bradbury, Wolverden!'

'Come away,' Maisie said, shuddering. 'I'm afraid of that woman. Why was she whispering at the doors of the vault down there? I don't like the look of her.'

'My dear,' Mrs. West answered, in no less terrified a tone, 'I will confess I don't like the look of her myself. I wish she'd leave the place. I've tried to make her. The Colonel offered her fifty pounds down and a nice cottage in Surrey if only she'd go—she frightens me so much; but she wouldn't hear of it. She said she must stop by the bodies of her dead—that's her style, don't you see: a sort of modern ghoul, a degenerate vampire—and from the bodies of her dead in Wolverden Church no living soul should ever move her.'

II

For dinner Maisie wore her white satin Empire dress, high-waisted, low-necked, and cut in the bodice with a certain baby-like simplicity of style which exactly suited her strange and uncanny type of beauty. She was very much admired. She felt it, and it pleased her. The young man who took her in, a subaltern of engineers, had no eyes for any one else; while old Admiral Wade, who sat opposite her with a plain and skinny dowager, made her positively uncomfortable by the persistent way in which he stared at her simple pearl necklet.

After dinner, the tableaux. They had been designed and managed by a famous Royal Academician, and were mostly got up by the members of the house-party. But two or three actresses from London had been specially invited to help in a few of the more mythological scenes; for, indeed, Mrs. West had prepared the entire entertainment with that topsy-turvy conscientiousness and scrupulous sense of responsibility to society which pervaded her view of millionaire morality. Having once decided to offer the county a set of tableaux, she felt that millionaire morality absolutely demanded of her the sacrifice of three weeks' time and several hundred pounds money in order to discharge her obligations to the county with becoming magnificence.

The first tableau, Maisie learned from the gorgeous programme, was 'Jephthah's Daughter.' The subject was represented at the pathetic moment when the doomed virgin goes forth from her father's house with her attendant maidens to bewail her virginity for two months upon the mountains, before the fulfilment of the awful vow which bound her father to offer her up for a burnt offering. Maisie thought it too solemn and tragic a scene for a festive occasion. But the famous R.A. had a taste for such themes, and his grouping was certainly most effectively dramatic.

'A perfect symphony in white and grey,' said Mr. Wills, the art critic.

'How awfully affecting!' said most of the young girls.

'Reminds me a little too much, my dear, of old Bessie's stories,' Mrs. West whispered low, leaning from her seat across two rows to Maisie.

A piano stood a little on one side of the platform, just in front of the curtain. The intervals between the pieces were filled up with songs, which, however, had been evidently arranged in keeping with the solemn and half-mystical tone of the tableaux. It is the habit of amateurs to take a long time in getting their scenes in order, so the interposition of the music was a happy thought as far as its prime intention went. But Maisie wondered they could not have chosen some livelier song for Christmas Eve than 'Oh, Mary, go and call the cattle home, and call the cattle home, and call the cattle home, across the sands of Dee.' Her own name was Mary when she signed it officially, and the sad lilt of the last line, 'But never home came she,' rang unpleasantly in her ear through the rest of the evening.

[115]

The second tableau was the 'Sacrifice of Iphigenia.' It was admirably rendered. The cold and dignified father, standing, apparently un-moved, by the pyre; the cruel faces of the attendant priests; the shrinking form of the immolated princess; the mere blank curiosity and inquiring interest of the helmeted heroes looking on, to whom this slaughter of a virgin victim was but an ordinary incident of the Achaean religion—all these had been arranged by the Academical director with consummate skill and pictorial cleverness. But the group that attracted Maisie most among the components of the scene was that of the attendant maidens, more conspicuous here in their flowing white chitons that even they had been when posed as companions of the beautiful and ill-fated Hebrew victim. Two in particular excited her close attention—two very graceful and spiritual-looking girls, in long white robes of no particular age or country, who stood at the very end near the right edge of the picture. 'How lovely they are, the two last on the right!' Maisie whispered to her neighbour—an Oxford undergraduate with a budding moustache. 'I do so admire them!'

'Do you?' he answered, fondling the moustache with one dubious finger. 'Well, now, do you know, I don't think I do. They're rather coarse-looking. And besides, I don't quite like the way they've got their hair done up in bunches; too fashionable, isn't it?—too much of the present day? I don't care to see a girl in a Greek costume, with her coiffure so evidently turned out by Truefitt's!'

'Oh, I don't mean those two,' Maisie answered, a little shocked he should think she had picked out such meretricious faces; 'I mean the two beyond them again—the two with their hair so simply and sweetly done—the ethereal-looking dark girls.'

The undergraduate opened his mouth, and stared at her in blank amazement for a moment. 'Well, I don't see—' he began, and broke off suddenly. Something in Maisie's eye seemed to give him pause. He fondled his moustache, hesitated, and was silent.

'How nice to have read the Greek and know what it all means!' Maisie went on, after a minute. 'It's a human sacrifice, of course; but, please, what is the story?'

The undergraduate hummed and hawed. 'Well, it's in Euripides, you know,' he said, trying to look impressive, 'and—er—and I haven't taken up Euripides for my next examination. But I *think* it's like this. Iphigenia was a daughter of Agamemnon's, don't you know, and he had offended Artemis or somebody—some other goddess; and he vowed to offer up to her the most beautiful thing that should be born that year, by way of reparation—just like Jephthah. Well, Iphigenia was considered the most beautiful product of the particular twelve-month—don't look at me like that, please! you—you make me nervous—and so, when the young woman grew up—well, I don't quite recollect the ins and outs of the details, but it's a human sacrifice business, don't you see; and they're just going to kill her, though I *believe* a hind was finally substituted for the girl, like the ram for Isaac; but I must confess I've a very vague recollection of it.' He rose from his seat uneasily. 'I'm afraid,' he went on, shuffling about for an excuse to move, 'these chairs are too close. I seem to be incommoding you.'

He moved away with a furtive air. At the end of the tableau one or two of the characters who were not needed in succeeding pieces came down from the stage and joined the body of spectators, as they often do, in their character-dresses—a good opportunity, in point of fact, for retaining through the evening the advantages conferred by theatrical costume, rouge, and pearl-powder. Among them the two girls Maisie had admired so much glided quietly toward her and took the two vacant seats on either side, one of which had just been quitted by the awkward undergraduate. They were not only beautiful in face and figure, on a closer view, but Maisie found them from the first extremely sympathetic. They burst into talk with her, frankly and at once, with charming ease and grace of manner. They were ladies in the grain, in instinct and breeding. The taller of the two, whom the other addressed as Yolande, seemed particularly pleasing. The very name charmed Maisie. She was friends with them at once. They both possessed a certain nameless attraction that constitutes in itself the best possible introduction. Maisie hesitated to ask them whence they came, but it was clear from their talk they knew Wolverden intimately.

After a minute the piano struck up once more. A famous Scotch vocalist, in a diamond necklet and a dress to match, took her place on the stage, just in front of the footlights. As chance would have it, she began singing the song Maisie most of all hated. It was Scott's ballad of 'Proud Maisie,' set to music by Carlo Ludovici—

> 'Proud Maisie is in the wood,
>   Walking so early;
> Sweet Robin sits on the bush,
>   Singing so rarely.

"Tell me, thou bonny bird
    When shall I marry me?"
"When six braw gentlemen
    Kirkward shall carry ye."

"Who makes the bridal bed,
    Birdie, say truly?"
"The grey-headed sexton
    That delves the grave duly.

"The glow-worm o'er grave and stone
    Shall light thee steady;
The owl from the steeple sing,
    'Welcome, proud lady.'" '

Maisie listened to the song with grave discomfort. She had never liked it, and to-night it appalled her. She did not know that just at that moment Mrs. West was whispering in a perfect fever of apology to a lady by her side, 'Oh dear! oh dear! what a dreadful thing of me ever to have permitted that song to be sung here to-night! It was horribly thoughtless! Why, now I remember, Miss Llewelyn's name, you know, is Maisie!—and there she is listening to it with a face like a sheet! I shall never forgive myself!'

The tall, dark girl by Maisie's side, whom the other called Yolande, leaned across to her sympathetically. 'You don't like that song?' she said, with just a tinge of reproach in her voice as she said it.

'I hate it!' Maisie answered, trying hard to compose herself.

'Why so?' the tall, dark girl asked, in a tone of calm and singular sweetness. 'It's sad, perhaps; but it's lovely—and natural!'

'My own name is Maisie,' her new friend replied, with an ill-repressed shudder. 'And somehow that song pursues me through life. I seem always to hear the horrid ring of the words, "When six braw gentlemen kirkward shall carry ye." I wish to Heaven my people had never called me Maisie!'

'And yet *why*?' the tall, dark girl asked again, with a sad, mysterious air. 'Why this clinging to life—this terror of death—this inexplicable attachment to a world of misery? And with such eyes as yours, too! Your eyes are like mine'—which was a compliment, certainly, for the dark girl's own pair were strangely deep and lustrous. 'People with eyes such as those, that can look into futurity, ought not surely to shrink from a mere gate like death! For death is but a gate—the gate

[118]

of life in its fullest beauty. It is written over the door, ' "Mors janua vitae." '

'What door?' Maisie asked—for she remembered having read those selfsame words, and tried in vain to translate them, that very day, though the meaning was now clear to her.

The answer electrified her: 'The gate of the vault in Wolverden churchyard.'

She said it very low, but with pregnant expression.

'Oh, how dreadful!' Maisie exclaimed, drawing back. The tall, dark girl half frightened her.

'Not at all,' the girl answered. 'This life is so short, so vain, so transitory! And beyond it is peace—eternal peace—the calm of rest— the joy of the spirit.'

'You come to anchor at last,' her companion added.

'But if—one has somebody one would not wish to leave behind?' Maisie suggested timidly.

'He will follow before long,' the dark girl replied with quiet decision, interpreting rightly the sex of the indefinite substantive. 'Time passes so quickly. And if time passes quickly in time, how much more, then, in eternity!'

'Hush, Yolande,' the other dark girl put in, with a warning glance; 'there's a new tableau coming. Let me see, is this "The Death of Ophelia"? No, that's number four; this is number three, "The Martyrdom of St. Agnes." '

III

'My dear,' Mrs. West said, positively oozing apology, when she met Maisie in the supper-room, 'I'm afraid you've been left in a corner by yourself almost all the evening!'

'Oh dear, no,' Maisie answered with a quiet smile. 'I had that Oxford undergraduate at my elbow at first; and afterwards those two nice girls, with the flowing white dresses and the beautiful eyes, came and sat beside me. What's their name, I wonder?'

'Which girls?' Mrs. West asked, with a little surprise in her tone, for her impression was rather that Maisie had been sitting between two empty chairs for the greater part of the evening, muttering at times to herself in the most uncanny way, but not talking to anybody.

Maisie glanced round the room in search of her new friends, and for some time could not see them. At last, she observed them in a remote alcove, drinking red wine by themselves out of Venetian-glass beakers. 'Those two,' she said, pointing towards them. 'They're such charming girls! Can you tell me who they are? I've quite taken a fancy to them.'

Mrs. West gazed at them for a second—or rather, at the recess towards which Maisie pointed—and then turned to Maisie with much the same oddly embarrassed look and manner as the undergraduate's. 'Oh, *those*!' she said slowly, peering through and through her, Maisie thought. 'Those—must be some of the professionals from London. At any rate—I'm not sure which you mean—over there by the curtain, in the Moorish nook, you say—well, I can't tell you their names! So they *must* be professionals.'

She went off with a singularly frightened manner. Maisie noticed it and wondered at it. But it made no great or lasting impression.

When the party broke up, about midnight or a little later, Maisie went along the corridor to her own bedroom. At the end, by the door, the two other girls happened to be standing, apparently gossiping.

'Oh, you've not gone home yet?' Maisie said, as she passed, to Yolande.

'No, we're stopping here,' the dark girl with the speaking eyes answered.

Maisie paused for a second. Then an impulse burst over her. 'Will you come and see my room?' she asked, a little timidly.

'Shall we go, Hedda?' Yolande said, with an inquiring glance at her companion.

Her friend nodded assent. Maisie opened the door, and ushered them into her bedroom.

The ostentatiously opulent fire was still burning brightly, the electric light flooded the room with its brilliancy, the curtains were drawn, and the shutters fastened. For a while the three girls sat together by the hearth and gossiped quietly. Maisie liked her new friends—their voices were so gentle, soft, and sympathetic, while for face and figure they might have sat as models to Burne-Jones or Botticelli. Their dresses, too, took her delicate Welsh fancy; they were so dainty, yet so simple. The soft silk fell in natural folds and dimples. The only ornaments they wore were two curious brooches of very antique workmanship—as Maisie supposed—somewhat Celtic in design, and enamelled in blood-red on a gold background. Each carried a flower laid loosely in her bosom. Yolande's was an orchid

[120]

with long, floating streamers, in colour and shape recalling some Southern lizard; dark purple spots dappled its lip and petals. Hedda's was a flower of a sort Maisie had never before seen—the stem spotted like a viper's skin, green flecked with russet-brown, and uncanny to look upon; on either side, great twisted spirals of red-and-blue blossoms, each curled after the fashion of a scorpion's tail, very strange and lurid. Something weird and witch-like about flowers and dresses rather attracted Maisie; they affected her with the half-repellent fascination of a snake for a bird; she felt such blossoms were fit for incantations and sorceries. But a lily-of-the-valley in Yolande's dark hair gave a sense of purity which assorted better with the girl's exquisitely calm and nun-like beauty.

After a while Hedda rose. 'This air is close,' she said. 'It ought to be warm outside to-night, if one may judge by the sunset. May I open the window?'

'Oh, certainly, if you like,' Maisie answered, a vague foreboding now struggling within her against innate politeness.

Hedda drew back the curtains and unfastened the shutters. It was a moonlit evening. The breeze hardly stirred the bare boughs of the silver birches. A sprinkling of soft snow on the terrace and the hills just whitened the ground. The moon lighted it up, falling full upon the Hall; the church and tower below stood silhouetted in dark against a cloudless expanse of starry sky in the background. Hedda opened the window. Cool, fresh air blew in, very soft and genial, in spite of the snow and the lateness of the season. 'What a glorious night!' she said, looking up at Orion overhead. 'Shall we stroll out for a while in it?'

If the suggestion had not thus been thrust upon her from outside, it would never have occurred to Maisie to walk abroad in a strange place, in evening dress, on a winter's night, with snow whitening the ground; but Hedda's voice sounded so sweetly persuasive, and the idea itself seemed so natural now she had once proposed it, that Maisie followed her two new friends on to the moonlit terrace without a moment's hesitation.

They paced once or twice up and down the gravelled walks. Strange to say, though a sprinkling of dry snow powdered the ground under foot, the air itself was soft and balmy. Stranger still, Maisie noticed, almost without noticing it, that though they walked three abreast, only one pair of footprints—her own—lay impressed on the snow in a long trail when they turned at either end and re-paced the platform. Yolande and Hedda must step lightly indeed; or perhaps her own feet

[121]

might be warmer or thinner shod, so as to melt the light layer of snow more readily.

The girls slipped their arms through hers. A little thrill coursed through her. Then, after three or four turns up and down the terrace, Yolande led the way quietly down the broad flight of steps in the direction of the church on the lower level. In that bright, broad moonlight Maisie went with them undeterred; the Hall was still alive with the glare of electric lights in bedroom windows; and the presence of the other girls, both wholly free from any signs of fear, took off all sense of terror or loneliness. They strolled on into the churchyard. Maisie's eyes were now fixed on the new white tower, which merged in the silhouette against the starry sky into much the same grey and indefinite hue as the older parts of the building. Before she quite knew where she was, she found herself at the head of the worn stone steps which led into the vault by whose doors she had seen old Bessie sitting. In the pallid moonlight, with the aid of the greenish reflection from the snow, she could just read the words inscribed over the portal, the words that Yolande had repeated in the drawing-room, 'Mors janua vitae.'

Yolande moved down one step. Maisie drew back for the first time with a faint access of alarm. 'You're—you're not *going down* there!' she exclaimed, catching her breath for a second.

'Yes, I am,' her new friend answered in a calmly quiet voice. 'Why not? We live here.'

'You live here?' Maisie echoed, freeing her arms by a sudden movement and standing away from her mysterious friends with a tremulous shudder.

'Yes, we live here,' Hedda broke in, without the slightest emotion. She said it in a voice of perfect calm, as one might say it of any house in a street in London.

Maisie was far less terrified than she might have imagined beforehand would be the case under such unexpected conditions. The two girls were so simple, so natural, so strangely like herself, that she could not say she was really afraid of them. She shrank, it is true, from the nature of the door at which they stood, but she received the unearthly announcement that they lived there with scarcely more than a slight tremor of surprise and astonishment.

'You will come in with us?' Hedda said in a gently enticing tone. 'We went into your bedroom.'

Maisie hardly liked to say no. They seemed so anxious to show her their home. With trembling feet she moved down the first step, and then the second. Yolande kept ever one pace in front of her. As Maisie reached the third step, the two girls, as if moved by one design, took her wrists in their hands, not unkindly, but coaxingly. They reached the actual doors of the vault itself—two heavy bronze valves, meeting in the centre. Each bore a ring for a handle, pierced through a Gorgon's head embossed upon the surface. Yolande pushed them with her hand. They yielded instantly to her light touch, and opened *inward.* Yolande, still in front, passed from the glow of the moon to the gloom of the vault, which a ray of moonlight just descended obliquely. As she passed, for a second, a weird sight met Maisie's eyes. Her face and hands and dress became momentarily self-luminous; but through them, as they glowed, she could descry within every bone and joint of her living skeleton, dimly shadowed in dark through the luminous haze that marked her body.

Maisie drew back once more, terrified. Yet her terror was not quite what one could describe as fear: it was rather a vague sense of the profoundly mystical. 'I can't! I can't!' she cried, with an appealing glance. 'Hedda! Yolande! I cannot go with you.'

Hedda held her hand tight, and almost seemed to force her. But Yolande, in front, like a mother with her child, turned round with a grave smile. 'No, no,' she said reprovingly. 'Let her come if she will, Hedda, of her own accord, not otherwise. The tower demands a willing victim.'

Her hand on Maisie's wrist was strong but persuasive. It drew her without exercising the faintest compulsion. 'Will you come with us, dear?' she said, in that winning silvery tone which had captivated Maisie's fancy from the very first moment they spoke together. Maisie's gazed into her eyes. They were deep and tender. A strange resolution seemed to nerve her for the effort. 'Yes, yes—I—will—come—with you,' she answered slowly.

Hedda on one side, Yolande on the other, now went before her, holding her wrists in their grasp, but rather enticing than drawing her. As each reached the gloom, the same luminous appearance which Maisie had noticed before spread over their bodies, and the same weird skeleton shape showed faintly through their limbs in darker shadow. Maisie crossed the threshold with a convulsive gasp. As she crossed it she looked down at her own dress and body. They were semi-transparent, like the others', though not quite so self-luminous; the framework of her limbs appeared within in less certain outline, yet quite dark and distinguishable.

[123]

The doors swung to of themselves behind her. Those three stood alone in the vault of Wolverden.

Alone, for a minute or two; and then, as her eyes grew accustomed to the grey dusk of the interior, Maisie began to perceive that the vault opened out into a large and beautiful hall or crypt, dimly lighted at first, but becoming each moment more vaguely clear and more dreamily definite. Gradually she could make out great rock-hewn pillars, Romanesque in their outline or dimly Oriental, like the sculptured columns in the caves of Ellora, supporting a roof of vague and uncertain dimensions, more or less strangely dome-shaped. The effect on the whole was like that of the second impression produced by some dim cathedral, such as Chartres or Milan, after the eyes have grown accustomed to the mellow light from the stained-glass windows, and have recovered from the blinding glare of the outer sunlight. But the architecture, if one may call it so, was more mosque-like and magical. She turned to her companions. Yolande and Hedda stood still by her side; their bodies were now self-luminous to a greater degree than even at the threshold; but the terrible transparency had disappeared altogether; they were once more but beautiful though strangely transfigured and more than mortal women.

Then Maisie understood in her own soul, dimly, the meaning of those mystic words written over the portal—'Mors janua vitae'— Death is the gate of life; and also the interpretation of that awful vision of death dwelling within them as they crossed the threshold; for through that gate they had passed to this underground palace.

Her two guides still held her hands, one on either side. But they seemed rather to lead her on now, seductively and resistlessly, than to draw or compel her. As she moved in through the hall, with its endless vistas of shadowy pillars, seen now behind, now in dim perspective, she was gradually aware that many other people crowded its aisles and corridors. Slowly they took shape as forms more or less clad, mysterious, varied, and of many ages. Some of them wore flowing robes, half mediaeval in shape, like the two friends who had brought her there. They looked like the saints on a stained-glass window. Others were girt merely with a light and flowing Coan sash; while some stood dimly nude in the darker recesses of the temple or palace. All leaned eagerly forward with one mind as she approached, and regarded her with deep and sympathetic interest. A few of them murmured words—mere cabalistic sounds which at first she could not understand; but as she moved further into the hall, and saw at each step more clearly into the gloom, they began to have a meaning for her. Before long, she was aware that she understood the mute tumult of voices at once by some internal instinct. The Shades addressed her; she answered them. She knew by intuition what tongue they spoke; it was the Language of the Dead; and, by passing that portal with her two companions, she had herself become enabled both to speak and understand it.

A soft and flowing tongue, this speech of the Nether World—all vowels it seemed, without distinguishable consonants; yet dimly recalling every other tongue, and compounded, as it were, of what was common to all of them. It flowed from those shadowy lips as clouds issue inchoate from a mountain valley; it was formless, uncertain, vague, but yet beautiful. She hardly knew, indeed, as it fell upon her senses, if it were sound or perfume.

Through this tenuous world Maisie moved as in a dream, her two companions still cheering and guiding her. When they reached an inner shrine or chantry of the temple she was dimly conscious of more terrible forms pervading the background than any of those that had yet appeared to her. This was a more austere and antique apartment than the rest; a shadowy cloister, prehistoric in its severity; it recalled to her mind something indefinitely intermediate between the huge unwrought trilithons of Stonehenge and the massive granite pillars of Philae and Luxor. At the further end of the sanctuary a sort of Sphinx looked down on her, smiling mysteriously. At its base, on a rude megalithic throne, in solitary state, a High Priest was seated. He bore in his hand a wand or sceptre. All round, a strange court of half-unseen acolytes and shadowy hierophants stood attentive. They were girt, as she fancied, in what looked like leopards' skins, or in the fells of some earlier prehistoric lion. These wore sabre-shaped teeth suspended by a string round their dusky necks; others had ornaments of uncut amber, or hatchets of jade threaded as collars on a cord of sinew. A few, more barbaric than savage in type, flaunted torques of gold as armlets and necklets.

The High Priest rose slowly and held out his two hands, just level with his head, the palms turned outward. 'You have brought a willing victim as Guardian of the Tower?' he asked, in that mystic tongue, of Yolande and Hedda.

'We have brought a willing victim,' the two girls answered.

The High Priest gazed at her. His glance was piercing. Maisie trembled less with fear than with a sense of strangeness, such as a

[125]

neophyte might feel on being first presented at some courtly pageant. 'You come of your own accord?' the Priest inquired of her in solemn accents.

'I come of my own accord,' Maisie answered, with an inner consciousness that she was bearing her part in some immemorial ritual. Ancestral memories seemed to stir within her.

'It is well,' the Priest murmured. Then he turned to her guides. 'She is of royal lineage?' he inquired, taking his wand in his hand again.

'She is a Llewelyn,' Yolande answered, 'of royal lineage, and of the race that, after your own, earliest bore sway in this land of Britain. She has in her veins the blood of Arthur, of Ambrosius, and of Vortigern.'

'It is well,' the Priest said again. 'I know these princes.' Then he turned to Maisie. 'This is the ritual of those who build,' he said, in a very deep voice. 'It has been the ritual of those who build from the days of the builders of Lokmariaker and Avebury. Every building man makes shall have its human soul, the soul of a virgin to guard and protect it. Three souls it requires as a living talisman against chance and change. One soul is the soul of the human victim slain beneath the foundation-stone; she is the guardian spirit against earthquake and ruin. One soul is the soul of the human victim slain when the building is half built up; she is the guardian spirit against battle and tempest. One soul is the soul of the human victim who flings herself of her own free will off tower or gable when the building is complete; she is the guardian spirit against thunder and lightning. Unless a building be duly fasted with these three, how can it hope to stand against the hostile powers of fire and flood and storm and earthquake?'

An assessor at his side, unnoticed till then, took up the parable. He had a stern Roman face, and bore a shadowy suit of Roman armour. 'In times of old,' he said, with iron austerity, 'all men knew well these rules of building. They built in solid stone to endure for ever: the works they erected have lasted to this day, in this land and others. So built we the amphitheatres of Rome and Verona; so built we the walls of Lincoln, York, and London. In the blood of a king's son laid we the foundation-stone: in the blood of a king's son laid we the coping-stone: in the blood of a maiden of royal line fasted we the bastions against fire and lightning. But in these latter days, since faith grows dim, men build with burnt brick and rubble of plaster; no foundation spirit or guardian soul do they give to their bridges, their walls, or their towers: so bridges break, and walls fall in, and towers crumble, and the art and mystery of building aright have perished from among you.'

He ceased. The High Priest held out his wand and spoke again. 'We are the Assembly of Dead Builders and Dead Victims,' he said, 'for this mark of Wolverden; all of whom have built or been built upon in this holy site of immemorial sanctity. We are the stones of a living fabric. Before this place was a Christian church, it was a temple of Woden. And before it was a temple of Woden, it was a shrine of Hercules. And before it was a shrine of Hercules, it was a grove of Nodens. And before it was a grove of Nodens, it was a Stone Circle of the Host of Heaven. And before it was a Stone Circle of the Host of Heaven, it was the grave and tumulus and underground palace of Me, who am the earliest builder of all in this place; and my name in my ancient tongue is Wolf, and I laid and hallowed it. And after me, Wolf, and my namesake Wulfhere, was this barrow called Ad Lupum and Wolverden. And all these that are here with me have built and been built upon in this holy site for all generations. And *you* are the last who come to join us.'

Maisie felt a cold thrill course down her spine as he spoke these words; but courage did not fail her. She was dimly aware that those who offer themselves as victims for service must offer themselves willingly; for the gods demand a voluntary victim; no beast can be slain unless it nod assent; and none can be made a guardian spirit who takes not the post upon him of his own free will. She turned meekly to Hedda. 'Who are you?' she asked, trembling.

'I am Hedda,' the girl answered, in the same soft sweet voice and winning tone as before; 'Hedda, the daughter of Gorm, the chief of the Northmen who settled in East Anglia. And I was a worshipper of Thor and Odin. And when my father, Gorm, fought against Alfred, King of Wessex, was I taken prisoner. And Wulfhere, the Kenting, was then building the first church and tower of Wolverden. And they baptized me, and shrived me, and I consented of my own free will to be built under the foundation-stone. And there my body lies built up to this day; and *I* am the guardian spirit against earthquake and ruin.'

'And who are you?' Maisie asked, turning again to Yolande.

'I am Yolande Fitz-Aylwin,' the tall dark girl answered; 'a royal maiden too, sprung from the blood of Henry Plantagenet. And when Roland Fitz-Stephen was building anew the choir and chancel of Wulfhere's minster, I chose to be immured in the fabric of the wall, for love of the Church and all holy saints; and there my body lies built up to this day; and *I* am the guardian against battle and tempest.'

Maisie held her friend's hand tight. Her voice hardly trembled. 'And I?' she asked once more. 'What fate for me? Tell me!'

'Your task is easier far,' Yolande answered gently. 'For *you* shall be the guardian of the new tower against thunder and lightning. Now, those who guard against earthquake and battle are buried alive under the foundation-stone or in the wall of the building; there they die a slow death of starvation and choking. But those who guard against thunder and lightning cast themselves alive of their own free will from the battlements of the tower, and die in the air before they reach the ground; so their fate is the easiest and the lightest of all who would serve mankind; and thenceforth they live with us here in our palace.'

Maisie clung to her hand still tighter. 'Must I do it?' she asked, pleading.

'It is not *must*,' Yolande replied in the same caressing tone, yet with a calmness as of one in whom earthly desires and earthly passions are quenched for ever. 'It is as you choose yourself. None but a willing victim may be a guardian spirit. This glorious privilege comes but to the purest and best amongst us. Yet what better end can you ask for your soul than to dwell here in our midst as our comrade for ever, where all is peace, and to preserve the tower whose guardian you are from evil assaults of lightning and thunderbolt?'

Maisie flung her arms round her friend's neck. 'But—I am afraid,' she murmured. Why she should even wish to consent she knew not, yet the strange serene peace in these strange girls' eyes made her mysteriously in love with them and with the fate they offered her. They seemed to move like the stars in their orbits. 'How shall I leap from the top?' she cried. 'How shall I have courage to mount the stairs alone, and fling myself off from the lonely battlement?'

Yolande unwound her arms with a gentle forbearance. She coaxed her as one coaxes an unwilling child. 'You will *not* be alone,' she said, with a tender pressure. 'We will all go with you. We will help you and encourage you. We will sing our sweet songs of life-in-death to you. Why should you draw back? All we have faced it in ten thousand ages, and we tell you with one voice, you need not fear it. 'Tis life you should fear—life, with its dangers, its toils, its heart-breakings. Here we dwell for ever in unbroken peace. Come, come, and join us!'

She held out her arms with an enticing gesture. Maisie sprang into them, sobbing. 'Yes, I will come,' she cried in an access of hysterical fervour. 'These are the arms of Death—I embrace them. These are the lips of Death—I kiss them. Yolande, Yolande, I will do as you ask me!'

The tall dark girl in the luminous white robe stooped down and kissed her twice on the forehead in return. Then she looked at the High Priest. 'We are ready,' she murmured in a low, grave voice. 'The Victim consents. The Virgin will die. Lead on to the tower. We are ready! We are ready!'

IV

From the recesses of the temple—if temple it were—from the inmost shrines of the shrouded cavern, unearthly music began to sound of itself, with wild modulation, on strange reeds and tabors. It swept through the aisles like a rushing wind on an Æolian harp; at times it wailed with a voice like a woman's; at times it rose loud in an organ-note of triumph; at times it sank low into a pensive and melancholy flute-like symphony. It waxed and waned; it swelled and died away again; but no man saw how or whence it proceeded. Wizard echoes issued from the crannies and vents in the invisible walls; they sighed from the ghostly interspaces of the pillars; they keened and moaned from the vast overhanging dome of the palace. Gradually the song shaped itself by weird stages into a processional measure. At its sound the High Priest rose slowly from his immemorial seat on the mightly cromlech which formed his throne. The Shades in leopards' skins ranged themselves in bodiless rows on either hand; the ghostly wearers of the sabre-toothed lions' fangs followed like ministrants in the footsteps of their hierarch.

Hedda and Yolande took their places in the procession. Maisie stood between the two, with hair floating on the air; she looked like a novice who goes up to take the veil, accompanied and cheered by two elder sisters.

The ghostly pageant began to move. Unseen music followed it with fitful gusts of melody. They passed down the main corridor, between shadowy Doric or Ionic pillars which grew dimmer and ever dimmer again in the distance as they approached, with slow steps, the earthward portal.

At the gate, the High Priest pushed against the valves with his hand. They opened *outward*.

He passed into the moonlight. The attendants thronged after him.

As each wild figure crossed the threshold the same strange sight as before met Maisie's eyes. For a second of time each ghostly body became self-luminous, as with some curious phosphorescence; and through each, at the moment of passing the portal, the dim outline of a skeleton loomed briefly visible. Next instant it had clothed itself as with earthly members.

Maisie reached the outer air. As she did so, she gasped. For a second, its chilliness and freshness almost choked her. She was conscious now that the atmosphere of the vault, though pleasant in its way, and warm and dry, had been loaded with fumes as of burning incense, and with somnolent vapours of poppy and mandragora. Its drowsy ether had cast her into a lethargy. But after the first minute in the outer world, the keen night air revived her. Snow lay still on the ground a little deeper than when she first came out, and the moon rode lower; otherwise, all was as before, save that only one or two lights till burned here and there in the great house on the terrace. Among them she could recognise her own room, on the ground floor in the new wing, by its open window.

The procession made its way across the churchyard towards the tower. As it wound among the graves an owl hooted. All at once Maisie remembered the lines that had so chilled her a few short hours before in the drawing-room —

> 'The glow-worm o'er grave and stone
> Shall light thee steady;
> The owl from the steeple sing,
> "Welcome, proud lady!"'

But, marvellous to relate, they no longer alarmed her. She felt rather that a friend was welcoming her home; she clung to Yolande's hand with a gentle pressure.

As they passed in front of the porch, with its ancient yew-tree, a stealthy figure glided out like a ghost from the darkling shadow. It was a woman, bent and bowed, with quivering limbs that shook half palsied. Maisie recognised old Bessie. 'I knew she would come!' the old hag muttered between her toothless jaws. 'I knew Wolverden Tower would yet be duly fasted!'

She put herself, as of right, at the head of the procession. They moved on to the tower, rather gliding than walking. Old Bessie drew a rusty key from her pocket, and fitted it with a twist into the brand-new lock. 'What turned the old will turn the new,' she murmured, looking round and grinning. Maisie shrank from her as she shrank from not one of the Dead; but she followed on still into the ringers' room at the base of the tower.

Thence a staircase in the corner led up to the summit. The High Priest mounted the stair, chanting a mystic refrain, whose runic sounds were no longer intelligible to Maisie. As she reached the outer air, the Tongue of the Dead seemed to have become a mere blank of mingled odours and murmurs to her. It was like a summer breeze, sighing through warm and resinous pinewoods. But Yolande and Hedda spoke to her yet, to cheer her, in the language of the living. She recognised that as *revenants* they were still in touch with the upper air and the world of the embodied.

They tempted her up the stair with encouraging fingers. Maisie followed them like a child, in implicit confidence. The steps wound round and round, spirally, and the staircase was dim; but a super-natural light seemed to fill the tower, diffused from the bodies or souls of its occupants. At the head of all, the High Priest still chanted as he went his unearthly litany; magic sounds of chimes seemed to swim in unison with his tune as they mounted. Were those floating notes material or spiritual? They passed the belfry; no tongue of metal wagged; but the rims of the great bells resounded and reverberated to the ghostly symphony with sympathetic music. Still they passed on and on, upward and upward. They reached the ladder that alone gave access to the final storey. Dust and cobwebs already clung to it. Once more Maisie drew back. It was dark overhead, and the luminous haze began to fail them. Her friends held her hands with the same kindly persuasive touch as ever. 'I cannot!' she cried, shrinking away from the tall, steep ladder. 'Oh, Yolande, I cannot!'

'Yes, dear,' Yolande whispered in a soothing voice. 'You can. It is but ten steps, and I will hold your hand tight. Be brave and mount them!'

The sweet voice encouraged her. It was like heavenly music. She knew not why she should submit, or, rather, consent; but none the less she consented. Some spell seemed cast over her. With tremulous feet, scarcely realising what she did, she mounted the ladder and went up four steps of it.

Then she turned and looked down again. Old Bessie's wrinkled face met her frightened eyes. It was smiling horribly. She shrank back once more, terrified. 'I can't do it,' she cried, 'if that woman comes up! I'm not afraid of *you*, dear'—she pressed Yolande's hand—'but she, she is too terrible!'

Hedda looked back and raised a warning finger. 'Let the woman stop below,' she said; 'she savours too much of the evil world. We must do nothing to frighten the willing victim.'

The High Priest by this time, with his ghostly fingers, had opened the trap-door that gave access to the summit. A ray of moonlight slanted through the aperture. The breeze blew down with it. Once more Maisie felt the stimulating and reviving effect of the open air. Vivified by its freshness, she struggled up to the top, passed out through the trap, and found herself standing on the open platform at the summit of the tower.

The moon had not yet quite set. The light on the snow shone pale green and mysterious. For miles and miles around she could just make out, by its aid, the dim contour of the downs, with their thin white mantle, in the solemn silence. Range behind range rose faintly shimmering. The chant had now ceased; the High Priest and his acolytes were mingling strange herbs in a mazar-bowl or chalice. Stray perfumes of myrrh and of cardamoms were wafted towards her. The men in leopards' skins burnt smouldering sticks of spikenard. Then Yolande led the postulant forward again, and placed her close up to the new white parapet. Stone heads of virgins smiled on her from the angles. 'She must front the east,' Hedda said in a tone of authority: and Yolande turned her face towards the rising sun accordingly. Then she opened her lips and spoke in a very solemn voice. 'From this new-built tower you fling yourself,' she said, or rather intoned, 'that you may serve mankind, and all the powers that be, as its guardian spirit against thunder and lightning. Judged a virgin, pure and unsullied in deed and word and thought, of royal race and ancient lineage—a Cymry of the Cymry—you are found worthy to be intrusted with this charge and this honour. Take care that never shall dart or thunderbolt assault this tower, as She that is below you takes care to preserve it from earthquake and ruin, and She that is midway takes care to preserve it from battle and tempest. This is your charge. See well that you keep it.'

She took her by both hands. 'Mary Llewelyn,' she said, 'you willing victim, step on to the battlement.'

Maisie knew not why, but with very little shrinking she stepped as she was told, by the aid of a wooden footstool, on to the eastward-looking parapet. There, in her loose white robe, with her arms spread abroad, and her hair flying free, she poised herself for a second, as if about to shake out some unseen wings and throw herself on the air like a swift or a swallow.

'Mary Llewelyn,' Yolande said once more, in a still deeper tone, with ineffable earnestness, 'cast yourself down, a willing sacrifice, for the service of man, and the security of this tower against thunderbolt and lightning.'

Maisie stretched her arms wider, and leaned forward in act to leap, from the edge of the parapet, on to the snow-clad churchyard.

V

One second more and the sacrifice would have been complete. But before she could launch herself from the tower, she felt suddenly a hand laid upon her shoulder from behind to restrain her. Even in her existing state of nervous exaltation she was aware at once that it was the hand of a living and solid mortal, not that of a soul or guardian spirit. It lay heavier upon her than Hedda's or Yolande's. It seemed to clog and burden her. With a violent effort she strove to shake herself free, and carry out her now fixed intention of self-immolation, for the safety of the tower. But the hand was too strong for her. She could not shake it off. It gripped and held her.

She yielded, and, reeling, fell back with a gasp on to the platform of the tower. At the selfsame moment a strange terror and commotion seemed to seize all at once on the assembled spirits. A weird cry rang voiceless through the shadowy company. Maisie heard it as in a dream, very dim and distant. It was thin as a bat's note; almost inaudible to the ear, yet perceived by the brain or at least by the spirit. It was a cry of alarm, of fright, of warning. With one accord, all the host of phantoms rushed hurriedly forward to the battlements and pinnacles. The ghostly High Priest went first, with his wand held downward; the men in leopards' skins and other assistants followed in confusion. Theirs was a reckless rout. They flung themselves from the top, like fugitives from a cliff, and floated fast through the air on invisible pinions. Hedda and Yolande, ambassadresses and inter-mediaries with the upper air, were the last to fly from the living presence. They clasped her hand silently, and looked deep into her eyes. There was something in that calm yet regretful look that seemed to say, 'Farewell! We have tried in vain to save you, sister, from the terrors of living.'

The horde of spirits floated away on the air, as in a witches' Sabbath, to the vault whence it issued. The doors swung on their rusty hinges, and closed behind them. Maisie stood alone with the hand that grasped her on the tower.

The shock of the grasp, and the sudden departure of the ghostly band in such wild dismay, threw Maisie for a while into a state of semi-unconsciousness. Her head reeled round; her brain swam faintly. She clutched for support at the parapet of the tower. But the hand that held her sustained her still. She felt herself gently drawn down with quiet mastery, and laid on the stone floor close by the trap-door that led to the ladder.

The next thing of which she could feel sure was the voice of the Oxford undergraduate. He was distinctly frightened and not a little tremulous. 'I think,' he said very softly, laying her head on his lap, 'you had better rest a while, Miss Llewelyn, before you try to get down again. I hope I didn't catch you and disturb you too hastily. But one step more, and you would have been over the edge. I really couldn't help it.'

'Let me go,' Maisie moaned, trying to raise herself again, but feeling too faint and ill to make the necessary effort to recover the power of motion. 'I *want* to go with them! I *want* to join them!'

'Some of the others will be up before long,' the undergraduate said, supporting her head in his hands; 'and they'll help me get you down again. Mr. Yates is in the belfry. Meanwhile, if I were you, I'd lie quite still, and take a drop or two of this brandy.'

He held it to her lips. Maisie drank a mouthful, hardly knowing what she did. Then she lay quiet where he placed her for some minutes. How they lifted her down and conveyed her to her bed she scarcely knew. She was dazed and terrified. She could only remember afterward that three or four gentlemen in roughly huddled clothes had carried or handed her down the ladder between them. The spiral stair and all the rest were a blank to her.

VI

When she next awoke she was lying in her bed in the same room at the hall, with Mrs. West by her side, leaning over her tenderly.

Maisie looked up through her closed eyes and just saw the motherly face and grey hair bending above her. Then voices came to her from the mist, vaguely: 'Yesterday was so hot for the time of year, you see!' 'Very unusual weather, of course, for Christmas.' 'But a thunderstorm! So strange! I put it down to that. The electrical disturbance must have affected the poor child's head.' Then it dawned upon her that the conversation she heard was passing between Mrs. West and a doctor.

She raised herself suddenly and wildly on her arms. The bed faced the windows. She looked out and beheld—the tower of Wolverden church, rent from top to bottom with a mighty rent, while half its height lay tossed in fragments on the ground in the churchyard.

'What is it?' she cried wildly, with a flush as of shame.

'Hush, hush!' the doctor said. 'Don't trouble! Don't look at it!'

'Was it—after I came down?' Maisie moaned in vague terror.

The doctor nodded. 'An hour after you were brought down,' he said, 'a thunderstorm broke over it. The lightning struck and shattered the tower. They had not yet put up the lightning-conductor. It was to have been done on Boxing Day.'

A weird remorse possessed Maisie's soul. 'My fault!' she cried, starting up. 'My fault, my fault! I have neglected my duty!'

'Don't talk,' the doctor answered, looking hard at her. 'It is always dangerous to be too suddenly aroused from these curious overwrought sleeps and trances.'

'And old Bessie?' Maisie exclaimed, trembling with an eerie presentiment.

The doctor glanced at Mrs. West. 'How did she know?' he whispered. Then he turned to Maisie. 'You may as well be told the truth as suspect it,' he said slowly. 'Old Bessie must have been watching there. She was crushed and half buried beneath the falling tower.'

'One more question, Mrs. West,' Maisie murmured, growing faint with an access of supernatural fear. 'Those two nice girls who sat on the chairs at each side of me through the tableaux—are they hurt? Were they in it?'

Mrs. West soothed her hand. 'My dear child,' she said gravely, with quiet emphasis, 'there were *no* other girls. This is mere hallucination. You sat alone by yourself through the whole of the evening.'

A GHOST-CHILD

by Bernard Capes

Bernard Capes (1854–1918) was another equally
popular and busy author at the turn of the century,
equally adept in the genres of romantic and mystery
fiction, especially the bizarre and the supernatural.
One of his most memorable tales is 'The Ghost-
Child'; written for the *Pall Mall Magazine*, January
1906, it appeared later that year in his collection
Loaves and Fishes.

I n making this confession public, I am aware that I am giving a
butterfly to be broken on a wheel. There is so much of delicacy in
its subject, that the mere resolve to handle it at all might seem to
imply a lack of the sensitiveness necessary to its understanding; and it
is certain that the more reverent the touch, the more irresistible will
figure its opportunity to the common scepticism which is bondslave to
its five senses. Moreover one cannot, in the reason of things, write to
publish for Aristarchus alone; but the gauntlet of Grub Street must be
run in any bid for truth and sincerity.

On the other hand, to withhold from evidence, in these days of
what one may call a zetetic psychology, anything which may appear
elucidatory, however exquisitely and rarely, of our spiritual relation-
ships, must be pronounced, I think, a sin against the Holy Ghost.

All in all, therefore, I decide to give, with every passage to personal
identification safeguarded, the story of a possession, or visitation,
which is signified in the title to my narrative.

Tryphena was the sole orphaned representative of an obscure but gentle family which had lived for generations in the east of England. The spirit of the fens, of the long grey marshes, whose shores are the neutral ground of two elements, slumbered in her eyes. Looking into them, one seemed to see little beds of tiny green mosses luminous under water, or stirred by the movement of microscopic life in their midst. Secrets, one felt, were shadowed in their depths, too frail and sweet for understanding. The pretty love-fancy of babies seen in the eyes of maidens, was in hers to be interpreted into the very cosmic dust of sea-urchins, sparkling like chrysoberyls. Her soul looked out through them, as if they were the windows of a water-nursery.

She was always a child among children, in heart and knowledge most innocent, until Jason came and stood in her field of vision. Then, spirit of the neutral ground as she was, inclining to earth or water with the sway of the tides, she came wondering and dripping, as it were, to land, and took up her abode for final choice among the daughters of the earth. She knew her woman's estate, in fact, and the irresistible attraction of all completed perfections to the light that burns to destroy them.

Tryphena was not only an orphan, but an heiress. Her considerable estate was administered by her guardian, Jason's father, a widower, who was possessed of this single adored child. The fruits of parental infatuation had come early to ripen on the seedling. The boy was self-willed and perverse, the more so as he was naturally of a hot-hearted disposition. Violence and remorse would sway him in alternate moods, and be made, each in its turn, a self-indulgence. He took a delight in crossing his father's wishes, and no less in atoning for his gracelessness with moving demonstrations of affection.

Foremost of the old man's most cherished projects was, very naturally, a union between the two young people. He planned, manœuvred, spoke for it with all his heart of love and eloquence. And, indeed, it seemed at last as if his hopes were to be crowned. Jason, returning from a lengthy voyage (for his enterprising spirit had early decided for the sea, and he was a naval officer), saw, and was struck amazed before, the transformed vision of his old child-play-fellow. She was an opened flower whom he had left a green bud—a thing so rare and flawless that it seemed a sacrilege for earthly passions to converse of her. Familiarity, however, and some sense of reciprocal attraction, quickly dethroned that eucharist. Tryphena could blush, could thrill, could solicit, in the sweet ways of innocent womanhood.

[137]

She loved him dearly, wholly, it was plain—had found the realisation of her old formless dreams in this wondrous birth of a desire for one, in whose new-impassioned eyes she had known herself reflected hitherto only for the most patronised of small gossips. And, for her part, fearless as nature, she made no secret of her love. She was absorbed in, a captive to, Jason from that moment and for ever.

He responded. What man, however perverse, could have resisted, on first appeal, the attraction of such beauty, the flower of a radiant soul? The two were betrothed; the old man's cup of happiness was brimmed.

Then came clouds and a cold wind, chilling the garden of Hesperis. Jason was always one of those who, possessing classic noses, will cut them off, on easy provocation, to spite their faces. He was so proudly independent, to himself, that he resented the least assumption of proprietorship in him on the part of other people—even of those who had the best claim to his love and submission. This pride was an obsession. It stultified the real good in him, which was considerable. Apart from it, he was a good, warm-tempered fellow, hasty but affectionate. Under its dominion, he would have broken his own heart on an imaginary grievance.

He found one, it is to be supposed, in the privileges assumed by love; in its exacting claims upon him; perhaps in its little unreasoning jealousies. He distorted these into an implied conceit of authority over him on the part of an heiress who was condescending to his meaner fortunes. The suggestion was quite base and without warrant; but pride has no balance. No doubt, moreover, the rather childish self-depreciations of the old man, his father, in his attitude towards a match he had so fondly desired, helped to aggravate this feeling. The upshot was that, when within a few months of the date which was to make his union with Tryphena eternal, Jason broke away from a restraint which his pride pictured to him as intolerable, and went on a yachting expedition with a friend.

Then, at once, and with characteristic violence, came the reaction. He wrote, impetuously, frenziedly, from a distant port, claiming himself Tryphena's, and Tryphena his, for ever and ever and ever. They were man and wife before God. He had behaved like an insensate brute, and he was at that moment starting to speed to her side, to beg her forgiveness and the return of her love.

He had no need to play the suitor afresh. She had never doubted or questioned their mutual bondage, and would have died a maid for his sake. Something of sweet exultation only seemed to quicken and leap in her body, that her faith in her dear love was vindicated.

But the joy came near to upset the reason of the old man, already tottering to its dotage; and what followed destroyed it utterly.

The yacht, flying home, was lost at sea, and Jason was drowned.

I once saw Tryphena about this time. She lived with her near mindless charge, lonely, in an old grey house upon the borders of a salt mere, and had little but the unearthly cries of seabirds to answer to the questions of her widowed heart. She worked, sweet in charity, among the marsh folk, a beautiful unearthly presence; and was especially to be found where infants and the troubles of child-bearing women called for her help and sympathy. She was a wife herself, she would say quaintly; and some day perhaps, by grace of the good spirits of the sea, would be a mother. None thought to cross her statement, put with so sweet a sanity; and, indeed, I have often noticed that the neighbour-hood of great waters breeds in souls a mysticism which is remote from the very understanding of land-dwellers.

How I saw her was thus:—

I was fishing, on a day of chill calm, in a dinghy off the flat coast. The stillness of the morning had tempted me some distance from the village where I was staying. Presently a sense of bad sport and healthy famine 'plumped' in me, so to speak, for luncheon, and I looked about for a spot picturesque enough to add a zest to sandwiches, whisky, and tobacco. Close by, a little creek or estuary ran up into a mere, between which and the sea lay a cluster of low sand-hills; and thither I pulled. The spot, when I reached it, was calm, chill desolation manifest—lifeless water and lifeless sand, with no traffic between them but the dead interchange of salt. Low sedges, at first, and behind them low woods were mirrored in the water at a distance, with an interval between me and them of sheeted glass; and right across this shining pool ran a dim, half-drowned causeway—the sea-path, it appeared, to and from a lonely house which I could just distinguish squatting among trees. It was Tryphena's house.

Now, paddling dispiritedly, I turned a cold dune, and saw a mermaid before me. At least, that was my instant impression. The creature sat coiled on the strand, combing her hair—that was certain, for I saw the gold-green tresses of it whisked by her action into rainbow threads. It appeared as certain that her upper half was flesh and her lower fish; and it was only on my nearer approach that this latter resolved itself into a pale green skirt, roped, owing to her posture, about her limbs, and the hem fanned out at her feet into a tail fin. Thus also her bosom, which had appeared naked, became a bodice, as near to her flesh in colour and texture as a smock is to a lady's-smock, which some call a cuckoo-flower.

It was plain enough now; yet the illusion for the moment had quite startled me.

As I came near, she paused in her strange business to canvass me. It was Tryphena herself, as after-inquiry informed me. I have never seen so lovely a creature. Her eyes, as they regarded me passing, were something to haunt a dream: so great in tragedy—not fathomless, but all in motion near their surfaces, it seemed, with green and rooted sorrows. They were the eyes, I thought, of an Undine late-humanised, late awakened to the rapturous and troubled knowledge of the woman's burden. Her forehead was most fair, and the glistening thatch divided on it like a golden cloud revealing the face of a wondering angel.

I passed, and a sand-heap stole my vision foot by foot. The vision was gone when I returned. I have reason to believe it was vouchsafed me within a few months of the coming of the ghost-child.

On the morning succeeding the night of the day on which Jason and Tryphena were to have been married, the girl came down from her bedroom with an extraordinary expression of still rapture on her face. After breakfast she took the old man into her confidence. She was childish still; her manner quite youthfully thrilling; but now there was a newborn wonder in it that hovered on the pink of shame.

'Father! I have been under the deep waters and found him. He came to me last night in my dreams—so sobbing, so impassioned—to assure me that he had never really ceased to love me, though he had near broken his own heart pretending it. Poor boy! poor ghost! What could I do but take him to my arms? And all night he lay there, blest and forgiven, till in the morning he melted away with a sigh that woke me; and it seemed to me that I came up dripping from the sea.'

'My boy! He has come back!' chuckled the old man. 'What have you done with him, Tryphena?'

'I will hold him tighter the next time,' she said.

But the spirit of Jason visited her dreams no more.

That was in March. In the Christmas following, when the mere was locked in stillness, and the wan reflection of snow mingled on the ceiling with the red dance of firelight, one morning the old man came hurrying and panting to Tryphena's door.

'Tryphena! Come down quickly! My boy, my Jason, has come back!

It was a lie that they told us about his being lost at sea!'

Her heart leapt like a candle-flame! What new delusion of the old man's was this? She hurried over her dressing and descended. A garrulous old voice mingled with a childish treble in the breakfast-room. Hardly breathing, she turned the handle of the door, and saw Jason before her.

But it was Jason, the prattling babe of her first knowledge; Jason, the flaxen-headed, apple-cheeked cherub of the nursery; Jason, the confiding, the merry, the loving, before pride had come to warp his innocence. She fell on her knees to the child, and with a burst of ecstasy caught him to her heart.

She asked no question of the old man as to when or whence this apparition had come, or why he was here. For some reason she dared not. She accepted him as some waif, whom an accidental likeness had made glorious to their hungering hearts. As for the father, he was utterly satisfied and content. He had heard a knock at the door, he said, and had opened it and found this. The child was naked, and his pink, wet body glazed with ice. Yet he seemed insensible to the killing cold. It was Jason—that was enough. There is no date nor time for imbecility. Its phantoms spring from the clash of ancient memories. This was just as actually his child as—more so, in fact, than—the grown young figure which, for all its manhood, had dissolved into the mist of waters. He was more familiar with, more confident of it, after all. It had come back to be unquestioningly dependent on him; and that was likest the real Jason, flesh of his flesh.

'Who are you, darling?' said Tryphena.

'I am Jason,' answered the child.

She wept, and fondled him rapturously.

'And who am I?' she asked. "If you are Jason, you must know what to call me.'

'I know,' he said; 'but I mustn't, unless you ask me.'

'I won't,' she answered, with a burst of weeping. 'It is Christmas Day, dearest, when the miracle of a little child was wrought. I will ask you nothing but to stay and bless our desolate home.'

He nodded, laughing.

'I will stay, until you ask me.'

They found some little old robes of the baby Jason, put away in lavender, and dressed him in them. All day he laughed and prattled; yet it was strange that, talk as he might, he never once referred to matters familiar to the childhood of the lost sailor.

[141]

In the early afternoon he asked to be taken out—seawards, that was his wish. Tryphena clothed him warmly, and, taking his little hand, led him away. They left the old man sleeping peacefully. He was never to wake again.

As they crossed the narrow causeway, snow, thick and silent, began to fall. Tryphena was not afraid, for herself or the child. A rapture upheld her; a sense of some compelling happiness, which she knew before long must take shape on her lips.

They reached the seaward dunes—mere ghosts of foothold in that smoke of flakes. The lap of vast waters seemed all around them, hollow and mysterious. The sound flooded Tryphena's ears, drowning her senses. She cried out, and stopped.

'Before they go,' she screamed—'before they go, tell me what you were to call me!'

The child sprang a little distance, and stood facing her. Already his lower limbs seemed dissolving in the mists.

'I was to call you "mother"!' he cried, with a smile and toss of his hand.

Even as he spoke, his pretty features wavered and vanished. The snow broke into him, or he became part with it. Where he had been, a gleam of iridescent dust seemed to show one moment before it sank and was extinguished in the falling cloud. Then there was only the snow, heaping an eternal chaos with nothingness.

Tryphena made this confession, on a Christmas Eve night, to one who was a believer in dreams. The next morning she was seen to cross the causeway, and thereafter was never seen again. But she left the sweetest memory behind her, for human charity, and an elf-life gift of loveliness.

THE KIT-BAG

by Algernon Blackwood

Algernon Blackwood (1869–1951) is undisputedly
one of the greatest writers of horror and ghost
stories of this century. Most of his classics like 'The
Willows' and 'The Wendigo' have been
consistently reprinted, but the fine ghost story 'The
Kit-Bag', which appears here, has *never* been
reprinted since it was first published exactly 80
years ago in the Christmas number of the *Pall Mall
Magazine* (December 1908).

When the words 'Not Guilty' sounded through the crowded court-room that dark December afternoon, Arthur Wilbraham, the great criminal K.C., and leader for the triumphant defence, was represented by his junior: but Johnson, his private secretary, carried the verdict across to his chambers like lightning.

'It's what we expected, I think,' said the barrister, without emotion; 'and, personally, I am glad the case is over.' There was no particular sign of pleasure that his defence of John Turk, the murderer, on a plea of insanity, had been successful, for no doubt he felt, as everybody who had watched the case felt, that no man had ever better deserved the gallows.

'I'm glad too,' said Johnson. He had sat in the court for ten days watching the face of the man who had carried out with callous detail one of the most brutal and cold-blooded murders of recent years.

The counsel glanced up at his secretary. They were more than employer and employed; for family and other reasons, they were friends. 'Ah, I remember; yes,' he said with a kind smile, 'and you want to get away for Christmas? You're going to skate and ski in the Alps, aren't you? If I was your age I'd come with you.'

Johnson laughed shortly. He was a young man of twenty-six, with a delicate face like a girl's. 'I can catch the morning boat now,' he said; 'but that's not the reason I'm glad the trial is over. I'm glad it's over because I've seen the last of that man's dreadful face. It positively haunted me. That white skin, with the black hair brushed low over the forehead, is a thing I shall never forget, and the description of the way the dismembered body was crammed and packed with lime into that—'

'Don't dwell on it, my dear fellow,' interrupted the other, looking at him curiously out of his keen eyes, 'don't think about it. Such pictures have a trick of coming back when one least wants them.' He paused a moment. 'Now go,' he added presently, 'and enjoy your holiday. I shall want all your energy for my Parliamentary work when you get back. And don't break your neck ski-ing.'

Johnson shook hands and took his leave. At the door he turned suddenly.

'I knew there was something I wanted to ask you,' he said. 'Would you mind lending me one of your kit-bags? It's too late to get one to-night, and I leave in the morning before the shops are open.'

'Of course; I'll send Henry over with it to your rooms. You shall have it the moment I get home.'

'I promise to take great care of it,' said Johnson gratefully, delighted to think that within thirty hours he would be nearing the brilliant sunshine of the high Alps in winter. The thought of that criminal court was like an evil dream in his mind.

He dined at his club and went on to Bloomsbury, where he occupied the top floor in one of those old, gaunt houses in which the rooms are large and lofty. The floor below his own was vacant and unfurnished, and below that were other lodgers whom he did not know. It was cheerless, and he looked forward heartily to a change. The night was even more cheerless: it was miserable, and few people were about. A cold, sleety rain was driving down the streets before the keenest east wind he had ever felt. It howled dismally among the big, gloomy houses of the great squares, and when he reached his rooms he heard it whistling and shouting over the world of black roofs beyond his windows.

In the hall he met his landlady, shading a candle from the draughts with her thin hand. 'This come by a man from Mr. Wilbr'im's, sir.'

She pointed to what was evidently the kit-bag, and Johnson thanked her and took it upstairs with him. 'I shall be going abroad in the morning for ten days, Mrs. Monks,' he said. 'I'll leave an address for letters.'

'And I hope you'll 'ave a merry Christmas, sir,' she said, in a raucous, wheezy voice that suggested spirits, 'and better weather than this.'

'I hope so too,' replied her lodger, shuddering a little as the wind went roaring down the street outside.

When he got upstairs he heard the sleet volleying against the window-panes. He put his kettle on to make a cup of hot coffee, and then set about putting a few things in order for his absence. 'And now I must pack—such as my packing is,' he laughed to himself, and set to work at once.

He liked the packing, for it brought the snow mountains so vividly before him, and made him forget the unpleasant scenes of the past ten days. Besides, it was not elaborate in nature. His friend had lent him the very thing—a stout canvas kit-bag, sack-shaped, with holes round the neck for the brass bar and padlock. It was a bit shapeless, true, and not much to look at, but its capacity was unlimited, and there was no need to pack carefully. He shoved in his water-proof coat, his fur cap and gloves, his skates and climbing boots, his sweaters, snow-boots, and ear-caps; and then on the top of these he piled his woollen shirts and underwear, his thick socks, puttees, and knickerbockers. The dress-suit came next, in case the hotel people dressed for dinner, and then, thinking of the best way to pack his white shirts, he paused a moment to reflect. 'That's the worst of these kit-bags,' he mused vaguely, standing in the centre of the sitting-room, where he had come to fetch some string.

It was after ten o'clock. A furious gust of wind rattled the windows as though to hurry him up, and he thought with pity of the poor Londoners whose Christmas would be spent in such a climate, whilst he was skimming over snowy slopes in bright sunshine, and dancing in the evening with rosy-cheeked girls—Ah! that reminded him; he must put in his dancing-pumps and evening socks. He crossed over from his sitting-room to the cupboard on the landing where he kept his linen.

And as he did so he heard some one coming softly up the stairs.

He stood still a moment on the landing to listen. It was Mrs. Monks's step, he thought; she must be coming up with the last post.

But then the steps ceased suddenly, and he heard no more. They were at least two flights down, and he came to the conclusion they were too heavy to be those of his bibulous landlady. No doubt they belonged to a late lodger who had mistaken his floor. He went into his bedroom and packed his pumps and dress-shirts as best he could.

The kit-bag by this time was two-thirds full, and stood upright on its own base like a sack of flour. For the first time he noticed that it was old and dirty, the canvas faded and worn, and that it had obviously been subjected to rather rough treatment. It was not a very nice bag to have sent him—certainly not a new one, or one that his chief valued. He gave the matter a passing thought, and went on with his packing. Once or twice, however, he caught himself wondering who it could have been wandering down below, for Mrs. Monks had not come up with letters, and the floor was empty and unfurnished. From time to time, moreover, he was almost certain he heard a soft tread of some one padding about over the bare boards—cautiously, stealthily, as silently as possible—and, further, that the sounds had been lately coming distinctly nearer.

For the first time in his life he began to feel a little creepy. Then, as though to emphasise this feeling, an odd thing happened: as he left the bedroom, having just packed his recalcitrant white shirts, he noticed that the top of the kit-bag lopped over towards him with an extraordinary resemblance to a human face. The canvas fell into a fold like a nose and forehead, and the brass rings for the padlock just filled the position of the eyes. A shadow—or was it a travel stain? for he could not tell exactly—looked like hair. It gave him rather a turn, for it was so absurdly, so outrageously, like the face of John Turk, the murderer.

He laughed, and went into the front room, where the light was stronger.

'That horrid case has got on my mind,' he thought; 'I shall be glad of a change of scene and air.' In the sitting-room, however, he was not pleased to hear again that stealthy tread upon the stairs, and to realise that it was much closer than before, as well as unmistakably real. And this time he got up and went out to see who it could be creeping about on the upper staircase at so late an hour.

But the sound ceased; there was no one visible on the stairs. He went to the floor below, not without trepidation, and turned on the electric light to make sure that no one was hiding in the empty rooms of the unoccupied suite. There was not a stick of furniture large enough to hide a dog. Then he called over the banisters to Mrs. Monks, but there was no answer, and his voice echoed down into the dark vault of the house, and was lost in the roar of the gale that howled outside. Everyone was in bed and asleep—everyone except himself and the owner of this soft and stealthy tread.

'My absurd imagination, I suppose,' he thought. 'It must have been the wind after all, although—it seemed so *very* real and close, I thought.' He went back to his packing. It was by this time getting on towards midnight. He drank his coffee up and lit another pipe—the last before turning in.

It is difficult to say exactly at what point fear begins, when the causes of that fear are not plainly before the eyes. Impressions gather on the surface of the mind, film by film, as ice gathers upon the surface of still water, but often so lightly that they claim no definite recognition from the consciousness. Then a point is reached where the accumulated impressions become a definite emotion, and the mind realises that something has happened. With something of a start, Johnson suddenly recognised that he felt nervous—oddly nervous; also, that for some time past the causes of this feeling had been gathering slowly in his mind, but that he had only just reached the point where he was forced to acknowledge them.

It was a singular and curious malaise that had come over him, and he hardly knew what to make of it. He felt as though he were doing something that was strongly objected to by another person, another person, moreover, who had some right to object. It was a most disturbing and disagreeable feeling, not unlike the persistent prompt- ings of conscience: almost, in fact, as if he were doing something he knew to be wrong. Yet, though he searched vigorously and honestly in his mind, he could nowhere lay his finger upon the secret of this growing uneasiness, and it perplexed him. More, it distressed and frightened him.

'Pure nerves, I suppose,' he said aloud with a forced laugh. 'Mountain air will cure all that! Ah,' he added, still speaking to himself, 'and that reminds me—my snow-glasses.'

He was standing by the door of the bedroom during this brief soliloquy, and as he passed quickly towards the sitting-room to fetch them from the cupboard he saw out of the corner of his eye the indistinct outline of a figure standing on the stairs, a few feet from the top. It was someone in a stooping position, with one hand on the banisters, and the face peering up towards the landing. And at the same moment he heard a shuffling footstep. The person who had been creeping about below all this time had at last come up to his own floor. Who in the world could it be? And what in the name of Heaven did he want?

Johnson caught his breath sharply and stood stock still. Then, after a few seconds' hesitation, he found his courage, and turned to investigate. The stairs, he saw to his utter amazement, were empty; there was no one. He felt a series of cold shivers run over him, and something about the muscles of his legs gave a little and grew weak. For the space of several minutes he peered steadily into the shadows that congregated about the top of the staircase where he had seen the figure, and then he walked fast—almost ran, in fact—into the light of the front room; but hardly had he passed inside the doorway when he heard someone come up the stairs behind him with a quick bound and go swiftly into his bedroom. It was a heavy, but at the same time a stealthy footstep—the tread of somebody who did not wish to be seen. And it was at this precise moment that the nervousness he had hitherto experienced leaped the boundary line, and entered the state of fear, almost of acute, unreasoning fear. Before it turned into terror there was a further boundary to cross, and beyond that again lay the region of pure horror. Johnson's position was an unenviable one.

'By Jove! That *was* someone on the stairs, then,' he muttered, his flesh crawling all over; 'and whoever it was has now gone into my bedroom.' His delicate, pale face turned absolutely white, and for some minutes he hardly knew what to think or do. Then he realised intuitively that delay only set a premium upon fear; and he crossed the landing boldly and went straight into the other room, where, a few seconds before, the steps had disappeared.

'Who's there? Is that you, Mrs. Monks?' he called aloud, as he went, and heard the first half of his words echo down the empty stairs, while the second half fell dead against the curtains in a room that apparently held no other human figure than his own.

'Who's there?' he called again, in a voice unnecessarily loud and that only just held firm. 'What do you want here?'

The curtains swayed very slightly, and, as he saw it, his heart felt as if it almost missed a beat; yet he dashed forward and drew them aside with a rush. A window, streaming with rain, was all that met his gaze. He continued his search, but in vain; the cupboards held nothing but rows of clothes, hanging motionless; and under the bed there was no sign of anyone hiding. He stepped backwards into the middle of the room, and, as he did so, something all but tripped him up. Turning with a sudden spring of alarm he saw—the kit-bag.

'Odd!' he thought. 'That's not where I left it!' A few moments before it had surely been on his right, between the bed and the bath; he did not remember having moved it. It was very curious. What in the world was the matter with everything? Were all his senses gone queer? A terrific gust of wind tore at the windows, dashing the sleet against the glass with the force of a small gun-shot, and then fled away howling dismally over the waste of Bloomsbury roofs. A sudden vision of the Channel next day rose in his mind and recalled him sharply to realities.

'There's no-one here at any rate; that's quite clear!' he exclaimed aloud. Yet at the time he uttered them he knew perfectly well that his words were not true and that he did not believe them himself. He felt exactly as though someone was hiding close about him, watching all his movements, trying to hinder his packing in some way. 'And two of my senses,' he added, keeping up the pretence, 'have played me the most absurd tricks: the steps I heard and the figure I saw were both entirely imaginary.'

He went back to the front room, poked the fire into a blaze, and sat down before it to think. What impressed him more than anything else was the fact that the kit-bag was no longer where he had left it. It had been dragged nearer to the door.

What happened afterwards that night happened, of course, to a man already excited by fear, and was perceived by a mind that had not the full and proper control, therefore, of the senses. Outwardly, Johnson remained calm and master of himself to the end, pretending to the very last that everything he witnessed had a natural explanation, or was merely delusions of his tired nerves. But inwardly, in his very heart, he knew all along that someone had been hiding downstairs in the empty suite when he came in, that this person had watched his opportunity and then stealthily made his way up to the bedroom, and that all he saw and heard afterwards, from the moving of the kit-bag to—well, to the other things this story has to tell—were caused directly by the presence of this invisible person.

And it was here, just when he most desired to keep his mind and thoughts controlled, that the vivid pictures received day after day upon the mental plates exposed in the court-room of the Old Bailey, came strongly to light and developed themselves in the dark room of his inner vision. Unpleasant, haunting memories have a way of coming to life again just when the mind least desires them—in the silent watches of the night, on sleepless pillows, during the lonely hours spent by sick and dying beds. And so now, in the same way, Johnson saw nothing but the dreadful face of John Turk, the murderer, lowering at him from every corner of his mental field of vision; the white skin, the evil eyes, and the fringe of black hair low over the forehead. All the pictures of those ten days in court crowded back into his mind unbidden, and very vivid.

'This is all rubbish and nerves,' he exclaimed at length, springing with sudden energy from his chair. 'I shall finish my packing and go to bed. I'm overwrought, overtired. No doubt, at this rate I shall hear steps and things all night!'

But his face was deadly white all the same. He snatched up his field-glasses and walked across to the bedroom, humming a music-hall song as he went—a trifle too loud to be natural; and the instant he crossed the threshold and stood within the room something turned cold about his heart, and he felt that every hair on his head stood up.

The kit-bag lay close in front of him, several feet nearer to the door than he had left it, and just over its crumpled top he saw a head and face slowly sinking down out of sight as though someone were crouching behind it to hide, and at the same moment a sound like a long-drawn sigh was distinctly audible in the still air about him between the gusts of the storm outside.

Johnson had more courage and will-power than the girlish indecision of his face indicated; but at first such a wave of terror came over him that for some seconds he could do nothing but stand and stare. A violent trembling ran down his back and legs, and he was conscious of a foolish, almost an hysterical, impulse to scream aloud. That sigh seemed in his very ear, and the air still quivered with it. It was unmistakably a human sigh.

'Who's there?' he said at length, finding his voice; but though he meant to speak with loud decision, the tones come out instead in a faint whisper, for he had partly lost the control of his tongue and lips.

He stepped forward, so that he could see all round and over the kit-bag. Of course there was nothing there, nothing but the faded carpet and the bulging canvas sides. He put out his hands and threw open the mouth of the sack where it had fallen over, being only three parts full, and then he saw for the first time that round the inside, some six inches from the top, there ran a broad smear of dull crimson. It was an old and faded blood stain. He uttered a scream, and drew back his hands as if they had been burnt. At the same moment the kit-bag gave a faint, but unmistakable, lurch forward towards the door.

Johnson collapsed backwards, searching with his hands for the support of something solid, and the door, being farther behind him than he realised, rceived his weight just in time to prevent his falling, and shut to with a resounding bang. At the same moment the swinging of his left arm accidentally touched the electric switch, and the light in the room went out.

It was an awkward and disagreeable predicament, and if Johnson had not been possessed of real pluck he might have done all manner of foolish things. As it was, however, he pulled himself together, and groped furiously for the little brass knob to turn the light on again. But the rapid closing of the door had set the coats hanging on it a-swinging, and his fingers became entangled in a confusion of sleeves and pockets, so that it was some moments before he found the switch. And in those few moments of bewilderment and terror two things happened that sent him beyond recall over the boundary into the region of genuine horror—he distinctly heard the kit-bag shuffling heavily across the floor in jerks, and close in front of his face sounded once again the sigh of a human being.

In his anguished efforts to find the brass button on the wall he nearly scraped the nails from his fingers, but even then, in those frenzied moments of alarm—so swift and alert are the impressions of a mind keyed up by a vivid emotion—he had time to realise that he dreaded the return of the light, and that it might be better for him to stay hidden in the merciful screen of darkness. It was but the impulse of a moment, however, and before he had time to act upon it he had yielded automatically to the original desire, and the room was flooded again with light.

But the second instinct had been right. It would have been better for him to have stayed in the shelter of the kind darkness. For there, close before him, bending over the half-packed kit-bag, clear as life in the merciless glare of the electric light, stood the figure of John Turk, the murderer. Not three feet from him the man stood, the fringe of black hair marked plainly against the pallor of the forehead, the whole horrible presentment of the scoundrel, as vivid as he had seen him day after day in the Old Bailey, when he stood there in the dock, cynical and callous, under the very shadow of the gallows.

In a flash Johnson realised what it all meant: the dirty and much-used bag; the smear of crimson within the top; the dreadful stretched condition of the bulging sides. He remembered how the victim's body had been stuffed into a canvas bag for burial, the ghastly, dismembered fragments forced with lime into this very bag; and the bag itself produced as evidence—it all came back to him as clear as day. . . .

Very softly and stealthily his hand groped behind him for the handle of the door, but before he could actually turn it the very thing that he most of all dreaded came about, and John Turk lifted his devil's face and looked at him. At the same moment that heavy sigh passed through the air of the room, formulated somehow into words: 'It's my bag. And I want it.'

Johnson just remembered clawing the door open, and then falling in a heap upon the floor of the landing, as he tried frantically to make his way into the front room.

He remained unconscious for a long time, and it was still dark when he opened his eyes and realised that he was lying, stiff and bruised, on the cold boards. Then the memory of what he had seen rushed back into his mind, and he promptly fainted again. When he woke the second time the wintry dawn was just beginning to peep in at the windows, painting the stairs a cheerless, dismal grey, and he managed to crawl into the front room, and cover himself with an overcoat in the armchair, where at length he fell asleep.

A great clamour woke him. He recognised Mrs. Monks's voice, loud and voluble.

'What! You ain't been to bed, sir! Are you ill, or has anything 'appened? And there's an urgent gentleman to see you, though, it ain't seven o'clock yet, and—'

'Who is it?' he stammered. 'I'm all right, thanks. Fell asleep in my chair, I suppose.'

'Someone from Mr. Wilb'rim's, and he says he ought to see you quick before you go abroad, and I told him—'

'Show him up, please, at once,' said Johnson, whose head was whirling, and his mind was still full of dreadful visions.

Mr. Wilbraham's man came in with many apologies, and explained briefly and quickly that an absurd mistake had been made, and that the wrong kit-bag had been sent over the night before.

'Henry somehow got hold of the one that came over from the court-room, and Mr. Wilbraham only discovered it when he saw his own lying in his room, and asked why it had not gone to you,' the man said.

'Oh!' said Johnson stupidly.

'And he must have brought you the one from the murder case instead, sir, I'm afraid,' the man continued, without the ghost of an expression on his face. 'The one John Turk packed the dead body in. Mr. Wilbraham's awful upset about it, sir, and told me to come over first thing this morning with the right one, as you were leaving by the boat.'

He pointed to a clean-looking kit-bag on the floor, which he had just brought. 'And I was to bring the other one back, sir,' he added casually.

For some minutes Johnson could not find his voice. At last he pointed in the direction of his bedroom. 'Perhaps you would kindly unpack it for me. Just empty the things out on the floor.'

The man disappeared into the other room, and was gone for five minutes. Johnson heard the shifting to and fro of the bag, and the rattle of the skates and boots being unpacked.

'Thank you, sir,' the man said, returning with the bag folded over his arm. 'And can I do anything more to help you, sir?'

'What is it?' asked Johnson, seeing that he still had something he wished to say.

The man shuffled and looked mysterious. 'Beg pardon, sir, but knowing your interest in the Turk case, I thought you'd maybe like to know what's happened—'

'Yes.'

'John Turk killed himself last night with poison immediately on getting his release, and he left a note for Mr. Wilbraham saying as he'd be much obliged if they'd have him put away, same as the woman he murdered, in the old kit-bag.'

'What time—did he do it?' asked Johnson.

'Ten o'clock last night, sir, the warder says.'

THE SHADOW

by E. Nesbit

Edith Nesbit (1858–1924) achieved her greatest
fame and popularity with *The Railway Children, The
Would-Be-Goods, The Treasure Seekers* and other
children's classics. Most of her adult fiction is
largely forgotten, although two or three of her
ghost stories—notably 'Man-Size in Marble'—have
often been anthologized. Less familiar is 'The
Shadow', which appeared in her collection aptly
entitled *Fear* (1910).

This is not an artistically rounded-off ghost story, and nothing is
explained in it, and there seems to be no reason why any of it
should have happened. But that is no reason why it should not
be told. You must have noticed that all the real ghost stories you have
ever come close to, are like this in these respects—no explanation, no
logical coherence. Here is the story.

There were three of us and another, but she had fainted suddenly
at the second extra of the Christmas dance, and had been put to bed
in the dressing-room next to the room which we three shared. It had
been one of those jolly, old-fashioned dances where nearly everybody
stays the night, and the big country house is stretched to its utmost
containing—guests harbouring on sofas, couches, settles, and even
mattresses on floors. Some of the young men actually, I believe, slept
on the great dining-table. We had talked of our partners, as girls will,
and then the stillness of the manor house, broken only by the whisper

of the wind in the cedar branches, and the scraping of their harsh fingers against our window panes, had pricked us to such a luxurious confidence in our surroundings of bright chintz and candle-flame and fire-light, that we had dared to talk of ghosts—in which, we all said, we did not believe one bit. We had told the story of the phantom coach, and the horribly strange bed, and the lady in the sacque, and the house in Berkeley Square.

We none of us believed in ghosts, but my heart, at least, seemed to leap to my throat and choke me there, when a tap came to our door— a tap faint, not to be mistaken.

'Who's there?' said the youngest of us, craning a lean neck towards the door. It opened slowly, and I give you my word the instant of suspense that followed is still reckoned among my life's least confident moments. Almost at once the door opened fully, and Miss Eastwich, my aunt's housekeeper, companion and general stand-by looked in on us.

We all said 'Come in,' but she stood there. She was, at all normal hours, the most silent woman I have ever known. She stood and looked at us, and shivered a little. So did we—for in those days corridors were not warmed by hot-water pipes, and the air from the door was keen.

'I saw your light,' she said at last, 'and I thought it was late for you to be up—after all this gaiety. I thought perhaps—' her glance turned towards the door of the dressing-room.

'No,' I said, 'she's fast asleep.' I should have added a good-night, but the youngest of us forestalled my speech. She did not know Miss Eastwich as we others did; did not know how her persistent silence had built a wall round her—a wall that no one dared to break down with the commonplaces of talk, or the littlenesses of mere human relation-ship. Miss Eastwich's silence had taught us to treat her as a machine; and as other than a machine we never dreamed of treating her. But the youngest of us had seen Miss Eastwich for the first time that day. She was young, crude, ill-balanced, subject to blind, calf-like impulses. She was also the heiress of a rich tallow-chandler, but that has nothing to do with this part of the story. She jumped up from the hearth-rug, her unsuitably rich silk lace-trimmed dressing-gown falling back from her thin collar-bones, and ran to the door and put an arm round Miss Eastwich's prim, lisse-encircled neck. I gasped. I should as soon have dared to embrace Cleopatra's Needle. 'Come in,' said the youngest of us—'come in and get warm. There's lots of cocoa left.' She drew Miss Eastwich in and shut the door.

[155]

The vivid light of pleasure in the housekeeper's pale eyes went through my heart like a knife. It would have been so easy to put an arm round her neck, if one had only thought she wanted an arm there. But it was not I who had thought that—and indeed, my arm might not have brought the light evoked by the thin arm of the youngest of us.

'Now,' the youngest went on eagerly, 'you shall have the very biggest, nicest chair, and the cocoa-pot's here on the hob as hot as hot—and we've all been telling ghost stories, only we don't believe in them a bit; and when you get warm you ought to tell one too.'

Miss Eastwich—that model of decorum and decently done duties, tell a ghost story!

'You're sure I'm not in your way,' Miss Eastwich said, stretching her hands to the blaze. I wondered whether housekeepers have fires in their rooms even at Christmas time. 'Not a bit'—I said it, and I hope I said it as warmly as I felt it. 'I—Miss Eastwich—I'd have asked you to come in other times—only I didn't think you'd care for girls' chatter.'

The third girl, who was really of no account, and that's why I have not said anything about her before, poured cocoa for our guest. I put my fleecy Madeira shawl round her shoulders. I could not think of anything else to do for her, and I found myself wishing desperately to do something. The smiles she gave us were quite pretty. People can smile prettily at forty or fifty, or even later, though girls don't realise this. It occurred to me, and this was another knife-thrust, that I had never seen Miss Eastwich smile—a real smile, before. The pale smiles of dutiful acquiescence were not of the same blood as this dimpling, happy, transfiguring look.

'This is very pleasant,' she said, and it seemed to me that I had never before heard her real voice. It did not please me to think that at the cost of cocoa, a fire, and my arm round her neck, I might have heard this new voice any time these six years.

'We've been telling ghost stories,' I said. 'The worst of it is, we don't believe in ghosts. No-one one knows has ever seen one.

'It's always what somebody told somebody, who told somebody you know,' said the youngest of us, 'and you can't believe that, can you?'

'What the soldier said, is not evidence,' said Miss Eastwich. Will it be believed that the little Dickens quotation pierced one more keenly than the new smile or the new voice?

'And all the ghost stories are so beautifully rounded off—a murder committed on the spot—or a hidden treasure, or a warning . . . I think that makes them harder to believe. The most horrid ghost-story I ever heard was one that was quite silly.'

'Tell it.'

'I can't—it doesn't sound anything to tell. Miss Eastwich ought to tell one.'

'Oh do,' said the youngest of us, and her salt cellars loomed dark, as she stretched her neck eagerly and laid an entreating arm on our guest's knee.

'The only thing that I ever knew of was—was hearsay,' she said slowly, 'till just the end.'

I knew she would tell her story, and I knew she had never before told it, and I knew she was only telling it now because she was proud, and this seemed the only way to pay for the fire and the cocoa, and the laying of that arm round her neck.

'Don't tell it,' I said suddenly. 'I know you'd rather not.'

'I daresay it would bore you,' she said meekly, and the youngest of us, who, after all, did not understand everything, glared resentfully at me.

'We should just *love* it,' she said. '*Do* tell us. Never mind if it isn't a real, proper, fixed up story. I'm certain anything *you* think ghostly would be quite too beautifully horrid for anything.'

Miss Eastwich finished her cocoa and reached up to set the cup on the mantelpiece.

'It can't do any harm,' she said half to herself, 'they don't believe in ghosts, and it wasn't exactly a ghost either. And they're all over twenty—they're not babies.'

There was a breathing time of hush and expectancy. The fire crackled and the gas suddenly glared higher because the billiard lights had been put out. We heard the steps and voices of the men going along the corridors.

'It is really hardly worth telling,' Miss Eastwich said doubtfully, shading her faded face from the fire with her thin hand.

We all said 'Go on—oh, go on—do!'

'Well,' she said, 'twenty years ago—and more than that—I had two friends, and I loved them more than anything in the world. And they married each other—'

She paused, and I knew just in what way she had loved each of them. The youngest of us said—

'How awfully nice for you. Do go on.'

She patted the youngest's shoulder, and I was glad that I had understood, and that the youngest of all hadn't. She went on.

'Well, after they were married, I did not see much of them for a year or two; and then he wrote and asked me to come and stay, because his wife was ill, and I should cheer her up, and cheer him up as well; for it was a gloomy house, and he himself was growing gloomy too.'

I knew, as she spoke, that she had every line of that letter by heart.

'Well, I went. The address was in Lee, near London; in those days there were streets and streets of new villa-houses growing up round old brick mansions standing in their own grounds, with red walls round, you know, and a sort of flavour of coaching days, and post chaises, and Blackheath highwaymen about them. He had said the house was gloomy, and it was called 'The Firs,' and I imagined my cab going through a dark, winding shrubbery, and drawing up in front of one of these sedate, old, square houses. Instead, we drew up in front of a large, smart villa, with iron railings, gay encaustic tiles leading from the iron gate to the stained-glass-panelled door, and for shrubbery only a few stunted cypresses and aucubas in the tiny front garden. But inside it was all warm and welcoming. He met me at the door.'

She was gazing into the fire, and I knew she had forgotten us. But the youngest girl of all still thought it was to us she was telling her story.

'He met me at the door,' she said again, 'and thanked me for coming, and asked me to forgive the past.'

'What past?' said that high priestess of the *inàpropos*, the youngest of all.

'Oh—I suppose he meant because they hadn't invited me before, or something,' said Miss Eastwich worriedly, 'but it's a very dull story, I find, after all, and—'

'Do go on,' I said—then I kicked the youngest of us, and got up to rearrange Miss Eastwich's shawl, and said in blatant dumb show, over the shawled shoulder: 'Shut up, you little idiot—'

After another silence, the housekeeper's new voice went on.

'They were very glad to see me, and I was very glad to be there. You girls, now, have such troops of friends, but these two were all I had— all I had ever had. Mabel wasn't exactly ill, only weak and excitable. I thought he seemed more ill than she did. She went to bed early and before she went, she asked me to keep him company through his last pipe, so we went into the dining-room and sat in the two arm chairs on each side of the fireplace. They were covered with green leather I remember. There were bronze groups of horses and a black marble clock on the mantelpiece—all wedding-presents. He poured out some whisky for himself, but he hardly touched it. He sat looking into the fire. At last I said:—

' "What's wrong? Mabel looks as well as you could expect."

'He said, "yes—but I don't know from one day to another that she won't begin to notice something wrong. That's why I wanted you to come. You were always so sensible and strong-minded, and Mabel's like a little bird on a flower."

'I said yes, of course, and waited for him to go on. I thought he must be in debt, or in trouble of some sort. So I just waited. Presently he said:

' "Margaret, this is a very peculiar house—" he always called me Margaret. You see we'd been such old friends. I told him I thought the house was very pretty, and fresh, and homelike—only a little too new—but that fault would mend with time. He said:—

' "It *is* new: that's just it. We're the first people who've ever lived in it. If it were an old house, Margaret, I should think it was haunted."

'I asked if he had seen anything. "No," he said "not yet."

' "Heard then?" said I.

' "No—not heard either," he said, "but there's a sort of feeling: I can't describe it—I've seen nothing and I've heard nothing, but I've been so near to seeing and hearing, just near, that's all. And something follows me about—only when I turn round, there's never anything, only my shadow. And I always feel that I *shall* see the thing next minute—but I never do—not quite—it's always just not visible."

'I thought he'd been working rather hard—and tried to cheer him up by making light of all this. It was just nerves, I said. Then he said he had thought I could help him, and did I think anyone he had wronged could have laid a curse on him, and did I believe in curses. I said I didn't—and the only person anyone could have said he had wronged forgave him freely, I knew, if there was anything to forgive. So I told him this too.'

It was I, not the youngest of us, who knew the name of that person, wronged and forgiving.

'So then I said he ought to take Mabel away from the house and have a complete change. But he said No; Mabel had got everything in order, and he could never manage to get her away just now without explaining everything—"and, above all," he said, "she musn't guess there's anything wrong. I daresay I shan't feel quite such a lunatic now you're here."

[159]

'So we said good-night.'

'Is that all the story?' said the third girl, striving to convey that even as it stood it was a good story.

'That's only the beginning,' said Miss Eastwich. 'Whenever I was alone with him he used to tell me the same thing over and over again, and at first when I began to notice things, I tried to think that it was his talk that had upset my nerves. The odd thing was that it wasn't only at night—but in broad daylight—and particularly on the stairs and passages. On the staircase the feeling used to be so awful that I have had to bite my lips till they bled to keep myself from running upstairs at full speed. Only I knew if I did I should go mad at the top. There was always something behind me—exactly as he had said— something that one could just not see. And a sound that one could just not hear. There was a long corridor at the top of the house. I have sometimes almost seen something—you know how one sees things without looking—but if I turned round, it seemed as if the thing drooped and melted into my shadow. There was a little window at the end of the corridor.

'Downstairs there was another corridor, something like it, with a cupboard at one end and the kitchen at the other. One night I went down into the kitchen to heat some milk for Mabel. The servants had gone to bed. As I stood by the fire, waiting for the milk to boil, I glanced through the open door and along the passage. I never could keep my eyes on what I was doing in that house. The cupboard door was partly open; they used to keep empty boxes and things in it. And, as I looked, I knew that now it was not going to be "almost" any more. Yet I said, "Mabel?" not because I thought it could be Mabel who was crouching down there, half in and half out of the cupboard. The thing was grey at first, and then it was black. And when I whispered, "Mabel," it seemed to sink down till it lay like a pool of ink on the floor, and then its edges drew in, and it seemed to flow, like ink when you tilt up the paper you have spilt it on; and it flowed into the cupboard till it was all gathered into the shadow there. I saw it go quite plainly. The gas was full on in the kitchen. I screamed aloud, but even then, I'm thankful to say, I had enough sense to upset the boiling milk, so that when he came downstairs three steps at a time, I had the excuse for my scream of a scalded hand. The explanation satisfied Mabel, but next night he said:—

' "Why didn't you tell me? It was that cupboard. All the horror of the house comes out of that. Tell me—have you seen anything yet? Or is it only the nearly seeing and nearly hearing still?"

[160]

'I said, "You must tell me first what you've seen." He told me, and his eyes wandered, as he spoke, to the shadows by the curtains, and I turned up all three gas lights, and lit the candles on the mantelpiece. Then we looked at each other and said we were both mad, and thanked God that Mabel at least was sane. For what he had seen was what I had seen.

'After that I hated to be alone with a shadow, because at any moment I might see something that would crouch, and sink, and lie like a black pool, and then slowly draw itself into the shadow that was nearest. Often that shadow was my own. The thing came first at night, but afterwards there was no hour safe from it. I saw it at dawn and at noon, in the dusk and in the firelight, and always it crouched and sank, and was a pool that flowed into some shadow and became part of it. And always I saw it with a straining of the eyes—a pricking and aching. It seemed as though I could only just see it, as if my sight, to see it, had to be strained to the uttermost. And still the sound was in the house—the sound that I could just not hear. At last, one morning early, I did hear it. It was close behind me, and it was only a sigh. It was worse than the thing that crept into the shadows.

'I don't know how I bore it. I couldn't have borne it, if I hadn't been so fond of them both. But I knew in my heart that, if he had no-one to whom he could speak openly, he would go mad, or tell Mabel. His was not a very strong character; very sweet, and kind, and gentle, but not strong. He was always easily led. So I stayed on and bore up, añ we were very cheerful, and made little jokes, and tried to be amusing when Mabel was with us. But when we were alone, we did not try to be amusing. And sometimes a day or two would go by without our seeing or hearing anything, and we should perhaps have fancied that we had fancied what we had seen and heard—only there was always the feeling of there being something about the house, that one could just not hear and not see. Sometimes we used to try not to talk about it, but generally we talked of nothing else at all. And the weeks went by, and Mabel's baby was born. The nurse and the doctor said that both mother and child were doing well. He and I sat late in the dining-room that night. We had neither of us seen or heard anything for three days; our anxiety about Mabel was lessened. We talked of the future—if seemed then so much brighter than the past. We arranged that, the moment she was fit to be moved, he should take her away to the sea, and I should superintend the moving of their furniture into the new house he had already chosen. He was gayer than I had seen him since his marriage—almost like his old self. When I said goodnight to him, he said a lot of things about my having been a comfort to them both. I hadn't done anything much, of course, but still I am glad he said them.

'Then I went upstairs, almost for the first time without the feeling of something following me. I listened at Mabel's door. Everything was quiet. I went on towards my own room, and in an instant I felt that there *was* something behind me. I turned. It was crouching there; it sank, and the black fluidness of it seemed to be sucked under the door of Mabel's room.

'I went back. I opened the door a listening inch. All was still. And then I heard a sigh close behind me. I opened the door and went in. The nurse and the baby were asleep. Mabel was asleep too—she looked so pretty—like a tired child—the baby was cuddled up into one of her arms with its tiny head against her side. I prayed then that Mabel might never know the terrors that he and I had known. That those little ears might never hear any but pretty sounds, those clear eyes never see any but pretty sights. I did not dare to pray for a long time after that. Because my prayer was answered. She never saw, she never heard anything more in this world. And now I could do nothing more for him or for her.

'When they had put her in her coffin, I lighted wax candles round her, and laid the horrible white flowers that people will send near her, and then I saw he had followed me. I took his hand to lead him away.

'At the door we both turned. It seemed to us that we heard a sigh. He would have sprung to her side, in I don't know what mad, glad hope. But at that instant we both saw it. Between us and the coffin, first grey, then black, it crouched an instant, then sank and liquefied—and was gathered together and drawn till it ran into the nearest shadow. And the nearest shadow was the shadow of Mabel's coffin. I left the next day. His mother came. She had never liked me.'

Miss Eastwich paused. I think she had quite forgotten us.

'Didn't you see him again?' asked the youngest of us all.

'Only once,' Miss Eastwich answered, 'and something black crouched then between him and me. But it was only his second wife, crying beside his coffin. It's not a cheerful story is it? And it doesn't lead anywhere. I've never told anyone else. I think it was seeing his daughter that brought it all back.'

She looked towards the dressing-room door.

'Mabel's baby?'

'Yes—and exactly like Mabel, only with his eyes.'

The youngest of all had Miss Eastwich's hands, and was petting them.

Suddenly the woman wrenched her hands away, and stood at her gaunt height, her hands clenched, eyes straining. She was looking at something that we could not see, and I know what the man in the Bible meant when he said: 'The hair of my flesh stood up.'

What she saw seemed not quite to reach the height of the dressing-room door handle. Her eyes followed it down, down—widening and widening. Mine followed them—all the nerves of them seemed strained to the uttermost—and I almost saw—or did I quite see? I can't be certain. But we all heard the long-drawn, quivering sigh. And to each of us it seemed to be breathed just behind us.

It was I who caught up the candle—it dripped all over my trembling hand—and was dragged by Miss Eastwich to the girl who had fainted during the second extra. But it was the youngest of all whose lean arms were round the housekeeper when we turned away, and that have been round her many a time since, in the new home where she keeps house for the youngest of us.

The doctor who came in the morning said that Mabel's daughter had died of heart disease—which she had inherited from her mother. It was that that had made her faint during the second extra. But I have sometimes wondered whether she may not have inherited something from her father. I have never been able to forget the look on her dead face.

THE IRTONWOOD
GHOST

by Elinor Glyn

Another woman writer much better known for her writings in an entirely different genre was Elinor Glyn (1864–1943), world-famous for her sensational novels and the creation of 'It' (the indefinable sex appeal, which catapulted Clara Bow to equal fame, under Elinor Glyn's tuition, in Hollywood during the 1920s). Four years after the tremendous success of her bestseller *Three Weeks* (1907), Elinor Glyn was commissioned to write this 'story of a strange haunting' for the Christmas Number of *Pearson's Magazine* in December 1911.

I

M rs. Charters arrived at Euston in plenty of time for the 2.30 train to Ileton. She was a woman who was well served, and her footman had already got her all that she required, and she retired with a paper to the farther side of the compartment.

'You need not wait, Thomas,' she said. 'There will probably be no-one else getting in, and it is a corridor train.'

So Thomas touched his hat and left.

Just before the guard gave the signal to start, a man—evidently a gentleman—opened the door of the carriage and entered.

He had been walking leisurely up and down the platform—and if she had known it, had observed her maid and footman, looked at her

luggage, and ascertained her destination. It was the same as his own—
Irtonwood Manor, that really charmingly romantic old place Ada
Hardress and her obedient husband had just taken from the Wal-
worths for a year.

'It is too exquisitely ghostly, pet!' she had written to Estelle
Charters. 'Creaking panelling, underground passages, haunted library,
and a big cedarwood bedroom where the White Lady appears. There is
no electric light, and a person with your sensibilities can be perfectly
certain to receive a thrill! Come and spend Christmas with us!'

And Mrs. Charters had accepted—won by this alluring description
—and was now, the day before Christmas Eve, on her way thither.

She was a tall, slender woman of twenty-eight or thirty, perhaps.
She was not beautiful, but every single thing she put on seemed to
enhance her grace. Rather plaintive and distinguished refinement
appeared to be the note which first struck strangers about her.

That bore, Algernon Alexander Charters, had joined friends in
another world some three years before this Christmas Eve, leaving his
widow most comfortably provided for. Only an unpleasant jar had
happened, not more than a week ago. The family lawyer had written
to inform Estelle that there might be serious trouble ahead, and it
might even eventualise in her loss of most of Algernon Alexander's
money if a certain marriage certificate could not be found. The whole
fortune was being claimed by a descendant of the great-great-
grandfather, who contended that Algernon Alexander himself had
enjoyed his ten or twelve thousand a year unlawfully.

It appeared that somewhere about 1795 the rich Alderman Charters'
son, delighting to move in circles above him, had contracted a marriage
secretly with the daughter of a decayed noble, who would have none
of him!—and the lady, regretting her mistake too late, had denied all
connection with him, and willingly relinquishing her son, whose
existence she had concealed, and of whom she was ashamed, she had
retired with her father to Italy, and there a year or two later had died,
the wife of an Italian count!

The abandoned rich City husband had apparently taken the casual
behaviour of the noble lady in a philosophical spirit, doting upon her
son to whom, although he married again, and had a number of other
children, he left the bulk of his great fortune.

These second family seemed to have been complacent people, and
had accepted their fate. But now one of their descendants had come
forward and claimed that, the will of John Charters expressly stating,

'To my legitimate eldest son and his heirs,' with no name given, the property should come to him as the lineal representative of the eldest son of the second family, there being no proof to be found anywhere of the first marriage with the Lady Marjory Wildacre.

Mrs. Charters thought of all these things as she sat in the train. Her attention had scarcely wandered from them even as she glanced up at the intruder in her carriage, but she did casually notice that he was a thin, dark man with something rather attractive-looking about him. And after a while she became conscious that his eyes were fixed upon her, and she felt compelled to look up.

They were too close together, the orbs that met hers, she decided, though their size and shape left nothing to be desired. She had a foolish shiver of foreboding and dislike as she turned away and let her mind revert to the ceaseless question of where on the face of the earth this certificate could be—and how were they to find it.

Presently the stranger leaned forward and said, in a most cultivated voice, which yet had a foreign accent somewhere lurking in the background:

'You are Mrs. Charters, I believe? We are both going to the same house. May I introduce myself, I am Ambrose Duval—I am afraid, not quite an Englishman!'

His smile was so pleasant, it made you forget the sinister impression left by his eyes.

Mrs. Charters was of the world and not easily disconcerted.

She bowed politely, and a conversation began, in the course of which it became apparent that Mr. Ambrose Duval (such a name, it reminds one of 'Claude,' she thought!) had met the Hardresses abroad, and had renewed his acquaintance lately, and was coming down now to this Christmas party.

Nothing could be more polished and smooth than his manner; it had that easy gliding from one subject to another, which makes so agreeable a conversationalist. He skimmed all sorts of interesting topics, and at last arrived at English architecture.

'Irtonwood is a very romantic old place, Mrs. Hardress tells me,' he said. 'A fine specimen of Tudor style, with additions of Jacobean. I am longing to study it. Do you know its history?'

'Not in the least,' Estelle replied. 'My friend, Ada Hardress, merely wrote I should be certain to see ghosts! I love the thought of them, although I have never been fortunate enough to encounter one, have you? and she smiled her fascinating, elusive smile, that was half

[166]

melancholy and half gay.

Sir George Seafield, who had already arrived at Irtonwood earlier in the day, thought Estelle Charters' smile the most divine thing in the world, but then he was in love—resentfully so at first, then resignedly, and now abjectly!

Ambrose Duval, on the contrary, mused: 'She is no fool for all her gentleness, it is a capable mouth, perhaps her innocence about Irtonwood is all bluff, and she is bent upon the same errand as myself. I must lose no time.'

By four o'clock, when they had reached Ileton, they had each taken stock of the other.

'He makes me creep down my back,' was Mrs. Charters' comment, 'although I do feel he is attractive.'

Some more guests got out of another carriage, and there were greetings and chaff, and the whole party entered motors and were whirled to their destination.

Here all was holly and mistletoe and everything to make a real English Christmas. Huge log fires in every grate, and quantities of wax candles tried to make up for the want of electric light.

Nothing could have looked more like a story-book description of things as they were once in the good old days.

Ada Hardress gave her friend a most gushing welcome, and contrived that Sir George Seafield secured a chance for a *tête-à-tête* word in a suitable window-seat, as they drank tea.

'You were cruel to me,' he said, looking devotedly at the lady of his heart with his keen blue eyes—'promising to be at the junction and never turning up by that train—I came down from Scotland on purpose, and thought I should have been allowed to take care of you from Crewe here.'

'I can take care of myself,' she protested softly, 'and I found I wanted to shop this morning before I left.'

'You think you are capable of looking after yourself always, under any circumstances, I suppose,' he hazarded.

'But, of course,—when I feel I cannot, then I shall tell you,' and she smiled.

'I pray fate to let the chance come sooner than you think!' he announced fervently.

But at this pious hope Mrs. Charters only looked sweetly disdainful, and changed the conversation to less personal things.

'You won't be a goose, darling, and snub Sir George to death, will you?' Ada Hardress begged, as she took her friend up the stairs. 'You are so provoking with your aloof air, and now wanting to rest until dinner when he is dying to talk to you!'

But Mrs. Charters was unimpressed.

'I am really tired, Ada—and it does Englishmen good to be made to wait. I learned that in America,' she said. 'Algernon took me there when I wanted to go to Rome, but I never regretted it—I acquired so many hints from those clever women—Oh! what a heavenly place,' she added, when they got to the Cedar chamber which had been allotted to her, 'fancy it's not having been spoilt in these modern days!'

For it was all panelled and hung with faded orange silk in its three tall windows and capacious four-post bed.

And presently, when Mrs. Charters was tucked up upon the rather hard sofa, preparing to have a siesta before dinner, she felt at peace with all the world. It was not long before she was sound asleep and here she had a strange dream.

She felt herself unaccountably moved and perturbed—she had a sensation of breathless, waiting tension, while she stood in some dark place, and suddenly it seemed as though only one spot in the blackness became illuminated, and then she saw an old escritoire. There was nothing else, no furniture, no room—nothing but this old writing bureau standing in space, and there, on it, lay unfolded a yellow parchment, upon which seemed to have fallen some drops of fresh blood!

Estelle woke with a sensation of supernatural excitement and fear. And then she reasoned with herself. Could anything have been more foolish! A dream with no incident, no personages, no action, to cause such a feeling! There was something uncanny about it though—what if the room were really haunted! She was not sure she liked it after all!

She got up quickly and rang for her maid, glad to have company and lights. But all the while she dressed, she saw nothing but the escritoire, the parchment, and the three drops of blood.

'You look pale and pathetic,' Sir George Seafield told her, with tender anxiety in his voice, as they went in to dinner. 'What has happened. I want to know?'

But it was not until about the first *entrée* that he could get her to unfold her dream.

Her other hand neighbour was the attractive half-foreigner who had come down in the train with her, and who had no intention of allowing her legitimate partner to monopolise the conversation. He listened attentively as she described minutely the strange incident to Sir George, bending forward so as not to lose a word, much to that gentleman's disgust.

'I hate the brute!' he thought. 'Why cannot he attend to the woman he has taken in?'

'What a very strange dream!' Mr. Ambrose Duval said. 'And where was the escritoire—you have no idea?'

'Not in the least,' replied Estelle. 'It was all in space—but why the blood?' And then a thought struck her. 'Of course!' she exclaimed. 'This is some vision sent to tell me where I am to find a most important document—how stupid of me never to have thought of it before!'

'A document?' both men asked; but while Sir George's eyes only expressed deep admiration for the lady herself, Mr. Ambrose Duval's had a concentrated eagerness to hear her words that was arresting.

'Why should this interest him so?' wondered Sir George, and it caused him to feel puzzled and irritated.

Mrs. Charters was no chatterer and not in the habit of imparting her private affairs to strangers, so she laughed and changed the conversation now to lighter things, dividing her time equally between the two men until the ladies rose to leave the room.

Sir George Seafield was incensed. Why had his good friend Ada Hardress asked this foreigner to Irtonwood? and why had she put him next to Estelle, the lady of his heart?

'I believe she is rather drawn towards the jackanapes,' he thought angrily to himself, and with difficulty kept from sparring with him as they sat over the port.

'Ada, where did you meet Mr. Duval?' Mrs. Charters asked, as a group of women hung over the big drawing-room fire. 'He seems an interesting creature.'

'Doesn't he!' several of them chimed in.

'Mysterious and delightful,' one affirmed.

'So good-looking,' another announced.

'His eyes are too close together,' old Miss Harcourt said in her sententious way. 'I shan't play bridge with him.'

'We met him in Hungary last summer,' the hostess at last got in—'It seems absurd, but he was an hotel acquaintance, only he knew such a lot of people we did, he seemed like an old friend, and we saw him often, and he was always cheery and nice. He has relations in England that he has come to look up. I am so glad you find him attractive—I do myself! He has been too charming this last fortnight when we were up in town for Christmas shopping, he had just arrived from Paris and I have never had so delightful a companion, so I asked him down for Christmas. He said he would be lonely, and is so absorbed in the study of old houses.'

Then someone began to play the piano and the group broke up, and soon the gentlemen joined them, and a general move to the big oak-panelled hall commenced, when the younger members started a valse, while the 'fiddlers three,' who had come down from London to entertain the Yuletide guests, played merrily.

Sir George Seafield was detained by his host for a second, and had the chagrin to see Mrs. Charters whirling in the arms of the foreigner! He shut his firm jaw with an ominous snap.

'I am dashed if I'll put up with it,' he muttered, and went and claimed the next turn the moment the pair paused for breath.

'How cross you look to-night, Sir George!' Mrs. Charters said, as they danced, 'My last partner was so agreeable and sympathetic!'

'I want to wring his neck,' was all the answer she got. And then he added, as they stopped and wandered off to a distant sofa in the gallery, 'I am sure he is up to no good, I'd watch the silver if I were Jack Hardress!'

'It is really remarkable to what depths of spite men will descend about one another,' Estelle laughed as they sat down. 'No woman would be so transparent, and all just because Mr. Duval is a foreigner and has good manners and does not show—moods!' And she leaned back provokingly among the cushions.

'You like him?' Sir George asked indignantly—and then aggrievedly —'but anyone can see that!'

'If you are going to be unpleasant.' Mrs. Charters said, 'I shall leave you and dance with him again, he valses divinely.'

Sir George's eyes blazed.

'If you do, I *will* wring his neck—I could easily,' he blurted out.

'Absurd brute force!' and she smiled plaintively—'Englishmen are so crude.'

'How you do tease me—Estelle—' Sir George said, and then stopped suddenly.

'Who told you you might call me that?' Mrs. Charters frowned. 'A piece of impertinence!'—but here her voice faltered, for she saw that her companion was no longer listening to her, his eyes were fixed with an intense interest upon a picture which hung upon the wall opposite them—the portrait of a lady in late eighteenth-century dress, with the rather high waist, and flowing white draperies, while her hair fell in ruffled, unpowdered curls. It was not by any celebrated artist; but was a pleasing picture, and, as Estelle's eyes took it in, she knew why Sir George was so absorbed—for it bore a most wonderful likeness to herself!

'By Jove!' was all he said.

'It certainly might have been painted from me,' she allowed. 'Who can it be?'

But they could not find out. Their host, whom they questioned, did not know—he happened to be passing at that moment and joined them with his foreign guest. They had only taken the place from the Walworths for a year, he said, and the Walworths had bought it just as it stood from someone else. It had changed hands once or twice, and he could not remember now who were the original owners.

'It is supposed to be a portrait of the ghost, I believe,' he told them. 'Some old retainer informed Ada when we came. The White Lady who haunts the library and the Cedar chamber—'

'Where I sleep!' cried Estelle with a note of distress. 'Oh! Jack, I believe I am half afraid!'

'I'll come and watch outside your door if you are,' said Sir George. 'Then you can call me if you feel frightened in the night and I will tackle any ghost for you—I should glory in the act!'

'I do not doubt it!' laughed the host and discreetly walked on.

But Mr. Ambrose Duval stayed behind, examining every turn of the brush in the picture with a critical eye.

Estelle had grown very quiet, Sir George noticed—she suddenly felt again that strange sense of excitement, a cold, unpleasant feeling of tension and dread; and she looked up into his face with an appealing pair of soft grey eyes.

'Let us go and dance again,' she said. 'I want to get warm once more—I feel cold.'

And Sir George joyfully encircled her slender waist and held her close as they rejoined the dancers and whirled about.

'Who sleeps next to me?' Mrs. Charters asked, as a laughing group of women went up to bed about one in the morning—but she heard with secret dismay that the only other room in this quaint square wing was a sitting-room with a little oratory attached.

'You have always said you adored ghosts and weird things,' Mrs.

Hardress said, 'or, dearest, I would not have put you in the Cedar room.'

'So I do—of course,' returned Estelle rather half-heartedly. She was a proud woman and ashamed to show her fears.

Everything looked most bright and comfortable when she got to her room, and her devoted maid had waited up for her, and now put her to bed with every care. So, tired out with her dance, Estelle forgot her sense of uneasiness and soon sank to sleep between the slippery, fine sheets, while the dying fire made flickering lights in the vast room.

But in the grey dawn she awoke in mortal fright, for she had dreamed again of the dark space, the escritoire, the parchment, and the drops of fresh blood.

II

Next day was Christmas Eve, and much occupied with all sorts of bygone amusements, in which a Christmas tree for the children figured in the late afternoon. Everyone was particularly gay and cheerful, only Estelle Charters felt heavy as lead. Her dream haunted her, it had certainly some meaning; it was the second time she had experienced it, and the certificate, the loss of which might make such a difference to her, could quite well look like the parchment on the desk. But why there should be any connection with it and this house, of which she had never heard until her friends had taken it, she could not imagine. And if there were some strange thread in it all, why should the picture of the ghost be like herself? The money she could be deprived of had been Algernon's money, and had not come to her through her own family at all, so it would be more sensible and seemingly in sequence if the ghost looked like him or one of her sisters-in-law.

But she could not shake off the unaccountable depression she was filled with, and she tried to divert herself with Mr. Ambrose Duval's inspiriting conversation, to the rage of Sir George, who had left Scotland on purpose to be present at this party, and press his suit, feeling full of hope that she would show him some grace. But, for some reason, all had been at sixes and sevens between them, and this hateful foreigner appeared to be the cause.

Towards the end of the day, Sir George's temper had got the better of him, and he had finally gone off and talked to another woman in pique and disgust.

And so once more the night came, and Estelle was left alone in the Cedar room.

Now the conduct of the foreign guest had excited suspicion as well as fury in the breast of Sir George; and he had watched him unconsciously most of the day.

'The brute' had come to Irtonwood with some purpose — he now felt sure of that.

Such extreme interest in all the rooms and the furniture was overdone, if it were really an innocent fancy for old things. The library in particular seemed to have attracted him, and he even contrived to be shown the famous Cedar chamber, while he said most insinuating and admiring things to its present occupant. They had gone there, a company of four or five, after lunch, old Miss Harcourt among them, torn from her bridge.

'I would not sleep here for the world,' she said. 'I wonder how you can, Estelle. You must have nerves of iron and a conscience of snow-like purity — it makes me creep even in broad daylight.'

'I am not afraid,' affirmed Mrs. Charters, raising her head.

From there the group had returned to the library, and here Mr. Duval pointed to an old escritoire which stood in one window, used now as a writing table. Its surface seemed a good deal warped from the sunlight, which had come in upon it, probably for many years.

'This could be as the one you told us about in your dream,' Mr. Duval said, furtively watching her face.

And Estelle recognised that it was, indeed, the same, with a sharp thrill. But she laughed a little nervously as she evaded a direct reply.

Mr. Duval was examining it closely, passing smooth, finely moving fingers over all its sides and top.

'There is probably some secret spring,' he said. 'It would be amusing if your dream came true, and it disclosed the parchment and the drops of blood.'

But for some reason Estelle did not wish him to find it — if there were any spring. She would examine it herself another time, with Ada alone.

And Sir George, watching now intently, felt all sorts of queer ideas come into his head.

By the time they said good-night, the feeling that there was something going on underneath grew so strong that he determined not to undress or go to bed.

'He is going to have a try at opening that old bureau, I'd make any bet,' he said to himself. 'And I'll baulk him if I can and discover what is up.'

So he pretended to be tired, and go on to his room when the other men moved to the smoking room, which was in a side wing, after the ladies had left, but in reality he waited until he thought the butler would have extinguished the lights in the library and the middle part of the house. Then he lit his candle and softly crept down, and stretched himself upon a sofa rather behind a screen, while the dying embers of the fire shed a mysterious glow all over the rest of the room.

And in the Cedar chamber, Estelle, tired out and rather saddened at the estrangement which she felt had grown up in the day, between herself and her hitherto ardent, would-be lover, got hastily into bed.

It was her own fault she knew; she had been most capricious, and talked far too much to the foreign man, whom she realised now she rather disliked underneath. She had been foolish and nervous and jumpy to-day and she felt quite ashamed of herself.

But in a very short time she grew sleepy, and all became a blank, until, with startling vividness, for the third time the dream returned and to it was added a dim figure, which seemed to beckon to her, and compel her to rise and follow from her warm soft bed.

It seemed that she crept across the room to a panel beside the fireplace, fascinated, but without fear, following the ghostly shape which, when it turned its face, looked so strangely like herself. And the panel glided back, disclosing a dark opening, and still she was impelled to enter its black depths, and all the while, as she felt herself descending a narrow stair, a dim iridescence seemed, like a nimbus, to encircle the head of that faint wraith which was leading her on. Whither?

Meanwhile, in the library, Sir George was almost dozing off to sleep on his sofa in the shadow of the screen. The clock had struck two, and the fire had burnt so very low that hardly a glow now illumined the room; but a broad shaft of moonlight came in from the top part of the window, to which the shutters did not reach. It was composed of small panes, with a coat of arms emblazoned in the centre, and the beams of the moon threw some weird shades upon the floor and upon the old escritoire, which happened to stand in its path of light.

Sir George thought to himself that he had, after all, perhaps been mistaken. The foreigner had probably gone to bed with the rest, and he, too, would turn in.

Then, just as his meditations reached thus far, he heard the faintest noise of the door opening, and someone, with stealthy foot-steps, cautiously advanced up the room.

As he sprang to his feet he felt, rather than saw, that it was Ambrose Duval; he, himself, was securely hidden in the black shadow of the screen.

The man went softly to the shutter of the moonlit window, and, with quiet, nervous hands, undid its old-fashioned bolt, letting in a still broader shaft of light, which now allowed every detail of the old bureau to be seen. Then he came eagerly to its side, and Sir Goerge held his breath and leaned forward, not to miss anything of what might be about to happen.

Mr. Duval seemed to be feeling the lid, which he opened with care, and then a search began for the secret spring. And once or twice, as he looked up as if for inspiration, his face seemed like a fiend's in the ashen light.

At last he appeared to have discovered something—a drawer flew open with a jerk, and he gave a sharp exclamation of pain. Some part of the steel spring had evidently wounded his hand. But his hesitation was only momentary; with frantic eagerness, he now drew forth a roll from the secret place.

It looked to Sir George like an old yellow parchment, and as Ambrose Duval bent to scrutinise it, with devilish satisfaction upon his face, there dropped from the cut on his hand some drops of blood.

The scene was the exact reproduction of Mrs. Charters' dream.

This was the moment, Sir George felt, for him to interfere; but before he could take more than a step, he was arrested by seeing the thief raise his head, and then start and grow livid and shaking with abject terror, as he gazed into a far corner, the parchment dropping from his nerveless fingers back on to the old desk.

And Sir George, following the direction of his eyes, also experienced a thrill which, even in him, was not unmixed with something akin to fear.

For both men could just distinguish, slowly and noiselessly advancing towards them out of the shadows, from a part of the room where there was no door, the tall, slender figure of a woman, in a rather short-waisted white garment, with ruffled curls of unpowdered hair.

She seemed to be ethereal and unreal; but when she got into the moonlight the likeness was unmistakable, the face was the same as the picture in the gallery, which the host had told them represented the Irtonwood Ghost.

The great grey eyes were wide and staring, like the eyes of a corpse, and the whole figure moved slowly with a gliding motion unlike life.

'My God! Is it Estelle?' Sir George gasped to himself, as he waited the turn of events.

If it were his well-beloved, then she must be walking in her sleep. If the denizen of some other world, then something strange and awful might develop when she got to the escritoire.

In either case his best course would be to watch and be ready to spring. For he fully realised the securing of the parchment was to Ambrose Duval, for some reason, a matter of desperate need.

The figure advanced, growing more clear as it reached the goal; Duval was now crouching, an almost inert mass, some paces back, in mortal fright.

The lady—whoever or whatever she was—put out a transparent-looking hand in the moonlight, and, seizing the parchment, was gliding back again from whence she came; but Ambrose Duval gave the hiss of a snake as he saw the precious paper being taken from his grasp, and, with a half articulate cry of rage and terror, bounded forward.

But Sir George was quicker than he, and, ere he could reach the ghost, or woman, he found himself pinioned in the Englishman's strong arms.

Then the two men struggled, Ambrose Duval with mad fear in his breast at this new foe, and Sir George with cool determination to frustrate his opponent's ends.

As they tottered together, they both saw, with an indescribable thrill, the figure disappear, as it were before their eyes, into the darkness of the wall.

And they knew they were alone.

Was she a ghost, or real flesh and blood? That was a question which neither could decide.

But now that there was no more reason to protect Estelle—if it were she—Sir George let Mr. Duval go.

He was breathless from rage and fright, and he staggered to a chair.

'How dare you attack me like this!' he exclaimed furiously, drawing a revolver from his pocket and pointing it at his foe.

But Sir George, far more perturbed at the thought of what might have become of his lady love, took no notice of him. He walked over to the fire and poked up the dying embers, which threw up a last small flame, giving enough light for him to find his candlestick, which he had put down beside the sofa in the gloom, beyond the shaft of moonlight. Mr. Duval followed him, still livid from fear of the supernatural, and mad with rage at his failure and loss.

'You shall answer to me for this, now, with your life!' he snarled.

'In that case you will be hanged for murder,' Sir George retorted , coolly. 'You had better go quietly in the morning, before I denounce you as a thief.'

'I am no thief!' Mr. Duval protested, violently. 'How dare you attack a guest in our friend's house in this murderous fashion! It is I who can denounce you. You must give me satisfaction for this!'

'I shall do nothing of the kind,' said Sir George. 'I should not think of duelling with a thief. Just take my advice and go in the morning without a scandal, and prosecute your scheming tricks elsewhere. I have seen all you did, remember, and can describe it well!'

Then the two men glared at one another there in the old library, the one candle illuminating their angry faces, and the great shaft of moonlight lighting the rifled escritoire. And then Sir George calmed himself.

'You can take what course you please,' he said. 'I have a pistol, too,' and he drew his small Derringer from the pocket where he had been holding it. 'I am rather a good shot sometimes, so we may each hit the other, but there is no use in it, and rats like you are fond of life.'

This reflection seemed to carry weight with Mr. Duval, unflattering as it was. For it is quite one thing to shoot at an unarmed man, and quite another to find him possessed of a pistol, too.

With what dignity he could, Mr. Duval now drew himself up, and prepared to leave the room.

'You have won this time,' he said, between his teeth, 'but some day I will level things up.'

'I am quite indifferent about that,' Sir George answered, hurriedly. 'Get out now, and get away by the earliest train, I shall give you so much start. Now I have other and more important things to do. Go!'

And he almost drove Duval to the door and up to his room. Then, when he had seen him safely shut in, he paused to think what was the next thing to be done.

To awaken Jack Hardress and his wife, and ascertain if Estelle was safe in her Cedar chamber, seemed to be the best move. So, after some difficulty, he found his host's apartment, and knocked firmly on the door.

'Yes, what is it?' Jack Hardress called out, sleepily.

And Ada's frightened voice piped, 'Oh! who is there?'

Then Sir George explained in as few words as he could, when his host and hostess, clothed in dressing-gowns, appeared in the passage, and they all three, carrying lights, set off for the Cedar room.

But here was deathly silence, no answer came to their knocks, nor could they enter—the door was locked from within.

A sickening icy hand clutched at Sir George's heart. What had happened? Some ill had befallen Estelle.

'If we both rush the door together we can break the lock, Jack,' he said, desperately. 'We must not delay an instant—now!'

And the two men hurled themselves against the stout panels; but, though they shivered, they held. Then, with the strength of despair, Sir George made a rush by himself, and the bolt gave, and he fell headlong into the room.

But, alas! Ada's two candles, which she held high, revealed no occupant. The bed had been slept in and left hastily, the clothes were turned back, but there was no sign of Estelle!

The three people looked at each other with blanched faces—what mystery was here? Sir George began hastily to examine the walls. It followed, his common-sense told him, if the door were locked from within, his beloved lady had left the apartment by some other means. The windows were out of the question; they were too high, and, besides were closed and the orange curtains drawn. There must be some secret panel, and Estelle must have walked in her sleep—but how weird it all was! And he was filled with dread and foreboding as he felt each part of the wall.

'We *must* discover the entrance, Jack,' he said. 'I saw Mrs. Charters—or her ghost—with my own eyes in the library and she disappeared at the end of the room.'

Now, with terrified eagerness, the three set to work, feeling and tapping each cedar panel, while Ada Hardress called continually: 'Estelle! Estelle! Answer if you are there and can hear us!'

But only silence greeted them.

And, as the hopelessness of their task made itself felt, a sickening fear grew and grew in each of their hearts.

What if she had fallen down some deep secret place—some

oubliette—and were dead? They might pull all the house down, and yet be too late.

At last Ada, almost weeping from grief and fright, subsided upon the sofa, while her husband and Sir George, rigid and grey with anxiety, faced each other, to decide what to do.

'Wake the servants and send for a mason and carpenter,' Sir George said. 'And, meanwhile, can't we get an axe and some tools? I will tear the woodwork down myself, when I have an implement.'

Mrs. Hardress went off to wake the household, and send for the required men.

'And get a doctor, too,' Sir George called, and when some tools were found by a frightened footman, and brought, he set to work with such a will that at last a steel bolt was discovered, and the panelling giving way by the fireplace, a very small, narrow door was disclosed in the stonework. The bolts in connection with it were stiff and rusted with age, and how a delicate woman could have moved them was a profound mystery.

The door gave way without much difficulty, and here by the light of a lamp held high, the very narrowest passage was revealed, which in three paces developed into a stair.

It was so extremely narrow that Sir George was obliged to force his broad shoulders through until he came to the descent. Suddenly, at a sharp turn, he could see the steps rising again on the opposite side, but there, in the space beneath, lay the figure of a woman in white.

With an exclamation of anguish, he saw that it was Estelle—but was she dead?

He handed the lamp to Jack Hardress, who was behind him, and in a second he was beside his love, and had raised her in his arms with difficulty in the confined space; and even in the excitement, he noticed that she still clutched in her hand the paper which seemed to have been the cause of all the tragic events of the night.

He detached it from her fingers, and saw that the blood drops had smeared her hand, as he put the paper in his pocket and lifted her in his arms to carry her back.

A bruise marked where her forehead had struck a projecting stone in the wall; perhaps she was only stunned, and not dead! This hope gave him the strength of a lion, and he clasped her close. But their exit was no easy task; the space had been narrow enough for one person here and there, and was impossible for a man cumbered with a woman in his arms.

Jack Hardress retreated before them, holding the lamp high, and when Sir George came to a turn that he could not pass, he was obliged to lay his precious burden down, and let Jack Hardress pull her through by the arms. Then he lifted her up again. And so, at last, all three were safe in the Cedar room, where a thrilled and excited group awaited them, including the doctor, who had now arrived.

The room was cleared of all but Ada, Sir George, and Estelle's maid, while the doctor bent over the inanimate form. And, at last, he looked up and announced, 'No—she is not dead,' and never were more grateful words sent up to heaven than Sir George's fervent, 'Thank God!'

She was not dead then, his darling, and soon she might open her eyes and look into his own.

He could afford to wait in the passage now, as he told the good news to the rest of the alarmed guests.

And presently the doctor and Mrs. Hardress came out, and he heard that his beloved was conscious, and rapidly recovering.

'She must have walked in her sleep,' the physician said, 'and her head struck a stone, but it was the stifling air which made her faint, though, no doubt, she was stunned, too, by the blow; if you had been an hour later in finding her, I think she could not have lived.'

So, after all, there were rejoicings on that Christmas morning, which seemed as though it was going to dawn so tragically; and in the excitement of it all no one thought then to remark upon Mr. Ambrose Duval's departure by the one and only early train.

His note of farewell to his hostess was a masterpiece, and caused Sir George to smile, as she handed it to him to read.

Late in the afternoon he was allowed to see his sweet lady in Ada's own sitting-room, alone, and in peace. She was lying on the sofa with a bandage round her forehead, and her small face looked ghastly pale against the blue silk cushions, but her eyes shone and she stretched out her hands, as he bent upon his knees to be near her.

'George—you were good to me!' she whispered. 'and I can't take care of myself—' But she could not say any more, because he stopped and kissed her lips. And for some while they were too happy to talk of even a subject so interesting as her dream and the adventure it produced.

But at last they became sane enough to examine the parchment, which proved to be the certificate of marriage between John Charters, bachelor, and Marjorie Wildacre, spinster, celebrated at a little village in Leicestershire, in the year 1795.

So the Irtonwood Ghost had stood Estelle in good stead! For here was her fortune secured beyond any doubt.

But who, then, was Mr. Ambrose Duval? and what was his connection with the affair? and why did Estelle, herself, resemble the picture of the Irtonwood Ghost? These were questions which it would take time to answer.

'Though what does anything matter,' exclaimed Sir George, after a while, 'since I have enough for us both? And since you cannot take care of yourself, and are going to let me.'

It was not before the happy pair returned from their honeymoon that all the mystery was unravelled. The lawyers had been busy investigating the while. It appeared that Lady Marjorie Wildacre had lived at Irtonwood, which was her old home, her father having sold it when they went to Italy.

She had had a daughter by her second husband, the Italian Count, who eventually married the great-grandfather of Estelle, thus carrying the likeness into her family.

And Estelle often loves to weave a romance round her dream, and imagine how, influenced by this far-back ancestress's unquiet spirit, she must have been drawn to go to the Irtonwood Christmas party and participate in the events which followed.

'You see, George, she probably loved the Italian Count,' Estelle told her husband, 'and wanted their descendant, by him, to benefit, too. That is why she directed me. But I cannot help being sorry for poor Mr. Duval.'

'Loathsome foreigner!' was all Sir George said.

His real name was Charters, and he was the claimant to the fortune; but he chose to take his mother's name — she had been a French-woman — the better to pursue his investigations unsuspected.

He had got hold of some letter, among the papers of his branch of the family, which referred to the certificate being at Irtonwood, and Lady Marjorie's residence there; and, hearing that his chance acquaintances, the Hardresses, had taken this place, he cultivated them in order to have access for his search, determining, when he found the certificate, he would destroy it, and then with certainty prosecute his claim.

But Fate takes care of things, and arranges what she thinks best. And even the thoroughly English Sir George Seafield is obliged to own that there are more things in heaven and earth than are dreamed of in our philosophy.

[181]

BONE TO HIS BONE

by E. G. Swain

Edmund Gill Swain (1861–1938) was Chaplain at
King's College, Cambridge (from 1892 to 1916),
where one of his best friends was M.R. James, the
great writer of ghost stories. Swain obviously fell
under his influence, and penned several 'Jamesian'
tales of his own, all collected in *The Stoneground
Ghost Tales* 'compiled from the recollections of the
Reverend Roland Batchel, Vicar of the Parish'
(published in Cambridge, 1912).
Swain became the Minor Canon and Librarian at
Peterborough Cathedral — 'Stoneground' being
directly based on the village of Stanground,
situated near Peterborough.

W illiam Whitehead, Fellow of Emmanuel College, in the
University of Cambridge, became Vicar of Stoneground in
the year 1731. The annals of his incumbency were doubtless short and simple: they have not survived. In his day were no
newspapers to collect gossip, no Parish Magazines to record the simple
events of parochial life. One event, however, of greater moment then
than now, is recorded in two places. Vicar Whitehead failed in health
after 23 years of work, and journeyed to Bath in what his monument
calls 'the vain hope of being restored.' The duration of his visit is
unknown; it is reasonable to suppose that he made his journey in the
summer, it is certain that by the month of November his physician
told him to lay aside all hope of recovery.

[182]

Then it was that the thoughts of the patient turned to the comfortable straggling vicarage he had left at Stoneground, in which he had hoped to end his days. He prayed that his successor might be as happy there as he had been himself. Setting his affairs in order, as became one who had but a short time to live, he executed a will, bequeathing to the Vicars of Stoneground, for ever, the close of ground he had recently purchased because it lay next the vicarage garden. And by a codicil, he added to the bequest his library of books. Within a few days, William Whitehead was gathered to his fathers.

A mural tablet in the north aisle of the church, records, in Latin, his services and his bequests, his two marriages, and his fruitless journey to Bath. The house he loved, but never again saw, was taken down 40 years later, and re-built by Vicar James Devie. The garden, with Vicar Whitehead's 'close of ground' and other adjacent lands, was opened out and planted, somewhat before 1850, by Vicar Robert Towerson. The aspect of everything has changed. But in a convenient chamber on the first floor of the present vicarage the library of Vicar Whitehead stands very much as he used it and loved it, and as he bequeathed it to his successors 'for ever.'

The books there are arranged as he arranged and ticketed them. Little slips of paper, sometimes bearing interesting fragments of writing, still mark his places. His marginal comments still give life to pages from which all other interest has faded, and he would have but a dull imagination who could sit in the chamber amidst these books without ever being carried back 180 years into the past, to the time when the newest of them left the printer's hands.

Of those into whose possession the books have come, some have doubtless loved them more, and some less; some, perhaps, have left them severely alone. But neither those who loved them, nor those who loved them not, have lost them, and they passed, some century and a half after William Whitehead's death, into the hands of Mr. Batchel, who loved them as a father loves his children. He lived alone, and had few domestic cares to distract his mind. He was able, therefore, to enjoy to the full what Vicar Whitehead had enjoyed so long before him. During many a long summer evening would he sit poring over long-forgotten books; and since the chamber, otherwise called the library, faced the south, he could also spend sunny winter mornings there without discomfort. Writing at a small table, or reading as he stood at a tall desk, he would browse amongst the books like an ox in a pleasant pasture.

There were other times also, at which Mr. Batchel would use the books. Not being a sound sleeper (for book-loving men seldom are), he elected to use as a bedroom one of the two chambers which opened at either side into the library. The arrangement enabled him to beguile many a sleepless hour amongst the books, and in view of these nocturnal visits he kept a candle standing in a sconce above the desk, and matches always ready to his hand.

There was one disadvantage in this close proximity of his bed to the library. Owing, apparently, to some defect in the fittings of the room, which, having no mechanical tastes, Mr. Batchel had never investigated, there could be heard, in the stillness of the night, exactly such sounds as might arise from a person moving about amongst the books. Visitors using the other adjacent room would often remark at breakfast, that they had heard their host in the library at one or two o'clock in the morning, when, in fact, he had not left his bed. Invariably Mr. Batchel allowed them to suppose that he had been where they thought him. He disliked idle controversy, and was unwilling to afford an opening for supernatural talk. Knowing well enough the sounds by which his guests had been deceived, he wanted no other explanation of them than his own, though it was of too vague a character to count as an explanation. He conjectured that the window-sashes, or the doors, or 'something,' were defective, and was too phlegmatic and too unpractical to make any investigation. The matter gave him no concern.

Persons whose sleep is uncertain are apt to have their worst nights when they would like their best. The consciousness of a special need for rest seems to bring enough mental disturbance to forbid it. So on Christmas Eve, in the year 1907, Mr. Batchel, who would have liked to sleep well, in view of the labours of Christmas Day, lay hopelessly wide awake. He exhausted all the known devices for courting sleep, and, at the end, found himself wider awake than ever. A brilliant moon shone into his room, for he hated window-blinds. There was a light wind blowing, and the sounds in the library were more than usually suggestive of a person moving about. He almost determined to have the sashes 'seen to,' although he could seldom be induced to have anything 'seen to.' He disliked changes, even for the better, and would submit to great inconvenience rather than have things altered with which he had become familiar.

As he revolved these matters in his mind, he heard the clocks strike the hour of midnight, and having now lost all hope of falling asleep, he rose from his bed, got into a large dressing gown which hung in readiness for such occasions, and passed into the library, with the intention of reading himself sleepy, if he could.

The moon, by this time, had passed out of the south, and the library seemed all the darker by contrast with the moonlit chamber he had left. He could see nothing but two blue-grey rectangles formed by the windows against the sky, the furniture of the room being altogether invisible. Groping along to where the table stood, Mr. Batchel felt over its surface for the matches which usually lay there; he found, however, that the table was cleared of everything. He raised his right hand, therefore, in order to feel his way to a shelf where the matches were sometimes mislaid, and at that moment, whilst his hand was in mid-air, the matchbox was gently put into it!

Such an incident could hardly fail to disturb even a phlegmatic person, and Mr. Batchel cried 'Who's this?' somewhat nervously. There was no answer. He struck a match, looked hastily round the room, and found it empty, as usual. There was everything, that is to say, that he was accustomed to see, but no other person than himself.

It is not quite accurate, however, to say that everything was in its usual state. Upon the tall desk lay a quarto volume that he had certainly not placed there. It was his quite invariable practice to replace his books upon the shelves after using them, and what we may call his library habits were precise and methodical. A book out of place like this, was not only an offence against good order, but a sign that his privacy had been intruded upon. With some surprise, therefore, he lit the candle standing ready in the sconce, and proceeded to examine the book, not sorry, in the disturbed condition in which he was, to have an occupation found for him.

The book proved to be one with which he was unfamiliar, and this made it certain that some other hand than his had removed it from its place. Its title was 'The Compleat Gard'ner' of M. de la Quintinye made English by John Evelyn Esquire. It was not a work in which Mr. Batchel felt any great interest. It consisted of divers reflections on various parts of husbandry, doubtless entertaining enough, but too deliberate and discursive for practical purposes. He had certainly never used the book, and growing restless now in mind, said to himself that some boy having the freedom of the house, had taken it down from its place in the hope of finding pictures.

But even whilst he made this explanation he felt its weakness. To begin with, the desk was too high for a boy. The improbability that any boy would place a book there was equalled by the improbability that he would leave it there. To discover its uninviting character would be the work only of a moment, and no boy would have brought it so far from its shelf.

Mr. Batchel had, however, come to read, and habit was too strong with him to be wholly set aside. Leaving 'The Compleat Gard'ner' on the desk, he turned round to the shelves to find some more congenial reading.

Hardly had he done this when he was startled by a sharp rap upon the desk behind him, followed by a rustling of paper. He turned quickly about and saw the quarto lying open. In obedience to the instinct of the moment, he at once sought a natural cause for what he saw. Only a wind, and that of the strongest, could have opened the book, and laid back its heavy cover; and though he accepted, for a brief moment, that explanation, he was too candid to retain it longer. The wind out of doors was very light. The window sash was closed and latched, and, to decide the matter finally, the book had its back, and not its edges, turned towards the only quarter from which a wind could strike.

Mr. Batchel approached the desk again and stood over the book. With increasing perturbation of mind (for he still thought of the matchbox) he looked upon the open page. Without much reason beyond that he felt constrained to do something, he read the words of the half completed sentence at the turn of the page—

'at dead of night he left the house and passed into the solitude of the garden.'

But he read no more, nor did he give himself the trouble of discovering whose midnight wandering was being described, although the habit was singularly like one of his own. He was in no condition for reading, and turning his back upon the volume he slowly paced the length of the chamber, 'wondering at that which had come to pass.'

He reached the opposite end of the chamber and was in the act of turning, when again he heard the rustling of paper, and by the time he had faced round, saw the leaves of the book again turning over. In a moment the volume lay at rest, open in another place, and there was no further movement as he approached it. To make sure that he had not been deceived, he read again the words as they entered the page. The author was following a not uncommon practice of the time, and throwing common speech into forms suggested by Holy Writ: 'So dig,' it said, 'that ye may obtain.'

This passage, which to Mr. Batchel seemed reprehensible in its levity, excited at once his interest and his disapproval. He was prepared to read more, but this time was not allowed. Before his eye could pass beyond the passage already cited, the leaves of the book slowly turned again, and presented but a termination of five words and a colophon.

The words were, 'to the North, an Ilex.' These three passages, in which he saw no meaning and no connection, began to entangle themselves together in Mr. Batchel's mind. He found himself repeating them in different orders, now beginning with one, and now with another. Any further attempt at reading he felt to be impossible, and he was in no mind for any more experiences of the unaccountable. Sleep was, of course, further from him than ever, if that were conceivable. What he did, therefore, was to blow out the candle, to return to his moonlit bedroom, and put on more clothing, and then to pass downstairs with the object of going out of doors.

It was not unusual with Mr. Batchel to walk about his garden at night-time. This form of exercise had often, after a wakeful hour, sent him back to his bed refreshed and ready for sleep. The convenient access to the garden at such times lay through his study, whose French windows opened on to a short flight of steps, and upon these he now paused for a moment to admire the snow-like appearance of the lawns, bathed as they were in the moonlight. As he paused, he heard the city clocks strike the half-hour after midnight, and he could not forbear repeating aloud:

'At dead of night he left the house, and passed into the solitude of the garden.'

It was solitary enough. At intervals the screech of an owl, and now and then the noise of a train, seemed to emphasise the solitude by drawing attention to it and then leaving it in possession of the night. Mr. Batchel found himself wondering and conjecturing what Vicar Whitehead, who had acquired the close of land to secure quiet and privacy for garden, would have thought of the railways to the west and north. He turned his face northwards, whence a whistle had just sounded, and saw a tree beautifully outlined against the sky. His breath caught at the sight. Not because the tree was unfamiliar. Mr. Batchel knew all his trees. But what he had seen was 'to the north, an Ilex.'

Mr. Batchel knew not what to make of it all. He had walked into

[187]

the garden hundreds of times and as often seen the Ilex, but the words out of the 'Compleat Gard'ner' seemed to be pursuing him in a way that made him almost afraid. His temperament, however, as has been said already, was phlegmatic. It was commonly said, and Mr. Batchel approved the verdict, whilst he condemned its inexactness, that 'his nerves were made of fiddle-string,' so be braced himself afresh and set upon his walk round the silent garden, which he was accustomed to begin in a northerly direction, and was now too proud to change. He usually passed the Ilex at the beginning of his perambulation, and so would pass it now.

He did not pass it. A small discovery, as he reached it, annoyed and disturbed him. His gardener, as careful and punctilious as himself, never failed to house all his tools at the end of a day's work. Yet there, under the Ilex, standing upright in moonlight brilliant enough to cast a shadow of it, was a spade.

Mr. Batchel's second thought was one of relief. After his extra-ordinary experiences in the library (he hardly knew now whether they had been real or not) something quite commonplace would act sedatively, and he determined to carry the spade to the tool-house.

The soil was quite dry, and the surface even a little frozen, so Mr. Batchel left the path, walked up to the spade, and would have drawn it towards him. But it was as if he had made the attempt upon the trunk of the Ilex itself. The spade would not be moved. Then, first with one hand, and then with both, he tried to raise it, and still it stood firm. Mr. Batchel, of course, attributed this to the frost, slight as it was. Wondering at the spade's being there, and annoyed at its being frozen, he was about to leave it and continue his walk, when the remaining words of the 'Compleat Gard'ner' seemed rather to utter themselves, than to await his will—

'So dig, that ye may obtain.'

Mr. Batchel's power of independent action now deserted him. He took the spade, which no longer resisted, and began to dig. 'Five spadefuls and no more,' he said aloud. 'This is all foolishness.'

Four spadefuls of earth he then raised and spread out before him in the moonlight. There was nothing unusual to be seen. Nor did Mr. Batchel decide what he would look for, whether coins, jewels, documents in canisters, or weapons. In point of fact, he dug against what he deemed his better judgement, and expected nothing. He spread before him the fifth and last spadeful of earth, not quite without result, but with no result that was at all sensational. The earth contained a bone. Mr. Batchel's knowledge of anatomy was sufficient to show him that it was a human bone. He identified it, even by moonlight, as the *radius*, a bone of the forearm, as he removed the earth from it, with his thumb.

Such a discovery might be thought worthy of more than the very ordinary interest Mr. Batchel showed. As a matter of fact, the presence of a human bone was easily to be accounted for. Recent excavations within the church had caused the upturning of number-less bones, which had been collected and reverently buried. But an earth-stained bone is also easily overlooked, and this *radius* had obviously found its way into the garden with some of the earth brought out of the church.

Mr. Batchel was glad, rather than regretful at this termination to his adventure. He was once more provided with something to do. The re-interment of such bones as this had been his constant care, and he decided at once to restore the bone to consecrated earth. The time seemed opportune. The eyes of the curious were closed in sleep, he himself was still alert and wakeful. The spade remained by his side and the bone in his hand. So he betook himself, there and then, to the churchyard. By the still generous light of the moon, he found a place where the earth yielded to his spade, and within a few minutes the bone was laid decently to earth, some 18 inches deep.

The city clocks struck one as he finished. The whole world seemed asleep, and Mr. Batchel slowly returned to the garden with his spade. As he hung it in its accustomed place he felt stealing over him the welcome desire to sleep. He walked quietly on to the house and ascended to his room. It was now dark: the moon had passed on and left the room in shadow. He lit a candle, and before undressing passed into the library. He had an irresistible curiosity to see the passages in John Evelyn's book which had so strangely adapted themselves to the events of the past hour.

In the library a last surprise awaited him. The desk upon which the book had lain was empty. 'The Compleat Gard'ner' stood in its place on the shelf. And then Mr. Batchel knew that he had handled bone of William Whitehead, and that in response to his own entreaty.

TRANSITION

by *Algernon Blackwood*

The second Christmas story in this anthology by
the redoubtable Algernon Blackwood.

J ohn Mudbury was on his way home from the shops, his arms full of
Christmas Presents. It was after six o'clock and the streets were
very crowded. He was an ordinary man, lived in an ordinary
suburban flat, with an ordinary wife and ordinary children. *He*
did not think them ordinary, but everybody else did. He had ordinary
presents for each one, a cheap blotter for his wife, a cheap air-gun for
the boy, and so forth. He was over fifty, bald, in an office, decent in
mind and habits, of uncertain opinions, uncertain politics, and
uncertain religion. Yet he considered himself a decided, positive
gentleman, quiet unaware that the morning newspaper determined his
opinions for the day. He just lived—from day to day. Physically,
he was fit enough, except for a weak heart (which never troubled
him); and his summer holiday was bad golf, while the children bathed
and his wife read Garvice on the sands. Like the majority of men,
he dreamed idly of the past, muddled away the present, and
guessed vaguely—after imaginative reading on occasions—at the
future.

'I'd like to survive all right,' he said, 'provided it's better than this,'
surveying his wife and children, and thinking of his daily toil.
'Otherwise—!' and he shrugged his shoulders as a brave man should.

[190]

He went to church regularly. But nothing in church convinced him that he did survive, just as nothing in church enticed him into hoping that he would. On the other hand, nothing in life persuaded him that he didn't, wouldn't, couldn't. 'I'm an Evolutionist,' he loved to say to thoughtful cronies (over a glass), having never heard that Darwinism had been questioned.

And so he came home gaily, happily, with his bunch of Christmas Presents 'for the wife and little ones,' stroking himself upon their keen enjoyment and excitement. The night before he had taken 'the wife' to see *Magic* at a select London theatre where the Intellectuals went—and had been extraordinarily stirred. He had gone questioningly, yet expecting something out of the common. 'It's *not* musical,' he warned her, 'nor farce, nor comedy, so to speak', and in answer to her question as to what the critics had said, he had wriggled, sighed, and put his gaudy neck-tie straight four times in quick succession. For no Man in the Street, with any claim to self-respect, could be expected to understand what the critics had said, even if he understood the Play. And John had answered truthfully: 'Oh, they just said things. But the theatre's always full—and that's the only test.'

And just now, as he crossed the crowded Circus to catch his 'bus, it chanced that his mind (having glimpsed an advertisement) was full of this particular Play, or, rather, of the effect it had produced upon him at the time. For it had thrilled him—inexplicably: with its marvellous speculative hint, its big audacity, its alert and spiritual beauty. . . . Thought plunged to find something—plunged after this bizarre suggestion of a bigger universe, after this quasi-jocular suggestion that man is not the only—then dashed full-tilt against a sentence that memory thrust beneath his nose: 'Science does *not* exhaust the Universe'—and at the same time dashed full-tilt against destruction of another kind as well . . . !

How it happened he never exactly knew. He saw a Monster glaring at him with eyes of blazing fire. It was horrible! It rushed upon him. He dodged. . . . Another monster met him round the corner. Both came at him simultaneously. He dodged again—a leap that might have cleared a hurdle easily, but was too late. Between the pair of them—his heart literally in his gullet—he was mercilessly caught. Bones crunched. . . . There was a soft sensation, icy cold and hot as fire. Horns and voices roared. Battering-rams he saw, and a carapace of iron. . . . Then dazzling light. . . . 'Always *face* the traffic!' he remembered with a frantic yell—and, by some extraordinary luck, escaped miraculously on to the opposite pavement.

There was no doubt about it. By the skin of his teeth he had dodged a rather ugly death. First. . . . he felt for his Presents—all were safe. And then, instead of congratulating himself and taking breath, he hurried homewards—on foot, which proved that his mind had lost control a bit!—thinking only how disappointed the wife and children would have been if—well, if anything had happened. Another thing he realised, oddly enough, was that he no longer really loved his wife, but had only great affection for her. What made him think of that, Heaven only knows, but he *did* think of it. He was an honest man without pretence. This came as a discovery somehow. He turned a moment, and saw the crowd gathered about the entangled taxi-cabs, policemen's helmets gleaming in the lights of the shop windows . . . then hurried on again, his thoughts full of the joy his Presents would give . . . of the scampering children . . . and of his wife—bless her silly heart!—eyeing the mysterious parcels. . . .

And, though he never could explain how, he presently stood at the door of the jail-like building that contained his flat, having walked the whole three miles. His thoughts had been so busy and absorbed that he had hardly noticed the length of weary trudge. 'Besides,' he reflected, thinking of the narrow escape, 'I've had a nasty shock. It was a damned near thing, now I come to think of it. . . .' He still felt a bit shaky and bewildered. Yet, at the same time, he felt extraordinarily jolly and light-hearted.

He counted his Christmas parcels . . . hugged himself in anticipatory joy – and let himself in swiftly with his latchkey. 'I'm late,' he realised, 'but when she sees the brown-paper parcels, she'll forget to say a word. God bless the old faithful soul.' And he softly used the key a second time and entered his flat on tiptoe. . . . In his mind was the master impulse of that afternoon—the pleasure these Christmas Presents would give his wife and children.

He heard a noise. He hung up hat and coat in the poky vestibule (they never called it 'hall') and moved softly towards the parlour door, holding the packages behind him. Only of them he thought, not of himself—of his family, that is, not of the packages. Pushing the door cunningly ajar, he peeped in shyly. To his amazement the room was full of people. He withdrew quickly, wondering what it meant. A party? And without his knowing about it? Extraordinary!. . . Keen disappointment came over him. But as he stepped back, the vestibule, he saw, was full of people too.

He was uncommonly surprised, yet somehow not surprised at all. People were congratulating him. There was a perfect mob of them. Moreover, he knew them all—vaguely remembered them, at least. And they all knew him.

'Isn't it a game?' laughed someone, patting him on the back. '*They* haven't the least idea . . . !'

And the speaker, it was old John Palmer, the bookkeeper at the office—emphasised the 'they.'

'Not the least idea,' he answered with a smile, saying something he didn't understand, yet knew was right.

His face, apparently, showed the utter bewilderment he felt. The shock of the collision had been greater than he realised evidently. His mind was wandering. . . . Possibly! Only the odd thing was—he had never felt so clear-headed in his life. Ten thousand things grew simple suddenly. But, how thickly these people pressed about him, and how—familiarly!

'My parcels,' he said, joyously pushing his way across the throng. 'These are Christmas Presents I've bought for them.' He nodded toward the room. 'I've saved for weeks—stopped cigars and billiards and—and several other good things—to buy them.'

'Good man!' said Palmer with a happy laugh. 'It's the heart that counts.'

Mudbury looked at him. Palmer had said an amazing truth, only—people would hardly understand and believe him. . . . Would they?

'Eh?' he asked, feeling stuffed and stupid, muddled somewhere between two meanings, one of which was gorgeous and the other stupid beyond belief.

'If you *please*, Mr. Mudbury, step inside. They are expecting you,' said a kindly, pompous voice. And, turning sharply, he met the gentle, foolish eyes of Sir James Epiphany, a director of the Bank where he worked.

The effect of the voice was instantaneous from long habit.

'They are,' he smiled from his heart, and advanced as from the custom of many years. Oh, how happy and gay he felt! His affection for his wife was real. Romance, indeed, had gone, but he needed her—and she needed him. And the children—Milly, Bill, and Jean—he deeply loved them. Life was worth living indeed!

In the room was a crowd, but—an astounding silence. John

[193]

Mudbury looked round him. He advanced towards his wife, who sat in the corner arm-chair with Milly on her knee. A lot of people talked and moved about. Momentarily the crowd increased. He stood in front of them—in front of Milly and his wife. And he spoke—holding out his packages. 'It's Christmas Eve,' he whispered shyly, 'and I've— brought you something—something for everybody. Look!' He held the packages before their eyes.

'Of course, of course,' said a voice behind him, 'but you may hold them out like that for a century. They'll *never* see them!'

'Of course they won't. But I love to do the old, sweet thing,' replied John Mudbury—then wondered with a gasp of stark amazement why he said it.

'I think—' whispered Milly, staring round her.

'Well what do you think?' her mother asked sharply. 'You're always thinking something odd.'

'I think,' the girl continued dreamily, 'that Daddy's already here.' She paused, then added with a child's impossible conviction, 'I'm sure he is. I *feel* him.'

There was an extraordinary laugh. Sir James Epiphany laughed. The others—the whole crowd of them—also turned their heads and smiled. But the mother, thrusting the child away from her, rose up suddenly with a violent start. Her face had turned to chalk. She stretched her arms out into the air before her. She gasped and shivered. There was anguish in her eyes.

'Look!' repeated John, 'these are the Presents that I brought.'

But his voice apparently was soundless. And, with a spasm of icy pain, he remembered that Palmer and Sir James—some years ago— had died.

'It's magic,' he cried, 'but—I love you, Jinny—I love you—and— and I have always been true to you—as true as steel. We need each other—oh, can't you see—we go on together—you and I—for ever and ever—'

'*Think*,' interrupted an exquisitely tender voice, 'don't shout! They can't *hear* you—now.' And, turning, John Mudbury met the eyes of Everard Minturn, their President of the year before. Minturn had gone down with the *Titanic*.

He dropped his parcels then. His heart gave an enormous leap of joy.

He saw her face—the face of his wife—look through him.

But the child gazed straight into his eyes. She *saw* him.

[194]

The next thing he knew was that he heard something tinkling . . . far, far away. It sounded miles below him—inside him—he was sounding himself—all utterly bewildering—like a bell. It *was* a bell.

Milly stopped down and picked the parcels up. Her face shone with happiness and laughter. . . .

But a man came in soon after, a man with a ridiculous, solemn face, a pencil and a notebook. He wore a dark blue helmet. Behind him came a string of other men. They carried something . . . something . . . he could not see exactly what it was. But, when he pressed forward through the laughing throng to gaze upon it, he dimly made out two eyes, a nose, a chin, a deep red smear, and a pair of folded hands upon an overcoat. A woman's form fell down upon them then, and he heard soft sounds of children weeping strangely . . . and other sounds . . . as of familiar voices laughing . . . laughing gaily.

'They'll join us presently. It goes like a flash . . .'

And, turning with great happiness in his heart, he saw that Sir James had said it, holding Palmer by the arm as with some natural yet unexpected love of sympathetic friendship.

'Come on,' said Palmer, smiling like a man who accepts a gift in universal fellowhip, 'let's help 'em. They'll never understand. . . . Still, we can always try.'

The entire throng moved up with laughter and amusement. It was a moment of hearty, genuine life at last. Delight and Joy and Peace were everywhere.

Then John Mudbury realised the truth—that he was dead.

THE STORY OF A DISAPPEARANCE AND AN APPEARANCE

by M. R. James

Montague Rhodes James (1862–1936) stands as
the great doyen of ghost story writers, and one of
the most influential forces in the genre. 'What first
interested me in ghosts?' he wrote later in his
career (in 1931). 'This I can tell you quite
definitely. In my childhood I chanced to see a toy
Punch and Judy set, with figures cut out in
cardboard. One of these was The Ghost. It was a
tall figure habited in white with an unnaturally
long and narrow head, also surrounded with white,
and a dismal visage. Upon this my conceptions of a
ghost were based, and for years it permeated my
dreams . . .' The veiled horrors of Punch and Judy
returned in this uncanny tale, which appeared in
his collection A *Thin Ghost, and others* (1919).

T he letters which I now publish were sent to me recently by a person who knows me to be interested in ghost stories. There is no doubt about their authenticity. The paper on which they are written, the ink, and the whole external aspect put their date beyond the reach of question.

The only point which they do not make clear is the identity of the writer. He signs with initials only, and as none of the envelopes of the letters are preserved, the surname of his correspondent—obviously a married brother—is as obscure as his own. No further preliminary explanation is needed, I think. Luckily the first letter supplies all that could be expected.

LETTER I

GREAT CHRISHALL, *Dec. 22, 1837.*

MY DEAR ROBERT,—It is with great regret for the enjoyment I am losing, and for a reason which you will deplore equally with myself, that I write to inform you that I am unable to join your circle for this Christmas: but you will agree with me that it is unavoidable when I say that I have within these few hours received a letter from Mrs. Hunt at B—, to the effect that our Uncle Henry has suddenly and mysteriously disappeared, and begging me to go down there immediately and join the search that is being made for him. Little as I, or you either, I think, have ever seen of Uncle, I naturally feel that this is not a request that can be regarded lightly, and accordingly I propose to go to B— by this afternoon's mail, reaching it late in the evening. I shall not go to the Rectory, but put up at the King's Head, and to which you may address letters. I enclose a small draft, which you will please make use of for the benefit of the young people. I shall write you daily (supposing me to be detained more than a single day) what goes on, and you may be sure, should the business be cleared up in time to permit of my coming to the Manor after all, I shall present myself. I have but a few minutes at disposal. With cordial greetings to you all, and many regrets, believe me, your affectionate Bro.,

W.R.

LETTER II

KING'S HEAD, *Dec. 23, '37.*

MY DEAR ROBERT,—In the first place, there is as yet no news of Uncle H., and I think you may finally dismiss any idea—I won't say hope—that I might after all 'turn up' for Xmas. However, my thoughts will be with you, and you have my best wishes for a really festive day. Mind that none of my nephews or nieces expend any fraction of their guineas on presents for me.

Since I got here I have been blaming myself for taking this affair of Uncle H. too easily. From what people here say, I gather that there is very little hope that he can still be alive; but whether it is accident or design that carried him off I cannot judge. The facts are these. On Friday the 19th, he went as usual shortly before five o'clock to read evening prayers at the Church; and when they were over the clerk brought him a message, in response to which he set off to pay a visit to a sick person at an outlying cottage the better part of two miles away. He paid the visit, and started on his return journey at about half-past six. This is the last that is known of him. The people here are very much grieved at his loss; he had been here many years, as you know, and though, as you also know, he was not the most genial of men, and had more than a little of the *martinet* in his composition, he seems to have been active in good works, and unsparing of trouble to himself.

Poor Mrs. Hunt, who has been his housekeeper ever since she left Woodley, is quite overcome: it seems like the end of the world to her. I am glad that I did not entertain the idea of taking quarters at the Rectory; and I have declined several kindly offers of hospitality from people in the place, preferring as I do to be independent, and finding myself very comfortable here.

You will, of course, wish to know what has been done in the way of inquiry and search. First, nothing was to be expected from investigation at the Rectory; and to be brief, nothing has transpired. I asked Mrs. Hunt—as others had done before—whether there was either any unfavourable symptom in her master such as might portend a sudden stroke, or attack of illness, or whether he had ever had reason to apprehend any such thing: but both she, and also his medical man, were clear that this was not the case. He was quite in his usual health. In the second place, natually, ponds and streams have been dragged, and fields in the neighbourhood which he is known to have visited last, have been searched—without result. I have myself talked to the parish clerk and—more important—have been to the house where he paid his visit.

There can be no question of any foul play on these people's part. The one man in the house is ill in bed and very weak: the wife and the children of course could do nothing themselves, nor is there the shadow of a probability that they or any of them should have agreed to decoy poor Uncle H. out in order that he might be attacked on the way back. They had told what they knew to several other inquirers already, but the woman repeated it to me. The Rector was looking just as usual: he wasn't very long with the sick man—'He ain't,' she said, 'like some what has a gift in prayer; but there, if we was all that way, 'owever would the chapel people get their living?' He left some money when he went away, and one of the children saw him cross the stile into the next field. He was dressed as he always was: wore his bands—I gather he is nearly the last man remaining who does so—at any rate in this district.

You see I am putting down everything. The fact is that I have nothing else to do, having brought no business papers with me; and, moreover, it serves to clear my own mind, and may suggest points which have been overlooked. So I shall continue to write all that passes, even to conversations if need be—you may read or not as you please, but pray keep the letters. I have another reason for writing so fully, but it is not a very tangible one.

You may ask if I have myself made any search in the fields near the cottage. Something—a good deal—has been done by others, as I mentioned; but I hope to go over the ground to-morrow. Bow Street has now been informed, and will send down by tonight's coach, but I do not think they will make much of the job. There is no snow, which might have helped us. The fields are all grass. Of course I was on the *qui vive* for any indication to-day both going and returning; but there was a thick mist on the way back, and I was not in trim for wandering about unknown pastures, especially on an evening when bushes looked like men, and a cow lowing in the distance might have been the last trump. I assure you, if Uncle Henry had stepped out from among the trees in a little copse which borders the path at one place, carrying his head under his arm, I should have been very little more uncomfortable than I was. To tell you the truth, I was rather expecting something of the kind. But I must drop my pen for the moment: Mr. Lucas, the curate, is announced.

Later. Mr Lucas has been, and gone, and there is not much beyond the decencies of ordinary sentiment to be got from him. I can see that he has given up any idea that the Rector can be alive, and that, so far as he can be, he is truly sorry. I can also discern that even in a more emotional person than Mr. Lucas, Uncle Henry was not likely to inspire strong attachment.

Besides Mr. Lucas, I have had another visitor in the shape of my Boniface—mine host of the 'King's Head'—who came to see whether I had everything I wished, and who really requires the pen of a Boz to do him justice. He was very solemn and weighty at first. 'Well, sir,' he said, 'I suppose we must bow our 'ead beneath the blow, as my poor wife had used to say. So far as I can gather there's been neither hide nor yet hair of out late respected incumbent scented out as yet; not that he was what the Scripture terms a hairy man in any sense of the word.'

I said—as well as I could—that I supposed not, but could not help adding that I had heard he was sometimes a little difficult to deal with. Mr. Bowman looked at me sharply for a moment, and then passed in a flash from solemn sympathy to impassioned declamation. 'When I think,' he said, 'of the language that man see fit to employ to me in this here parlour over no more a matter than a cask of beer—such a thing as I told him might happen any day of the week to a man with a family—though as it turned out he was quite under a mistake, and that I knew at the time, only I was that shocked to hear him I couldn't lay my tongue to the right expression.'

He stopped abruptly and eyed me with some embarrassment. I only said, 'Dear me, I'm sorry to hear you had any little differences: I suppose my uncle will be a good deal missed in the parish?' Mr. Bowman drew a long breath. 'Ah, yes!' he said; 'your uncle! You'll understand me when I say that for the moment it had slipped my remembrance that he was a relative; and natural enough, I must say, as it should, for as to you bearing any resemblance to—to him, the notion of any such a thing is clean ridiculous. All the same, 'ad I 'ave bore it in my mind, you'll be among the first to feel, I'm sure, as I should have abstained my lips, or rather I should *not* have abstained my lips with no such reflections.'

I assured him that I quite understood, and was going to have asked him some further questions, but he was called away to see after some business. By the way, you need not take it into your head that he has anything to fear from the inquiry into poor Uncle Henry's disappearance—though, no doubt, in the watches of the night it will occur to him that I think he has, and I may expect explanations to-morrow.

I must close this letter: it has to go by the late coach.

LETTER III

Dec. 25, '37.

MY DEAR ROBERT,—This is a curious letter to be writing on Christmas Day, and yet after all there is nothing much in it. Or there may be—you shall be the judge. At least, nothing decisive. The Bow Street men practically say that they have no clue. The length of time and the weather conditions have made all tracks so faint as to be quite useless: nothing that belonged to the dead man—I'm afraid no other word will do—has been picked up.

As I expected, Mr. Bowman was uneasy in his mind this morning;

quite early I heard him holding forth in a very distinct voice—purposely so, I thought—to the Bow Street officers in the bar, as to the loss that the town had sustained in their Rector, and as to the necessity of leaving no stone unturned (he was very great on this phrase) in order to come at the truth. I suspect him of being an orator of repute at convivial meetings.

When I was at breakfast he came to wait on me, and took an opportunity when handling a muffin to say in a low tone, 'I 'ope, sir, you recognize as my feelings towards your relative is not actuated by any taint of what you may call melignity—you can leave the room, Eliza, I will see the gentleman 'as all he requires with my own hands—I ask your pardon, sir, but you must be well aware a man is not always master of himself: and when that man has been 'urt in his mind by the application of expressions which I will go so far as to say 'ad not ought to have been made use of (his voice was rising all this time and his face growing redder); no, sir; and 'ere, if you will permit of it, I should like to explain to you in a very few words the exact state of the bone of contention. This cask—I might more truly call it a firkin—of beer—'

I felt it was time to interpose, and said that I did not see that it would help us very much to go into that matter in detail. Mr. Bowman acquiesced, and resumed more calmly:

'Well, sir, I bow to your ruling, and as you say, be that here or be it there, it don't contribute a great deal, perhaps, to the present question. All I wish you to understand is that I am as prepared as you are yourself to lend every hand to the business we have afore us, and—as I took the opportunity to say as much to the Orficers not three-quarters of an hour ago—to leave no stone unturned as may throw even a spark of light on this painful matter.'

In fact, Mr. Bowman did accompany us on our exploration, but though I am sure his genuine wish was to be helpful, I am afraid he did not contribute to the serious side of it. He appeared to be under the impression that we were likely to meet either Uncle Henry or the person responsible for his disappearance, walking about the fields, and did a great deal of shading his eyes with his hand and calling our attention, by pointing with his stick, to distant cattle and labourers. He held several long conversations with old women whom we met, and was very strict and severe in his manner, but on each occasion returned to our party saying, 'Well, I find she don't seem to 'ave no connexion with this sad affair. I think you may take it from me, sir, as there's little or no light to be looked for from that quarter; not without she's keeping somethink back intentional.'

We gained no appreciable result, as I told you at starting; the Bow Street men have left the town, whether for London or not I am not sure.

This evening I had company in the shape of a bagman, a smartish fellow. He knew what was going forward, but though he has been on the roads for some days about here, he had nothing to tell of suspicious characters—tramps, wandering sailors or gipsies. He was very full of a capital Punch and Judy Show he had seen this same day at W—, and asked if it had been here yet, and advised me by no means to miss it if it does come. The best Punch and the best Toby dog, he said, he had ever come across. Toby dogs, you know, are the last new thing in the shows. I have only seen one myself, but before long all the men will have them.

Now why, you will want to know, do I trouble to write all this to you? I am obliged to do it, because it has something to do with another absurd trifle (as you will inevitably say), which in my present state of rather unquiet fancy—nothing more, perhaps—I have to put down. It is a dream, sir, which I am going to record, and I must say it is one of the oddest I have had. Is there anything in it beyond what the bagman's talk and Uncle Henry's disappearance could have suggested? You, I repeat, shall judge: I am not in a sufficiently cool and judicial frame to do so.

It began with what I can only describe as a pulling aside of curtains: and I found myself seated in a place—I don't know whether indoors or out. There were people—only a few—on either side of me, but I did not recognize them, or indeed think much about them. They never spoke, but, so far as I remember, were all grave and pale-faced and looked fixedly before them. Facing me there was a Punch and Judy Show, perhaps rather larger than the ordinary ones, painted with black figures on a reddish-yellow ground. Behind it and on each side was only darkness, but in front there was a sufficiency of light. I was 'strung up' to a high degree of expectation and looked every moment to hear the pan-pipes and the Roo-too-too-it. Instead of that there came suddenly an enormous—I can use no other word—an enormous single toll of a bell, I don't know from how far off—somewhere behind. The little curtain flew up and the drama began.

I believe someone once tried to re-write Punch as a serious tragedy; but whoever he may have been, this performance would have suited him exactly. There was something Satanic about the hero. He varied his methods of attack: for some of his victims he lay in wait, and to see his horrible face—it was yellowish white, I may remark—peering round the wings made me think of the Vampyre in Fuseli's foul sketch. To others he was polite and carneying—particularly to the unfortunate alien who can only say *Shallabalah*—though what Punch said I never could catch. But with all of them I came to dread the moment of death. The crack of the stick on their skulls, which in the ordinary way delights me, had here a crushing sound as if the bone was giving way, and the victims quivered and kicked as they lay. The baby—it sounds more ridiculous as I go on—the baby, I am sure, was alive. Punch wrung its neck, and if the choke or squeak which it gave were not real, I know nothing of reality.

The stage got perceptibly darker as each crime was consummated, and at last there was one murder which was done quite in the dark, so that I could see nothing of the victim, and took some time to effect. It was accompanied by hard breathing and horrid muffled sounds, and after it Punch came and sat on the footboard and fanned himself and looked at his shoes, which were bloody, and hung his head on one side, and sniggered in so deadly a fashion that I saw some of those beside me cover their faces, and I would gladly have done the same. But in the meantime the scene behind Punch was clearing, and showed, not the usual house front, but something more ambitious—a grove of trees and the gentle slope of a hill, with a very natural—in fact, I should say a real—moon shining on it. Over this there rose slowly an object which I soon perceived to be a human figure with something peculiar about the head—what, I was unable at first to see. It did not stand on its feet, but began creeping or dragging itself across the middle distance towards Punch, who still sat back to it; and by this time, I may remark (though it did not occur to me at the moment) that all pretence of this being a puppet show had vanished. Punch was still Punch, it is true, but, like the others, was in some sense a live creature, and both moved themselves at their own will.

When I next glanced at him he was sitting in malignant reflection; but in another instant something seemed to attract his attention, and he first sat up sharply and then turned round, and evidently caught sight of the person that was approaching him and was in fact now very near. Then, indeed, did he show unmistakable signs of terror: catching up his stick, he rushed towards the wood, only just eluding the arm of his pursuer, which was suddenly flung out to intercept him.

It was with a revulsion which I cannot easily express that I now saw more or less clearly what this pursuer was like. He was a sturdy figure clad in black, and, as I thought, wearing bands: his head was covered with a whitish bag.

The chase which now began lasted I do not know how long, now among the trees, now along the slope of the field, sometimes both figures disappearing wholly for a few seconds, and only some uncertain sounds letting one know that they were still afoot. At length there came a moment when Punch, evidently exhausted, staggered in from the left and threw himself down among the trees. His pursuer was not long after him, and came looking uncertainly from side to side. Then, catching sight of the figure on the ground, he too threw himself down—his back was turned to the audience—with a swift motion twitched the covering from his head, and thrust his face into that of Punch. Everything on the instant grew dark.

There was one long, loud, shuddering scream, and I awoke to find myself looking straight into the face of—what in all the world do you think? but—a large owl, which was seated on my window-sill immediately opposite my bed-foot, holding up its wings like two shrouded arms. I caught the fierce glance of its yellow eyes, and then it was gone. I heard the single enormous bell again—very likely, as you are saying to yourself, the church clock; but I do not think so—and then I was broad awake.

All this, I may say, happened within the last half-hour. There was no probability of my getting to sleep again, so I got up, put on clothes enough to keep me warm, and am writing this rigmarole in the first hours of Christmas Day. Have I left out anything? Yes; there was no Toby dog, and the names over the front of the Punch and Judy booth were Kidman and Gallop, which were certainly not what the bagman told me to look out for.

By this time, I feel a little more as if I could sleep, so this shall be sealed and wafered.

LETTER IV

Dec. 26, '37.

MY DEAR ROBERT,—All is over. The body has been found. I do not make excuses for not having sent off my news by last night's mail, for the simple reason that I was incapable of putting pen to paper. The events that attended the discovery bewildered me so completely that I needed what I could get of a night's rest to enable me to face the situation at all. Now I can give you my journal of the day, certainly the strangest Christmas Day that ever I spent or am likely to spend.

The first incident was not very serious. Mr. Bowman had, I think, been keeping Christmas Eve, and was a little inclined to be captious: at least, he was not on foot very early, and to judge from what I could hear, neither men or maids could do anything to please him. The latter were certainly reduced to tears; nor am I sure that Mr. Bowman succeeded in preserving a manly composure. At any rate, when I came downstairs, it was in a broken voice that he wished me the compliments of the season, and a little later on, when he paid his visit of ceremony at breakfast, he was far from cheerful: even Byronic, I might almost say, in his outlook on life.

'I don't know,' he said, 'if you think with me, sir; but every Christmas as comes round the world seems a hollerer thing to me. Why, take an example now from what lays under my own eye. There's my servant Eliza—been with me now for going on fifteen years. I thought I could have placed my confidence in Eliza, and yet this very morning—Christmas morning too, of all the blessed days in the year—with the bells a ringing and—and—all like that—I say, this very morning, had it not have been for Providence watching over us all, that girl would have put—indeed I may go so far to say, 'ad put the cheese on your breakfast-table—' He saw I was about to speak, and waved his hand at me. 'It's all very well for you to say, 'Yes, Mr. Bowman, but you took away the cheese and locked it up in the cupboard,' which I did, and have the key here, or if not the actual key, one very much about the same size. That's true enough, sir, but what do you think is the effect of that action on me? Why, it's no exaggeration for me to say that the ground is cut from under my feet. And yet when I said as much to Eliza, not nasty, mind you, but just firm-like, what was my return? 'Oh,' she says: 'well,' she says, 'there wasn't no bones broke, I suppose.' Well, sir, it 'urt me, that's all I can say: it 'urt me, and I don't like to think of it now.'

There was an ominous pause here, in which I ventured to say something like, 'Yes, very trying,' and then asked at what hour the church service was to be. 'Eleven o'clock,' Mr. Bowman said with a heavy sigh. 'Ah, you won't have no such discourse from poor Mr. Lucas as what you would have done from our late Rector. Him and me may have had our little differences, and did do, more's the pity.'

I could see that a powerful effort was needed to keep him off the vexed question of the cask of beer, but he made it. 'But I will say this, that a better preacher, nor yet one to stand faster by his rights, or what he considered to be his rights—however, that's not the question now—I for one, never set under. Some might say, 'Was he an eloquent man?' and to that my answer would be: 'Well, there you've a better right per'aps to speak of your own uncle than what I have.' Others might ask, 'Did he keep a hold of his congregation?' and there again I should reply, 'That depends.' But as I say—yes, Eliza, my girl, I'm coming—eleven o'clock, sir, and you inquire for the King's Head pew.' I believe Eliza had been very near the door, and shall consider it in my vail.

The next episode was church: I felt Mr. Lucas had a difficult task in doing justice to Christmas sentiments, and also to the feeling of disquiet and regret which, whatever Mr. Bowman might say, was clearly prevalent. I do not think he rose to the occasion. I was uncomfortable. The organ wolved—you know what I mean: the wind died—twice in the Christman Hymn, and the tenor bell, I suppose owing to some negligence on the part of the ringers, kept sounding faintly about once in a minute during the sermon. The clerk sent up a man to see to it, but he seemed unable to do much. I was glad when it was over. There was an odd incident, too, before the service. I went in rather early, and came upon two men carrying the parish bier back to its place under the tower. From what I overheard them saying, it appeared that it had been put out by mistake, by someone who was not there. I also saw the clerk busy folding up a moth-eaten velvet pall— not a sight for Christmas Day.

I dined soon after this, and then, feeling disinclined to go out, took my seat by the fire in the parlour, with the last number of *Pickwick*, which I had been saving up for some days. I thought I could be sure of keeping awake over this, but I turned out as bad as our friend Smith. I suppose it was half-past two when I was roused by a piercing whistle and laughing and talking voices outside in the market-place. It was a Punch and Judy—I had no doubt the one that my bagman had seen at W—. I was half delighted, half not—the latter because my unpleasant dream came back to me so vividly; but, anyhow, I determined to see it through, and I sent Eliza out with a crown-piece to the performers and a request that they would face my window if they could manage it.

The show was a very smart new one; the names of the proprietors, I need hardly tell you, were Italian, Foresta and Calpigi. The Toby dog was there, as I had been led to expect. All B— turned out, but did not obstruct my view, for I was at the large first-floor window and not ten yards away.

The play began on the stroke of a quarter to three by the church clock. Certainly it was very good; and I was soon relieved to find that the disgust my dream had given me for Punch's onslaughts on his ill-starred visitors was only transient. I laughed at the demise of the Turncock, the Foreigner, the Beadle, and even the baby. The only drawback was the Toby dog's developing a tendency to howl in the wrong place. Something had occurred, I suppose, to upset him, and something considerable: for, I forget exactly at what point, he gave a most lamentable cry, leapt off the footboard, and shot away across the market-place and down a side street. There was a stage-wait, but only a brief one. I suppose the men decided that it was no good going after him, and that he was likely to turn up again at night.

We went on. Punch dealt faithfully with Judy, and in fact with all comers; and then came the moment when the gallows was erected, and the great scene with Mr. Ketch was to be enacted. It was now that something happened of which I can certainly not yet see the import fully. You have witnessed an execution, and know what the criminal's head looks like with the cap on. If you are like me, you never wish to think of it again, and I do not willingly remind you of it. It was just such a head as that, that I, from my somewhat higher post, saw in the inside of the show-box; but at first the audience did not see it. I expected it to emerge into their view, but instead of that there slowly rose for a few seconds an uncovered face, with an expression of terror upon it, of which I have never imagined the like. It seemed as if the man, whoever he was, was being forcibly lifted, with his arms somehow pinioned or held back, towards the little gibbet on the stage. I could just see the nightcapped head behind him. Then there was a cry and a crash. The whole showbox fell over backwards; kicking legs were seen among the ruins, and then two figures—as some said; I can only answer for one—were visible running at top speed across the square and disappearing in a lane which leads to the fields.

Of course everybody gave chase. I followed; but the pace was killing, and very few were in, literally, at the death. It happened in a chalk pit: the man went over the edge quite blindly and broke his neck. They searched everywhere for the other, until it occurred to me to ask whether he had ever left the market-place. At first everyone was sure that he had; but when we came to look, he was there, under the showbox, dead too.

But in the chalk pit it was that poor Uncle Henry's body was found, with a sack over the head, the throat horribly mangled. It was a peaked corner of the sack sticking out of the soil that attracted attention. I cannot bring myself to write in greater detail.

I forgot to say the men's real names were Kidman and Gallop. I feel sure I have heard them, but no one here seems to know anything about them.

I am coming to you as soon as I can after the funeral. I must tell you when we meet what I think of it all.

THE SCULPTOR'S ANGEL

by Marie Corelli

Marie Corelli (pseudonym of Mary Mackay,
1855–1924) was much derided but tremendously
successful during her lifetime, with several of her
novels like *Thelma* exceeding 50 editions each. Her
short stories are now similarly neglected, but one of
the best examples of her style is this story, taken
from her collection *The Love of Long Ago* (1920).

'You are a great artist, my son'—said the Abbot, with a
favouring smile—'and, what is far better, you are noble and
pure-hearted. And to you we entrust the high task of filling
the vacant niche in our church with an Angel of Peace and Blessing.
We will give you all possible freedom and leisure for the work, so that
you may complete it before Christmas. On the Feast of the Nativity of
our Blessed Lord we shall hope, God willing, to see your Angel in the
chancel.'

He, the renowned and wellnigh saintly head of one of the most
famous among England's early monasteries, spoke with an authoritative dignity which gave his words, though gently uttered, the weight
of a command, and the monk Anselmus whom he addressed heard
him in submissive silence. They were standing together in one of the
side chapels of a magnificent Abbey Church—the creation of devout
and prayerful men who gave their highest thought and most fervent
toil to the service and praise of their Maker, and the days were those

when implicit belief in a Divine Power, strong to guard and to defend the right, was the chief saving grace of the nation. The blind and unruly passions of that age were held in salutary check by the spiritual force and sanctity of the Church—and neither priest nor layman then foresaw the coming time of terror when desecrating hands should violate and pillage the holy shrines so patiently upbuilt to the honour and glory of God, leaving of them nothing but the ruins of their grandeur—the melancholy emblems of a faith more ruined even than they.

'You will'—continued the Abbot—'have your time to yourself— that is, of course, such time as is not occupied by the holy services, and we will take good care that nothing shall disturb the flow of what must be a truly divine inspiration. Yes, my son!—all labour is divine— and our best thoughts come from God alone, so that we of ourselves dare claim no merit. In the making of an Angel's likeness angels must surely guide the sculptor's hand—and bring his work to ultimate perfection! Is this not so? You hear me?—you understand?'

Anselmus had remained mute, but now he raised his bent head. He was not a young man—youth seemed to have passed him by in haste and left him old before his time. His face was worn and thin, and showed deep furrows of pain and sorrow—only his eyes, sunken, yet bright and almost feverish in their lustre, flashed with the smouldering fires of suppressed and dying energy.

'I hear—and I understand'—he answered, slowly—'But why not choose a better man—a better sculptor? I am not worthy.'

The Abbot laid a kindly hand upon his arm.

'Who among us is more worthy?' he said—'Have you not bestowed upon us the treasures of your genius, and do we not owe much of the greatest beauty of our Abbey Church to your designs? Good son, humility is becoming in you as in us all—each one of us is indeed unworthy so far as he himself is concerned—but your gift of art is from God, and therefore of its worthiness neither you nor I must presume to doubt! It is a gift that you are bound to use for highest purpose—need I say more? You accept the task?'

'Father, when you command I must obey'—replied the monk— 'Nevertheless, I say I am not worthy of so much as the passing dream of an Angel!—but to satisfy you and our brethren I will do my best.'

'That best will be sufficient for us'—said the Abbot—'And while you work, you must relax a little in the rigorous discipline to which you so constantly submit yourself by your own choice. You fast too long and sleep too lightly—take more food and rest, Anselmus!—or the spirit will chafe the flesh with so much sharpness that the end will be disaster to both brain and body. Ease and freedom are as air and light to the artist—we give you both, my son, as far as may be given without trespass against our rules—work at your own time and pleasure—and we will make it a sacred charge to ourselves and our brethren not to break in upon the solitude of your studio—we will leave you alone with your Angel!'

He nodded, smiling graciously—and, making the sign of the cross in the air, paced slowly out of the chapel into the nave, and out of the nave again into the cloisters beyond, where among the many arches his tall and stately figure in its flowing robes disappeared.

The monk Anselmus stood for a few moments gazing after him— then with a deep sigh that was almost a groan, turned back into the deeper and more shadowed seclusion of the chapel, where with a movement of utter abandonment and despair he threw himself on his knees before the great Crucifix which had lately been sent as a gift to the monastery from the Holy Father in Rome.

'O God, God!' he prayed, under his breath—'Have mercy upon me, Thy wicked and treacherous servant! Lift from my soul the heavy burden of its secret sin! Teach me the way to win Thy pardon and recover the peace that I have lost! Lighten my darkness, for the shadow of my crime is ever black before my eyes! Spare me, O Redeemer of souls!—for my remorse is greater than I can bear!'

He covered his face with his hands, and crouched rather than knelt before the sculptured figure of the crucified Christ, shuddering with the suppressed agony which seemed to rack his body with positive physical pain. His own thoughts whipped him as with a million lashes—they drove him through every memory of the past, sparing no detail, as they had driven him remorselessly over and over again till at times he had felt himself almost on the verge of madness. He looked back to his early days of boyhood and manhood in Rome, when as a young and ardent student of art, working under one of the master sculptors of that period, he had hewn life out of senseless marble with a power and perfection which had astonished his fellows in the school—he remembered how just when the wreath of fame seemed his to win and to hold, he had suddenly become possessed and inspired by an enthusiastic faith and exaltation towards the highest things—a faith and exaltation which had moved him to consecrate his life and genius to the Church—and how, convinced of his vocation, he had voluntarily severed all ties of natural affection, leaving father, mother and home to take the monastic vows and devote himself to the service of God, and how, when this was done, he had gladly joined a band of earnest and devoted brethren who were sent from Rome to England to assist by their labours the completion and perfecting of one of the greatest abbeys ever founded in Britain. And then he recalled the almost passionate love of his work which had filled his brain and strengthened his hands when he first saw the splendid church and monastery, a vision of architectural magnificence and purity; lifting its towers heavenward in the midst of a landscape so peaceful and fair, so set about with noble trees and broad green fields and crystal streams that it seemed like an earthly realization of the dream of Paradise. And he had laboured so lovingly and patiently, and done so much to adorn and beautify the sacred shrine, that he had endeared himself greatly to the Abbot, who knew that in Anselmus he had a sculptor of rare genius—one who if he had chosen to follow a worldly career rather than embrace the religious life, would have made a name not easily forgotten. As it was, however, he seemed entirely content—he was as careful in his religious rule as in his art labours—and the wonderful chancel screen which he, alone and unaided, had wrought out of the native stone of which the monastery itself was built, was not more perfect than the discipline and obedience to which he had submitted himself for many peaceful years. Then—all suddenly—the great test presented itself—the fiery trial from which he did not come out unscathed. And thus it happened:-

Among his many duties he was sent out from the monastery twice every week among the scattered villages lying about the church lands to inquire into the needs of the sick and the poor—and on one of these occasions he met the fate that befalls all men sooner or later— love. A mere glance, a touch of hands—and the whole bulwark of a life can be swept away by the storm of a sudden irresistible passion— and so, unhappily, it chanced to the monk Anselmus. And yet it was only a very loving, foolish, trusting little maid, who had in all ignorance and innocence beguiled him from his monastic vows—a little peasant, with cheeks like the wild rose and eyes blue as the summer sea, whom he had found tending unaided upon an aged and sick woman, her grandmother, working for her uncomplainingly, and keeping the poor cottage in which they lived clean and sweet as a lady's bower, though there was hardly any food to share between them. Touched to the earth by the sight of so young and fair a creature

[212]

bearing her daily lot of hard privation with such gentle patience and content, Anselmus brought much needed relief from the monastery—medicines and wine for the aged sufferer, and supplies of bread and new milk and eggs and fowls for the better help and sustenance of the girl, who, however, asked for no assistance, and could hardly be induced to accept it even from the bounty of Mother Church. And Anselmus saw her again and yet again—together they talked of many things, and often at the monk's request she would walk with him from her cottage door through the long deeply-shaded avenue of thickly-branched trees that led to the gates of the monastery—till at last—one fateful evening, when she had accompanied him thus and was about to turn back alone, his long-suppressed man's heart arose within him, and yielding to a reckless impulse, he caught her in his arms. Their lips met—and as he felt the tender, clinging warmth of that first kiss of love, he suddenly experienced a sense of happiness he had never yet known—an ecstasy so intense that it seemed to lift him to a heaven far beyond even that of which he had dreamed in long nightly vigils of prayer.

This was the beginning of many secret meetings—meetings fraught with fear and joy. He, the ascetic monk, scholar and rigid disciplinarian in all the duties of an exacting religious Order, became an ardent, passionate and selfish lover—while she, poor child, overcome and carried away by the burning warmth of his eager caresses and words of endearment, asked nothing better than to be loved by him, and in return loved him herself with all the strength and devotion of her fond little heart and soul. Their dream-like idyll of forbidden love was brief; Anselmus, like the rest of his sex, soon tired of what he had too easily obtained, and in order to escape from the tender tie he had so willingly fastened upon himself, began, somewhat late in the day, to consider the dangers he ran by his unlawful conduct. His own safety and convenience now seemed to him of far greater importance than the peace or the happiness of the loving soul he had set himself to conquer and contaminate—and the more he dwelt upon his position the more irksome and unbearable it proved. One day, goaded beyond endurance by her gentle solicitude and wonderment at his altered manner, he harshly told her that they must meet no more.

'I have,' he said, 'committed an unpardonable sin in allowing myself to be entangled by your company—I must do penance for it with many years of fasting and of prayer. You tempted me!—it was not I!—*you*, with your appealing eyes and smile—*you* led me from the path of purity and honour—surely God knows it was more your fault than mine! I am sorry for you, poor child!'—here his accents were softer and almost paternal—'Forgive me for any wrong I have done you, and forget me! You are young—you will be happy yet!'

And then, having spoken as he thought reasonably and sensibly, and being too hardened to realize that his words were as death-blows dealt brutally on the tender heart of the girl who loved him, he waited for tears, reproaches, the bitter abandonment of grief and despair. But she gave him no trouble or pain of this kind. All she did was to raise her pretty sea-blue eyes to his face with a look in them which he never forgot—a look of sorrow, pity and pardon—then she caught his hand, kissed it, and turned away.

'Stay! Are you going?' he called—'Without one word?'

She made no reply. On she went, steadily—a little figure, glimmering whitely through the shadows of the bending trees—and without giving him so much as a backward glance, she disappeared.

He never saw her again. But that same week, when he went on his usual rounds of charity through the district, he learned that she had been found drowned among the reeds of the slowly flowing river that wound its clear ribbon of liquid light through the monastery lands. And the old grandmother she had so loyally cared for, and to whom she was more than the sunshine itself, hearing she was dead, would not believe it, and sat chattering stupidly all day about the hour when she would return to prepare the food for supper—and even when the small frail corpse was brought into the cottage dripping with its weight of water and clinging weed, she would not look at it or accept it as the body of her grandchild, but merely said—'No, no! It is not she—God gave her to me and He is good!—He would not rob me of her in my age—He would remember how much I need her!'

And the monk Anselmus, proffering spiritual consolation, trembled within himself, knowing the guilt of his own conscience which branded him as the murderer of the dead girl. But he kept his secret and betrayed no sign of his inward torment. And so, like all things sad or pleasant, humorous or pathetic, the little tragedy of a lost life was soon forgotten. No one ever knew that the poor drowned child had had a lover—and certainly no one in their wildest conjectures would have suspected that a monk could be that lover—a monk of austere reputation, who was sometimes called by his brethen 'our heavenly sculptor, Anselmus.'

Years passed—and his sin had never found him out, save in secret hours when the rememberance of his little dead love's last look haunted him with a kind of ghostly terror, and he could feel her last kiss upon his hand like a scorching coal of fire. Just in these latter days the thought of her had been so prominent in his brain as to leave him no peace. There was no especial reason why he should perpetually dwell upon the recollection of her sea-blue eyes and child's smile—yet somehow he could not shut her memory from his mind. And it was because of this constant remorseful impression and the knowledge of the irreparable wrong he had wrought upon her, that he had almost involuntarily told the Abbot that he was unworthy to perform the task for which he was commissioned, namely, to fill the last remaining empty niche in the chancel with the statue of an Angel. Burdened with the hidden weight of his sin, and feeling that even in his most rigorous fastings and penances he was nothing more than a hypocrite in the sight of the all All-Knowing God, he wrestled with himself in prayer, and with tears, but all in vain. And even now, abased in supplication before the crucifix, he felt no answering thrill of hope or consolation, so that when he rose from his knees it was with a kind of desperate resignation to the inevitable—a resolve to do the work he was set to do, not with pride or gladness, but by way of punishment. In this spirit—so far removed from the joyous elation of an artist who knows that his hand can accomplish what his brain conceives, he began his labours. Carefully taking the exact measurement of the niche to be filled, he made a similarly-sized one of rough wood and set it up in his own workshop or studio, so that he might study its height and breadth and try to realize within his mind the attitude and appearance the 'Angel' should assume. Sitting opposite to it, and looking attentively at its interior vacancy, he saw that the figure would have to be life-size—and he presently began to draw on paper in charcoal the suggestion of a form and face, but without success or satisfaction in any actual conception.

'It is not for me to see divine things!' he said, bitterly—'Such inspiration as I once had is killed at its very source by sin! Shame on my weak soul that it should be trapped by a woman's eyes! If she had not looked at me—if her smile had not been so sweet!—if she had resisted my passion, she might have saved herself and me!'

So he argued—as Adam argued before him—'The woman tempted me.' So will men, in their pitiless egotism, argue in their own defence till time shall be no more.

All that first afternoon of attempted 'work' he sat, weary and puzzled, alternately gazing at the empty niche and at the paper on his drawing-board, where as yet he had only traced a few unmeaning lines. The sun began to sink, and through the broad mullioned windows of his monastic studio he saw the western sky glowing like melted rubies in a belt of sapphire blue. The bright glow flared dazzlingly upon his eyes and made them ache—he covered them with one hand for a minute's space. Then, uncovering them again, he looked away from the sunset light towards the niche he had been studying all day, and—looking—uttered a smothered cry of mingled terror and rapture, and fell on his knees! For the niche was no longer empty—an Angel stood within it!—a Figure delicate, brilliant and surpassingly beautiful, with folded wings like rays of light on either side, and a Face fair, radiant and full of an exquisite tenderness such as is never seen on any features of mere mortality. Awed and over-whelmed beyond all power of speech, Anselmus, kneeling, gazed upward at the ravishing Vision which bent its star-like eyes upon him with a look of divine and affectionate compassion. The red glow of the sunset deepened, and within the studio all the lights of heaven seemed transfused, circling gloriously around the one white uplifted Wonder that shone forth from the niche like a lily illumined with some pale hidden fire—then almost mechanically—Anselmus groped for his pencil and his drawing-board, and trembling with fear, essayed to make a hasty similitude of the gracious Loveliness which, like a beautiful dream, confronted him. But, gradually as the sunset-light faded into grey shadow, the vision faded also—and by the time darkness began to steal slowly over all visible things, it had vanished! In a kind of mingled ecstasy and anguish Anselmus rose slowly from his kneeling attitude—the Angelus was ringing—it was time for him to leave his work for the day and betake himself to prayer and vigil. Like a man too suddenly awakened from deep sleep he walked slowly, absorbed in thought, and the brethren who watched him enter his choir-stall to join them in the singing of the vespers, glanced at each other with meaning in their looks—one or two murmuring to each other—'Our Anselmus is at work! He has the air of one inspired by Heaven!'

The next morning dawned fair and bright, and as soon as the light had fully come Anselmus hastened to his studio. Full of an almost feverish haste and eagerness, he caught up the drawing he had attempted—the picture of the visionary Angel—but alas!—there was nothing suggestive enough for any attempt at further elaboration or completion, and he flung it aside with a sigh of bitter disappointment. The sun peeped sparkling through the windows, shooting rays of light along the stone floor—and Anselmus, seating himself in his accustomed working place, slowly and half-fearfully raised his eyes toward the niche which on the previous night had held, as he now thought, a dream of his own brain—then—he caught his breath and remained still, not daring to move—for there again—there stood the Angel! In full daylight—and whiter than the whitest cloud tipped by the sun— there, with folded wings and divine, inscrutable smile it waited, as though it sought to be commanded—its delicate hands outstretched in an attitude of mingled protection and blessing! And now Anselmus did not kneel—for, more than ever convinced that this miraculous sight was the chimera of his own mind, he resolved to turn it to use.

'It is my own creation!' he said—'A vision evoked from my own thoughts, and from my desire to fulfil the task our father Abbot has set upon me. Let me therefore work while it is day—' And he did not finish the sentence: 'For the night cometh when no man can work.'

He began to draw—and everything came to him easily as in the former days of his early skill and power—with light and facile touch he soon completed a rough outline of the form and luminous drapery of his heavenly visitant—and then—then, when he attempted to get some idea of the divinely fair face and features his hand trembled—he looked again and again, and his heart suddenly failed him! For surely he had seen those eyes before?—that wistful child's smile? Shuddering as with icy cold, he murmured:-

'God have mercy upon me! Spare me my brain, O Lord! Let me not go mad until my work is done! Is this Thy punishment?—and can the dead arise before Thy Judgment Day? It is not yet the time!—not yet!'

His eyes smarted with the pain of unshed tears as he lifted them to the Angel in the niche—a Vision silent as the light itself—but expressive of all sweetness—all patience. Seeing that it did not move, but remained quite still as though it were in very truth a model posed for his study and treatment, he fell to work again with a sort of passion that consumed his energies as though with a devouring fire.

Day after day he toiled unceasingly, giving himself scarcely any leisure for food or sleep, and for the first time in his life almost grudging the hours he was compelled to pass in the duties of his religious Order. Day after day, with miraculous fidelity, the Angel stood in the niche confronting him, and never stirred! Treating the vision as a delusion or imaginary creation of his own brain, he worked

[217]

from it steadily—knowing that it was a perfect presentment of the ideal 'Angel' he sought to create—and very soon after his drawings were made he began to mould the figure in clay. Slowly, but surely, it grew up in his hands towards a beautiful completeness—and still the Angel stayed with him, apparently watching with steadfast, sweet eyes the modelling of its own likeness.

More than a month passed in this way, and the Angel in the niche became so much a part of the life and work of Anselmus that he could not imagine himself able to accomplish any good thing without the influence of its shining presence. The autumn deepened into winter— the withered leaves fell in rustling heaps on the gravel-paths and disfigured the smooth green grass-walks round the monastery, and bitter winds blew from the north-east, bringing sudden gusts of sleet and snow. The bare room or studio where Anselmus worked became very cold—sometimes he felt a chill as of death upon him while modelling the figure of his 'Angel' in the damp clay. Yet from the niche where the heavenly Vision faithfully remained, streamed an unearthly light that was almost warmth, and Anselmus would have died rather than have left the spot for a better room in the monastery, which the Abbot had offered him in kindly solicitude for his health.

'We do not seek to know what you are doing'—he said—'nor would we look upon your work till you yourself summon us to see it finished. But you appear to suffer—you are worn to the merest shadow of a man!—let me entreat you, my son, to take more care and rest—or cease work for a while—'

'No, no!' interrupted Anselmus, excitedly—'I cannot cease work, or I must cease to live! I am well—quite well! Have no trouble concerning me—let me finish my task—or else the Angel'—here he smiled a strange, bewildered smile—'Yes!—the Angel may leave me!'

The Abbot was puzzled by his manner, but forbore to press any further advice upon him, though both he and all the brethren of the Abbey noticed with deep and regretful concern that their 'heavenly sculptor' seemed stricken with some strange mortal illness which, though he did not complain of any ailment, was visibly breaking him down.

Things went better for him, and he appeared to suffer less, when, having finished his model in the clay, he began to hew out his 'Angel' in stone. He was an adept at this kind of hard work, and the physical exertion needed for it did him good and restored to him something of his old vigour and elasticity. From dawn to dusk every day he worked steadily and ardently—and from dawn to dusk every day the radiant Vision filled the niche and adorned it with rays of light more brilliant than the sunbeams. From dawn to dusk the sweet, mysterious Angel-eyes watched him as he hammered and carved the rigid stone, forming it into an apparently pliable grace and beauty—till at last the day came when, having spent all his thought and energy on the last few fine perfecting touches—looking every moment at the delicate features, the eyes and divine smile of his visionary model, and making sure that he had rendered them as faithfully as only a great artist can, he realized that his task was done. Throwing down his tools, he fell on his knees, stretching out his hands in an agony of appeal. For there was now no longer any need to try and deceive himself—or to feign to his own accusing conscience that he had not recognized the face he had sculptured—the sweet lips he had so tenderly chiselled—the dimple in the soft cheek—the down-dropping eyelids—he knew it well!—it was the face of an Angel truly or the face of a Vision—but more than all it was the face of the little dead girl who had loved him and given him all her life.

'Angel of my soul!'—he murmured—'Angel of my dreams!—Spirit of my work!—Speak to me! Oh speak, and tell me why you are here!—why you have stayed so patiently and long!—you, who are the heavenly likeness of one whom I wronged!—why have you come to me?'

There followed a moment's silence—a silence so tense and deep as to be fraught with ineffable torment to the mind of the suffering man. Then—the answer came—in a voice sweeter than the sound of a crystal bell:—

'Because I love you!'

Thrilled by these words, and gazing upward, he met the sea-blue radiance of those angelic eyes in mingled fear and rapture.

'Because I love you!' repeated the Voice—'Because I have always loved you!'

He heard—incredulous.

'I am mad!—or dreaming!' he whispered, tremulously—'This Miracle speaks as She would have spoken!'

'Love is the only miracle!' went on the Voice—'It cannot die—it is immortal! Oh, my Beloved! Your sin before God was not the breaking of a religious vow but the breaking of a human heart—the ruin of a human life!—a heart that trusted you!—a life that gave itself to you!'

The unhappy monk wrung his hands in despair.

[219]

'Punish me!' he cried—'Wreak lightning vengeance now upon me, O Angel of the Most High! Slay me with one look of those sweet eyes, O spirit of my murdered love! Let me not live to lose the memory of this day!'

The figure of the Angel stirred—its folded wings quivered and began to expand slowly, like great fans of light on either side.

'Love has no vengeance in its hands!' said the Voice, in accents surpassingly tender—'All is pardoned, my Beloved!—all is finished save the story of our joy which no mortal shall ever know!—a joy beginning, but never ending! Out of my death I give you life—and for the wrong you wrought upon my soul, I bring you, in the Name of God, pardon and peace! Beloved, your work is done!'

And now the radiant Form rose slowly, like a fine mist coloured through by the rays of the sun—it floated out of the niche where it had stood so long and patiently—and soaring upward, upward—melted away on a flashing stream of light into vaporous air.

Late that evening, as Anselmus did not appear in his place at vespers, some of the brethren sought the Abbot's permission to go to his studio and see if anything ailed him. The Abbot himself readily accompanied them—and by the light of a pale moon they found their 'heavenly sculptor' lying unconscious before the empty niche—while, standing on a rough pedestal was the completed statue of an angel, more angelic in form and feature than any they had ever yet seen. Full of wonder and compassion, they raised the sculptor's senseless body and bore him to his cell, where after some hours he revived sufficiently to recognize his surroundings and to express with pathetic humility his gratitude for the Abbot's fatherly solicitude and the brethren's anxious care. He was too feeble and ill to suffer much converse, therefore they humoured him in his evident desire to be spared all praise for the noble work of art he had achieved. All he would say when the Abbot expressed his admiration and reverence for what he justly considered the most perfect statue of an angel that had ever adorned any church was—

'God made it—not I!'

And he lay quiet for many days, without the strength to move—till at last the hours wore peacefully on to the blessed time of Christ's Nativity. Anselmus, brooding on this, began to rouse himself from his painful torpor and feebleness—nothing should prevent him, he said, with gentle, smiling earnestness, from standing in the choir with his 'Angel' on Christmas Day!

So, when the glorious morning came he went to Mass, supported by two of the brethren, one on each side to guide his faltering steps—and took his own place, his stall being immediately opposite the niche where his sculptured Angel was now set up in all its glory—a beauteous figure so instinct with genius as to be almost living, stretching out its hands in Peace and Blessing. White, worn and weary, Anselmus was the centre of sorrowful interest among all the brethren who looked upon him—his thin, intellectual face and great burning eyes suggested some haunting tragedy in his brain—and they watched him in a kind of fear, feeling that he had about him the sense of something supernatural and strange.

The music surged around him, and the chanting voices of the monks made a deep, rhythmic wave of melody upon the air—the light through the stained-glass windows glittered and glowed, throwing long rays of purple and emerald, rose and blue across the steps of the altar, and Anselmus listened, looking at all things vaguely as one far off may look from some great height at the little plots of land and houses spread below—wondering within himself at the curious impression he had of unreality in all these sights and sounds, and more conscious of the statue of his Angel opposite to him than of anything else. The stately ritual went on till it reached the supreme moment of the oblation of the Host, when all were seated with heads bent in profound meditation and prayer. The bell rang, and the resonant voices of the brethren chanted solemnly—'Sanctus, Sanctus, Sanctus! Dominus Deus Sabaoth! Plein sunt cœli et terra gloria tua!'—when Anselmus, suddenly looking up, was struck across the eyes, as it were, by lightning. Thrilled by the shock, he sprang to his feet. There, on a shaft of dazzling luminance far brighter than the day, and poised on radiant wings between him and the statue he had wrought, was the Angel of his vision!—the Angel with the face of the little maiden he had wronged—the Angel of his inspiration—the Angel of his finished work! Ah, what tenderness now in the sea-blue eyes!—what sweetness in the divine smile!—what heavenly welcome in the outstretched arms and beckoning white hands!

'Beloved!—Beloved!' he cried—then with a choking sound in his throat he staggered and fell foward. The chanting ceased—the Abbot at the altar paused, with the sacred chalice in his hand—the brethren gathered hastily round the prone figure in consternation and sorrow— but all was over. Anselmus was dead.

A cloud swept across the sun, and for a moment the chancel was

[221]

darkened—then, while two of the monks knelt by the fallen man and gently covered his face, the Abbot, with tears rising thickly in his eyes, again lifted the Chalice. The sun came out anew, shining brilliantly through the chancel and lighting up the Angel-statue with a sudden whiteness as of snow—and with trembling voices the brethren resumed the interrupted service, making the arches of the noble Abbey resound and respond to a mystic Truth which the world is slow to recognize—

Benedictus qui venit in nomine Domini!

THE SNOW

by Hugh Walpole

Sir Hugh Walpole (1884–1941) is best known for
his novels of cathedral life, and the large 'Herries'
Lakeland saga. A macabre vein runs through much
of his work, and he was a regular contributor to
Cynthia Asquith's early ghost anthologies. She
commissioned 'The Snow' for the *Shudders* volume
in 1929; and the story also later appeared in his
collection *All Souls' Night* (1933).

The second Mrs. Ryder was a young woman not easily frightened, but now she stood in the dusk of the passage leaning
back against the wall, her hand on her heart, looking at the
grey-faced window beyond which the snow was steadily falling against
the lamplight.

The passage where she was led from the study to the dining-room,
and the window looked out on to the little paved path that ran at the
edge of the Cathedral green. As she stared down the passage she
couldn't be sure whether the woman was there or no. How absurd of
her! She knew the woman was not there. But if the woman was not,
how was it that she could discern so clearly the old-fashioned grey
cloak, the untidy grey hair and the sharp outline of the pale cheek and
pointed chin? Yes, and more than that, the long sweep of the grey
dress, falling in folds to the ground, the flash of a gold ring on the
white hand. No. No. NO. This was madness. There was no one and
nothing there. Hallucination . . .

[223]

Very faintly a voice seemed to come to her: 'I warned you. This is for the last time. . . .'

The nonsense! How far now was her imagination to carry her? Tiny sounds about the house, the running of a tap somewhere, a faint voice from the kitchen, these and something more had translated themselves into an imagined voice. 'The last time . . .'

But her terror was real. She was not normally frightened by anything. She was young and healthy and bold, fond of sport, hunting, shooting, taking any risk. Now she was truly *stiffened* with terror—she could not move, could not advance down the passage as she wanted to and find light, warmth, safety in the dining-room. All the time the snow fell steadily, stealthily, with its own secret purpose, maliciously, beyond the window in the pale glow of the lamplight.

Then unexpectedly there was noise from the hall, opening of doors, a rush of feet, a pause and then in clear beautiful voices the well-known strains of 'Good King Wenceslas.' It was the Cathedral choir boys on their regular Christmas round. This was Christmas Eve. They always came just at this hour on Christmas Eve.

With an intense, almost incredible relief she turned back into the hall. At the same moment her husband came out of the study. They stood together smiling at the little group of mufflered, becoated boys who were singing, heart and soul in the job, so that the old house simply rang with their melody.

Reassured by the warmth and human company, she lost her terror. It had been her imagination. Of late she had been none too well. That was why she had been so irritable. Old Doctor Bernard was no good: he didn't understand her case at all. After Christmas she would go to London and have the very best advice . . .

Had she been well she could not, half an hour ago, have shown such miserable temper over nothing. She knew that it was over nothing and yet that knowledge did not make it any easier for her to restrain herself. After every bout of temper she told herself that there should never be another—and then Herbert said something irritating, one of his silly muddle-headed stupidities, and she was off again!

She could see now as she stood beside him at the bottom of the staircase, that he was still feeling it. She had certainly half an hour ago said some abominably rude personal things—things that she had not at all meant—and he had taken them in his meek, quiet way. Were he not so meek and quiet, did he only pay her back in her own coin, she would never lose her temper. Of that she was sure. But who wouldn't be irritated by that meekness and by the only reproachful thing that he ever said to her: 'Elinor understood me better, my dear'? To throw the first wife up against the second! Wasn't that the most tactless thing that a man could possibly do? And Elinor, that worn elderly woman, the very opposite of her own gay, bright, amusing self! That was why Herbert had loved her, because she was gay and bright and young. It was true that Elinor had been devoted, that she had been so utterly wrapped up in Herbert that she lived only for him. People were always recalling her devotion, which was sufficiently rude and tactless of them.

Well, she could not give anyone that kind of old-fashioned sugary devotion; it wasn't in her, and Herbert knew it by this time.

Nevertheless she loved Herbert in her own way, as he must know, know it so well that he ought to pay no attention to the bursts of temper. She wasn't well. She would see a doctor in London . . .

The little boys finished their carols, were properly rewarded, and tumbled like feathery birds out into the snow again. They went into the study, the two of them, and stood beside the big open log-fire. She put her hand up and stroked his thin beautiful cheek.

'I'm so sorry to have been cross just now, Bertie. I didn't mean half I said, you know.'

But he didn't, as he usually did, kiss her and tell her that it didn't matter. Looking straight in front of him, he answered:

'Well, Alice, I do wish you wouldn't. It hurts, horribly. It upsets me more than you think. And it's growing on you. You make me miserable. I don't know what to do about it. And it's all about nothing.'

Irritated at not receiving the usual commendation for her sweetness in making it up again, she withdrew a little and answered:

'Oh, all right. I've said I'm sorry. I can't do any more.'

'But tell me,' he insisted, 'I want to know. What makes you so angry, so suddenly?—and about nothing at all.'

She was about to let her anger rise, her anger at his obtuseness, obstinacy, when some fear checked her, a strange unanalysed fear, as though someone had whispered to her, 'Look out! This is the last time!'

'It's not altogether my own fault,' she answered, and left the room.

She stood in the cold hall, wondering where to go. She could feel the snow falling outside the house and shivered. She hated the snow, she hated the winter, this beastly, cold dark English winter that went on and on, only at last to change into a damp, soggy English spring.

It had been snowing all day. In Polchester it was unusual to have so heavy a snowfall. This was the hardest winter that they had known for many years.

When she urged Herbert to winter abroad—which he could quite easily do—he answered her impatiently; he had the strongest affection for this poky dead-and-alive Cathedral town. The Cathedral seemed to be precious to him; he wasn't happy if he didn't go and see it every day! She wouldn't wonder if he didn't think more of the Cathedral than he did of herself. Elinor had been the same; she had even written a little book about the Cathedral, about the Black Bishop's Tomb and the stained glass and the rest . . .

What was the Cathedral after all? Only a building!

She was standing in the drawing-room looking out over the dusky ghostly snow to the great hulk of the Cathedral that Herbert said was like a flying ship, but to herself was more like a crouching beast licking its lips over the miserable sinners that it was for ever devouring.

As she looked and shivered, feeling that in spite of herself her temper and misery were rising so that they threatened to choke her, it seemed to her that her bright and cheerful fire-lit drawing-room was suddenly open to the snow. It was exactly as though cracks had appeared everywhere, in the ceiling, the walls, the windows, and that through these cracks the snow was filtering, dribbling in little tracks of wet down the walls, already perhaps making pools of water on the carpet.

This was of course imagination, but it was a fact that the room was most dreadfully cold although a great fire was burning and it was the cosiest room in the house.

Then, turning, she saw the figure standing by the door. This time there could be no mistake. It was a grey shadow, and yet a shadow with form and outline—the untidy grey hair, the pale face like a moon-lit leaf, the long grey clothes, and something obstinate, vindictive, terribly menacing in its pose.

She moved and the figure was gone; there was nothing there and the room was warm again, quite hot in fact. But young Mrs. Ryder, who had never feared anything in all her life save the vanishing of her youth, was trembling so that she had to sit down, and even then her trembling did not cease. Her hand shook on the arm of her chair.

She had created this thing out of her imagination of Elinor's hatred of her and her own hatred of Elinor. It was true that they had never met, but who knew but that the spiritualists were right, and Elinor's spirit, jealous of Herbert's love for her, had been there driving them apart, forcing her to lose her temper and then hating her for losing it? Such things might be! But she had not much time for speculation. She was preoccupied with her fear. It was a definite, positive fear, the kind of fear that one has just before one goes under an operation. Someone or something was threatening her. She clung to her chair as though to leave it were to plunge into disaster. She looked around her every-where; all the familiar things, the pictures, the books, the little tables, the piano were different now, isolated, strange, hostile, as though they had been won over by some enemy power.

She longed for Herbert to come and protect her; she felt most kindly to him. She would never lose her temper with him again—and at that same moment some cold voice seemed to whisper in her ear: 'You had better not. It will be for the last time.'

At length she found courage to rise, cross the room and go up to dress for dinner. In her bedroom courage came to her once more. It was certainly very cold, and the snow, as she could see when she looked between her curtains, was falling more heavily than ever, but she had a warm bath, sat in front of her fire and was sensible again.

For many months this odd sense that she was watched and accompanied by someone hostile to her had been growing. It was the stronger perhaps because of the things that Herbert told her about Elinor; she was the kind of woman, he said, who, once she loved anyone, would never relinquish her grasp; she was utterly faithful. He implied that her tenacious fidelity had been at times a little difficult.

'She always said,' he added once, 'that she would watch over me until I rejoined her in the next world. Poor Elinor!' he sighed. 'She had a fine religious faith, stronger than mine, I fear.'

It was always after one of her tantrums that young Mrs. Ryder had been most conscious of this hallucination, this dreadful discomfort of feeling that someone was near you who hated you—but it was only during the last week that she began to fancy that she actually saw anyone, and with every day her sense of this figure had grown stronger.

It was, of course, only nerves, but it was one of those nervous afflictions that became tiresome indeed if you did not rid yourself of it. Mrs. Ryder, secure now in the warmth and intimacy of her bedroom, determined that henceforth everything should be sweetness and light. No more tempers! Those were the things that did her harm.

Even though Herbert were a little trying, was not that the case with every husband in the world? And was it not Christmas time? Peace and Good Will to men! Peace and Good Will to Herbert!

They sat down opposite to one another in the pretty little dining-room hung with Chinese woodcuts, the table gleaming and the amber curtains richly dark in the firelight.

But Herbert was not himself. He was still brooding, she supposed, over their quarrel of the afternoon. Weren't men children? Incredible the children that they were!

So when the maid was out of the room she went over to him, bent down and kissed his forehead.

'Darling . . . you're still cross, I can see you are. You mustn't be. Really you mustn't. It's Christmas time and, if I forgive you, you must forgive me.'

'You forgive me?' he asked, looking at her in his most aggravating way. 'What have you to forgive me for?'

Well, that was really too much. When she had taken all the steps, humbled her pride.

She went back to her seat, but for a while could not answer him because the maid was there. When they were alone again she said, summoning all her patience:

'Bertie dear, do you really think that there's anything to be gained by sulking like this? It isn't worthy of you. It isn't really.'

He answered her quietly.

'Sulking? No, that's not the right word. But I've got to keep quiet. If I don't I shall say something I'm sorry for.' Then, after a pause, in a low voice, as though to himself: 'These constant rows are awful.'

Her temper was rising again; another self that had nothing to do with her real self, a stranger to her and yet a very old familiar friend.

'Don't be so self-righteous,' she answered, her voice trembling a little. 'These quarrels are entirely my own fault, aren't they?'

'Elinor and I never quarrelled,' he said, so softly that she scarcely heard him.

'No! Because Elinor thought you perfect. She adored you. You've often told me. I don't think you perfect. I'm not perfect either. But we've both got faults. I'm not the only one to blame.'

'We'd better separate,' he said, suddenly looking up. 'We don't get on now. We used to. I don't know what's changed everything. But, as things are, we'd better separate.'

She looked at him and knew that she loved him more than ever, but because she loved him so much she wanted to hurt him, and because he had said that he thought he could get on without her she was so angry that she forgot all caution. Her love and her anger helped one another. The more angry she became the more she loved him.

'I know why you want to separate,' she said. 'It's because you're in love with someone else. ('How funny,' something inside her said. 'You don't mean a word of this.') You've treated me as you have and then you leave me.'

'I'm not in love with anyone else,' he answered her steadily, 'and you know it. But we are so unhappy together that it's silly to go on . . . silly . . . The whole thing has failed.'

There was so much unhappiness, so much bitterness, in his voice that she realised that at last she had truly gone too far. She had lost him. She had not meant this. She was frightened and her fear made her so angry that she went across to him.

'Very well then . . . I'll tell everyone . . . what you've been. How you've treated me.'

'Not another scene,' he answered wearily. 'I can't stand any more. Let's wait. Tomorrow is Christmas Day . . .'

He was so unhappy that her anger with herself maddened her. She couldn't bear his sad, hopeless disappointment with herself, their life together, everything.

In a fury of blind temper she struck him; it was as though she were striking herself. He got up and without a word left the room. There was a pause, and then she heard the hall door close. He had left the house.

She stood there, slowly coming to her control again. When she lost her temper it was as though she sank under water. When it was all over she came one more to the surface of life, wondering where she'd been and what she had been doing. Now she stood there, bewildered, and then at once she was aware of two things, one that the room was bitterly cold and the other that someone was in the room with her.

This time she did not need to look around her. She did not turn at all, but only stared straight at the curtained windows, seeing them very carefully, as though she were summing them up for some future analysis, with their thick amber folds, gold rod, white lines—and beyond them the snow was falling.

[229]

She did not need to turn, but, with a shiver of terror, she was aware that that grey figure who had, all these last weeks, been approaching ever more closely, was almost at her very elbow. She heard quite clearly: 'I warned you. That was the last time.'

At the same moment Onslow the butler came in. Onslow was broad, fat and rubicund—a good faithful butler with a passion for church music. He was a bachelor and, it was said, disappointed of women. He had an old mother in Liverpool to whom he was greatly attached.

In a flash of consciousness she thought of all these things when he came in. She expected him also to see the grey figure at her side. But he was undisturbed, his ceremonial complacency clothed him securely.

'Mr. Fairfax has gone out,' she said firmly. Oh, surely he must see something, feel something?

'Yes, Madam!' Then, smiling rather grandly: 'It's snowing hard. Never seen it harder here. Shall I build up the fire in the drawing-room, Madam?'

'No, thank you. But Mr. Fairfax's study . . .

'Yes, Madam. I only thought that as this room was so warm you might find it chilly in the drawing-room.'

This room warm, when she was shivering from head to foot; but holding herself lest he should see . . . She longed to keep him there, to implore him to remain; but in a moment he was gone, softly closing the door behind him.

Then a mad longing for flight seized her, and she could not move. She was rooted there to the floor, and even as, wildly trying to cry, to scream, to shriek the house down, she found that only a little whisper would come, she felt the cold touch of a hand on hers.

She did not turn her head: her whole personality, all her past life, her poor little courage, her miserable fortitude were summoned to meet this sense of approaching death which was as unmistakable as a certain smell, or the familiar ringing of a gong. She had dreamt in nightmares of approaching death and it had always been like this, a fearful constriction of the heart, a paralysis of the limbs, a choking sense of disaster like an anaesthetic.

'You were warned,' something said to her again.

She knew that if she turned she would see Elinor's face, set, white, remorseless. The woman had always hated her, been vilely jealous of her, protecting her wretched Herbert.

[230]

A certain vindictiveness seemed to release her. She found that she could move, her limbs were free.

She passed to the door, ran down the passage, into the hall. Where would she be safe? She thought of the Cathedral, where to-night there was a carol service. She opened the hall door and just as she was, meeting the thick, involving, muffling snow, she ran out.

She started across the green towards the Cathedral door. Her thin black slippers sank in the snow. Snow was everywhere—in her hair, her eyes, her nostrils, her mouth, on her bare neck, between her breasts.

'Help! Help! Help!' she wanted to cry, but the snow choked her. Lights whirled about her. The Cathedral rose like a huge black eagle and flew towards her.

She fell forward, and even as she fell a hand, far colder than the snow, caught her neck. She lay struggling in the snow and as she struggled there two hands of an icy fleshless chill closed about her throat.

Her last knowledge was of the hard outline of a ring pressing into her neck. Then she lay still, her face in the snow, and the flakes eagerly, savagely, covered her.

SMEE

by A.M. Burrage

Alfred McLelland Burrage (1889–1956) was
another prolific writer and contributor of short
stories in every conceivable genre to the pre-war
popular monthly magazines. His most controversial
novel *War is War* was published by Victor Gollancz
under the pseudonym 'Ex-Private X'. The same
alias was used on the now extremely rare collection
of ghost stories, *Someone in the Room* (1931), from
which 'Smee' is taken.

'No,' said Jackson, with a deprecatory smile, 'I'm sorry. I don't want to upset your game. I shan't be doing that because you'll have plenty without me. But I'm not playing any games of hide-and-seek.'

It was Christmas Eve, and we were a party of fourteen with just the proper leavening of youth. We had dined well; it was the season for childish games, and we were all in the mood for playing them—all, that is, except Jackson. When somebody suggested hide-and-seek there was rapturous and almost unanimous approval. His was the one dissentient voice.

It was not like Jackson to spoil sport or refuse to do as others wanted. Somebody asked him if he were feeling seedy.

'No,' he answered. 'I feel perfectly fit, thanks. But,' he added with a smile which softened without retracting the flat refusal, 'I'm not playing hide-and-seek.'

One of us asked him why not. He hesitated for some seconds before replying.

[232]

'I sometimes go and stay at a house where a girl was killed through playing hide-and-seek in the dark. She didn't know the house very well. There was a servant's staircase with a door to it. When she was pursued she opened the door and jumped into what she must have thought was one of the bedrooms—and she broke her neck at the bottom of the stairs.'

We all looked concerned, and Mrs. Fernley said:

'How awful! And you were there when it happened?'

Jackson shook his head very gravely. 'No,' he said, 'but I was there when something else happened. Something worse.'

'I shouldn't have thought anything could be worse.'

'This was,' said Jackson, and shuddered visibly. 'Or so it seemed to me.'

I think he wanted to tell the story and was angling for encouragement. A few requests which may have seemed to him to lack urgency, he affected to ignore and went off at a tangent.

'I wonder if any of you have played a game called "Smee". It's a great improvement on the ordinary game of hide-and-seek. The name derives from the ungrammatical colloquialism, "It's me." You might care to play if you're going to play a game of that sort. Let me tell you the rules.

'Every player is presented with a sheet of paper. All the sheets are blank except one, on which is written "Smee". Nobody knows who is "Smee" except "Smee" himself—or herself, as the case may be. The lights are then turned out and "Smee" slips from the room and goes off to hide, and after an interval the other players go off in search, without knowing whom they are actually in search of. One player meeting another challenges with the word "Smee" and the other player, if not the one concerned, answers "Smee".

'The real "Smee" makes no answer when challenged, and the second player remains quietly by him. Presently they will be discovered by a third player, who, having challenged and received no answer, will link up with the first two. This goes on until all the players have formed a chain, and the last to join is marked down for a forfeit. It's a good noisy, romping game, and in a big house it often takes a long time to complete the chain. You might care to try it; and I'll pay my forfeit and smoke one of Tim's excellent cigars here by the fire until you get tired of it.'

I remarked that it sounded a good game and asked Jackson if he had played it himself.

[233]

'Yes,' he answered; 'I played it in the house I was telling you about.'

'And *she* was there? The girl who broke—'

'No, no,' Mrs. Fernley interrupted. 'He told us he wasn't there when it happened.'

Jackson considered. 'I don't know if she was there or not. I'm afraid she was. I know that there were thirteen of us and there ought only to have been twelve. And I'll swear that I didn't know her name, or I think I should have gone clean off my head when I heard that whisper in the dark. No, you don't catch me playing that game, or any other like it, any more. It spoiled my nerve quite a while, and I can't afford to take long holidays. Besides, it saves a lot of trouble and inconvenience to own up at once to being a coward.'

Tim Vouce, the best of hosts, smiled around at us, and in that smile there was a meaning which is sometimes vulgarly expressed by the slow closing of an eye. 'There's a story coming,' he announced.

'There's certainly a story of sorts,' said Jackson, 'but whether it's coming or not—' He paused and shrugged his shoulders.

'Well, you're going to pay a forfeit instead of playing?'

'Please. But have a heart and let me down lightly. It's not just a sheer cussedness on my part.'

'Payment in advance,' said Tim, 'insures honesty and promotes good feeling. You are therefore sentenced to tell the story here and now.'

And here follows Jackson's story, unrevised by me and passed on without comment to a wider public:—

Some of you, I know, have run across the Sangstons. Christopher Sangston and his wife, I mean. They're distant connections of mine—at least, Violet Sangston is. About eight years ago they bought a house between the North and South Downs on the Surrey and Sussex border, and five years ago they invited me to come and spend Christmas with them.

It was a fairly old house—I couldn't say exactly of what period—and it certainly deserved the epithet 'rambling'. It wasn't a particularly big house, but the original architect, whoever he may have been, had not concerned himself with economising in space, and at first you could get lost in it quite easily.

Well, I went down for that Christmas, assured by Violet's letter that I knew most of my fellow-guests and that the two or three who might be strangers to me were all 'lambs'. Unfortunately, I'm one of the world's workers, and I couldn't get away until Christmas Eve, although the other members of the party had assembled on the preceding day. Even then I had to cut it rather fine to be there for dinner on my first night. They were all dressing when I arrived and I had to go straight to my room and waste no time. I may even have kept dinner waiting a bit, for I was last down, and it was announced within a minute of my entering the drawing-room. There was just time to say 'hullo' to everybody I knew, to be briefly introduced to the two or three I didn't know, and then I had to give my arm to Mrs. Gorman.

I mention this as the reason why I didn't catch the name of a tall dark, handsome girl I hadn't met before. Everything was rather hurried and I am always bad at catching people's names. She looked cold and clever and rather forbidding, the sort of girl who gives the impression of knowing all about men and the more she knows of them the less she likes them. I felt that I wasn't going to hit it off with this particular 'lamb' of Violet's, but she looked interesting all the same, and I wondered who she was. I didn't ask, because I was pretty sure of hearing somebody address her by name before very long.

Unluckily, though, I was a long way off her at table, and as Mrs. Gorman was at the top of her form that night I soon forgot to worry about who she might be. Mrs. Gorman is one of the most amusing women I know, an outrageous but quite innocent flirt, with a very sprightly wit which isn't always unkind. She can think half a dozen moves ahead in conversation just as an expert can in a game of chess. We were soon sparring, or, rather, I was 'covering' against the ropes, and I quite forgot to ask her in an undertone the name of the cold, proud beauty. The lady on the other side of me was a stranger, or had been until a few minutes since, and I didn't think of seeking information in that quarter.

There was a round dozen of us, including the Sangstons themselves, and we were all young or trying to be. The Sangstons themselves were the oldest members of the party and their son Reggie, in his last year at Marlborough, must have been the youngest. When there was talk of playing games after dinner it was he who suggested 'Smee'. He told us how to play it just as I've described it to you.

His father chipped in as soon as we all understood what was going to be required of us. 'If there are any games of that sort going on in the house,' he said, 'for goodness' sake be careful of the back stairs on the first-floor landing. There's a door to them and I've often meant to take it down. In the dark anybody who doesn't know the house very well might think they were walking into a room. A girl actually did break her neck on those stairs about ten years ago when the Ainsties lived here.'

I asked how it happened.

'Oh,' said Sangston, 'there was a party here one Christmas time and they were playing hide-and-seek as you propose doing. This girl was one of the hiders. She heard somebody coming, ran along the passage to get away, and opened the door of what she thought was a bedroom, evidently with the intention of hiding behind it while her pursuer went past. Unfortunately it was the door leading to the back stairs, and that staircase is as straight and almost as steep as the shaft of a pit. She was dead when they picked her up.'

We all promised for our own sakes to be careful. Mrs. Gorman said that she was sure nothing could happen to her, since she was insured by three different firms, and her next-of-kin was a brother whose consistent ill-luck was a byword in the family. You see, none of us had known the unfortunate girl, and as the tragedy was ten years old there was no need to pull long faces about it.

Well, we started the game almost immediately after dinner. The men allowed themselves only five minutes before joining the ladies, and then young Reggie Sangston went round and assured himself that the lights were out all over the house except in the servants' quarters and in the drawing-room where we were assembled. We then got busy with twelve sheets of paper which he twisted into pellets and shook up between his hands before passing them round. Eleven of them were blank, and 'Smee' was written on the twelfth. The person drawing the latter was the one who had to hide. I looked and saw that mine was a blank. A moment later out went the electric lights, and in the darkness I heard somebody get up and creep to the door.

After a minute or so somebody gave a signal and we made a rush for the door. I for one hadn't the least idea which of the party was 'Smee'. For five or ten minutes we were all rushing up and down passages and in and out of rooms challenging one another and answering, 'Smee? — Smee!'

After a bit the alarums and excursions died down, and I guessed that 'Smee' was found. Eventually I found a chain of people all sitting still and holding their breath on some narrow stairs leading up to a row of attics. I hastily joined it, having challenged and been answered with silence, and presently two more stragglers arrived, each racing the other to avoid being last. Sangston was one of them, indeed it was he who was marked down for a forfeit, and after a little while he remarked in an undertone, 'I think we're all here now, aren't we?'

He struck a match; looked up the shaft of the staircase, and began to count. It wasn't hard, although we just about filled the staircase, for we were sitting each a step or two above the next, and all our heads were visible.

'. . . nine, ten, eleven, twelve—*thirteen*,' he concluded, and then laughed. 'Dash it all, that's one too many!'

The match had burned out and he struck another and began to count. He got as far as twelve, and then uttered an exclamation.

'There are thirteen people here!' he exclaimed. 'I haven't counted myself yet.'

'Oh, nonsense!' I laughed. 'You probably began with yourself, and now you want to count yourself twice.'

Out came his son's electric torch, giving a brighter and steadier light and we all began to count. Of course we numbered twelve.

Sangston laughed.

'Well', he said, 'I could have sworn I counted thirteen twice.'

From halfway up the stairs came Violet Sangston's voice with a little nervous trill in it. 'I thought there was somebody sitting two steps above me. Have you moved up, Captain Ransome?'

Ransome said that he hadn't: He also said that he thought there was somebody sitting between Violet and himself. Just for a moment there was an uncomfortable Something in the air, a little cold ripple which touched us all. For that little moment it seemed to all of us, I think, that something odd and unpleasant had happened and was liable to happen again. Then we laughed at ourselves and at one another and were comfortable once more. There *were* only twelve of us, and there *could* only have been twelve of us, and there was no argument about it. Still laughing we trooped back to the drawing-room to begin again.

This time I was 'Smee', and Violet Sangston ran me to earth while I was still looking for a hiding-place. That round didn't last long, and we were a chain of twelve within two or three minutes. Afterwards there was a short interval. Violet wanted a wrap fetched for her, and her husband went up to get it from her room. He was no sooner gone than Reggie pulled me by the sleeve. I saw that he was looking pale and sick.

'Quick!' he whispered, 'while father's out of the way. Take me into the smoke room and give me a brandy or a whisky or something.'

Outside the room I asked him what was the matter, but he didn't answer at first, and I thought it better to dose him first and question him afterward. So I mixed him a pretty dark-complexioned brandy and soda which he drank at a gulp and then began to puff as if he had been running.

'I've had rather a turn,' he said to me with a sheepish grin.

'What's the matter?'

'I don't know. You were "Smee" just now, weren't you? Well, of course I didn't know who "Smee" was, and while mother and the others ran into the west wing and found you, I turned east. There's a deep clothes cupboard in my bedroom—I'd marked it down as a good place to hide when it was my turn, and I had an idea that "Smee" might be there. I opened the door in the dark, felt round, and touched somebody's hand. "Smee?" I whispered, and not getting any answer I thought I had found "Smee".'

'Well, I don't know how it was, but an odd creepy feeling came over me, I can't describe it, but I felt that something was wrong. So I turned on my electric torch and there was nobody there. Now, I swear I touched a hand, and I was filling up the doorway of the cupboard at the time, so nobody could get out and past me.' He puffed again. 'What do you make of it?' he asked.

'You imagined that you had touched a hand,' I answered, naturally enough.

He uttered a short laugh. 'Of course I knew you were going to say that,' he said. 'I must have imagined it, mustn't I?' He paused and swallowed. 'I mean, it couldn't have been anything else *but* imagination, could it?'

I assured him that it couldn't, meaning what I said, and he accepted this, but rather with the philosophy of one who knows he is right but doesn't expect to be believed. We returned together to the drawing-room where, by that time, they were all waiting for us and ready to start again.

It may have been my imagination—although I'm almost sure it wasn't—but it seemed to me that all enthusiasm for the game had suddenly melted like a white frost in strong sunlight. If anybody had suggested another game I'm sure we should all have been grateful and abandoned 'Smee'. Only nobody did. Nobody seemed to like to. I for one, and I can speak for some of the others too, was oppressed with the feeling that there was something wrong. I couldn't have said what I thought was wrong, indeed I didn't think about it at all, but somehow all the sparkle had gone out of the fun, and hovering over my mind like a shadow was the warning of some sixth sense which told me that there was an influence in the house which was neither sane, sound nor healthy. Why did I feel like that? Because Sangston had counted thirteen of us instead of twelve, and his son had thought he had touched somebody in an empty cupboard. No, there was more in it than just that. One would have laughed at such things in the ordinary way, and it was just that feeling of something being wrong which stopped me from laughing.

Well, we started again, and when we went in pursuit of the unknown 'Smee', we were as noisy as ever, but it seemed to me that most of us were acting. Frankly, for no reason other than the one I've given you, we'd stopped enjoying the game. I had an instinct to hunt with the main pack, but after a few minutes, during which no 'Smee' had been found, my instinct to play winning games and be first if possible, set me searching on my own account. And on the first floor of the west wing following the wall which was actually the shell of the house, I blundered against a pair of human knees.

I put out my hand and touched a soft, heavy curtain. Then I knew where I was. There were tall, deeply-recessed windows with seats along the landing, and curtains over the recesses to the ground. Somebody was sitting in a corner of this window-seat behind the curtain. Aha, I had caught 'Smee!' So I drew the curtain aside, stepped in, and touched the bare arm of a woman.

It was a dark night outside, and, moreover, the window was not only curtained but a blind hung down to where the bottom panes joined up with the frame. Between the curtain and the window it was as dark as the plague of Egypt. I could not have seen my hand held six inches before my face, much less the woman sitting in the corner.

'Smee?' I whispered.

I had no answer. 'Smee' when challenged does not answer. So I sat down beside her, first in the field, to await the others. Then, having settled myself I leaned over to her and whispered:

'Who is it? What's your name, "Smee?" '

And out of the darkness beside me the whisper came back: 'Brenda Ford.'

I didn't know the name, but because I didn't know it I guessed at once who she was. The tall, pale, dark girl was the only person in the house I didn't know by name. Ergo my companion was the tall, pale, dark girl. It seemed rather intriguing to be there with her, shut in between a heavy curtain and a window, and I rather wondered whether she was enjoying the game we were all playing. Somehow she hadn't seemed to me to be one of the romping sort. I muttered one or two commonplace questions to her and had no answer.

'Smee' is a game of silence. 'Smee' and the person or persons who have found 'Smee' are supposed to keep quiet to make it hard for the others. But there was nobody else about, and it occurred to me that she was playing the game a little too much to the letter. I spoke again and got no answer, and then I began to be annoyed. She was of that cold, 'superior' type which affects to despise men; she didn't like me; and she was sheltering behind the rules of a game for children to be discourteous. Well, if she didn't like sitting there with me, I certainly didn't want to be sitting there with her! I half turned from her and began to hope that we should both be discovered without much more delay.

Having discovered that I didn't like being there alone with her, it was queer how soon I found myself hating it, and that for a reason very different from the one which had at first whetted my annoyance. The girl I had met for the first time before dinner, and seen diagonally across the table, had a sort of cold charm about her which had attracted while it had half angered me. For the girl who was with me, imprisoned in the opaque darkness between the curtain and the window, I felt no attraction at all. It was so very much the reverse that I should have wondered at myself if, after the first shock of the discovery that she had suddenly become repellent to me, I had no room in my mind for anything besides the consciousness that her close presence was an increasing horror to me.

It came upon me just as quickly as I've uttered the words. My flesh suddenly shrank from her as you see a strip of gelatine shrink and wither before the heat of a fire. That feeling of something being wrong had come back to me, but multiplied to an extent which turned foreboding into actual terror. I firmly believe that I should have got up and run if I had not felt that at my first movement she would have divined my intention and compelled me to stay, by some means of which I could not bear to think. The memory of having touched her bare arm made me wince and draw in my lips. I prayed that somebody else would come along soon.

My prayer was answered. Light footfalls sounded on the landing. Somebody on the other side of the curtain brushed against my knees. The curtain was drawn aside and a woman's hand, fumbling in the darkness, presently rested on my shoulder. 'Smee?' whispered a voice which I instantly recognised as Mrs. Gorman's.

Of course she received no answer. She came and settled down beside me with a rustle, and I can't describe the sense of relief she brought me.

'It's Tony, isn't it?' she whispered.

'Yes', I whispered back.

'You're not "Smee" are you?'

'No, she's on my other side.'

She reached a hand across me, and I heard one of her nails scratch the surface of a woman's silk gown.

'Hullo, "Smee!" How are you? *Who* are you? Oh, is it against the rules to talk? Never mind, Tony, we'll break the rules. Do you know, Tony, this game is beginning to irk me a little. I hope they're not going to run it to death by playing it all the evening. I'd like to play some game where we can all be together in the same room with a nice bright fire.'

'Same here,' I agreed fervently.

'Can't you suggest something when we go down? There's something rather uncanny in this particular amusement. I can't quite shed the delusion that there's somebody in this game who oughtn't to be in it at all.'

That was just how I had been feeling, but I didn't say so. But for my part the worst of my qualms were now gone; the arrival of Mrs. Gorman had dissipated them. We sat on talking, wondering from time to time when the rest of the party would arrive.

I don't know how long elapsed before we heard a clatter of feet on the landing and young Reggie's voice shouting, 'Hullo! Hullo, there! Anybody there?'

'Yes,' I answered.

'Mrs. Gorman with you?'

'Yes.'

'Well, you're a nice pair! You've both forfeited. We've all been waiting for you for hours.'

'Why, you haven't found "Smee" yet,' I objected.

'*You* haven't, you mean. I happen to have been "Smee" myself.'

'But "Smee's" here with us,' I cried.

'Yes,' agreed Mrs. Gorman.

The curtain was stripped aside and in a moment we were blinking into the eye of Reggie's electric torch. I looked at Mrs. Gorman and

[241]

then on my other side. Between me and the wall there was an empty space on the window seat. I stood up at once and wished I hadn't, for I found myself sick and dizzy.

'There *was* somebody there,' I maintained, 'because I touched her.'

'So did I,' said Mrs. Gorman in a voice which had lost its steadiness. 'And I don't see how she could have got up and gone without our knowing it.'

Reggie uttered a queer, shaken laugh. He, too, had had an unpleasant experience that evening. 'Somebody's been playing the goat,' he remarked. 'Coming down?'

We were not very popular when we arrived in the drawing-room. Reggie rather tactlessly gave it out that he had found us sitting on a window seat behind a curtain. I taxed the tall, dark girl with having pretended to be 'Smee' and afterwards slipping away. She denied it. After which we settled down and played other games. 'Smee' was done with for the evening, and I for one was glad of it.

Some long while later, during an interval, Sangston told me, if I wanted a drink, to go into the smoke room and help myself. I went, and he presently followed me. I could see that he was rather peeved with me, and the reason came out during the following minute or two. It seemed that, in his opinion, if I must sit out and flirt with Mrs. Gorman—in circumstances which would have been considered highly compromising in his young days—I needn't do it during a round game and keep everybody waiting for us.

'But there was somebody else there,' I protested, 'somebody pretending to be "Smee". I believe it was that tall, dark girl, Miss Ford, although she denied it. She even whispered her name to me.'

Sangston stared at me and nearly dropped his glass.

'Miss *Who?*' he shouted.

'Brenda Ford—she told me her name was.'

Sangston put down his glass and laid a hand on my shoulder.

'Look here, old man,' he said, 'I don't mind a joke, but don't let it go too far. We don't want all the women in the house getting hysterical. Brenda Ford is the name of the girl who broke her neck on the stairs playing hide-and-seek here ten years ago.'

THE PRESCRIPTION

by Marjorie Bowen

Marjorie Bowen (1886–1952; pseudonym of Mrs
Gabrielle Margaret Vere Campbell Long) had over
180 novels and collections to her credit, using a
variety of male and female pseudonyms. Her best
'twilight tales' (as she preferred to call them) were
collected together in *The Last Bouquet* (1933). This
fine selection contains 'The Fair Hair of
Ambrosine', which Arthur Conan Doyle
considered to be one of the finest stories of the
occult he had ever read; 'The Crown Derby Plate',
'Florence Flannery', and the Christmas story
'The Prescription'.

J ohn Cuming collected ghost stories; he always declared that this
was the best that he knew, although it was partially second-hand
and contained a mystery that had no reasonably solution, while
most really good ghost stories allow of a plausible explanation,
even if it is one as feeble as a dream, excusing all; or an hallucination
or a crude deception. Cuming told the story rather well. The first part
of it at least had come under his own observation and been carefully
noted by him in the flat green book which he kept for the record of all
curious cases of this sort. He was a shrewd and trained observer; he
honestly restrained his love of drama from leading him into embellish-
ing facts. Cuming told the story to us all on the most suitable
occasion—Christmas Eve—and prefaced it with a little homily.

'You all know the good old saw— "The more it changes the more it is the same thing'—and I should like you to notice that this extremely up-to-date ultra-modern ghost story is really almost exactly the same as one that might have puzzled Babylonian or Assyrian sages. I can give you the first start of the tale in my own words, but the second part will have to be in the words of someone else. They were, however, most carefully and scrupulously taken down. As for the conclusion, I must leave you to draw that for yourselves—each according to your own mood, fancy, and temperament; it may be that you will all think of the same solution, it may be that you will each think of a different one, and it may be that every one will be left wondering.'

Having thus enjoyed himself by whetting our curiousity, Cuming settled himself down comfortably in his deep arm-chair and unfolded his tale.

'It was about five years ago. I don't wish to be exact with time, and of course I shall alter names—that's one of the first rules of the game, isn't it? Well, whenever it was, I was the guest of a—Mrs. Janey we will call her—who was, to some extent, a friend of mine; an intelligent, lively, rather bustling sort of woman who had the knack of gathering interesting people about her. She had lately taken a new house in Buckinghamshire. It stood in the grounds of one of those large estates which are now so frequently being broken up. She was very pleased with the house, which was quite new and had only been finished a year, and seemed, according to her own rather excited imagination, in every way desirable. I don't want to emphasize anything about the house except that it *was* new and did stand on the verge, as it were, of this large old estate, which had belonged to one of those notable English families now extinct and completely forgotten. I am no antiquarian or connoisseur in architecture, and the rather blatant modernity of the house did not offend me. I was able to appreciate its comfort and to enjoy what Mrs. Janey rather maddeningly called "the old-world gardens," which were really a section of the larger gardens of the vanished mansion which had once commanded this domain. Mrs. Janey, I should tell you, knew nothing about the neighbourhood nor anyone who lived there, except that for the first it was very convenient for town, and for the second she believed that they were all "nice" people, not likely to bother one. I was slightly disappointed with the crowd she had gathered together at Christmas. They were all people whom either I knew too well or whom I didn't wish to know at all, and at first the party showed signs of being extremely flat. Mrs. Janey seemed to perceive this too, and with rather nervous haste produced, on Christmas Eve, a trump card in the way of amusement—a professional medium, called Mrs. Mahogany, because that could not possibly have been her name. Some of us "believed in," as the saying goes, mediums, and some didn't; but we were all willing to be diverted by the experiment. Mrs. Janey continually lamented that a certain Dr. Dilke would not be present. He was going to be one of the party, but had been detained in town and would not reach Verrall, which was the name of the house, until later, and the medium, it seemed, could not stay; for she, being a personage in great demand, must go on to a further engagement. I, of course, like every one else possessed of an intelligent curiosity and a certain amount of leisure, had been to mediums before. I had been slightly impressed, slightly disgusted, and very much bewildered, and on the whole had decided to let the matter alone, considering that I really preferred the more direct and old-fashioned method of getting in touch with what we used to call "The Unseen." This sitting in the great new house seemed rather banal. I could understand in some haunted old manor that a clairvoyant, or a clairaudient, or a trance-medium might have found something interesting to say, but what was she going to get out of Mrs. Janey's bright, brilliant, and comfortable dwelling?

'Mrs. Mahogany was a nondescript sort of woman—neither young nor old, neither clever nor stupid, neither dark nor fair, placid, and not in the least self-conscious. After an extremely good luncheon (it was a gloomy, stormy afternoon) we all sat down in a circle in the cheerful drawing-room; the curtains were pulled across the dreary prospect of grey sky and grey landscape, and we had merely the light of the fire. We sat quite close together in order to increase "the power," as Mrs. Mahogany said, and the medium sat in the middle, with no special precautions against trickery; but we all knew that trickery would have been really impossible, and we were quite prepared to be tremendously impressed and startled if any manifestations took place. I think we all felt rather foolish, as we did not know each other very well, sitting round there, staring at this very ordinary, rather common, stout little woman, who kept nervously pulling a little tippet of grey wool over her shoulders, closing her eyes and muttering, while she twisted her fingers together. When we had sat silent for about ten minutes Mrs. Janey announced in a rather raw whisper that the medium had gone into a trance. "Beautifully," she added. I thought that Mrs. Mahogany did not look at all beautiful. Her communication began with a lot of rambling talk which had no point at all, and a good deal of generalisation under which I think we all became a little restive. There was too much of various spirits who had all sorts of ordinary names, just regular Toms, Dicks, and Harrys of the spirit world, floating round behind us, their arms full of flowers and their mouths of goodwill, all rather pointless. And though, occasionally, a Tom, Dick, or a Harry was identified by some of us, it wasn't very convincing, and, what was worse, not very interesting. We got, however, our surprise and our shock, because Mrs. Mahogany began suddenly to writhe into ugly contortions and called out in a loud voice, quite different from the one that she had hitherto used:

' "Murder!"

'This word gave us all a little thrill, and we leant forward eagerly to hear what further she had to say. With every sign of distress and horror Mrs. Mahogany began to speak:

' "He's murdered her. Oh, how dreadful. Look at him! Can't somebody stop him? It's so near here, too. He tried to save her. He was sorry, you know. Oh, how dreadful! Look at him—he's borne it as long as he can, and now he's murdered her! I see him mixing it in a glass. Oh, isn't it awful that no one could have saved her—and he was so terribly remorseful afterwards. Oh, how dreadful! How horrible!"

'She ended in a whimpering of fright and horror, and Mrs. Janey, who seemed an adept at this sort of thing, leant forward and asked eagerly:

' "Can't you get the name—can't you find out who it is? Why do you get that here?"

' "I don't know," muttered the medium, "it's somewhere near here—a house, an old dark house, and there are curtains of mauve velvet—do you call it mauve?, a kind of blue red—at the windows. There's a garden outside with a fishpond and you go through a low door-way and down stone steps."

' "It isn't near here," said Mrs. Janey decidedly, "all the houses are new."

' "The house is near here," persisted the medium. "I am walking through it now; I can see the room, I can see that poor, poor woman, and a glass of milk—"

' "I wish you'd get the name," insisted Mrs. Janey, and she cast a look, as I thought not without suspicion, round the circle. "You can't be getting this from my house, you know, Mrs. Mahogany," she added decidedly, "it must be given out by someone here—something they've

[246]

read or seen, you know," she said, to reassure us that our characters were not in dispute.

'But the medium replied drowsily, "No, it's somewhere near here. I see a light dress covered with small roses. If he could have got help he would have gone for it, but there was no one; so all his remorse was useless . . ."

'No further urging would induce the medium to say more; soon afterwards she came out of the trance, and all of us, I think, felt that she had made rather a stupid blunder by introducing this vague piece of melodrama, and if it was, as we suspected, a cheap attempt to give a ghostly and mysterious atmosphere to Christmas Eve, it was a failure.

'When Mrs. Mahogany, blinking round her, said brightly, "Well, here I am again! I wonder if I said anything that interested you?" we all replied rather coldly, "Of course it has been most interesting, but there hasn't been anything definite." And I think that even Mrs. Janey felt that the sitting had been rather a disappointment, and she suggested that if the weather was really too horrible to venture out of doors we should sit round the fire and tell old-fashioned ghost stories. "The kind," she said brightly, "that are about bones and chairs and shrouds. I really think that is the most thrilling kind after all." Then, with some embarrassment, and when Mrs. Mahogany had left the room, she suggested that not one of us should say anything about what the medium had said in her trance.

' "It really was rather absurd," said our hostess, "and it would make me look a little foolish if it got about; you know some people think these mediums are absolute fakes, and anyhow, the whole thing, I am afraid, was quite stupid. She must have got her contacts mixed. There is no old house about here and never has been since the original Verrall was pulled down, and that's a good fifty years ago, I believe, from what the estate agent told me; and as for a murder, I never heard the shadow of any such story."

'We all agreed not to mention what the medium had said, and did this with the more heartiness as we were, not any one of us, impressed. The feeling was rather that Mrs. Mahogany had been obliged to say something and had said that . . .

'Well,' said Cuming comfortably, 'that is the first part of my story, and I daresay you'll think it's dull enough. Now we come to the second part.

'Lateish that evening Dr. Dilke arrived. He was not in any way a remarkable man, just an ordinary successful physician, and I refuse to say that he was suffering from overwork or nervous strain; you know that is so often put into this kind of story as a sort of excuse for what happens afterwards. On the contrary, Dr. Dilke seemed to be in the most robust of health and the most cheerful frame of mind, and quite prepared to make the most of his brief holiday. The car that fetched him from the station was taking Mrs. Mahogany away, and the doctor and the medium met for just a moment in the hall. Mrs. Janey did not trouble to introduce them, but without waiting for this Mrs. Mahogany turned to the doctor, and looking at him fixedly, said, "You're very psychic, aren't you?" And upon that Mrs. Janey was forced to say hastily: "This is Mrs. Mahogany, Dr. Dilke, the famous medium."

'The physician was indifferently impressed: "I really don't know," he answered smiling, "I have never gone in for that sort of thing. I shouldn't think I am what you call 'psychic' really; I have had a hard, scientific training, and that rather knocks the bottom out of fantasies."

' "Well, you are, you know," said Mrs. Mahogany; "I felt it at once; I shouldn't be at all surprised if you had some strange experience one of these days."

'Mrs. Mahogany left the house and was duly driven away to the station. I want to make the point very clear that she and Dr. Dilke did not meet again and that they held no communication except those few words in the hall spoken in the presence of Mrs. Janey. Of course Dr. Dilke got twitted a good deal about what the medium had said; it made quite a topic of conversation during dinner and after dinner, and we all had queer little ghost stories or incidents of what we considered "psychic" experiences to trot out and discuss. Dr. Dilke remained civil, amused, but entirely unconvinced. He had what he called a material, or physical, or medical explanation for almost everything that we said, and, apart from all these explanations he added, with some justice, that human credulity was such that there was always some one who would accept and embellish anything, however wild, unlikely, or grotesque it was.

' "I should rather like to hear what you would say if such an experience happened to you," Mrs. Janey challenged him; "whether you use the ancient terms of 'ghost,' 'witches,' 'black magic,' and so on, or whether you speak in modern terms like 'medium,' 'clairvoyance,' 'psychic contacts,' and all the rest of it; well, it seems one is in a bit of a tangle anyhow, and if any queer thing ever happens to you—"

'Dr. Dilke broke in pleasantly: "Well, if it ever does I will let you all know about it, and I dare say I shall have an explanation to add at the end of the tale."

'When we all met again the next morning we rather hoped that Dr. Dilke *would* have something to tell us—some odd experience that might have befallen him in the night, new as the house was, and banal as was his bedroom. He told us, of course, that he had passed a perfectly good night.

'We most of us went to the morning service in the small church that had once been the chapel belonging to the demolished mansion, and which had some rather curious monuments inside and in the church-yard. As I went in I noticed a mortuary chapel with niches for the coffins to be stood upright, now whitewashed and used as a sacristy. The monuments and mural tablets were mostly to the memory of members of the family of Verrall—the Verralls of Verrall Hall, who appeared to have been people of little interest or distinction. Dr. Dilke sat beside me, and I, having nothing better to do through the more familiar and monotonous portions of the service, found myself idly looking at the mural table beyond him. This was a large slab of black marble deeply cut with a very worn Latin inscription which I found, unconsciously, I was spelling out. The stone, it seemed, commemorated a woman who had been, of course, the possessor of all the virtues; her name was Philadelphia Carwithen, and I rather pleasantly sampled the flavour of that ancient name—Philadelphia. Then I noticed a smaller inscription at the bottom of the slab, which indicated that the lady's husband also rested in the vault; he had died suddenly about six months after her—of grief at her loss, no doubt, I thought, scenting out a pretty romance.

'As we walked home across the frost-bitten fields and icy lanes Dr. Dilke, who walked beside me, as he had sat beside me in church, began to complain of cold; he said he believed that he had caught a chill. I was rather amused to hear this old-womanish expression on the lips of so distinguished a physician, and I told him that I had been taught in my more enlightened days that there was no such thing as "catching a chill." To my surprise he did not laugh at this, but said:

' "Oh, yes, there is, and I believe I've got it—I keep on shivering; I think it was that slab of black stone I was sitting next. It was as cold as ice, for I touched it, and it seemed to me exuding moisture—some of that old stone does, you know, it's always, as it were, sweating; and I felt exactly as if I were sitting next a slab of ice from which a cold wind was blowing; it was really as if it penetrated my flesh."

'He looked pale, and I thought how disagreeable it would be for us all, and particularly for Mrs. Janey, if the good man was to be taken ill in the midst of her already not too successful Christmas party. Dr. Dilke seemed, too, in that ill-humour which so often presages an illness; he was quite peevish about the church and the service, and the fact that he had been asked to go there.

' "These places are nothing but charnel-houses, after all," he said fretfully; "one sits there among all those rotting bones, with that damp marble at one's side . . ."

' "It is supposed to give you 'atmosphere,' " I said. "The atmosphere of an old-fashioned Christmas. . . . Did you notice who your black stone was erected "to the memory of"?' I asked, and the doctor replied that he had not.

' "It was to a young woman—a young woman, I took it, and her husband: 'Philadelphia Carwithen,' I noticed that, and of course there was a long eulogy of her virtues, and then underneath it just said that he had died a few months afterwards. As far as I could see it was the only example of that name in the church—all the rest were Verralls. I suppose they were strangers here."

' "What was the date?" asked the doctor, and I replied that really I had not been able to make it out, for where the roman figures came the stone had been very worn.

'The day ambled along somehow, with games, diversions, and plenty of good food and drink, and towards the evening we began to feel a little more satisfied with each other and our hostess. Only Dr. Dilke remained a little peevish and apart, and this was remarkable in one who was obviously of a robust temperament and an even temper. He still continued to talk of a "chill," and I did notice that he shuddered once or twice, and continually sat near the large fire which Mrs. Janey had rather laboriously arranged in imitation of what she would call "the good old times."

'That evening, the evening of Christmas Day, there was no talk whatever of ghosts or psychic matters; our discussions were entirely topical and of mundane matters, in which Dr. Dilke, who seemed to have recovered his spirits, took his part with ability and agreeableness. When it was time to break up I asked him, half in jest, about his mysterious chill, and he looked at me with some surprise and appeared to have forgotten that he had ever said he had got such a thing; the impression, whatever it was, which he had received in the church, had evidently been effaced from his mind. I wish to make that quite clear.

'The next morning Dr. Dilke appeared very late at the breakfast table, and when he did so his looks were matter for hints and comment; he was pale, distracted, troubled, untidy in his dress, absent in his manner, and I, at least, instantly recalled what he had said yesterday, and feared he was sickening for some illness.

'On Mrs. Janey putting to him some direct question as to his looks and manner, so strange and so troubled, he replied rather sharply, "Well, I don't know what you can expect from a fellow who's been up all night. I thought I came down here for a rest."

'We all looked at him as he dropped into his place and began to drink his coffee with eager gusto; I noticed that he continually shivered. There was something about this astounding statement and his curious appearance which held us all discreetly silent. We waited for further developments before committing ourselves; even Mrs. Janey, whom I had never thought of as tactful, contrived to say casually:

' "Up all night, doctor. Couldn't you sleep, then? I'm so sorry if your bed wasn't comfortable."

' "The bed was all right," he answered, "that made me the more sorry to leave it. Haven't you got a local doctor who can take the local cases?" he added.

' "Why, of course we have; there's Dr. Armstrong and Dr. Fraser—I made sure about that before I came here."

' "Well, then," demanded Dr. Dilke angrily, "why on earth couldn't one of them have gone last night?"

'Mrs. Janey looked at me helplessly, and I, obeying her glance, took up the matter.

' "What do you mean, doctor? Do you mean that you were called out of your bed last night to attend a case?" I asked deliberately.

' "Of course I was—I only got back with the dawn."

'Here Mrs. Janey could not forbear breaking in.

' "But whoever could it have been? I know nobody about here yet, at least, only one or two people by name, and they would not be aware that you were here. And how did you get out of the house? It's locked every night."

'Then the doctor gave his story in rather, I must confess, a confused fashion, and yet with an earnest conviction that he was speaking the simple truth. It was broken up a good deal by ejaculations and comments from the rest of us, but I give it you here shorn of all that and exactly as I put it down in my notebook afterwards.

' "I was awoken by a tap at the door. I was instantly wide awake and I said, 'Come in.' I thought immediately that probably someone in the house was ill—a doctor, you know, is always ready for these emergencies. The door opened at once, and a man entered holding a small ordinary storm-lantern. I noticed nothing peculiar about the man. He had a dark greatcoat on, and appeared extremely anxious. 'I am sorry to disturb you,' he said at once, 'but there is a young woman dangerously ill. I want you to come and see her.' I, somehow, did not think of arguing or of suggesting that there were other medical men in the neighbourhood, or of asking how it was he knew of my presence at Verrall. I dressed myself quickly and accompanied him out of the house. He opened the front door without any trouble, and it did not occur to me to ask him how it was he had obtained either admission or egress. There was a small carriage outside the door, such a one as you may still see in isolated country places, but such a one as I was certainly surprised to see here. I could not very well make out either the horse or the driver, for, though the moon was high in the heavens, it was frequently obscured by clouds. I got into the carriage and noticed, as I have often noticed before in these ancient vehicles, a most repulsive smell of decay and damp. My companion got in beside me. He did not speak a word during the whole of the journey, which was, I have the impression, extremely long. I had also the sense that he was in the greatest trouble, anguish, and almost despair; I do not know why I did not question him. I should tell you that he had drawn down the blinds of the carriage and we travelled in darkness, yet I was perfectly aware of his presence and seemed to see him in his heavy dark greatcoat turned up round the chin, his black hair low on his forehead, and his anxious, furtive dark eyes. I think I may have gone to sleep in the carriage, I was tired and cold. I was aware, however, when it stopped, and of my companion opening the door and helping me out. We went through a garden, down some steps and past a fishpond; I could see by the moonlight the silver and gold shapes of fishes slipping in and out of the black water. We entered the house by a side-door—I remember that very distinctly—and went up what seemed to be some secret or seldom-used stairs, and into a bedroom. I was, by now, quite alert, as one is when one gets into the presence of the patient, and said to myself, 'What a fool I've been, I've brought nothing with me,' and I tried to remember, but could not quite do so, whether or not I had brought anything with me—my cases and so on—to Verrall. The room was very badly lit, but a certain illumination—I could not say whether it came from any artificial light within the room or merely from the moonlight through the open window, draped with mauve velvet curtains—fell on the bed, and there I saw my patient. She was a young woman, who, I surmised, would have been, when in health, of considerable though coarse charm. She was now in great suffering, twisted and contorted with agony, and in her struggles of anguish had pulled and torn the bedclothes into a heap. I noticed that she wore a dress of some light material spotted with small roses, and it occurred to me at once that she had been taken ill during the daytime and must have lain thus in great pain for many hours, and I turned with some reproach to the man who had fetched me and demanded why help had not been sought sooner. For answer he wrung his hands—a gesture that I do not remember having noticed in any human being before; one hears a great deal of hands being wrung, but one does not so often see it. This man, I remember distinctly, wrung his hands, and muttered, 'Do what you can for her—do what you can!' I feared that this would be very little. I endeavoured to make an examination of the patient, but owing to her half-delirious struggles this was very difficult; she was, however, I thought, likely to die, and of what malady I could not determine. There was a table nearby on which lay some papers—one I took to be a will—and a glass in which there had been milk. I do not remember seeing anything else in the room—the light was so bad. I endeavoured to question the man, whom I took to be the husband, but without any success. He merely repeated his monotonous appeal for me to save her. Then I was aware of a sound outside the room—of a woman laughing, perpetually and shrilly laughing. 'Pray stop that,' I cried to the man; 'who have you got in the house—a lunatic?' But he took no notice of my appeal, merely repeating his own hushed lamentations. The sick woman appeared to hear that demoniacal laughter outside, and raising herself on one elbow said, 'You have destroyed me and you may well laugh.'

'I sat down at the table on which were the papers and the glass half full of milk, and wrote a prescription on a sheet torn out of my notebook. The man snatched it eagerly. 'I don't know when and where you can get that made up,' I said, 'but it's the only hope.' At this he seemed wishful for me to depart, as wishful as he had been for me to come. 'That's all I want,' he said. He took me by the arm and led me out of the house by the same back stairs. As I descended I still heard those two dreadful sounds—the thin laughter of the woman I had not seen, and the groans, becoming every moment fainter, of the young woman whom I had seen. The carriage was waiting for me, and I was driven back by the same way I had come. When I reached the house and my room I saw the dawn just breaking. I rested till I heard the breakfast gong. I suppose some time had gone by since I returned to the house, but I wasn't quite aware of it; all through the night I had rather lost the sense of time."

'When Dr. Dilke had finished his narrative, which I give here baldly—but, I hope, to the point—we all glanced at each other rather uncomfortably, for who was to tell a man like Dr. Dilke that he had been suffering from a severe hallucination? It was, of course, quite impossible that he could have left the house and gone through the peculiar scenes he had described, and it seemed extraordinary that he could for a moment have believed that he had done so. What was even more remarkable was that so many points of his story agreed with what the medium, Mrs. Mahogany, had said in her trance. We recognised the frock with the roses, the mauve velvet curtains, the glass of milk, the man who had fetched Dr. Dilke sounded like the murderer, and the unfortunate woman writhing on the bed sounded like the victim; but how had the doctor got hold of these particulars? We all knew that he had not spoken to Mrs. Mahogany, and each suspected the other of having told him what the medium had said, and that this having wrought on his mind he had the dream, vision, or hallucination he had just described to us. I must add that this was found afterwards to be wholly false; we were all reliable people and there was not a shadow of doubt we had all kept our counsel about Mrs. Mahogany. In fact, none of us had been alone with Dr. Dilke the previous day for more than a moment or so save myself, who had walked with him from the church, when we had certainly spoken of nothing except the black stone in the church and the chill which he had said emanated from it. . . . Well, to put the matter as briefly as possible, and to leave out a great deal of amazement and wonder, explanation, and so on, we will come to the point when Dr. Dilke was finally persuaded that he had not left Verrall all the night. When his story was taken to pieces and put before him, as it were, in the raw, he himself recognised many absurdities: How could the man have come straight to his bedroom? How could he have left the house?—the doors were locked every night, there was no doubt about that. Where did the carriage come from and where was the house to which he had been taken? And who could possibly have known of his presence in the neighbourhood? Had not, too, the scene in the house to which he was taken all the resemblance of a nightmare? Who was it laughing in the other room? What was the mysterious illness that was destroying the young woman? Who was the black-browed man who had fetched him? And, in these days of telephone and motor-cars, people didn't go out in the old-fashioned one-horse carriages to fetch doctors from miles away in the case of dangerous illness.

'Dr. Dilke was finally silenced, uneasy, but not convinced. I could see that he disliked intensely the idea that he had been the victim of an hallucination and that he equally intensely regretted the impulse which had made him relate his extraordinary adventure of the night. I could only conclude that he must have done so while still, to an extent, under the influence of his delusion, which had been so strong that never for a moment had he questioned the reality of it. Though he was forced at last to allow us to put the whole thing down as a most remarkable dream, I could see that he did not intend to let the matter rest there, and later in the day (out of good manners we had eventually ceased discussing the story) he asked me if I would accompany him on some investigation in the neighbourhood.

' "I think I should know the house," he said, "even though I saw it in the dark. I was impressed by the fishpond and the low doorway through which I had to stoop in order to pass without knocking my head."

'I did not tell him that Mrs. Mahogany had also mentioned a fishpond and a low door.

'We made the excuse of some old brasses we wished to discover in a nearby church to take my car and go out that afternoon on an investigation of the neighbourhood in the hope of discovering Dr. Dilke's dream house.

'We covered a good deal of distance and spent a good deal of time without any success at all, and the short day was already darkening when we came upon a row of almshouses in which, for no reason at all that I could discern, Dr. Dilke showed an interest and insisted on stopping before them. He pointed out an inscription cut in the centre gable, which said that there had been built by a certain Richard Carwithen in memory of Philadelphia, his wife.

' "The people whose tablet you sat next in the church," I remarked.

' "Yes," murmured Dr. Dilke, "when I felt the chill," and he added, "when I *first* felt the chill. You see, the date is 1830. That would be about right."

'We stopped in the little village, which was a good many miles from Verrall, and after some tedious delays because everything was shut up for the holiday, we did discover an old man who was willing to tell us something about the almshouses, though there was nothing much to be said about them. They had been founded by a certain Mr. Richard Carwithen with his wife's fortune. He had been a poor man, a kind of adventurer, our informant thought, who had married a wealthy woman; they had not been at all happy. There had been quarrels and disputes, and a separation (at least, so the gossip went, as his father had told it to him); finally, the Carwithens had taken a house here in this village of Sunford—a large house it was and it still stood. The Carwithens weren't buried in this village though, but at Verrall; she had been a Verrall by birth—perhaps that's why they came to this neighbourhood—it was the name of a great family in those days, you know. . . . There was another woman in the old story, as it went, and she got hold of Mr. Carwithen and was for making him put his wife aside; and so, perhaps, he would have done, but the poor lady died suddenly, and there was some talk about it, having the other woman in the house at the time, and it being so convenient for both of them. . . . But he didn't marry the other woman, because he died six months after his wife. . . . By his will he left all his wife's money to found these almshouses.

'Dr. Dilke asked if he could see the house where the Carwithens had lived.

' "It belongs to a London gentleman," the old man said, "who never comes here. It's going to be pulled down and the land sold in building lots; why, it's been locked up these ten years or more. I don't suppose it's been inhabited since—no, not for a hundred years."

' "Well, I'm looking for a house round about here. I don't mind spending a little money on repairs if that house is in the market."

'The old man didn't know whether it was in the market or not, but kept repeating that the property was to be sold and broken up for building lots.

'I won't bother you with all our delays and arguments, but merely tell you that we did finally discover the lodgekeeper of the estate, who gave us the key. It was not such a very large estate, nothing to be compared to Verrall, but had been, in its time, of some pretension. Builders' boards had already been raised along the high road frontage.

There were some fine old trees, black and bare, in a little park. As we turned in through the rusty gates and motored towards the house it was nearly dark, but we had our electric torches and the powerful headlamps of the car. Dr. Dilke made no comment on what we had found, but he reconstructed the story of the Carwithens whose names were on that black stone in Verrall church.

' "They were quarrelling over money, he was trying to get her to sign a will in his favour; she had some little sickness perhaps—brought on probably by rage—he had got the other woman in the house, remember; I expect he was no good. There was some sort of poison about—perhaps for a face-wash, perhaps as a drug. He put it in the milk and gave it to her."

'Here I interrupted: "How do you know it was in the milk?"

'The doctor did not reply to this. I had now swung the car round to the front of the ancient mansion—a poor, pretentious place, sinister in the half-darkness.

' "And then, when he had done it," continued Dr. Dilke, mounting the steps of the house, "he repented most horribly; he wanted to fly for a doctor to get some antidote for the poison with the idea in his head that if he could have got help he could have saved her himself. The other woman kept on laughing. He couldn't forgive her that—that she could laugh at a moment like that; he couldn't get help! He couldn't find a doctor. His wife died. No one suspected foul play—they seldom did in those days as long as the people were respectable; you must remember the state in which medical knowledge was in 1830. He couldn't marry the other woman, and he couldn't touch the money; he left it all to found the almshouses; then he died himself, six months afterwards, leaving instructions that his name should be added to that black stone. I dare say he died by his own hand. Probably he loved her through it all, you know—it was only the money, that cursed money, a fortune just within his grasp, but which he couldn't take."

' "A pretty romance," I suggested, as we entered the house; "I am sure there is a three-volume novel in it of what Mrs. Janey would call 'the good old-fashioned' sort."

'To this Dr. Dilke answered: "Suppose the miserable man can't rest? Supposing he is still searching for a doctor?"

'We passed from one room to another of the dismal, dusty, dismantled house. Dr. Dilke opened a damaged shutter which concealed one of the windows at the back, and pointed out in the waning light a decayed garden with stone steps and a fishpond; and a low

[257]

gateway to pass through which a man of his height would have had to stoop. We could just discern this in the twilight. He made no comment. We went upstairs.'

Here Cuming paused dramatically to give us the full flavour of the final part of his story. He reminded us, rather unnecessarily, for somehow he had convinced us that this was all perfectly true.

'I am not romancing; I won't answer for what Dr. Dilke said or did, or his adventure of the night before, or the story of the Carwithens as he constructed it, but *this* is actually what happened. . . . We went upstairs by the wide main stairs. Dr. Dilke searched about for and found a door which opened on to the back stairs, and then he said: "This must be the room." It was entirely devoid of any furniture, and stained with damp, the walls stripped of panelling and cheaply covered with decayed paper, peeling, and in parts fallen.

' "What's this?" said Dr. Dilke.

'He picked up a scrap of paper that showed vivid on the dusty floor and handed it to me. It was a prescription. He took out his notebook and showed me the page where this fitted in.

' "This page I tore out last night when I wrote that prescription in this room. The bed was just there, and there was the table on which were the papers and the glass of milk."

' "But you couldn't have been here last night," I protested feebly, the locked doors — the whole thing! . . ."

'Dr. Dilke said nothing. After a while neither did I. "Let's get out of this place," I said. Then another thought struck me. "What is your prescription?" I asked.

'He said: "A very uncommon kind of prescription, a very desperate sort of prescription, one that I've never written before, nor I hope shall again — an antidote for severe arsenical poisoning."

'I leave you,' smiled Cuming, 'to your various attitudes of incredulity or explanation.'

THE DEMON KING

by J. B. Priestley

John Boynton Priestley (1894–1984), one of the
most successful playwrights and novelists this
century, wrote this fantastic and strange little tale
shortly after his classic treatment of the British
vaudeville circuit, *The Good Companions*. 'The
Demon King' was included in his collection *Four in
Hand* (1934).

Among the company assembled for Mr. Tom Burt's Grand
Annual Pantomime at the old Theatre Royal, Bruddersford,
there was a good deal of disagreement. They were not quite
'the jolly, friendly party' they pretended to be—through the good
offices of 'Thespian'—to the readers of *The Bruddersford Herald* and
Weekly Herald Budget. The Principal Boy told her husband and about
fifty-five other people that she could work with anybody, was famous
for being able to work with anybody, but that nevertheless the
management had gone and engaged, as Principal Girl, the one woman
in the profession who made it almost impossible for anybody to work
with anybody. The Principal Girl told her friend, the Second Boy,
that the Principal Boy and the Second Girl were spoiling everything
and might easily ruin the show. The Fairy Queen went about pointing
out that she did not want to make trouble, being notoriously easy-
going, but that sooner or later the Second Girl would hear a few things
that she would not like. Johnny Wingfield had been heard to declare
that some people did not realize even yet that what audiences wanted
from a panto was some good fast comedy work by the chief comedian,

who had to have all the scope he required. Dippy and Doppy, the broker's men, hinted that even if there were two stages, Johnny Wingfield would want them both all the time.

But they were all agreed on one point, namely, that there was not a better demon in provincial panto than Mr. Kirk Ireton, who had been engaged by Mr. Tom Burt for this particular show. The pantomime was *Jack and Jill,* and those people who are puzzled to know what demons have to do with Jack and Jill, those innocent water-fetchers, should pay a visit to the nearest pantomime, which will teach them a lot they did not know about fairy tales. Kirk Ireton was not merely a demon, but the Demon King, and when the curtain first went up, you saw him on a darkened stage standing in front of a little chorus of attendant demons, made up of local baritones at ten shillings a night. Ireton looked the part, for he was tall and rather satanically featured and was known to be very clever with his make-up; and what was more important, he sounded the part too, for he had a tremendous bass voice, of most demonish quality. He had played Mephistopheles in *Faust* many times with a good touring opera company. He was, indeed, a man with a fine future behind him. If it had not been for one weakness, pantomime would never have seen him. The trouble was that for years now he had been in the habit of 'lifting the elbow' too much. That was how they all put it. Nobody said that he drank too much, but all agreed that he lifted the elbow. And the problem now was—would there be trouble because of this elbow-lifting?

He had rehearsed with enthusiasm, sending his great voice to the back of the empty, forlorn gallery in the two numbers allotted to him, but at the later rehearsals there had been ominous signs of elbow-lifting.

'Going to be all right, Mr. Ireton?' the stage-manager inquired anxiously.

Ireton raised his formidable and satanic eyebrows. 'Of course it is,' he replied, somewhat hoarsely. 'What's worrying you, old man?'

The other explained hastily that he wasn't worried. 'You'll go well here,' he went on. 'They'll eat those two numbers of yours. Very musical in these parts. But you know Bruddersford, of course. You've played here before.'

'I have,' replied Ireton grimly. 'And I loathe the damn' place. Bores me stiff. Nothing to do in it.'

This was not reassuring. The stage-manager knew only too well Mr. Ireton was already finding something to do in the town, and his enthusiastic description of the local golf courses had no effect. Ireton loathed golf too, it seemed. All very ominous.

They were opening on Boxing Day night. By the afternoon, it was known that Kirk Ireton had been observed lifting the elbow very determinedly in the smoke-room of The Cooper's Arms, near the theatre. One of the stage-hands had seen him: 'And by gow, he wor lapping it up an' all,' said this gentleman, no bad judge of anybody's power of suction. From there, it appeared, he had vanished, along with several other riotous persons, two of them thought to be Leeds men—and in Bruddersford they know what Leeds men are.

The curtain was due to rise at seven-fifteen sharp. Most members of the company arrived at the theatre very early. Kirk Ireton was not one of them. He was still absent at six-thirty, though he had to wear an elaborate make-up, with glittering tinselled eyelids and all the rest of it, and had to be on the stage when the curtain rose. A messenger was dispatched to his lodgings, which were not far from the theatre. Even before the messenger returned, to say that Mr. Ireton had not been in since noon, the stage-manager was desperately coaching one of the local baritones, the best of a stiff and stupid lot, in the part of the Demon King. At six-forty-five, no Ireton; at seven, no Ireton. It was hopeless.

'All right, that fellow's done for himself now,' said the great Mr. Burt, who had come to give his Grand Annual his blessing. 'He doesn't get another engagement from me as long as he lives. What's this local chap like?'

The stage-manager groaned and wiped his brow. 'Like nothing on earth except a bow-legged baritone from a Wesleyan choir.'

'He'll have to manage somehow. You'll have to cut the part.'

'Cut it, Mr. Burt! I've slaughtered it, and what's left of it, he'll slaughter.'

Mr. Tom Burt, like the sensible manager he was, believed in a pantomime opening in the old-fashioned way, with a mysterious dark scene among the supernaturals. Here it was a cavern in the hill beneath the Magic Well, and in these dismal recesses the Demon King and his attendants were to be discovered waving their crimson cloaks and plotting evil in good, round chest-notes. Then the Demon King would sing his number (which had nothing whatever to do with Jack and Jill or demonology either), the Fairy Queen would appear, accompanied by a white spotlight, there would be a little dialogue between them, and then a short duet.

[261]

The cavern scene was all set, the five attendant demons were in their places, while the sixth, now acting as King, was receiving a few last instructions from the stage-manager, and the orchestra, beyond the curtain, were coming to the end of the overture, when suddenly, from nowhere, there appeared on the dimly-lighted stage a tall and terrifically imposing figure.

'My God! There's Ireton,' cried the stage-manager, and bustled across, leaving the temporary Demon King abandoned, a pitiful makeshift now. The new arrival was coolly taking his place in the centre. He looked superb. The costume a skin-tight crimson affair touched with a baleful green, was far better than the one provided by the management. And the make-up was better still. The face had a greenish phosphorescent glow, and its eyes flashed between glittering lids. When he first caught sight of the face, the stage-manager felt a sudden idiotic tremor of fear, but being a stage-manager first and a human being afterwards (as all stage-managers have to be), he did not feel that tremor long, for it was soon chased away by a sense of elation. It flashed across his mind that Ireton must have gone running off to Leeds or somewhere in search of this stupendous costume and make-up. Good old Ireton! He had given them all a fright, but it had been worth it.

'All right, Ireton?' said the stage-manager quickly.

'All right,' replied the Demon King, with a magnificent, careless gesture.

'Well, you get back in the chorus then,' said the stage-manager to the Wesleyan baritone.

'That'll do me champion,' said the gentleman, with a sigh of relief. He was not ambitious.

'All ready.'

The violins began playing a shivery sort of music, and up the curtain went. The six attendant demons, led by the Wesleyan, who was in good voice now that he felt such a sense of relief, told the audience who they were and hailed their monarch in appropriate form. The Demon King, towering above them, dominating the scene superbly, replied in a voice of astonishing strength and richness. Then he sang the number allotted to him. It had nothing to do with Jack and Jill and very little to do with demons, being a rather commonplace bass song about sailors and shipwrecks and storms, with thunder and lightning effects supplied by the theatre. Undoubtedly this was the same song that had been rehearsed; the words were the same; the music was the same. Yet it all seemed different. It was really sinister. As you listened, you saw the great waves breaking over the doomed ships, and the pitiful little white faces disappearing in the dark flood. Somehow, the storm was much stormier. There was one great clap of thunder and flash of lightning that made all the attendant demons, the conductor of the orchestra, and a number of people in the wings, nearly jump out of their skins.

'And how the devil did you do that?' said the stage-manager, after running round to the other wing.

'That's what I said to 'Orace 'ere,' said the man in charge of the two sheets of tin and the cannon ball.

'Didn't touch a thing that time, did we, mate?' said Horace.

'If you ask me, somebody let off a firework, one o' them big Chinese crackers, for that one,' his mate continued. 'Somebody monkeying about, that's what it is.'

And now a white spotlight had found its way on to the stage, and there, shining in its pure ray, was Miss Dulcie Farrar, the Fairy Queen, who was busy waving a silver wand. She was also busy controlling her emotions, for somehow she felt unaccountably nervous. Opening night is opening night, of course, but Miss Farrar had been playing Fairy Queen for the last ten years (and Principal Girls for the ten years before them), and there was nothing in this part to worry her. She rapidly came to the conclusion that it was Mr. Ireton's sudden reappearance, after she had made up her mind that he was not turning up, that had made her feel so shaky, and this caused her to feel rather resentful. Moreover, as an experienced Fairy Queen who had had trouble with demons before, she was convinced that he was about to take more than his share of the stage. Just because he had hit upon such a good make-up! And it *was* a good make-up, there could be no question about that. That greenish face, those glittering eyes—really, it was awful. Overdoing it, she called it. After all, a panto *was* a panto.

Miss Farrar, still waving her wand, moved a step or two nearer, and cried:

> 'I know your horrid plot, you evil thing,
> And I defy you, though you are the Demon King.'

'What, you?' he roared, contemptuously, pointing a long forefinger at her.

Miss Farrar should have replied: 'Yes, I, the Queen of Fairyland,' but for a minute she could not get out a word. As that horribly long

[263]

forefinger shot out at her, she had felt a sudden sharp pain and had then found herself unable to move. She stood there, her wand held out at a ridiculous angle, motionless, silent, her mouth wide open. But her mind was active enough. 'Is it a stroke?' it was asking feverishly. 'Like Uncle Edgar had that time at Greenwich. Oo, it must be. Oo, whatever shall I do? Oo. Oo. Ooooo.'

'Ho-ho-ho-ho-ho.' The Demon King's sinister baying mirth resounded through the theatre.

'Ha-ha-ha-ha-ha.' This was from the Wesleyan and his friends, and was a very poor chorus of laughs, dubious, almost apologetic. It suggested that the Wesleyan and his friends were out of their depth, the depth of respectable Bruddersfordian demons.

Their king now made a quick little gesture with one hand, and Miss Farrar found herself able to move and speak again. Indeed, the next second, she was not sure that she had ever been *unable* to speak and move. That horrible minute had vanished like a tiny bad dream. She defied him again, and this time nothing happened beyond an exchange of bad lines of lame verse. There were not many of these, however, for there was the duet to be fitted in, and the whole scene had to be played in as short a time as possible. The duet, in which the two supernaturals only defied one another all over again, was early Verdi by way of the local musical director.

After singing a few bars each, they had a rest while the musical director exercised his fourteen instrumentalists in a most imposing operatic passage. It was during this half that Miss Farrar, who was now quite close to her fellow-duettist, whispered: 'You're in great voice, tonight, Mr. Ireton. Wish I was. Too nervous. Don't know why, but I am. Wish I could get it out like you.'

She received, as a reply, a flash of those glittering eyes (it really was an astonishing make-up) and a curious little signal with the long forefinger. There was no time for more, for now the voice part began again.

Nobody in the theatre was more surprised by what happened then than the Fairy Queen herself. She could not believe that the marvellously rich soprano voice that came pealing and soaring belonged to her. It was tremendous. Covent Garden would have acclaimed it. Never before, in all her twenty years of hard vocalism, had Miss Dulcie Farrar sung like that, though she had always felt that *somewhere* inside her there was a voice of that quality only waiting the proper signal to emerge and then astonish the world. Now, in some fantastic fashion, it had received that signal.

Not that the Fairy Queen overshadowed her supernatural colleague. There was no overshadowing *him*. He trolled in a diapason bass, and with a fine fury of gesture. The pair of them turned that stolen and botched duet into a work of art and significance. You could hear Heaven and Hell at battle in it. The curtain came down on a good rattle of applause. They are very fond of music in Bruddersford, but unfortunately the people who attend the first night of the pantomime are not the people who are most fond of music, otherwise there would have been a furore.

'Great stuff that,' said Mr. Tom Burt, who was on the spot. 'Never mind, Jim. Let 'em take a curtain. Go on, you two, take the curtain.' And when they had both bowed their acknowledgments, Miss Farrar excited and trembling, the Demon King cool and amused, almost contemptuous, Mr. Burt continued: 'That would have stopped the show in some places, absolutely stopped the show. But the trouble here is, they won't applaud, won't get going easily.'

'That's true, Mr. Burt,' Miss Farrar observed. 'They take a lot of warming up here. I wish they didn't. Don't you, Mr. Ireton?'

'Easy to warm them,' said the tall crimson figure.

'Well, if anything could, that ought to have done,' the lady remarked.

'That's so,' said Mr. Burt condescendingly. 'You were great, Ireton. But they won't let themselves go.'

'Yes, they will.' The Demon King, who appeared to be taking his part very seriously, for he had not yet dropped into his ordinary tones, flicked his long fingers in the air, roughly in the direction of the auditorium, gave a short laugh, turned away, and then somehow completely vanished, though it was not difficult to do that in those crowded wings.

Half an hour later, Mr. Burt, his manager, and the stage-manager, all decided that something must have gone wrong with Bruddersford. Liquor must have been flowing like water in the town. That was the only explanation.

'Either they're all drunk or I am,' cried the stage-manager.

'I've been giving 'em pantomime here for five-and-twenty years,' said Mr. Burt, 'and I've never known it happen before.'

'Well, nobody can say they're not enjoying it.'

'Enjoying it! They're enjoying it too much. They're going daft. Honestly, I don't like it. It's too much of a good thing.'

The stage-manager looked at his watch. 'It's holding up the show, that's certain. God knows when we're going to get through at this rate. If they're going to behave like this every night, we'll have to cut an hour out of it.

'Listen to 'em now,' said Mr. Burt. 'And that's one of the oldest gags in the show. Listen to 'em. Nay, dash it, they must be all half-seas over.'

What had happened? Why—this: that the audience had suddenly decided to let itself go in a fashion never known in Bruddersford before. The Bruddersfordians are notoriously difficult to please, not so much because their taste is so exquisite but rather because, having paid out money, they insist upon having their money's worth, and usually arrive at a place of entertainment in a gloomy and suspicious frame of mind. Really tough managers like to open a new show in Bruddersford, knowing very well that if it will go there, it will go anywhere. But for the last half-hour of this pantomime there had been more laughter and applause than the Theatre Royal had known for the past six months. Every entrance produced a storm of welcome. The smallest and stalest gags set the whole house screaming, roaring, and rocking. Every song was determinedly encored. If the people had been specially brought out of jail for the performance, they could not have been more easily pleased.

'Here,' said Johnny Wingfield, as he made an exit as a Dame pursued by a cow, 'this is frightening me. What's the matter with 'em? Is this a new way of giving the bird?'

'Don't ask me,' said the Principal Boy. 'I wasn't surprised they gave me such a nice welcome when I went on, because I've always been a favourite here, as Mr. Burt'll tell you, but the way they're carrying on now, making such a fuss over nothing, it's simply ridiculous. Slowing up the show, too.'

After another quarter of an hour of this monstrous enthusiasm, this delirium, Mr. Burt could be heard grumbling to the Principal Girl, with whom he was standing in that close proximity which Principal Girls somehow invite. 'I'll tell you what it is, Alice,' Mr. Burt was saying. 'If this goes on much longer, I'll make a speech from the stage, asking 'em to draw it mild. Never known 'em to behave like this. And it's a funny thing, I was only saying to somebody—now who was it that I said that to?—anyhow, I was only saying to somebody that I wished this audience would let themselves go a bit more. Well, now I wish they wouldn't. And that's that.'

There was a chuckle, not loud, but rich, and distinctly audible.

'Here,' cried Mr. Burt, 'who's that? What's the joke?'

It was obviously nobody in their immediate vicinity. 'It sounded like Kirk Ireton,' said the Principal Girl, 'judging by the voice.' But Ireton was nowhere to be seen. Indeed, one or two people who had been looking for him, both in his dressing-room and behind, had not been able to find him. But he would not be on again for another hour, and nobody had time to discover whether Ireton was drinking or not. The odd thing was, though, that the audience lost its wild enthusiasm just as suddenly as it had found it, and long before the interval had turned itself into the familiar stolid Bruddersford crowd, grimly waiting for its money's worth. The pantomime went on its way exactly as rehearsed, until it came to the time when the demons had to put in another appearance.

Jack, having found the magic water and tumbled down the hill, had to wander into the mysterious cavern and there rest awhile. At least, he declared that he would rest, but being played by a large and shapely female, and probably having that restless feminine temperament, what he did do was to sing a popular song with immense gusto. At the end of that song, when Jack once more declared that he would rest, the Demon King had to make a sudden appearance through a trap-door. And it was reported from below, where a spring-board was in readiness, that no Demon King had arrived to be shot on to the stage.

'Now where—oh, where—the devil has Ireton got to?' moaned the stage-manager, sending people right and left, up and down, to find him.

The moment arrived. Jack spoke his and her cue, and the stage-manager was making frantic signals to her from the wings.

'Ouh-wer,' screamed Jack, and produced the most realistic bit of business in the whole pantomime. For the stage directions read *shows fright*, and Jack undoubtedly did show fright, as well he (or she) might, for no sooner was the cue spoken than there came a horrible green flash, followed by a crimson glare, and standing before her, having apparently arrived from nowhere, was the Demon King. Jack was now in the power of the Demon King and would remain in those evil clutches until rescued by Jill and the Fairy Queen. And it seemed as if the Principal Boy had suddenly developed a capacity for acting (of which nobody had ever suspected her before), or else that she was thoroughly frightened, for now she behaved like a large rabbit in tights. The unrehearsed appearance of the Demon King seemed to have upset her, and now and then she sent uneasy glances into the wings.

It had been decided, after a great deal of talk and drinks round, to introduce a rather novel dancing scene into this pantomime, in the form of a sort of infernal ballet. The Demon King, in order to show his power and to impress his captive, would command his subjects to dance—that is, after he himself had indulged in a little singing, assisted by his faithful six. They talk of that scene yet in Bruddersford. It was only witnessed in its full glory on this one night, but that was enough, for it passed into civic history, and local landlords were often called in to settle bets about it in the pubs. First, the Demon King sang his second number, assisted by the Wesleyan and his friends. He made a glorious job of it too. Then the Demon King had to call for his dancing subjects, who were made up of the troupe of girls known as Tom Burt's Happy Yorkshire Lasses, daintily but demonishly tricked out in red and green. While the Happy Yorkshire Lasses pranced in the foreground, the six attendants were supposed to make a few rhythmical movements in the background, enough to suggest that, if they wanted to dance, they could dance, a suggestion that the stage-manager and the producer knew to be entirely false. The six, in fact, could not dance and would not try very hard, being not only wooden but also stubborn Bruddersford baritones.

But now, the Happy Yorkshire Lasses having tripped a measure, the Demon King sprang to his full height, which seemed to be about seven feet two inches, swept an arm along the Wesleyan six, and command-ed them harshly to dance. And they did dance, they danced like men possessed. The King himself beat time for them, flashing an eye at the conductor now and again to quicken that gentleman's baton, and his faithful six, all with the most grotesque and puzzled expressions on their faces, cut the most amazing capers, bounding high into the air, tumbling over one another, flinging their arms and legs about in an ecstasy, and all in time to the music. The sweat shone on their faces; their eyes rolled forlornly; but still they did not stop, but went on in crazier and crazier fashion, like genuine demons at play.

'All dance!' roared the Demon King, cracking his long fingers like a whip, and it seemed as if something had inspired the fourteen cynical men in the orchestra pit, for they played like madmen grown tuneful, and on came the Happy Yorkshire Lasses again, to fling themselves into the wild sport, not as if they were doing something they had rehearsed a hundred times, but as if they, too, were inspired. They joined the orgy of the bounding six, and now, instead of there being only eighteen Happy Lasses in red and green, there seemed to be dozens and dozens of them. The very stage seemed to get bigger and bigger, to give space to all these whirling figures of demoniac revelry. And as they all went spinning, leaping, cavorting crazily, the audience, shaken at last out of its stolidity, cheered them on, and all was one wild insanity.

Yet when it was done, when the King cried, 'Stop!' and all was over, it was as if it had never been, as if everybody had dreamed it, so that nobody was ready to swear that it had really happened. The Wesleyan and the other five all felt a certain faintness but each was convinced that he had imagined all that wild activity while he was making a few sedate movements in the background. Nobody could be quite certain about anything. The pantomime went on its way; Jack was rescued by Jill and the Fairy Queen (who was now complaining of neuralgia); and the Demon King allowed himself to be foiled after which he quietly disappeared again. They were looking for him when the whole thing was over except for that grand entry of all the characters at the very end. It was his business to march in with the Fairy Queen, the pair of them dividing between them all the applause for the supernaturals. Miss Farrar, feeling very miserable with her neuralgia, delayed her entrance for him, but as he was not to be found, she climbed the little ladder at the back alone, to march solemnly down the steps towards the audience. And the extraordinary thing was then when she was actually making her entrance, at the top of those steps, she discovered that she was not alone, that her fellow-supernatural was there too, and that he must have slipped away to freshen his make-up. He was more demonish than ever.

As they walked down between the files of Happy Yorkshire Lasses, now armed to the teeth with tinsel spears and shields, Miss Farrar whispered: 'Wish I'd arranged for a bouquet. You never get anything here.'

'You'd like some flowers?' said the fantastic figure at her elbow.

'Think I would! So would everybody else.'

'Quite easy,' he remarked, bowing slowly to the footlights. He took her hand and led her to one side, and it is a fact—as Miss Farrar will tell you, within half an hour of your making her acquaintance—that the moment their hands met, her neuralgia completely vanished. And now came the time for the bouquets. Miss Farrar knew what they would be: there would be one for the Principal Girl, bought by the management, and one for the Principal Boy, bought by herself.

'Oo, look!' cried the Second Boy. 'My gosh!—Bruddersford's gone mad.'

The space between the orchestra pit and the front row of stalls had been turned into a hothouse. The conductor was so busy passing up bouquets that he was no longer visible. There were dozens of bouquets, and all of them beautiful. It was monstrous. Somebody must have spent a fortune on flowers. Up they came, while everybody cheered, and every woman with a part had at least two or three. Miss Farrar, pink and wide-eyed above a mass of orchids, turned to her colleague among the supernaturals, only to find that once again he had quietly disappeared. Down came the curtain for the last time, but everybody remained standing there, with arms filled with expensive flowers, chattering excitedly. Then suddenly somebody cried, 'Oo!' and dropped *their* flowers, until at last everybody who had had a bouquet had dropped it and cried, 'Oo!'

'Hot,' cried the Principal Girl, blowing on her fingers, 'hot as anything, weren't they? Burnt me properly. That's a nice trick.'

'Oo, look!' said the Second Boy, once more. 'Look at 'em all. Withering away.' And they were, every one of them, all shedding their colour and bloom, curling, writhing, withering away. . . .

'Message come through for you, sir, an hour since,' said the doorkeeper to the manager, 'only I couldn't get at yer. From the Leeds Infirmary, it is. Says Mr. Ireton was knocked down in Board Lane by a car this afternoon, but he'll be all right to-morrow. Didn't know who he was at first, so couldn't let anybody know.'

The manager stared at him, made a number of strange noises, then fled, singing various imaginary temperance pledges as he went.

'And another thing,' said the stage-hand to the stage-manager. 'That's where I saw the bloke last. He was there one minute and next minute he wasn't. And look at the place. All scorched.'

'That's right,' said his mate, 'and what's more, just you take a whiff—that's all, just take a whiff. Oo's started using brimstone in this the-ater? Not me nor you neither. But I've a good idea who it is.'

LUCKY'S GROVE

by H. Russell Wakefield

Herbert Russell Wakefield (1888–1964) is another
of the great hallowed names in the history of
English ghost story literature, with several classic
collections to his credit. This remarkable tale of an
extremely weird Christmas tree first appeared in
The Clock Strikes Twelve (1940).

'And Loki begat Hel, Goddess of the Grave, Fenris, the Great
Wolf, and the Serpent, Nidnogg, who lives beneath The Tree.'

M r. Braxton strolled with his land-agent, Curtis, into the
Great Barn.
'There you are,' said Curtis, in a satisfied tone, 'the finest
little fir I ever saw, and the kiddies will never set eyes on a lovelier
Christmas tree.'
Mr. Braxton examined it; it stood twenty feet from huge green pot
to crisp, straight peak, and was exquisitely sturdy, fresh and symmetri-
cal.
'Yes, it's a beauty,' he agreed. 'Where did you find it?'
'In that odd little spinney they call Lucky's Grove in the long
meadow near the river boundary.'
'Oh!' remarked Mr. Braxton uncertainly. To himself he was saying
vaguely, 'He shouldn't have got it from there, of course he wouldn't
realize it, but he shouldn't have got it from there.'
'Of course we'll replant it,' said Curtis, noticing his employer's
diminished enthusiasm. 'It's a curious thing, but it isn't a young tree;

[271]

it's apparently fullgrown. Must be a dwarf variety, but I don't know as much about trees as I should like.'

Mr. Braxton was surprised to find there was one branch of country lore on which Curtis was not an expert; for he was about the best-known man at his job in the British Isles. Pigs, bees, chickens, cattle, crops, running a shoot, he had mastered them one and all. He paid him two thousand a year with house and car. He was worth treble.

'I expect it's all right,' said Mr. Braxton; 'it is just that Lucky's Grove is—is—well, "sacred" is perhaps too strong a word. Maybe I should have told you, but I expect it's all right.'

'That accounts for it then,' laughed Curtis. 'I thought there seemed some reluctance on the part of the men while we were yanking it up and getting it on the lorry. They handled it a bit gingerly; on the part of the older men, I mean; the youngsters didn't worry.'

'Yes, there would be,' said Mr. Braxton. 'But never mind, it'll be back in a few days and it's a superb little tree. I'll bring Mrs. Braxton along to see it after lunch,' and he strolled back into Abingdale Hall.

Fifty-five years ago Mr. Braxton's father had been a labourer on this very estate, and in that year young Percy, aged eight, had got an errand boy's job in Oxford. Twenty years later he'd owned one small shop. Twenty-five years after that fifty big shops. Now, though he had finally retired, he owned two hundred and eighty vast shops and was a millionaire whichever way you added it up. How had this happened? No one can quite answer such questions. Certainly he'd worked like a brigade of Trojans, but midnight oil has to burn in Aladdin's Lamp before it can transform ninepence into one million pounds. It was just that he asked no quarter from the unforgiving minute, but squeezed from it the fruit of others many hours. Those like Mr. Braxton seem to have their own time-scale; they just say the word and up springs a fine castle of commerce, but the knowledge of that word cannot be imparted; it is as mysterious as the Logos. But all through his great labours he had been moved by one fixed resolve—to avenge his father—that fettered spirit—for he had been an able, intelligent man who had had no earthly chance of revealing the fact to the world. Always the categorical determination had blazed in his son's brain, 'I will own Abingdale Hall, and, where my father sweated, I will rule and be lord.' And of course it had happened. Fate accepts the dictates of such men as Mr. Braxton, shrugs its shoulders, and leaves its revenge to Death. The Hall had come on the market just when he was about to retire, and with an odd delight, an obscure sense of homecoming, the native returned, and his riding boots, shooting boots, golf shoes, and all the many glittering guineas' worth, stamped in and obliterated the prints of his father's hob-nails.

That was the picture he often re-visualized, the way it amused him to 'put it to himself,' as he roamed his broad acres and surveyed the many glowing triumphs of his model husbandry.

Some credit was due to buxom, blithe and debonair Mrs. Braxton, kindly, competent and innately adaptable. She was awaiting him in the morning-room and they went in solitary state to luncheon. But it was the last peaceful lunch they would have for a spell—'The Families' were pouring in on the morrow.

As a footman was helping them to Sole Meunière Mr. Braxton said, 'Curtis has found a very fine Christmas tree. It's in the barn. You must come and look at it after lunch.'

'That *is* good,' replied his wife. 'Where did he get it from?'

Mr. Braxton hesitated for a moment.

'From Lucky's Grove.'

Mrs. Braxton looked up sharply.

'From the grove!' she said, surprised.

'Yes, of course he didn't realize—anyway it'll be all right, it's all rather ridiculous, and it'll be replanted before the New Year.'

'Oh, yes,' agreed Mrs. Braxton. 'After all it's only a clump of trees.'

'Quite. And it's just the right height for the ballroom. It'll be taken in there tomorrow morning and the electricians will work on it in the afternoon.'

'I heard from Lady Pounser just now,' said Mrs. Braxton. 'She's bringing six over, that'll make seventy-four; only two refusals. The presents are arriving this afternoon.'

They discussed the party discursively over the cutlets and Pêche Melba and soon after lunch walked across to the barn. Mr. Braxton waved to Curtis, who was examining a new tractor in the garage fifty yards away, and he came over.

Mrs. Braxton looked the tree over and was graciously delighted with it, but remarked that the pot could have done with another coat of paint. She pointed to several streaks, rust-coloured, running through the green. 'Of course it won't show when it's wrapped, but they didn't do a very good job.'

Curtis leant down. 'They certainly didn't,' he answered irritably. 'I'll see to it. I think it's spilled over from the soil; that copse is on a curious patch of red sand—there are some at Frilford too. When we pulled it up I noticed the roots were stained a dark crimson.' He put his hand down and scraped at the stains with his thumb. He seemed a shade puzzled.

'It shall have another coat at once, he said. 'What did you think of Lampson and Colletts' scheme for the barn?'

'Quite good,' replied Mrs. Braxton, 'but the sketches for the chairs are too fancy.'

'I agree,' said Curtis, who usually did so in the case of unessentials, reserving his tactful vetoes for the others.

The Great Barn was by far the most aesthetically satisfying as it was the oldest feature of the Hall buildings: it was vast, exquisitely proportioned and mellow. That could hardly be said of the house itself, which the 4th Baron of Abingdale had rebuilt on the cinders of its predecessor in 1752.

This nobleman had travelled abroad extensively and returned with most enthusiastic, grandiose and indigestible ideas of architecture. The result was a gargantuan piece of rococo-jocoso which only an entirely humourless pedant could condemn. It contained forty-two bedrooms and eighteen reception rooms—so Mrs. Braxton had made it at the last recount. But Mr. Braxton had not repeated with the interior the errors of the 4th Baron. He'd briefed the greatest expert in Europe with the result that that interior was quite tasteful and sublimely comfortable.

'Ugh!' he exclaimed, as they stepped out into the air, 'it *is* getting nippy!'

'Yes,' said Curtis, 'there's a nor'-easter blowing up—may be snow for Christmas.'

On getting back to the house Mrs. Braxton went into a huddle with butler and housekeeper and Mr. Braxton retired to his study for a doze. But instead his mind settled on Lucky's Grove. When he's first seen it again after buying the estate, it seemed as if fifty years had rolled away, and he realised that Abingdale was far more summed up to him in the little copse than in the gigantic barracks two miles away. At once he felt at home again. Yet, just as when he'd been a small boy, the emotion the Grove had aroused in him had been sharply tinged with awe, so it had been now, half a century later. He still had a sneaking dread of it. How precisely he could see it, glowing darkly in the womb of the fire before him, standing starkly there in the centre of the big, fallow field, a perfect circle; and first, a ring of holm-oaks and, facing east, a breach therein to the firs and past them on the west a gap to the yews. It had always required a tug at his courage—not always forthcoming—to pass through them and face the mighty Scotch fir, rearing up its great bole from the grass mound. And when he stood before it, he'd always known an odd longing to fling himself down and—well, worship—it was the only word—the towering tree. His father had told him his forebears had done that very thing, but always when alone and at certain seasons of the year; and that no bird or beast was ever seen there. A lot of traditional nonsense, no doubt, but he himself had absorbed the spirit of the place and knew it would always be so.

One afternoon in late November, a few weeks after they had moved in, he'd gone off alone in the drowsing misty dark; and when he'd reached the holm-oak bastion and seen the great tree surrounded by its sentinels, he'd known again that quick turmoil of confused emotions. As he'd walked slowly towards it, it had seemed to quicken and be aware of his coming. As he passed the shallow grassy fosse and entered the oak ring he felt there was something he ought to say, some greeting, password or prayer. It was the most aloof, silent little place under the sun, and oh, so old. He'd tiptoed past the firs and faced the barrier of yews. He'd stood there for a long musing minute, tingling with the sensation that he was being watched and regarded. At length he stepped forward and stood before the God—that mighty word came abruptly and unforeseen—and he felt a wild desire to fling himself down on the mound and do obeisance. And then he'd hurried home. As he recalled all this most vividly and minutely, he was seized with a sudden gust of uncontrollable anger at the thought of the desecration of the grove. He knew now that if he'd had the slightest idea of Curtis's purpose he'd have resisted and opposed it. It was too late now. He realised he'd 'worked himself up' rather absurdly. What could it matter! He was still a superstitious bumpkin at heart. Anyway it was no fault of Curtis. It was the finest Christmas tree anyone could hope for, and the whole thing was too nonsensical for words. The general tone of these cadentic conclusions did not quite accurately represent his thoughts—a very rare failing with Mr. Braxton.

About dinner-time the blizzard set furiously in, and the snow was flying.

'Chains on the cars tomorrow,' Mrs. Braxton told the head chauffeur.

'Boar's Hill'll be a beggar,' thought that person.

Mr. and Mrs. Braxton dined early, casually examined the presents, and went to bed. Mr. Braxton was asleep at once as usual, but was awakened by the beating of a blind which had slipped its moorings. Reluctantly he got out of bed and went to fix it. As he was doing so he became conscious of the frenzied hysterical barking of a dog. The sound, muffled by the gale, came, he judged, from the barn. He believed the underkeeper kept his whippet there. Scared by the storm, he supposed, and returned to bed.

The morning was brilliantly fine and cold, but the snowfall had been heavy.

'I heard a dog howling in the night, Perkins,' said Mr. Braxton to the butler at breakfast; 'Drake's I imagine. What's the matter with it?'

'I will ascertain, sir,' replied Perkins.

'It was Drake's dog,' he announced a little later, 'apparently something alarmed the animal, for when Drake went to let it out this morning, it appeared to be extremely frightened. When the barn door was opened, it took to its heels and, although Drake pursued it, it jumped into the river and Drake fears it was drowned.'

'Um,' said Mr. Braxton, 'must have been the storm; whippets are nervous dogs.'

'So I understand, sir.'

'Drake was so fond of it,' said Mrs. Braxton, 'though it always looked so naked and shivering to me.'

'Yes, madam,' agreed Perkins, 'it had that appearance.'

Soon after Mr. Braxton sauntered out into the blinding glitter. Curtis came over from the garage. He was heavily muffled up.

'They've got the chains on all the cars,' he said. 'Very seasonable and all that, but farmers have another word for it.' His voice was thick and hoarse.

'Yes,' said Mr. Braxton. 'You're not looking very fit.'

'Not feeling it. Had to get up in the night. Thought I heard someone trying to break into the house, thought I saw him, too.'

'Indeed,' said Mr. Braxton. 'Did you see what he was like?'

'No,' replied Curtis uncertainly. 'It was snowing like the devil. Anyway, I got properly chilled to the marrow, skipping around in my nightie.'

'You'd better get to bed,' said Mr. Braxton solicitously. He had affection and a great respect for Curtis.

'I'll stick it out today and see how I feel tomorrow. We're going to get the tree across in a few minutes. Can I borrow the two footmen? I want another couple of pullers and haulers.'

Mr. Braxton consented, and went off on his favourite little stroll across the sparkling meadows to the river and the pool where the big trout set their cunning noses to the stream.

Half an hour later Curtis had mobilised his scratch team of sleeve-rolled assistants and, with Perkins steering and himself breaking, they got to grips with the tree and bore it like a camouflaged battering-ram towards the ball-room, which occupied the left centre of the frenetic frontage of the ground floor. There was a good deal of bumping and boring and genial blasphemy before the tree was manoeuvred into the middle of the room and levered by rope and muscle into position. As it came up its pinnacle just cleared the ceiling. Sam, a cow-man, whose ginger mob had been buried in the foliage for some time, exclaimed tartly as he slapped the trunk, 'There ye are, ye old sod! Thanks for the scratches on me mug, ye old—!'

The next moment he was lying on his back, a livid weal across his right cheek.

This caused general merriment, and even Perkins permitted himself a spectral smile. There was more astonishment than pain on the face of Sam. He stared at the tree in a humble way for a moment, like a chastised and guilty dog, and then slunk from the room. The merriment of the others died away.

'More spring in these branches than you'd think,' said Curtis to Perkins.

'No doubt, sir, that is due to the abrupt release of the tension,' replied Perkins scientifically.

The 'Families' met at Paddington and travelled down together so at five o'clock three car-loads drew up at the Hall. There were Jack and Mary with Paddy aged eight, Walter and Pamela with Jane and Peter, seven and five respectively, and George and Gloria with Gregory and Phyllis, ten and eight.

Jack and Walter were sons of the house. They were much of a muchness, burly, handsome and as dominating as their sire; a fine pair of commercial kings, entirely capable rulers, but just lacking that something which founds dynasties. Their wives conformed equally to the social type to which they belonged, good-lookers, smart dressers, excellent wives and mothers, but rather coolly colourless, spiritually. Their offspring were 'charming children,' flawless products of the English matrix, though Paddy showed signs of some obstreperous originality. 'George' was the Honourable George, Calvin, Roderick, et cetera Penables, and Gloria was Mr. and Mrs. Braxton's only daughter. George had inherited half a million and had started off at twenty-four to be something big in the City. In a sense he achieved his ambition, for two years later he was generally reckoned the biggest 'Something' in the City, from which he then withdrew, desperately clutching his last hundred thousand and vowing lachrymose repentance. He had kept his word and his wad, hunted and shot six days a week in the winter, and spent most of the summer wrestling with the two dozen devils in his golf bag. According to current jargon he was the complete extrovert, but what a relief are such, in spite of the pitying shrugs of those who for ever are peering into the septic recesses of their souls.

Gloria had inherited some of her father's force. She was rather overwhelmingly primed with energy and pep for her opportunities of releasing it. So she was always rather pent up and explosive, though maternity had kept the pressure down. She was dispassionately fond of George who had presented her with a nice little title and aristocratic background and two 'charming children.' Phyllis gave promise of such extreme beauty that, beyond being the cynosure of every press-camera's eye, and making a resounding match, no more was to be expected of her. Gregory, however, on the strength of some artistic precocity and a violent temper was already somewhat prematurely marked down as a genius to be.

Such were the 'Families.'

During the afternoon four engineers arrived from one of the Braxton factories to fix up the lighting of the tree. The fairy lamps for this had been specially designed and executed for the occasion. Disney figures had been grafted upon them and made to revolve by an ingenious mechanism; the effect being to give the tree, when illuminated, an aspect of whirling life meant to be very cheerful and pleasing.

Mr. Braxton happened to see these electricians departing in their lorry and noticed one of them had a bandaged arm and a rather white face. He asked Perkins what had happened.

'A slight accident, sir. A bulb burst and burnt him in some manner. But the injury is, I understand, not of a very serious nature.'

'He looked a bit white.'

'Apparently, sir, he got a fright, a shock of some kind, when the bulb exploded.'

After dinner the grown-ups went to the ball-room. Mr. Braxton switched on the mechanism and great enthusiasm was shown. 'Won't the kiddies love it,' said George, grinning at the kaleidoscope. 'Look at the Big Bad Wolf. He looks so darn realistic I'm not sure I'd give him a "U" certificate.'

'It's almost frightening,' said Pamela, 'they look incredibly real. Daddie, you really are rather bright, darling.'

It was arranged that the work of decoration should be tackled on the morrow and finished on Christmas Eve.

'All the presents have arrived,' said Mrs. Braxton, 'and are being unpacked. But I'll explain about them tomorrow.'

They went back to the drawing-room. Presently Gloria puffed and remarked.

'Papa, aren't you keeping the house rather too hot?'

'I noticed the same thing,' said Mrs. Braxton.

Mr. Braxton walked over to a thermometer on the wall. 'You're right,' he remarked, 'seventy.' He rang the bell.

'Perkins,' he asked, 'who's on the furnace?'

'Churchill, sir.'

'Well, he's overdoing it. It's seventy. Tell him to get it back to fifty-seven.'

Perkins departed and returned shortly after.

'Churchill informs me he has damped down and cannot account for the increasing warmth, sir.'

'Tell him to get it back to fifty-seven at once,' rapped Mr. Braxton.

'Very good, sir.'

'Open a window,' said Mrs. Braxton.

'It is snowing again, madam.'

'Never mind.'

'My God!' exclaimed Mary, when she and Jack went up to bed. 'That furnace-man is certainly stepping on it. Open all the windows.'

A wild flurry of snow beat against the curtains.

Mr. Braxton did what he very seldom did, woke up in the early hours. He awoke sweating from a furtive and demoralising dream. It had seemed to him that he had been crouching down in the fosse round Lucky's Grove and peering beneath the holm-oaks, and that there had been activity of a sort vaguely to be discerned therein, some quick, shadowy business. He knew a very tight terror at the thought of being detected at this spying, but he could not wrench himself away. That was all and he awoke still trembling and troubled. No wonder he'd had such a nightmare, the room seemed like a stokehold. He went to the windows and flung another open, and as he did so he

[279]

glanced out. His room looked over the rock garden and down the path to the maze. Something moved just outside, it caught his eye. He thought he knew what it was, that big Alsatian which had been sheep-worrying in the neighbourhood. What an enormous brute. Or was it just because it was outlined against the snow? It vanished suddenly, apparently into the maze. He'd organize a hunt for it after Christmas; if the snow lay, it should be easy to track.

The first thing he did after breakfast was to send for Churchill, severely reprimand him and threaten him with dismissal from his ship. That person was almost tearfully insistent that he had obeyed orders and kept his jets low. 'I can't make it out, sir. It's got no right to be as 'ot as what it is.'

'That's nonsense!' said Mr. Braxton. 'The system has been perfected and cannot take charge, as you suggest. See to it. You don't want me to get an engineer down, do you?'

'No, sir.'

'That's enough, Get it to fifty-seven and keep it there.'

Shortly after Mrs. Curtis rang up to say her husband was quite ill with a temperature and that the Doctor was coming. Mr. Braxton asked her to ring him again after he'd been.

During the morning the children played in the snow. After a pitched battle in which the girls lost their tempers, Gregory organized the erection of a snowman. He designed, the others fetched the material. He knew he had a reputation for brilliance to maintain and produce something Epsteinish, huge and squat. The other children regarded it with little enthusiasm, but, being Gregory, they supposed it must be admired. When it was finished Gregory wandered off by himself while the others went in to dry. He came in a little late for lunch during which he was silent and preoccupied. Afterwards the grown-ups sallied forth.

'Let's see your snowman, Greg,' said Gloria, in a mother-of-genius tone.

'It isn't all his, we helped,' said Phyllis, voicing a point of view which was to have many echoes in the coming years.

'Why, he's changed it!' exclaimed a chorus two minutes later.

'What an ugly thing!' exclaimed Mary, rather pleased at being able to say so with conviction.

Gregory had certainly given his imagination its head, for now the squat, inert truck was topped by a big wolf's head with open jaw and ears snarlingly laid back, surprisingly well modelled. Trailing behind it was a coiled, serpentine tail.

'Whatever gave you the idea for that?' asked Jack.

Usually Gregory was facile and eloquent in explaining his inspiration, but this time he refused to be drawn, bit his lip and turned away.

There was a moment's silence and then Gloria said with convincing emphasis, 'I think it's wonderful, Greg!'

And then they strolled off to examine the pigs and the poultry and the Suffolk punches.

They had just got back for tea when the telephone bell rang in Mr. Braxton's study. It was Mrs. Curtis. The patient was no better and Doctor Knowles had seemed rather worried, and so on. So Mr. Braxton rang up the doctor.

'I haven't diagnosed his trouble yet,' he said. 'And I'm going to watch him carefully and take a blood-test if he's not better tomorrow. He has a temperature of a hundred and two, but no other superficial symptoms, which is rather peculiar. By the way, one of your cow-men, Sam Colley, got a nasty wound on the face yesterday and shows signs of blood poisoning. I'm considering sending him to hospital. Some of your other men have been in to see me—quite a little outbreak of illness since Tuesday. However, I hope we'll have a clean bill again soon. I'll keep you informed about Curtis.'

Mr. Braxton was one of those incredible people who never have a day's illness—till their first and last. Consequently his conception of disease was unimaginative and mechanical. If one of his more essential human machines was running unsatisfactorily, there was a machine-mender called a doctor whose business it was to ensure that all the plug leads were attached firmly and that the manifold drain-pipe was not blocked. But he found himself beginning to worry about Curtis, and this little epidemic amongst his henchmen affected him disagreeably—there was something disturbing to his spirit about it. But just what and why, he couldn't analyse and decide.

After dinner, with the children out of the way, the business of decorating the tree was begun. The general scheme had been sketched out and coloured by one of the Braxton display experts and the company consulted this as they worked, which they did rather silently; possibly Mr. Braxton's palpable anxiety somewhat affected them.

Pamela stayed behind after the others had left the ball-room to put some finishing touches to her section of the tree. When she rejoined the others she was looking rather white and tight-lipped. She said

[281]

good night a shade abruptly and went to her room. Walter, a very, very good husband, quickly joined her.

'Anything the matter, old girl?' he asked anxiously.

'Yes,' replied Pamela, 'I'm frightened.'

'Frightened! What d'you mean?'

'You'll think it's all rot, but I'll tell you. When you'd all left the ball-room, I suddenly felt very uneasy—you know the sort of feeling when one keeps on looking round and can't concentrate. However, I stuck at it. I was a little way up the steps when I heard a sharp hiss from above me in the tree. I jumped back to the floor and looked up; now, of course, you won't believe me, but the trunk of the tree was moving—it was like the coils of a snake writhing upward, and there was something at the top of the tree, horrid-looking, peering at me. I know you won't believe me.'

Walter didn't, but he also didn't know what to make of it. 'I know what happened!' he improvised slightly. 'You'd been staring in at that trunk for nearly two hours and you got dizzy—like staring at the sun on the sea; and that snow dazzle this afternoon helped it. You've heard of snow-blindness—something like that, it still echoes form the retina or whatever. . . .'

'You think it might have been that?'

'I'm sure of it.'

'And that horrible head?'

'Well, as George put it rather brightly, I don't think some of those figures on the lamps should get a "U" certificate. There's the wolf to which he referred, and the witch.'

'Which witch?' laughed Pamela a little hysterically. 'I didn't notice one.'

'I did. I was working just near it, at least, I suppose it's meant to be a witch. A figure in black squinting round from behind a tree. As a matter of fact fairies never seemed all fun and frolic to me, there's often something diabolical about them—or rather casually cruel. Disney knows that.'

'Yes, there is,' agreed Pamela. 'So you think that's all there was to it?'

'I'm certain. One's eyes can play tricks on one.'

'Yes,' said Pamela, 'I know what you mean, as if they saw what one knew wasn't there or was different. Though who would "one" be then?'

'Oh, don't ask me that sort of question!' laughed Walter. 'Probably Master Gregory will be able to tell you in a year or two.'

'He's a nice little boy, really,' protested Pamela. 'Gloria just spoils him and it's natural.'

'I know he is, it's not his fault, but they will *force* him. Look at that snow-man—and staying behind to do it. A foul-looking thing!'

'Perhaps his eyes played funny tricks with him,' said Pamela.

'What d'you mean by that?'

'I don't know why I said it,' said Pamela frowning. 'Sort of echo, I suppose. Let's go to bed.'

Walter kissed her gently but fervently, as he loved her. He was a one-lady's man and had felt a bit nervous about her for a moment or two.

Was the house a little cooler? wondered Mr. Braxton, as he was undressing, or was it that he was getting more used to it? He was now convinced there was something wrong with the installation; he'd get an expert down. Meanwhile they must stick it. He yawned, wondered how Curtis was, and switched off the light.

Soon all the occupants were at rest and the great house swinging silently against the stars. *Should* have been at rest, rather, for one and all recalled that night with reluctance and dread. Their dreams were harsh and unhallowed, yet oddly related, being concerned with dim, uncertain and yet somehow urgent happenings in and around the house, as though some thing or things were stirring while they slept and communicated their motions to their dreaming consciousness. They awoke tired with a sense of unaccountable malaise.

Mrs. Curtis rang up during breakfast and her voice revealed her distress. Timothy was delirious and much worse. The doctor was coming at 10.30.

Mr. and Mrs. Braxton decided to go over there, and sent for the car. Knowles was waiting just outside the house when they arrived.

'He's very bad,' he said quietly. 'I've sent for two nurses and Sir Arthur Galley; I want another opinion. Has he had some trouble with a tree?'

'Trouble with a tree!' said Mr. Braxton, his nerves giving a flick.

'Yes, it's probably just a haphazard, irrational idea of delirium, but he continually fusses about some tree.'

'How bad is he?' asked Mrs. Braxton.

The doctor frowned. 'I wish I knew. I'm fairly out of my depth. He's keeping up his strength fairly well, but he can't go on like this.'

'As bad as that!' exclaimed Mr. Braxton.

'I'm very much afraid so. I'm anxiously awaiting Sir Arthur's verdict. By the way, that cow-man is very ill indeed; I'm sending him into hospital.'

'What happened to him?' asked Mr. Braxton, absently, his mind on Curtis.

'Apparently a branch of your Christmas tree snapped back at him and struck his face. Blood-poisoning set in almost at once.'

Mr. Braxton felt that tremor again, but merely nodded.

'I was just wondering if there might be some connection between the two, that Curtis is blaming himself for the accident. Seems an absurd idea, but judging from his ravings he appears to think he is lashed to some tree and that the great heat he feels comes from it.'

They went into the house and did their best to comfort and reassure Mrs. Curtis, instructed Knowles to ring up as soon as Sir Arthur's verdict was known, and then drove home.

The children had just come in from playing in the snow.

'Grandpa, the snow-man's melted,' said Paddy, 'did it thaw in the night?'

'Must have done,' replied Mr. Braxton, forcing a smile.

'Come and look, Grandpa,' persisted Paddy, 'there's nothing left of it.'

'Grandpa doesn't want to be bothered,' said Mary, noticing his troubled face.

'I'll come,' said Mr. Braxton. When he reached the site of the snow-man his thoughts were still elsewhere, but his mind quickly re-focused itself, for he was faced with something a little strange. Not a vestige of the statue remained, though the snow was frozen crisp and crunched hard beneath their feet; and yet that snow-man was completely obliterated and where it had stood was a circle of bare, brown grass.

'It must have thawed in the night and then frozen again,' he said uncertainly.

'Then why—' began Paddy.

'Don't bother Grandpa,' said Mary sharply. 'He's told you what happened.'

They wandered off toward the heavy, hurrying river.

'Are those dog-paw marks?' asked Phyllis.

That reminded Mr. Braxton. He peered down. 'Yes,' he replied. 'And I bet they're those of that brute of an Alsatian; it must be a colossal beast.'

'And it must have paws like a young bear,' laughed Mary. 'They're funny dogs, sort of Jekyll and Hydes. I rather adore them.'

[284]

'You wouldn't adore this devil. He's all Hyde.' (I'm in the wrong mood for these festivities, he thought irritably.)

During the afternoon George and Walter took the kids to a cinema in Oxford; the others finished the decoration of the tree.

The presents, labelled with the names of their recipients, were arranged on tables round the room and the huge cracker, ten feet long and forty inches in circumference, was placed on its gaily-decorated trestle near the tree. Just as the job was finished, Mary did a three-quarters faint, but was quickly revived with brandy.

'It's the simply ghastly heat in the house!' exclaimed Gloria, who was not looking too grand herself. 'The installation must be completely diseased. Ours always works perfectly.' Mary had her dinner in bed and Jack came up to her immediately he had finished his.

'How are you feeling, darling?' he asked.

'Oh, I'm all right.'

'It *was* just the heat, of course?'

'Oh, yes,' replied Mary with rather forced emphasis.

'Scared you a bit, going off like that?' suggested Jack, regarding her rather sharply.

'I'm quite all right, thank you,' said Mary in the tone she always adopted when she'd had enough of a subject. 'I'd like to rest. Switch off the light.'

But when Jack had gone, she didn't close her eyes, but lay on her back staring up at the faint outline of the ceiling. She frowned and lightly chewed the little finger of her left hand, a habit of hers when unpleasantly puzzled. Mary, like most people of strong character and limited imagination, hated to be puzzled. Everything she considered ought to have a simple explanation if one tried hard enough to find it. But how could one explain this odd thing that had happened to her? Besides the grandiose gifts on the tables which bore a number, as well as the recipient's name, a small present for everyone was hung on the tree. This also bore a number, the same one as the lordly gift, so easing the Braxton's task of handing these out to the right people. Mary had just fixed Curtis's label to a cigarette lighter and tied it on the tree when it swung on its silk thread, so that the back of the card was visible; and on it was this inscription: 'Died, December 25th, 1938.' It spun away again and back and the inscription was no longer there.

Now Mary came of a family which rather prided itself on being unimaginative. Her father had confined his flights of fancy to the Annual Meeting of his Shareholders, while to her mother, imagination and mendacity were at least first cousins. So Mary could hardly credit the explanation that, being remotely worried about Mr. Curtis, she had subconsciously concocted that sinister sentence. On the other hand she knew poor Mr. Curtis was very ill and, therefore, perhaps, if her brain had played that malign little trick on her, it might have done so in 'tombstone writing.'

This was a considerable logical exercise for Mary, the effort tired her, the impression began to fade and she started wondering how much longer Jack was going to sit up. She dozed off and there, as if flashed on the screen 'inside her head' was 'Died, December 25th, 1938.' This, oddly enough, completely reassured her. There was 'nothing there' this time. There had been nothing that other time. She'd been very weak and imaginative even to think otherwise.

While she was deciding this, Dr. Knowles rang up. 'Sir Arthur has just been,' he said. 'And I'm sorry to say he's pessimistic. He says Curtis is very weak.'

'But what's the matter with him?' asked Mr. Braxton urgently.

'He doesn't know. He calls it P.U.O., which really means nothing.'

'But what's it stand for?'

'Pyrexia unknown origin. There are some fevers which cannot be described more precisely.'

'How ill is he really?'

'All I can say is, we must hope for the best.'

'My God!' exclaimed Mr. Braxton. 'When's Sir Arthur coming again?'

'At eleven tomorrow. I'll ring you up after he's been.'

Mr. Braxton excused himself and went to his room. Like many men of his dominating, sometimes ruthless type, he was capable of an intensity of feeling, anger, resolution, desire for revenge, but also affection and sympathy, unknown to more superficially Christian and kindly souls. He was genuinely attached to Curtis and his wife and very harshly and poignantly moved by this news which, he realised, could hardly have been worse. He would have to exercise all his will power if he was to sleep.

If on the preceding night the rest of the sleepers had been broken by influences which had insinuated themselves into their dreams, that which caused the night of that Christmas Eve to be unforgettable was the demoniacal violence of the elements. The northeaster had been waxing steadily all the evening and by midnight reached hurrican force, driving before it an almost impenetrable wall of snow. Not only so, but continually all through the night the wall was enflamed, and the roar of the hurricane silenced, by fearful flashes of lightning and claps of thunder. The combination was almost intolerably menacing. As the great house shook from the gale and trembled at the blasts and the windows blazed with strange polychoromatic balls of flame, all were tense and troubled. The children fought or succumbed to their terror according to their natures; their parents soothed and reassured them.

Mr. Braxton was convinced the lightning conductors were struck three times within ten minutes, and he could imagine them recoiling from the mighty impacts and seething from the terrific charges. Not till a dilatory, chaotic dawn staggered up the sky did the storm temporarily lull. For a time the sky cleared and the frost came hard. It was a yawning and haggard company which assembled at breakfast. But determined efforts were made to engender a communal cheerfulness. Mr. Braxton did his best to contribute his quota of seasonal bonhomie, but his mind was plagued by thoughts of Curtis. Before the meal was finished the vicar rang up to say the church tower had been struck and almost demolished, so there could be no services. It rang again to say that Brent's farmhouse had been burnt to the ground.

While the others went off to inspect the Church Mr. Braxton remained in the study. Presently Knowles rang to say Sir Arthur had been and pronounced Curtis weaker, but his condition was not quite hopeless. One of the most ominous symptoms was the violence of the delirium. Curtis appeared to be in great terror and sedatives had no effect.

'How's that cow-man?' asked Mr. Braxton.

'He died in the night, I'm sorry to say.'

Whereupon Mr. Braxton broke one of his strictest rules by drinking a very stiff whisky with very little soda.

Christmas dinner was tolerably hilarious, and after it, the children, bulging and incipiently bilious, slept some of it off, while their elders put the final touches to the preparations for the party.

In spite of the weather, not a single 'cry-off' was telephoned. There was a good reason for this, Mr. Braxton's entertainments were justly famous.

So from four-thirty onwards the 'Cream of North Berkshire Society' came ploughing through the snow to the Hall; Lady Pounser and party bringing up the rear in her heirloom Rolls which was dribbling steam from its ancient and aristocratic beak. A tea of teas, not merely a high-tea, an Everest tea, towering, skyscraping, was then attacked by the already stuffed juveniles who, by the end of it, were almost livid with repletion, finding even the efforts of cracker-pulling almost beyond them.

They were then propelled into the library where rows of chairs had been provided for them. There was a screen at one end of the room, a projector at the other. Mr. Braxton had provided one of his famous surprises! The room was darkened and on the screen was flashed the sentence: 'The North Berks News Reel.'

During the last few weeks Mr. Braxton had had a sharp-witted and discreetly furtive camera-man at work shooting some of the guests while busy about their more or less lawful occasions.

For example, there was a sentence from a speech by Lord Gallen, the Socialist Peer: 'It is a damnable and calculated lie for our opponents to suggest we aim at a proposterous and essentially *inequitable* equalisation of income—' And then there was His Lordship just entering his limousine, and an obsequious footman, rug in hand, holding the door open for him.

His Lordship's laughter was raucous and vehement, though he *would* have liked to have said a few words in rebuttal.

And there was Lady Pounser's Rolls, locally known as 'the hippo-griffe,' stuck in a snow-drift and enveloped in steam, with the caption, 'Oh, Mr. Mercury, *do* give me a start!' And other kindly, slightly sardonic japes at the expense of the North Berks Cream.

The last scene was meant as an appropriate prelude to the climax of the festivities. It showed Curtis and his crew digging up the tree from Lucky's Grove. Out they came from the holm-oaks straining under their load, but close observers noticed there was one who remained behind, standing menacing and motionless, a very tall, dark, brooding figure. There came a blinding lightning flash which seemed to blaze sparking round the room and a fearsome metallic bang. The storm had returned with rasping and imperious salute.

The lights immediately came on and the children were marshalled into the ball-room. As they entered and saw the high tree shining there and the little people so lively upon its branches a prolonged 'O—h!' of astonishment was exhorted from the blasé brats. But there was another wave of flame against the windows which rattled wildly at the ensuing roar, and the cries of delight were tinged with terror. And, indeed, the hard, blue glare flung a sinister glow on the tree and its whirling throng.

The grown-ups hastened to restore equanimity and, forming rings of children, circled round the tree.

Presently Mrs. Braxton exclaimed: 'Now then, look for your names on the cards and see what Father Christmas has brought you.'

Though hardly one of the disillusioned infants retained any belief in that superannuated Deliverer of Goods, the response was immediate. For they had sharp ears which had eagerly absorbed the tales of Braxton munificence. (At the same time it was noticeable that some approached the tree with diffidence, almost reluctance, and started back as a livid flare broke against the window-blinds and the dread peals shook the streaming snow from the eaves.)

Mary had just picked up little Angela Rayner so that she could reach her card, when the child screamed out and pulled away her hand.

'The worm!' she cried, and a thick, black-grey squirming maggot fell from her fingers to the floor and writhed away. George, who was near, put his shoe on it with a squish.

One of the Pounser tribe, whose card was just below the Big Bad Wolf, refused to approach it. No wonder, thought Walter, for it looked horribly hunting and alive. There were other mischances too. The witch behind the sombre tree seemed to pounce out at Clarissa Balder, so she tearfully complained, and Gloria had to pull off her card for her. Of course Gregory was temperamental, seeming to stare at a spot just below the taut peak of the tree, as if mazed and entranced. But the presents were wonderful and more than worth the small ordeal of finding one's card and pretending not to be frightened when the whole room seemed full of fiery hands and the thunder cracked against one's ear-drums and shook one's teeth. Easy to be afraid!

At length the last present had been bestowed and it was time for the *pièce de résistance*, the pulling of the great cracker. Long, silken cords streamed from each end with room among them for fifty chubby fists, and a great surprise inside, for sure. The languid, uneasy troop were lined up at each end and took a grip on the silken cords.

At that moment a footman came in and told Mr. Braxton he was wanted on the telephone.

Filled with foreboding he went to his study. He heard the voice of Knowles—

'I'm afraid I have very bad news for you . . .'

The chubby fists gripped the silken cords.

'Now pull!' cried Mrs. Braxton.

The opposing teams took the strain.

A leaping flash and a blasting roar. The children were hurled, writhing and screaming over each other.

Up from the middle of the cracker leapt a rosy shaft of flame which, as it reached the ceiling, seemed to flatten its peak so that it resembled a great snake of fire which turned and hurled itself against the tree in a blinding embrace. There was a fierce sustained 'Hiss,' the tree flamed like a torch, and all the fairy globes upon it burst and splintered. And then the roaring torch cast itself down amongst the screaming chaos. For a moment the great pot, swathed in green, was a carmine cauldron and its paint streamed like blood upon the floor. Then the big room was a dream of fire and those within it driven wildly from its heat.

Phil Tangler, whose farmhouse, on the early slopes of Missen Rise, overlooked both Lucky's Grove and the Hall, solemnly declared that at 7.30 on Christmas Day, 1938, he was watching from a window and marvelling at the dense and boiling race of snow, the bitter gale, and the wicked flame and fury of the storm, when he saw a high fist of fire form in a rift in the cloud-rack, a fist with two huge blazing fingers, one of which speared down on the Hall, another touched and kindled the towering fir in Lucky's Grove, as though saluting it. Five minutes later he was racing through the hurricane to join in a vain night-long fight to save the Hall, already blazing from stem to stern.

'I SHALL TAKE PROPER PRECAUTIONS'

by George H. Bushnell

George Herbert Bushnell (1896–1973) was a
distinguished art historican, literary critic, and
Librarian to the University of St. Andrews for
many years. This story is taken from his collection
A *Handful of Ghosts* (1945), tales inspired by M.R.
James and similar antiquarian masters of the ghost
story.

I t was almost closing time in the University Library on Christmas
Eve in the first year of the war. Fiona Proctor, an assistant at the
counter, whom some of you may remember under another name,
was wearily shelving returned books. Her mind was not on her work
for she was anxious to get home to make her final preparations for
Christmas Day. Glancing hastily at the last book that had been
handed in she prepared to shelve it before hurrying home. To her
surprise the book did not belong to the Library at all but bore the
name and address of one Harry Dairsie of Dairsie Hall, Kemback, and
the date December 24th, 1939. Although the book had no dust
wrapper it was obviously quite new, but even so the date surprised her,
for it indicated that the book had only been acquired that very day.
Turning to the title page Fiona was further intrigued to observe that
the owner was apparently the author, Mr Dairsie, and that the book
had only been published that year. For a moment she hesitated. The

[291]

Library attendant was already switching off the lights and preparing to lock up. If she reported the matter to the Assistant-in-Charge, as of course she should have done, it would delay her considerably. Fiona glanced at the clock and decided not to do her duty but to take the book home with her.

She had never visited Kemback but knew that it was only a few miles from her new bunk at Strathkinness. During the bus ride home the already half-formed idea developed that if Christmas Day dawned in proper Christmas-card style it would be pleasant to walk through snow-covered lanes to the village of Kemback and personally deliver the book to its owner. Her fiance, Harry Nelson, was to call for her at midday to run her out to his mother's home for Christmas dinner at one o'clock, an afternoon party and a dance at night. She had no particular plans for the morning and there would be ample time to return the book to Mr Dairsie and to enjoy herself thoroughly with Harry afterwards. Or so she thought.

For some reason, perhaps over-tiredness or perhaps anticipation of the morrow, Fiona did not find sleep a willing bedfellow. For a long time she turned over and over restlessly and then, tired of trying to get to sleep sat up, switched on the bedside lamp and prepared to try to read herself to sleep. Now according to her very distinct recollection she had left Mr Dairsie's book downstairs on the hall table ready to pick it up on the following morning: of this she felt quite certain: yet there it was, obviously inviting her to read it, on the bedside table between Fiona and the novel she remembered putting there. Of course I have often told Fiona what a rotten memory she has, but. . . .

The light from the lamp fell full on the book. It was, as you will remember a new book, only published that year. Was it? Somehow it did not look so new in that bright electric light. Indeed it looked old and hand-worn. Fiona woke up thoroughly, shook herself, brushed back some errant strands of wayward hair and bent thoughtful brown eyes upon the book. Gingerly she picked it up.

Yes, there was the name, there was the address, and there, as Scrooge might have said, was December 24th, 1939, on the fly-leaf. Yet the ink no longer looked fresh. On the contrary it was fading and yellowing. Her smooth white forehead shallowed in faint wrinkles for a moment. Then Fiona laughed. How very curious, this effect of a different light, she thought. But nevertheless she glanced quickly round the room—why, she hardly knew. Yes, everything else seemed to be perfectly normal and ordinary. Fiona grinned at herself and turned to the book again. Soon she was quite absorbed in its account of the turbulent lives of the unruly family of Dairsie. One of them particularly attracted her attention, a scholar, Harry Dairsie by name—perhaps it was the name 'Harry' which attracted her, perhaps it was not—who became a priest in the reign of Mary Queen of Scots, truckled with queer people to such effect that he was called the Wizard of Kemback and was shunned by most people. When remonstrated with by his few remaining friends, who were troubled by reports of his unwholesome meddlings with magic, Harry Dairsie merely laughed and had but one answer: 'I shall take proper precautions!' Fiona read on with ever-increasing interest. But a disappointment was in wait for her.

The last few pages of the book were missing. This surprised Fiona intensely for there was no appearance of them having been torn out, and, indeed, in a newly-published book that seemed most unlikely. But was it *really* a new book? In the Library she had had no doubt about it but certainly it had no appearance of newness now. Mildewed, stained and dog-eared pages stared back at a now drowsy Fiona. 'Nuts', she murmured inelegantly to herself, flung the book down and switched off the light.

. . . And contrary to the law of probability she enjoyed the calm dreamless sleep of complete mental repose. Which is more than I should have done!

Throughout the night snow fell fast, but the gentle pattering drifts of snowflakes on the blacked-out windowpanes did not disturb the sleeping girl. Fiona awoke late—to the uncommon spectacle of a white Christmas. She felt more than usually refreshed, and the thought of the gay day in front of her provoked her to song. Like Pooh, the bear of little brain, she hummed to herself as she went down to breakfast. I am sorry to say that it was not a carol she sang, but 'Roll out the Barrel. Roll out the Barrel with me'. . . . At the foot of the stairs Fiona recollected the proverbial saying that it is unlucky to sing before breakfast, but she dismissed such old-fashioned superstition with light-hearted scorn. The truth is, as a wiser person—I myself for instance—could have told her, she was altogether too gay, too light-hearted for so early in the day. It is by no means a good omen to feel that the world is at your feet before you have started on the marmalade at least. Now had I been there I should most certainly have warned her—no doubt with little effect—to watch her step that day. But unfortunately I was not there. . . .

By nine o'clock Fiona was stepping out gaily on her way to Kemback to find Dairsie Hall and return the book to its owner. It was only a four-mile walk to Kemback and even allowing plenty of time to find the Hall and explain to Mr Dairsie how she came to have the book, Fiona decided that she had more than ample time to get back before Harry called for her. Still, just in case he arrived early, as he usually did, she left a brief note for him with the bunkwife.

I should like to tell of the landscape, of the play of sunlight through the snow-laden boughs, of the glistening crystals lightly crackling underfoot, but Fiona told me nothing of these things and my imaginings can be of no interest to you. If the blood of youth is still hot in your veins you would be more interested in the sort of picture my young friend Harry Nelson would draw, of a slim, but not *too* slim body, of twinkling, shapely silk-clad legs and all those other things so pleasant to the eyes of youth. . . . But I may be allowed to advise new students to take the walk: it is far more beautiful than the traditional student walk 'out by Cameron and in by the Grange'.

Fiona followed the main road past haunted Magus Muir until she reached Blebo, where a steeply rising lane on the right took her through Blebo Craigs, skirted Kemback Wood and brought her gently down the brae into Dura Den. Here her way lay along the side of the Eden.

She reached Kemback village shortly after ten o'clock, crossed the old hump-backed bridge supposed to have been built by Archbishop Sharp when Chancellor of the University, the bridge which carried the road over the now lightly frozen burn, and made her way past the old Church and the few white-walled cottages. Obviously none of these was Dairsie Hall. Of course Fiona did not know it, but somewhere outside the Holy Ground around the Church lay what was left of the wizard Harry Dairsie. Some hundred yards beyond the last little cottage a narrow lane, hardly wider than a cart track, slid almost imperceptibly into and across the high road. Fiona halted at the cross-roads. Perhaps she would have moved had she known that immediately below her feet lay the remains of the wizard. In front of her the main road was barren of houses as far as eye could see. She decided to try the lane, and if that yielded no result to go back to the cottages and enquire the way. That was typically what I call Fionese: any sensible person would have asked at the first cottage. Not so Fiona.

High red-berried bushes, weighed down under their white cloaks, framed the lane for a good distance, but at last Fiona reached a gap in the bushes, which, on closer inspection, proved to contain an almost overgrown wrought-iron gate. And on the gate was a worn coat of arms, now outlined by snow. Evidently, she not unreasonably concluded, this was the end of her journey, for the arms on the gate were the same as those of the Dairsie family which were illustrated in the book she carried.

It was quite a business getting the gate to open, for snow had drifted down the drive and lodged against it, but at last she succeeded and went marching briskly up the crunching drive.

For some distance up the drive there was no sign of a house, only snow-covered grounds with a few bare, half frozen trees here and there which might, she thought, at one time have turned the drive into an avenue but which were now scattered and neglected and their ranks woefully thinned. A little distance ahead of her the drive seemed to take a bend to the right and still there was no house in sight. But just at the corner, framed in a half moon of larch she found an ancient stone sundial, somewhat broken and decayed but seemingly in fair condition for its age. Momentarily interested in this first real sign of habitation Fiona paused at the dial and idly brushed away the snow which covered the face. With the cuts that marked the hours, some deeply incised letters came into view, and with little difficulty Fiona made them out to read:

'I doe not mark the houres to bee
Nor e'en the houres that are:
Who scans my face is apt to see
The doore of the past a-jar.'

Fiona read the verse a second time, frowned and then laughed. 'Some poor mutt trying to find an original verse for his old sundial, I suppose', she said to herself and turned away.

And, as she turned, the wintry sun shone full in her eyes across the snow and the bright whiteness made her blink. It was only a momentary reaction of the muscles of her eyes and they adjusted themselves to the intense brightness almost instantly, showing her, a mere stone's throw in front, the house for which she was seeking. The house, of course, was covered with snow and that, no doubt, explained why she had not seen it earlier: it partook so completely of the wintry landscape that only the glinting sun on its windows threw it now into relief.

Fiona fell in love with the old Hall immediately, with its crow-stepped gables, twisted chimneys and high mullioned windows, all diamond-paned. No smoke was issuing from any of the chimneys and at first it seemed to Fiona that the house must be deserted. But almost at once she realised that this could not be the case for a youngish-looking man was on the steps, apparently just on the point of entering the house. His lithe, athletic figure seemed very familiar to Fiona and when he brushed the palm of his right hand down the seam of his trousers she recognised him at once, although only his back was visible.

'Harry!' she called, and broke into a run.

Now a moment's thought, as I told her, would have made her realise that it could not possibly be her fiance: but of course giving a moment's thought to anything would have been quite unlike Fiona.

The man turned and regarded her quizzically—at least that is the expression she used—personally I suspect that the look he gave her was sardonic.

'Good morning', he remarked, 'Did you call me?'

Now Fiona is never nonplussed for more than a second and she explained quite readily her mistake, following up with an account of her errand. On closer acquaintance she realised that the man's resemblance to Harry Nelson was really very slight indeed. This was a much older man. What there was of resemblance was pretty well confined to a certain similarity of build and the characteristic stroking of the palm along the seam of the trousers.

For a few moments the two stood on the steps of the house, talking. Fiona expressed her admiration for the lovely old house and Mr Dairsie thereupon invited her to look over it. As I said to Fiona afterwards, how in the world could he have done otherwise after she had made her desire so obvious?

They went in.

The Hall, though externally of much earlier date, was all eighteenth century decoration inside. And although it was obviously inhabited, strangely enough in no room was any fire burning. Fiona indeed found the place icy cold though her escort did not seem to feel the cold at all. Several times she was on the point of remarking both upon his own imperviousness to lack of warmth and on the utter absence of fires and servants. But each time at the crucial moment Mr Dairsie turned the conversation in some other direction. By the time they had been over most of the house and had entered what Dairsie described as his own particular sanctum Fiona was half dead with the intense cold. Now Fiona is by no means a sensitive girl and I have never known her to express herself rhetorically, yet in this instance she says it seemed to her as if she was surrounded by snow in the house through which she had to force her way, and that an icy north wind was blowing straight through all the rooms and passages, from which walls and doors afforded no protection whatever, although they somehow managed to obscure every ray of sunshine. The sensation was apparently hateful; which is not surprising.

She looked round Mr Dairsie's sanctum and found it by far the least attractive room in the house, sparsely furnished with only one chair—and that a plain deal one—a long low white-scrubbed table and a few objects as unfamiliar as they were uninteresting to her. Fiona mentally contrasted this room, in which the owner evidently had great pride, with her fiance's comfortable book-lined study.

Dairsie closed the door behind him and crossed to her side.

A momentary Victorian qualm assailed Fiona, for this was the first time he had closed the door of a room which she was in it.

But the qualm passed immediately to give place to a new sensation. From overhead came the drone of 'planes and almost as Mr Dairsie reached her side the noise of an exploding bomb rent the air. Evidently it had fallen quite close to the Hall for the floor of the room shivered.

Another and yet another followed—and then came the sound of rattles and of whistles blowing.

'Does that mean gas?' Fiona asked. She was quite calm, or so she assures me. And we must remember that in December 1939 we were constantly expecting the use of gas.

'Yes. I am afraid there *is* gas about', Dairsie replied casually. And Fiona says she positively hated the expression on his face as he spoke, thought she cannot or will not describe it to me. Why she should look at *me* so oddly every time I ask her to describe his expression I have no idea.

'Then I suppose we had better put on our gas masks,' she suggested, pulling hers out of her handbag, where it had so far kept undisturbed company in a compartment adjacent to the one which contained lipstick, cigarettes and what-not.

'By all means put yours on if it will make you feel safer', Dairsie smiled, sarcastically. Fiona fought down her rising dislike of the man and managed to remark fairly normally:—

'But what about you? Won't you go and fetch yours?'

'I do not possess one, my young friend. But do not allow yourself to worry about *me. I* shall take proper precautions!'

Those were the last words Fiona heard Dairsie utter. Hardly were they out of his mouth when a high explosive bomb struck the house and the ceiling of the sanctum crashed down on them both.

Fiona passed into unconsciousness struggling to remember where she had heard those words before.

What sounded like the hammerings of thousands of riveters became the shouting of hundreds of people . . . of dozens of people . . . of one man . . . Harry Nelson. And gradually Fiona opened her eyes. Promptly she choked. And the whisky Harry was perhaps unwisely trying to force down her throat ran over her chin and down into the almost imperceptible little salt-cellars of her throat.

With his left hand Harry was dabbing away at a cut on Fiona's forehead, with a very blood-stained handkerchief. More blood from the same source had formed bright red poppies on the deep snow at her side. Near by, half buried in the snow, lay a broken signpost, on which the painted notice 'This desirable building site to be sold' had been partly obscured by a more recent poster conveying information about Air-Raid Precautions.

Apart from the three figures of Fiona, Harry Nelson and the broken signpost, the snow-covered field was completely empty, except for an untidy, ragged half-moon of larches just behind the signpost.

Overhead there were no 'planes; only a few birds twittering in a blue sky, revelling in the peaceful winter sunshine.

Fiona was very slow in regaining full consciousness, and apparently was thoroughly bewildered by Harry's confused mixture of explanation and solicitation. His confusion was natural enough in such circumstances: indeed the poor fellow was by no means clear about the whole business himself. All he knew was that on reaching Fiona's digs he had found her note and had followed her to Kemback. There he had discovered her lying in the field with the broken signpost on top of her. How it had come to fall and strike her on the forehead he had, of course, no idea, and Fiona had less. But quite obviously that is what had happened. An equally inexplicable fact was that Fiona's gas mask was half pulled out of her handbag. Of course there had been no air raid, nor even a warning, yet when the post had struck her it seems that she must have been in the very act of taking out her gas mask. And underneath the handbag, fallen open at the account of Harry Dairsie's dealings in the black arts, was the ill-starred book which had been the cause of all the trouble.

A smear of Fiona's blood underlined the words: 'I shall take proper precautions!'

As soon as Fiona was sufficiently herself again Nelson carried her to his car and drove her home, where she was put to bed with hot-water bottles, by her landlady, and dosed with hot whisky and lemon. The cut on her forehead proved not to be serious, though there was a bad bruise below and around it. After it had been dressed and the hot drink had taken good effect Fiona stoutly declared that she felt O.K. again. But she was still thoroughly bewildered (as well she might have been). Despite protests from her landlady she absolutely refused to attempt to go to sleep until Harry had gone over the whole business with her again.

And so, at half past three on that Christmas Day the dinnerless, worried and wondering pair were pooling their stories, aided by cups of strong tea and mince pies.

Fiona's story was, of course, much as I have just given it to you, and, of course, it explained nothing. But Harry was able to add a few points which, if they do not explain anything, at least suggest food for thought.

It seems that he was quite familiar with the field in which he had found Fiona. Indeed he had good reason to be, for his great-grandmother had been a Dairsie and was the only child of the last owner of Dairsie Hall. And, until the eighteen-thirties the Hall had stood in what was now the 'Desirable building site' where Harry had found Fiona. Knowing well that the Hall itself had long ceased to exist, Harry had been utterly bewildered and intensely worried when he read Fiona's notes saying that she had set out to go to the Hall.

The last owner of Dairsie Hall, he told Fiona, had dabbled in much more ordinary affairs than his predecessor the wizard. He was, in fact, an amateur chemist. This innocent hobby nevertheless proved serious enough for himself and for Dairsie Hall. One of this Harry Dairsie's former friends was the famous William Murdoch, who, as everyone knows, at the time of his death in 1839 was still experimenting with gas for street lighting and for domestic purposes. Harry Dairsie was interested in the same project and in that year believed that he had perfected his own experiments for the use of a new gas which he thought would be far superior to the gas made by Murdoch. One test only remained to be applied to it and this he felt sure would prove successful.

The great Murdoch was far from sharing his friend's confidence and with almost his dying words warned his friend to be very careful. But

[299]

Dairsie merely smiled confidently and replied '*I shall take proper precautions!*'

Dairsie carried out his final test on the morning of December 25th, 1839. But instead of proving successful there was almost immediately a series of small explosions, followed by a tremendous one which killed him instantly and destroyed most of the Hall. Fortunately, as it happened, his wife had taken their baby daughter to spend Christmas with her parents in London or they too would have suffered the fate of Mr Dairsie and the servants.

And had that happened there would have been no Harry Nelson, and my assistant Fiona Proctor would have been spared an experience of a gap in space and time such as many have written about but few have known.

And now we come to perhaps the strangest feature of those events of that first war-time Christmas. So far all that Harry Nelson had been able to add to the story had contributed little more than somewhat hazy but perhaps suggestive coincidences. And what he was able to add served only to further bewilder both Fiona and himself.

'If only you had read right on to the end of the book!' he exclaimed.

'To the end? But . . . how do you mean?' Fiona wondered.

'Why, if you had *finished* the book you would have read all about the explosion and about the destruction of the Hall. And then, of course, you would not have gone to Kemback at all.'

'But . . . if I had read to the end? But I *couldn't*. I told you that the pages were torn out! And how on earth do *you* know that they contained an account of the explosions, anyway? *You* haven't read the book, have you?'

Harry hesitated, and reddened.

'Yes', he admitted slowly. 'Yes. *I* have read it.' He paused again and then added, with a strange hint of uncertainty in his voice—'You see *I* wrote it!'

Fiona gazed at him in utter amazement. I think that for a moment she wondered if both of them were mad.

'*You* wrote it?' she gasped, unbelievingly.

'Yes. You see it was to have been a surprise—a Christmas surprise for you. That's why I dedicated it to you. And that's why I sent it to you on Christmas Eve.'

Fiona sat up. She stared at her fiance. She could find no words suitable for such a situation as this. At last, with great deliberation she reached for the book and carefully inspected the outside. It was *quite new*: so new in appearance that it might have been printed and bound that very day. Wrinkling her forehead she opened the book. Sure enough there on the fly-leaf was an inscription in Harry's well-known hand: 'To my darling Fiona, with all my love, Harry, December 24th, 1939.'

Fiona read the inscription through three times, passing a white red-tipped finger over it, as if to make quite sure that it was really there, before she turned to the title-page.

And there, as Harry had said, was the title: 'The Dairsies of Dairsie Hall. By H. Nelson.' Again she turned a page, and read a charming little dedication to herself. Then, with, it seemed, an effort which required all her strength of will, Fiona looked at the end of the book.

It was complete. Not a single page was missing. . . .

At last she put the book down, sank back upon the pillows and looked straight into the worried eyes of the author.

Harry got up and came over to her, but for a while neither spoke. Then Fiona, still staring intently into his eyes, broke the silence.

'Yes . . .' she murmured. 'Yes, you are certainly my Harry, not . . .' She did not need to finish the sentence.

They were married in the Spring and I lost my most attractive if not my most competent assistant. Harry now intends to buy what is left of the Dairsie Hall estate, to build a new Hall on the old site and to settle there with his bride.

I think it will be the height of folly to do so, and I cannot understand Fiona agreeing to such a project. But then I cannot understand the ways of any of the young people of to-day. In my young days we should have taken their extraordinary experiences as a warning, but to them the affair has already become a standing joke. . . . But what annoys me most of all when I remonstrate with Harry on his unwise plan is his invariable laughing reply:

'O.K. Don't worry. I shall take proper precautions!'

Tchah!

CHRISTMAS MEETING

by Rosemary Timperley

This superb vignette was the first of over 150 fine
ghost stories written by Rosemary Timperley
(B.1920), Britain's leading female writer of horror
and supernatural fiction. It first appeared in *Truth*,
and Cynthia Asquith's anthology *The Second Ghost
Book* in 1952.

I have never spent Christmas alone before.

It gives me an uncanny feeling, sitting alone in my 'furnished room,' with my head full of ghosts, and the room full of voices of the past. It's a drowning feeling—all the Christmases of the past coming back in a mad jumble: the childish Christmas, with a house full of relations, a tree in the window, sixpences in the pudding, and the delicious, crinkly stocking in the dark morning; the adolescent Christmas, with mother and father, the War and the bitter cold, and the letters from abroad; the first really grown-up Christmas, with a lover—the snow and the enchantment, red wine and kisses, and the walk in the dark before midnight, with the grounds so white, and the stars diamond bright in a black sky—so many Christmases through the years.

And, now, the first Christmas alone.

But not quite loneliness. A feeling of companionship with all the other people who are spending Christmas alone—millions of them—past and present. A feeling that, if I close my eyes, there will be no past or future, only an endless present which *is* time, because it is all we ever have.

Yes, however cynical you are, however irreligious, it makes you feel queer to be alone at Christmas time.

So I'm absurdly relieved when the young man walks in. There's nothing romantic about it—I'm a woman of nearly fifty, a spinster schoolma'am with grim, dark hair, and myopic eyes that once were beautiful, and he's a kid of twenty, rather unconventionally dressed with a flowing, wine-coloured tie and black velvet jacket, and brown curls which could do with a taste of the barber's scissors. The effeminacy of his dress is belied by his features—narrow, piercing, blue eyes, and arrogant, jutting nose and chin. Not that he looks strong. The skin is fine-drawn over the prominent features, and he is very white.

He bursts in without knocking, then pauses, says: 'I'm so sorry. I thought this was my room.' He begins to go out, then hesitates and says: 'Are you alone?'

'Yes.'

'It's—queer, being alone at Christmas, isn't it? May I stay and talk?'

'I'd be glad if you would.'

He comes right in, and sits down by the fire.

'I hope you don't think I came in here on purpose, I really did think it was my room,' he explains.

'I'm glad you made the mistake. But you're a very young person to be alone at Christmas time.'

'I wouldn't go back to the country to my family. It would hold up my work. I'm a writer.'

'I see.' I can't help smiling a little. That explains his rather unusual dress. And he takes himself so seriously, this young man! 'Of course, you mustn't waste a precious moment of writing,' I say with a twinkle.

'No, not a moment! That's what my family won't see. They don't appreciate urgency.'

'Families are never appreciative of the artistic nature.'

'No, they aren't,' he agrees seriously.

'What are you writing?'

'Poetry and a diary combined. It's called My *Poems and I*, by Francis Randel. That's my name. My family say there's no point in my writing, that I'm too young. But I don't feel young. Sometimes I feel like an old man, with too much to do before he dies.'

'Revolving faster and faster on the wheel of creativeness.'

[303]

'Yes! Yes, exactly! You understand! You must read my work some time. Please read my work! Read my work!' A note of desperation in his voice, a look of fear in his eyes, makes me say:

'We're both getting much too solemn for Christmas Day. I'm going to make you some coffee. And I have a plum cake.'

I move about, clattering cups, spooning coffee into my percolator. But I must have offended him, for, when I look round, I find he has left me. I am absurdly disappointed.

I finish making coffee, however, then turn to the bookshelf in the room. It is piled high with volumes, for which the landlady has apologised profusely: 'Hope you don't mind the books, Miss, but my husband won't part with them, and there's nowhere else to put them. We charge a bit less for the room for that reason.'

'I don't mind,' I said. 'Books are good friends.'

But these aren't very friendly-looking books. I take one at random. Or does some strange fate guide my hand?

Sipping my coffee, inhaling my cigarette smoke, I begin to read the battered little book, published, I see, in Spring, 1852. It's mainly poetry—immature stuff, but vivid. Then there's a kind of diary. More realistic, less affected. Out of curiosity, to see if there are any amusing comparisons, I turn to the entry for Christmas Day, 1851. I read:

'My first Christmas Day alone. I had rather an odd experience. When I went back to my lodgings after a walk, there was a middle-aged woman in my room. I thought, at first, I'd walked into the wrong room, but this was not so, and later, after a pleasant talk, she—disappeared. I suppose she was a ghost. But I wasn't frightened. I liked her. But I do not feel well to-night. Not at all well. I have never felt ill at Christmas before.'

A publishers' note followed the last entry: FRANCIS RANDEL DIED FROM A SUDDEN HEART ATTACK ON THE NIGHT OF CHRISTMAS DAY, 1851. THE WOMAN MENTIONED IN THIS FINAL ENTRY IN HIS DIARY WAS THE LAST PERSON TO SEE HIM ALIVE. IN SPITE OF REQUESTS FOR HER TO COME FORWARD, SHE NEVER DID SO. HER IDENTITY REMAINS A MYSTERY.

SOMEONE IN THE LIFT

by L. P. Hartley

Leslie Poles Hartley (1895–1972) is celebrated for
his sensitive novels of country life, notable *Eustace
and Hilda* and *The Go-Between*. He was also a
regular contributor to the *Ghost Book* series,
'Someone in the Lift' first appearing in *The Third
Ghost Book* (1955).

'There's someone coming down in the lift, Mummy!'

'No, my darling, you're wrong, there isn't.'

'But I can see him through the bars—a tall gentleman.'

'You think you can, but it's only a shadow. Now, you'll see,
the lift's empty.'

And it always was.

This piece of dialogue, or variations of it, had been repeated at
intervals ever since Mr and Mrs Maldon and their son Peter
had arrived at the Brompton Court Hotel, where, owing to a
domestic crisis, they were going to spend Christmas. New to hotel life,
the little boy had never seen a lift before and he was fascinated by it.
When either of his parents pressed the button to summon it he would
take up his stand some distance away to watch it coming down.

The ground floor had a high ceiling, so the lift was visible for some
seconds before it touched floor level: and it was then, at its first
appearance, that Peter saw the figure. It was always in the same place,

[305]

facing him in the left-hand corner. He couldn't see it plainly, of course, because of the double grille, the gate of the lift and the gate of the lift-shaft, both of which had to be firmly closed before the lift would work.

He had been told not to use the lift by himself—an unnecessary warning, because he connected the lift with the things that grown-up people did, and unlike most small boys he wasn't over-anxious to share the privileges of his elders: he was content to wonder and admire. The lift appealed to him more as magic than as mechanism. Acceptance of magic made it possible for him to believe that the lift had an occupant when he first saw it, in spite of the demonstrable fact that when it came to rest, giving its fascinating click of finality, the occupant had disappeared.

'If you don't believe me, ask Daddy,' his mother said.

Peter didn't want to do this, and for two reasons, one of which was easier to explain than the other.

'Daddy would say I was being silly,' he said.

'Oh, no, he wouldn't; he never says you're silly.'

This was not quite true. Like all well-regulated modern fathers, Mr Maldon was aware of the danger of offending a son of tender years: the psychological results might be regrettable. But Freud or no Freud, fathers are still fathers, and sometimes when Peter irritated him Mr Maldon would let fly. Although he was fond of him, Peter's private vision of his father was of someone more authoritative and awe-inspiring than a stranger, seeing them together, would have guessed.

The other reason, which Peter didn't divulge, was more fantastic. He hadn't asked his father because, when his father was with him, he couldn't see the figure in the lift.

Mrs Maldon remembered the conversation and told her husband of it. 'The lift's in a dark place,' she said, 'and I dare say he does see something, he's so much nearer to the ground than we are. The bars may cast a shadow and make a sort of pattern that we can't see. I don't know if it's frightening him, but you might have a word with him about it.'

At first Peter was more interested than frightened. Then he began to evolve a theory. If the figure only appeared in his father's absence, didn't it follow that the figure might be, could be, must be, his own father? In what region of his consciousness Peter believed this it would be hard to say; but for imaginative purposes he did believe it and the figure became for him 'Daddy in the lift'. The thought of Daddy in the lift did frighten him, and the neighbourhood of the lift-shaft, in which he felt compelled to hang about, became a place of dread.

Christmas Day was drawing near and the hotel began to deck itself with evergreens. Suspended at the foot of the staircase, in front of the lift, was a bunch of mistletoe, and it was this that gave Mr Maldon his idea.

As they were standing under it, waiting for the lift, he said to Peter:

'Your mother tells me you've seen someone in the lift who isn't there.'

His voice sounded more accusing than he meant it to, and Peter shrank.

'Oh, not now,' he said, truthfully enough. 'Only sometimes.'

'Your mother told me that you always saw it,' his father said, again more sternly than he meant to. 'And do you know who I think it may be?'

Caught by a gust of terror Peter cried, 'Oh please don't tell me!'

'Why, you silly boy,' said his father reasonably. 'Don't you want to know?'

Ashamed of his cowardice, Peter said he did.

'Why, it's Father Christmas, of course!'

Relief surged through Peter.

'But doesn't Father Christmas come down the chimney?' he asked.

'That was in the old days. He doesn't now. Now he takes the lift!'

Peter thought a moment.

'Will you dress up as Father Christmas this year,' he asked, 'even though it's an hotel?'

'I might.'

'And come down in the lift?'

'Why yes, that's what it's for.'

After this Peter felt happier about the shadowy passenger behind the bars. Father Christmas couldn't hurt anyone, even if he was (as Peter now believed him to be) his own father. Peter was only six but he could remember two Christmas Eves when his father had dressed up as Santa Claus and given him a delicious thrill. He could hardly wait for this one, when the apparition in the corner would at last become a reality.

Alas, two days before Christmas Day the lift broke down. On every floor it served, and there were five (six counting the basement), the forbidding notice 'Out of Order' dangled from the door-handle. Peter complained as loudly as anyone, though secretly, he couldn't have told why, he was glad that the lift no longer functioned; and he didn't mind climbing the four flights to his room, which opened out of his parents' room but had its own door too. By using the stairs he met the workmen (he never knew on which floor they would be) and from them gleaned the latest news about the lift-crisis. They were working overtime, they told him, and were just as anxious as he to see the last of the job. Sometimes they even told each other to put a jerk into it. Always Peter asked them when they would be finished, and they always answered, 'Christmas Eve at latest.'

Peter didn't doubt this. To him the workmen were infallible, possessed of magic powers capable of suspending the ordinary laws that governed lifts. Look how they left the gates open, and shouted to each other up and down the awesome lift-shaft, paying as little attention to the other hotel visitors as if they didn't exist! Only to Peter did they vouchsafe a word.

But Christmas Eve came, the morning passed, the afternoon passed, and still the lift didn't go. The men were working with set faces and a controlled hurry in their movements; they didn't even return Peter's 'Good night' when he passed them on his way to bed. Bed! He had begged to be allowed to stay up this once for dinner; he knew he wouldn't go to sleep, he said, till Father Christmas came. He lay awake, listening to the urgent voices of the men, wondering if each hammer stroke would be the last; and then, just as the clamour was subsiding, he dropped off.

Dreaming, he felt adrift in time. Could it be midnight? No, because his parents had after all consented to his going down to dinner. Now was the time. Averting his eyes from the forbidden lift he stole downstairs. There was a clock in the hall, but it had stopped. In the dining-room there was another clock; but dared he go into the dining-room alone, with no one to guide him and everybody looking at him?

He ventured in, and there, at their table, which he couldn't always pick out, he saw his mother. She saw him, too, and came towards him, threading her way between the tables as if they were just bits of furniture, not alien islands under hostile sway.

'Darling,' she said, 'I couldn't find you—nobody could, but here you are!' She led him back and they sat down. 'Daddy will be with us in a minute.' The minutes passed; suddenly there was a crash. It seemed to come from within, from the kitchen, perhaps. Smiles lit up the faces of the diners. A man at a near-by table laughed and said, 'Something's on the floor! Somebody'll be for it!' 'What is it?' whispered Peter, too excited to speak out loud. 'Is anyone hurt?' 'Oh no, darling, somebody's dropped a tray, that's all.'

To Peter it seemed an anti-climax, this paltry accident that had stolen the thunder of his father's entry, for he didn't doubt that his father would come in as Father Christmas. The suspense was unbearable. 'Can I go into the hall and wait for him?' His mother hesitated and then said yes.

The hall was deserted, even the porter was off duty. Would it be fair, Peter wondered, or would it be cheating and doing himself out of a surprise, if he waited for Father Christmas by the lift? Magic has its rules which mustn't be disobeyed. But he was there now, at his old place in front of the lift; and the lift would come down if he pressed the button.

He knew he mustn't, that it was forbidden, that his father would be angry if he did; yet he reached up and pressed it.

But nothing happened, the lift didn't come, and why? Because some careless person had forgotten to shut the gates—'monkeying with the lift', his father called it. Perhaps the workmen had forgotten, in their hurry to get home. There was only one thing to do—find out on which floor the gates had been left open, and then shut them.

On their own floor it was, and in his dream it didn't seem strange to Peter that the lift wasn't there, blocking the black hole of the liftshaft, though he daren't look down it. The gates clicked to. Triumph possessed him, triumph lent him wings; he was back on the ground floor, with his finger on the button. A thrill of power such as he had never known ran through him when the machinery answered to his touch.

But what was this? The lift was coming up from below, not down from above, and there was something wrong with its roof—a jagged hole that let the light through. But the figure was there in its accustomed corner, and this time it hadn't disappeared, it was still there, he could see it through the mazy criss-cross of the bars, a figure in a red robe with white edges, and wearing a red cowl on its head: his father, Father Christmas, Daddy in the lift. But why didn't he look at Peter, and why was his white beard streaked with red?

The two grilles folded back when Peter pushed them. Toys were lying at his father's feet, but he couldn't touch them for they too were red, red and wet as the floor of the lift, red as the jag of lightning that tore through his brain. . . .

THE CHRISTMAS PRESENT

by Ramsey Campbell

Ramsey Campbell (b. 1946) has been described as
'The John Le Carre of horror fiction' (on *Bookshelf*,
Radio 4), and his style is unsurpassed in the subtle
manipulation of mood, and suggestion of
supernatural presence in the normal everyday
world. He has written several horror & ghost
stories set in the Christmas season including the
much anthologised gems 'The Chimney' and
'Calling Card', and the less familiar tale reprinted
here—'The Christmas Present'—which was
originally written for BBC Radio Merseyside in
December 1969.

(A slightly different version of this story was broadcast on BBC Radio
Merseyside on December 24, 1969; it was produced by Tony Wolfe,
read by Gavin Richards, with a specially composed electronic score by
Donald Henshilwood, and for these reasons the story is dedicated to
them.)

Y ou scarcely notice Christmas in Liverpool 8, except that there
are more parties. On Christmas Eve I made my way early to the
pub; as I hurried along Gambier Terrace I glanced up in search
of party-goers, but most of the rooms of students and writers of

ephemeral verse were unlit, blackly rattling in the wind which swept up from the river around the horned tower of the Anglican cathedral and across the sloughed graveyard, recently scraped clean of graves. Still, by ten o'clock in The Grapes bottles of California Chablis were gathering on the tables; my table had collected three and a half of anonymous Riesling. Not that I knew all the people behind the names: only Bill and Les and Desmond and Jill, just back from London for Christmas, whose hand I was holding. I couldn't place the mute student on the other side of Jill; I'd caught his name and let it drift away among the stained glasses. He was one of those people you always seem to meet in the neurotics ward of O'Connor's Tavern or arguing with the Marxists at the Phil, a face everyone knows and nobody can name, and I didn't know what to do with him.

We hadn't objected when he joined us, thrust smiling hopefully against our table by the deafening scarved crowd, a drooping streamer supporting his head like a red chin strap—but he'd shown no inclination to provide a bottle. I couldn't bring myself to say 'Look, there are enough of us already'; it was Christmas. Perhaps if we waited he might go away. But at other tables groups were clutching bottles like truncheons and rising, and outside the first police cars were howling their way to Upper Parliament and Lime Streets. 'We might as well go,' I said and stood with Jill, followed by the others.

At last the student spoke. Jarred, I realized that I hadn't heard his voice, aggressive beneath the deprecating Southern whine. 'I've got a present here for someone,' he told his hands lurking under the table. 'I wanted to be sure it'd be appreciated. Shall I give it to you, then?' he asked me.

'Do I take it you've been watching me to make sure?'

'It was a nice thought,' Jill said, squeezing my hand and watching my face. 'Wasn't it?'

I knew she needed to believe in the Christmas spirit. 'Well, thank you very much,' I told the student. 'We're going back to my place for a party if you're free.'

'Great,' he said. His hands ventured forth and passed me a small box wrapped in black paper, tightly sealed and Sellotaped. 'I'd like to be there when you open it,' he said.

We forced out way through brimming tables and discussions of the art of cinema and emerged into Catherine Street. Fragmented by shadows of branches hard and sharp as black ice, we made our way through to Gambier Terrace, but Diana and Beatrice were out, for

[311]

their cacti clawed at an unlit window. For a second I thought I hard the tin choirboys singing carols in the tree outside the Jacey Cinema, but as they faded, buffeted out of shape by the wind, I decided that they were trapped in a radio. Jill was peering through the hedge opposite the cathedral; beyond the Mersey glittered, and at Birkenhead the dinosaur skeletons of cranes had come down to the water to drink in darkness. My hand was frozen around the cardboard box. I hid Jill's in my pocket and we turned into Canning Street,

As we did so I heard the student say 'Look at the face on that cathedral.'

We looked. An edge of the night-wind slipped into me as I took in the image; the tower's horns had pricked up triumphant and mocking, the long windows were eyes, drawn down and slitted into static evil. 'I wish it had a mouth. Then at least we could guess its thoughts,' I said.

'It looks as if it's shouldering its way up from the graveyards,' Jill said, and then immediately: 'Don't make me say things like that.'

'Don't worry,' I said. 'There no longer is a graveyard.'

'Thanks for trying,' said Jill. 'I've just been staring into that graveyard. If you hadn't pulled me away I might still be there. Why is it so crowded? And why in heaven's name do they have to light it up at night?'

'Come on, Jill, this is no party mood,' I protested and hurried her back to the corner of Hope Street, the others curving back in formation and following us like a tail. 'They've cleared the graveyard out completely. I'll show you.'

'No, John, please don't!' Jill cried.

'Look, don't force her,' the student intervened. 'He's quite right, you know. No graveyard at all.'

Jill steered us back toward my flat. I nodded thanks to the student. 'What is your name, by the way?' I asked.

'I'll tell you later,' he promised.

'When you've decided in our favour?'

'If you like.'

'My God!' I shouted beerily, but Jill gripped my arm.

'Look!' she said. 'We're being followed.'

'By what?'

'Darkness.'

I persuaded myself to relax. Turning, I saw that the light at the end of Canning Street was unlit. Behind us our procession plodded; a dark figure, probably Bill, waved a bottle at me. Briefly I thought: surely there were only eight more of us in the pub? How many are there now? But as they stepped one by one over the edge of light, I saw that there were no more than eight—certainly not the few dozen dark shapes that for a moment I thought I'd seen.

When the second light went out I said quickly to Jill: 'Someone in the power station is stoned.'

'Surely they can't turn off individual lamps,' she whispered.

'Of course they can,' I said, letting her cling to me as she strode on.

The third light vanished almost before we reached it, transformed into a dwindling image of brightness which receded like hope. Behind us the others shouted comments. There wasn't a car to be seen in Canning Street except the shells at the kerb, and there were two more lights ahead to be passed. Jill was almost running, snatching at the light before it was extinguished. I gripped my present and hurried with her. Beside her the student moved with us. His face suggested an expression which I couldn't read; as it seemed about to identify itself a fist of darkness clamped over his face. We were running. His face reappeared, expressionless, and we'd reached my flat. I glanced back; the others, however many there were, arrived panting. On the steps I hesitated, staring back along the fake Regency facades; surely some of the houses had been lit when we passed? But, an incoherent singing bus weaved past on Catherine Street, my key slipped into the lock, and we piled inside.

Jill and I plunged straight into the party, filling glasses where I'd placed them ready on the mantelpiece, sweeping up my abandoned afternoon's manuscript and burying it in the bedroom beneath coats, drawing back the curtains to attract those who might still be wandering with bottles, lighting the fire and throwing up the window. A record smacked the turntable and caught the needle. A bottle drained; conversations intertwined; laughter sprang up. Someone was dancing; a corner of my Beatles poster tore from the wall, but I'd meant to throw it out a month ago. Jill and I leaned against the chiming mantelpiece and sipped. Jill saw the student before I did, standing at the open window, staring down the lightless street toward the cathedral. As the next record hung alert for the needle, Jill cried: 'Listen, everyone! John's had a present!'

'Well, open it,' Bill called.

I tooked the sealed box from among the glasses on the mantelpiece, but the student turned. 'No, not yet,' he said. 'Wait until midnight.'

'Why midnight?' Bill demanded.

[313]

'Christmas Day.'

'Well, that's right,' Bill agreed. 'That's tradition.'

'Tradition,' Jill hissed. I could feel her tensing.

'Come on, Jill, sit down, love,' I said.

But Bill called: 'What's wrong with tradition?'

'Oh, not tradition,' Jill said from the couch. 'Myths. How can we all stop for a couple of days and get stoned on the myth of human fellowship when people are being murdered in Vietnam?'

'Oh, come on,' Bill said, offering a bottle. 'Never mind that for now. It's Christmas.'

'In Vietnam too?'

'You can't ignore myths,' the student interrupted. 'A war is a clash between a myth and its antithesis.'

'Don't be pretentious,' Jill said.

'All right, you stay on your debating-society level, but you wait. I'll show you that myths are dangerous.'

Jill recoiled. The arrested dancers looked uneasy. 'That's a hell of a generalization,' I intervened. 'How dangerous?'

'All belief needs is a mob to give it form,' he said. 'Listen, mate, there's nothing more frightening than people gathering round a belief. And I'll tell you why. Because if a belief exists it must have an opposite. That exists too but they try to ignore it. That's why people in a group are dangerous.'

He'd given me a present but I couldn't resist saying: 'In that case I'm surprised you came here.'

'Ah, well,' he said. 'I'm safe now.'

I think all this was above most of our heads. The second record had fallen unheard, but the touch of the needle on the third galvanized us all; we danced frenetically. Someone tried to draw the student into the dance, but he shook her off and returned to the window. As I whirled with Jill I saw him push the window up and climb into the balcony, his hair springing up against the darkness. The record spin to a climax and lost the needle, and in the suspended silence we all heard the bell.

At least, we couldn't imagine what else it might be. 'It's the cathedral. What's wrong?' Bill demanded. For the bell sounded drowned, its note boomed and then choked, muffled, swept away screaming and was engulfed. It dragged itself back, clanged unbearably loud and then dulled, thudded tonelessly in mud. We all stared at the student's intent back, but he never turned.

'It must be the electricity, like the lights,' Bill said, and was about to go when the voices began. 'Carol-singers,' he said happily.

Yes, we thought, carol-singers, they can't be anything else. But there seemed to be so many coming up from the cathedral, an entire choir. I didn't recognize the tune, and I could tell that everyone was baffled, for the tune led toward recognition and then fled squealing and growling into impossible extremes, notes leaping like frogs and falling dead. The voices squirmed between the suffocated tones of the bell, voices thin and cold as the wind, thick and black as wet earth, and paced toward us up Canning Street.

'What are they singing?' Bill said desperately.

'Does it matter?' Jill muttered.

I pushed past the student and gripped the chill iron of the balcony. But Canning Street was an abyss of blackness, leading to the powerful horned form of the cathedral. I could see nothing, only hear their voices fling a contorted mass of sound toward the sky and into the earth, and wonder whether they were moving to the music. I could only imagine their faces turned up to me as they chanted and knocked at the door beneath my feet.

When I thrust my head back through the window it was too late. 'I'll go and give them something,' Bill said. 'After all, it's Christmas,' and he'd gone.

Nobody else moved. Perhaps they were right; perhaps Bill was right. The bell swung reverberating through the sky. I peered down through the mesh of the balcony. Before I could strain sight from the darkness, I heard the street door open. I listened for minutes, waiting to hear more than the clangour of the bell and the packed insistent voices. But there was nothing, except determined conversation in the room behind me, until Jill gripped my arm through the window and whispered urgently: 'John, they're in the house. They're coming upstairs.'

I dragged myself over the sill and fell into the room. I could hear the voices turn at the first landing, mount the stairs lethargically like a gigantic worm. 'Where's Bill?' I demanded.

'I don't know.'

'Quickly,' I shouted. The voices were bursting forth at the top of the stairs. 'Everyone. We'll take a collection. Give them money, Jill, you collect half.'

But she was staring aghast out of the window. I whirled. On the balcony the student bent ecstatic against the gale of sound. Jill stood, a cry blocking her mouth; her face drained of colour and wrinkled like

GEBAL AND AMMON AND AMALEK

by David G. Rowlands

David G. Rowlands (B. 1941), a biochemist by
profession, is one of England's most talented
writers in the classic ghost story tradition. He has
had many excellent and original tales published
over the past twenty years, and is a regular
contributor to the *Holly Bough*, a Christmas
magazine published by the *Cork Examiner*. This
unusual Christmas tale, specially written for this
anthology, is previously unpublished.

Fancy his fright, When, with all his might
Having forced up the lid, which they'd not fastened quite,
Of the marble sarcophagus—'All in white'
The dead Bishop started up, bolt upright
On his hinder end,—and grasped him so tight . . .
And having thus 'tackled him'—blew out his light!!

Ingoldsby: Lay of St. Aloys

G reat Flaxted in Essex was formerly a rather isolated community known to a few antiquarians for its prehistoric ditch, the brick porch and wooden font at the church of St. Osyth, and at one time also to certain epicurean persons as a name on the label of a jam pot. For in the nineteenth century an enterprising Squire had filled his family coffers by developing a local aptitude for the making of

syrups and preserves. This time was long past, however, for in the 1940s the works and its patents had been purchased from the family holding. The refined local preserve which was costly to produce was discontinued, its label transferred to an amorphous Company product, and the Flaxted factory closed. Only until the 1950s did the willow-herb and nettles flourish on the site, however. The estate lands were acquired and the wilderness of former strawberry and fruit fields sold for a big housing development to accommodate 'London Overspill' as it
was called; within four years the population of Flaxted had increased four hundredfold.

The little village survived as a quaint anachronism, surrounded on all sides by jerry-building and plate glass and a few straggling remains of former blackberry hedges. At first the influx did little to swell congregations of the churches, though there were a few more christen-ings, marriages and funerals, courtesy of the immigrants. ('See Flaxted and Die' said the wags). The older generation stirred uneasily as a Catholic church was built on the estate and mumbled about 'popery', while the Nonconformists had sufficient augmentation to begin a church building of their own. To be sure, some newcomers joined the ranks of the Anglicans but it was not for many years that their presence and procreation began to comprise the greater proportion of the worshippers.

As the community entered the 1970s, however, there were few of the old-time Anglicans left. A new Vicar cared little for the Thirty-nine articles and less for the antiquities of his charge. He was keen on choral music and picturesque ritual though, and selected an organist whose voluntaries had a modern astringency little suited to the venerable pipe organ. The Rev Hayward capitalised on the scrap value of his church bells, which needed rehanging, and instead installed a tape-recorder and loudspeakers, so that the bells of St. Mary-le-Bow, Cheapside, boomed electronically up the main street at service times. The money from the bell metal went to provide an electronic organ of wide tonal range, new vestments adorned with much lace-work and embroidery, and an incense burner and censers. In these matters he was fully supported by his Churchwardens (the legal custodians of the church effects) and his parochial church council.

Opposition to these changes had come to reside within the venerable frame of one survivor. Old William Stokes had been Sexton, bell-ringer and chorister at the church since the 1890s, and he had come to see all his old cronies depart to their final dissolution in the churchyard, or—under pressure from the PCC—the crematorium. An old merchant seaman, he had survived the first world war, only to lose his son in the second and his wife but ten years later. Deprived of his bellringing by the sale of the bells; of his Sexton's duties by age and arthritis, and of stoking the furnace by gas-firing, he yet remained an incongruous has-been in the choir. His rumbling, slow bass was symptomatic (or so it seemed to the frustrated organist) of his reactionary outlook. He stumbled over the new pointing and only took to using the *Revised Psalter* when his venerable text was removed and thrown away by the organist. He was incapable of the more florid 'service settings', though he knew the Stanfords, the Woods and even some of the Dysons by heart. He refused point black to wear the new surplices ('Loike a lass's petticoat it be') and took his plain cotton garment home each weekend to wash and iron it ready for the next service; for being an old sailor, he managed his house well.

He had his minor triumphs too—over the red cassocks for instance. ('Onlee Royals can order red, see?'). He was right, as the Vicar found from the Diocesan Office, and the red had to be changed to blue, and it rankled. But it was the substitution of the old familiar archaic Book of Common Prayer and order of service by the 'Alternative Service' in modern English, that really finished the old man's resistance. That and the effects of the incense (which he loathed) on his chest and eyes. When twenty years younger, he had managed to accept the New English Bible as a necessary evil, because 'Old Vicar' had instituted its use, and he'd even developed a trick of hearing the 'proper' words as a reflex action in his mind. Sadly he was now too inflexible to do the same for the 'mucked about' Litany, without distress and vexation. ('If that be noo Christianity, it ain't for me!' was his cry.)

To do the Vicar justice he put no pressure on the old fellow: at least none that he was aware of; though the organist was less scrupulous. But after all time was on their side, and with the onset of winter's inflamed chest 'Old Bill' gave in his resignation after evensong, one Sunday in the run-up to Christmas.

They did him proud . . . there was a little presentation ceremony (a cheque) after 'Sung Eucharist', and for his final Evensong in the choir Bill was allowed to choose the hymns, the psalms, canticles and anthem as a final send-off and good riddance.

He had chosen psalms 83, 84 and 85, more for the Soper and Attwood set chants than for their words, though he was ready enough to identify 'Oh, how amiable are thy dwellings' of Ps 84 with his familiar parish church, despite the incense burner and 'odour of sanctity'. Lost in the harmony of the chants he loved, he had not given much attention to the words of Ps 83, but verse five suddenly registered as his own situation: 'For they have cast their heads together with one consent, and are confederate against thee', and he looked sideways at the Vicar, and craned round to the organ as he sang the words. Catching the Rev Hayward's eye briefly Bill thought he detected a flush on the man's countenance. . . . but the verses were running on. . . . 'the tabernacles of the Edomites' . . . Then, suddenly, his blood ran cold as the words 'Gebal and Ammon and Amalek' came to be sung. . . . and his mind instantly went back over seventy-five years to when he had been a young choirboy in these same stalls; but in the front row.

From the treble row of the *decani* side one could see opposite a hideous family tomb and memorial in Italian marble to the first Preserve King, Squire Jasper Fortescue; and at its base — level with the eyes of a lad of ten — was a ledge on which sat three symbolic figures. They had orginally been intended as new-born, maturity and old-age, but the detail was indistinct, and they might have been anything. But as young Will first noticed them from where he stood singing, the verse that came up was 'Gebal and Ammon and Amalek; the philistines that dwell with them at Tyre' . . . . and he decided to name them thus.

After the service he had crept back to look more closely at the figures. Cowls and robes hid their forms to a great extent, but each carried a staff or sceptre. While he looked at them, absorbed with interest, the Vicar came by and patted his shoulder, 'Fortescue tomb, eh?', he sighed. 'Philistines, my dear Willie, the lot of them; and old Jasper a philistine and a sodomite'. He carried on down the church, leaving Willie — who did not know what a sodomite was — amazed at his own accuracy in naming the figures. . . . 'the Philistines with them' . . . so that they became something of an obsession. He was not given to Bible study, though supposedly his Sunday afternoons and evenings at the kitchen table were so employed. For the first time he turned avidly to his Bible for information. . . . about the Philistines. He was supposed to be learning the Catechism, for his Confirmation a month hence; instead he studied the Philistines — 'Blood sacrifices are their delight'.

On his way to school next day he found the fresh corpse of a shrew decapitated by an owl. Without further thought, young Will picked it up and slipped into the nearby church, laying it on the ledge before the three marble figures. He bowed, and made his way to school.

That night Will had dreamed of a little girl he liked in the Bible class on Sundays. But he wasn't sure, for the dream girl wore an old smock like girls in the old picture book he was given to 'read' as an occasional treat. Then he wished he could wake up, for the girl was gone and was screaming. Another figure had come into his dream . . . . a figure like the three on the wall tablet. He could see its hands and feet projecting from the robe, and they were like the dead shrew's but much bigger . . . and he felt that it had no head, though something filled the cowl. Willie found his voice, 'You are real, then'. It was a statement rather than a question. The cowl inclined. 'Who was that screaming?' Willie wanted to know. And a voice came from the obscurity of the cowl: 'Pay no attention. She is in a different dream'.

'Am I dreaming, then?'

'We exist because you believe we are real. You gave us blood. What do you want in return?'

Now it happened there was something Will wanted very much indeed . . . the downfall of a bigger lad who was making his life a misery at the Board School. He was about to mention this, when the figure made a gesture with its pinkish, sinewy hands.

'We know. Trust us. Read about the Philistines, the Amalekites, the Chaldeans, the Persians in your Bible. Do not say your Litany; do not learn your Catechism. . . . or we shall be unable to help you.'

Next morning, young Will remembered much of his dream, and so he was quite dashed to meet Tom Hicks swaggering down the lane with a stick: a stick that was obviously intended to smite his, Will's, person. 'So much for Gebal, and Ammon and Amalek' he thought as he looked desperately for a way of escape. An opening in the hawthorn hedge beckoned, and he was through it in a trice, completely forgetting that the bull was in the field, and known to be dangerous. Hicks was at his very heels, swiping with the stick, when the thunder of hooves on the ground reminded him. He fell, winding himself, as Hicks—also now in terror—just failed to clear his recumbent form . . . then from his abject position he saw Hicks impaled, and the blood, and a lot more beside. . . .

All this was recalled instantly in old William's mind, and he had to bring himself back to a realisation that they were well into Psalm 84. His hands trembled and his voice faltered 'Who going through the vale of misery use it for a well'. He remembered his horror—suddenly as fresh as the day it had happend. His instant rejection of this evil. How morbidly he had prayed; how tenaciously he had learned his Catechism and recited his Litany, indeed: just as they were singing now 'I had rather be a doorkeeper in the house of my God: than to dwell in the tents of ungodliness'. How he had put himself to sleep nightly, shutting out other thoughts by reciting over and over again The Lord's Prayer . . . how he had gone with the school to Tom Hicks' funeral and heard that whisper in his ear 'You fool, you fool . . . we can do big things for you . . . give us blood sacrifice . . . you are damned—he who ill-wishes his brother is accursed . . .' How he had resolutely avoided looking at the wall tablet for week upon week until his confirmation. And the calm that the 'Laying on of hands' had brought.

Old Bill returned again to the present. The Gloria had finished and choir and congregation were settling down to the Lesson. The Organist had elected to read the Old Testament passage, droning on until he came to the words 'and let the aged and the infirm be gone hence'. Old Bill was conscious of a mounting anger as he sensed a smirk on that aquiline face, reflected in an answering grin—swiftly erased by a tactful hand—by the Vicar. Bill calmed down during the Magnificat, but when the Vicar read the second lesson, the words came, 'the long rest awaiteth thee', and he had some difficulty in pronouncing them; at the same time Bill saw—reflected in his glasses— the organist behind him, convulsed with a fit of coughing; he could no longer doubt that he was being mocked. Of course the 'Nunc Dimittis' followed, and the opening words of Stanford's setting in A, were heralded by some fumbled organ notes.. 'Lord now lettest thou thy servant depart in peace; . . .' In peace indeed!

Old Bill's blood was up, and he simmered for the rest of the service, oblivious even of the Vicar's words of appreciation of his long service—surely a record?—before the sermon, and after the vestry prayer.

The choir members, well used to 'Old Bill's ways' put his extreme gruffness down to sadness or embarrassment, rather than to rage . . . and made their farewells. And Bill did an unusual thing—he went across to the 'Fortescue Arms' and downed six pints of draught ale before going home.

That night, for the first time in seventy-five years, he dreamed again of Gebal and Ammon and Amalek.

It was almost as before. . . . he saw a little girl, but now in modern dress, who was in a garden surrounded by toys with which she was playing. Then a shadow fell over her and she began to scream. The screams ended suddenly as an all-too-familiar figure became the focus of William's attention. The voice came from within the cowl. . . .

'You do not like the modern services, nor do we. Now the people think more of what they are saying than of the tunes, and that is bad for us . . . they even *think* about their prayers and that gives us pain. You love the old services, see—we can help . . .' and William saw a dark, hunched figure stealing into the church and gathering up the 'brighter, modern' hymn books and the 'Alternative Service' booklets. There was something about its swooping but mechanical movement that made him hope he could avoid seeing it closer. It was piling up the books in the chancel and pouring liquid over them. Flames engulfed the scene, and William awoke in his bed, bolt upright and panting, with a last whisper still in his ear. 'Give us blood, give . . . us . . . blood'.

It was 1am by his old Hunter. He pulled on some clothes and crept downstairs.

It was the week before Christmas, and Father Denis of the Catholic church in the centre of the large Flaxted Estate woke to a thunderous banging at his front door. He looked at his bedside clock: 1.30am.

A young couple from his community, Tom and Alice Carter, had a problem. Their small daughter, Sarah, was a sunny child, keen on her school, Sunday classes and full of fun. Within the last week, however, she had startled her parents by having vivid nightmares on several consecutive nights . . . waking up, shrieking 'Keep it away! Mummy! Save Me!' When pressed for details of her dreams, they seemed to be the same—at first she would see herself playing with her toys in the garden; then she would smell a hot smell—like Mummy's jam—and the gate would open and a figure come up the path toward her. It was 'like a toffee bitten off at the end' and made crying noises and seemed sticky. Just as it was about to flop on her, she would wake up.

What puzzled her parents most, was the positive and undeniable smell of hot jam remaining in her room.

Next night they settled the little girl down with a milk drink and Alice stayed until she went to sleep. They were swiftly awoken by the same screams, and the same story . . . and the same strong smell of jam. Sarah was sent to stay the week with a school-friend who lived on a different estate on the other side of the village. Apart from the strangeness of her surroundings, she spent a peaceful night. Not so her parents.

Tom had decided to sleep on the child's bed as best he could. He was tall and found it cramped, but finally dozed off. He did not dream, but he woke suddenly to an overpowering smell of hot jam. Jumping up, he walked straight into a sticky mess that enveloped him—like a mass of cold treacle he described it; but there was a skeleton structure of some sort, because he felt bones and a form within the encroaching mass. He reached the light with some difficulty, and there was nothing to be seen—just the smell of hot jam everywhere, and particularly in his nose. Thoroughly frightened, he ran for his Priest's house. The day that had now begun was the 23rd, and the weather was turning seasonable, the North wind bringing a flurry of snow. As he sped past St Osyth's church, Tom noted the rather obvious figures of 'concealed' police constables keeping watch. Their presence reassured him of normal things, and he remembered hearing that on the past two or three nights vandals had done damage within the church. Reaching Father Denis's door he banged vigorously.

It was this, of course, that roused the priest. Poor Father Denis was somewhat nonplussed at Tom's story, but sent him home to his wife, promising to follow on his bicycle. In doing so, Fr. Denis turned the corner by St. Osyth's and almost ran down an old man who slipped out from behind the churchyard wall and ducked into the shadow of a cottage opposite. His mind full of the errand, and the cold wind he was cycling against, he gave the incident no further thought. At the Carter's house, he spent some time soothing Alice, comfirmed for himself the smell of hot sugar or syrup, and walked round the house, blessing each room in turn.

Cycling home again a couple of hours later, he found a commotion at St. Osyth's; a fire engine and several bystanders milling about. From one of these he gathered that mischief had been done inside the church, under the very noses of the police; modern prayer books and carol sheets held in readiness for the Christmas Eve midnight service had been burned . . . but little damage done to anything else. Fr Denis thought of the old superstition whereby the Midnight Mass was a power to quell the forces of evil which were at their peak, just prior to the symbolic birth of the Saviour. He remounted his bicycle and rode thoughtfully and sleepily home, on a road that was becoming dusted with snow.

[333]

Next day it snowed steadily. At breakfast, after early Mass, Fr Denis pondered whether he should tell the police or the Anglican Vicar what he had seen; but on his way to see Alice and Tom, he decided that he would do a little detective work, concealing himself near St. Osyth's and see if anything occurred. It was not like him to be so nosy, he thought in mild surprise; but he was conscious of a growing conviction that it somehow linked with his own problem.

He found Tom and Alice understandably worried and confused, but no little relieved to hear that Sarah had spent a peaceful night.

By evening it had stopped snowing, and was very cold with a prospect of moonlight and frost, and Fr Denis—mindful of the approaching Festival with its extra duties—was inclined to seek his bed and stay there. However at 11.30 he let himself out of the house and made his way through the ankle-deep snow to St Osyth's church. He stationed himself in an alleyway opposite, glad of his muffler and mittens and extra pairs of socks. The church clock no longer announced the quarters (there were no bells) so he glanced at the luminous dial of his watch; several times he thought it must have stopped.

At length his patience and freezing feet were rewarded. An old man emerged furtively from the cottage opposite the church and crept across the road and over the churchyard wall. If there was a police presence it was more skilfully placed, for none was in evidence. Father Denis followed cautiously, mindful that he had no local knowledge of obstacles in the dark; but the moon had emerged and the snowy ground made his task quite easy. He saw the old man descend the stoke hold steps beside the Vestry. From there he used a torch which helped the priest to follow his movements. The old chap was carrying a bundle of newspaper under his arm, and he slipped round a rusty, defunct coke boiler and seemingly into a niche in the wall. This proved to be a slipway upward, which emerged into the chancel of the church between a pillar and a recess where the Rood Screen had fitted centuries earlier. The old man had dimmed his torch, but the snow outside reflected the moonlight and gave a dullish lighting. By craning his neck from the recess, Fr Denis could see the old man crouching down by a monument close to the *cantoris* choir stalls and fumbling with the string of his package. He momentarily held up a dead bird by its legs, then laid it on the ledge of the monument. He seemed to sway, then placed his forehead against the marble slab, and with a sigh, slumped like a bundle of old clothes. The priest was about to

[334]

start forward to help him when he became aware of a strong smell of jam pervading the stale incense, and of a cloud of brownish smoke emerging from the tomb itself, that agglomerated into a shapeless mass of pulpy material. Then just as suddenly, it thinned as if dispersing, and was gone . . . leaving the old man breathing stertorously.

Fr Denis looked at his watch: it was 1.20 am—Christmas Eve—and debated what to do. Horridly unsure of himself in this bizarre situation but calling on the saints departed to aid him, he crept toward the crumpled old man. Even as he did so, the heap of clothes stirred and shook and began to tremble . . . and again came the fruity, hot smell so that the priest felt he was choking, so overpowering was it. There before his eyes was the hideous pulpy ruin of a human frame, with what seemed to be staring eyes. Taken off guard, and swallowing furiously with nausea, the priest tried to find words to ward off the power of malice he felt, but fell senseless instead on top of the old man's body.

He was shaken roughly to his senses, to find it daylight and two police constables and an Inspector helping him into a pew. The old man was gone and so was the dead pigeon, but there was a mess around of torn drugget and ruined hymn books. The Rev Hayward, the Anglican priest, was there too, with a look of incredulity on his face.

'Father Denis', he gasped, 'What on earth are you doing here? Surely this is not your work?'

The poor Father, feeling faint and ill, shook his head wanly; in no wise heartened to hear the Inspector say, 'Better not say anything now, sir; we shall have to ask you for a formal statement about this matter as there will be charges.'

All Father Denis could do was groan, and to think to himself 'The power of evil is indeed triumphant at present!'

He pulled himself together, and persuaded them to accompany him home first, from where he could phone his Bishop. The police agreed, and the five of them—including the nonplussed Hayward—walked through the snow to the Catholic church house.

There they found a further complication: not only a few anxious inquirers who were wondering why the early celebration had not been held, but also a near-hysterical Tom Carter with the story that Sarah had had the nightmare at her friend's house, and that the friend had woken and *both* had seen the dreadful shape that terrified her dreams.

Suddenly everyone present was looking at Fr Denis, who felt his head was going to burst. Then, like a wondrous inspiration, a course of action occurred to him.

He sent Tom home with as much reassurance as he could muster; promising him a visit within a few hours; though clearly it did not carry much conviction for the poor fellow.

'Now, Inspector and gentlemen,' he said, 'You have been very patient. I need to make one phone call, to Malmesford Abbey, to summon an old Priest here. Do you think you could get him collected in a police car? It will take hours for him to get here by public transport now there is no railway. It really is important that he attend. I will then make a full statement of what occurred last night: it is very complicated and I don't feel up to telling it several times over.'

The Inspector looked dubious, but the Rev Haywood took a positive lead and said, 'Please do it Inspector. Since it will fall to me to make any formal charge, I am not willing to do so until we have sifted the matter thoroughly. I am willing to accept Fr Denis's assurance that this person is necessary to clearing the matter up.'

Father O'Connor, the old priest summoned so dramatically to Flaxted, seemed so large and benevolent and childishly entertained at his ride in a police car, that things immediately took on a better aspect.

He listened attentively to Fr Denis's story, as did the Rev Hayward, the Inspector and the Constable taking shorthand notes. The last two looked decidedly incredulous (as well they might) at the strange story, but Fr O'Connor who seemed to have automatically presided over the session, simply murmured 'Yes, yes', soothingly.

They went out to inspect the snow and tracks across the churchyard to the stoke hold, which partly confirmed the priest's story, for clearly his steps had followed the other. They squeezed into the hidden passage into the church. 'I didn't even know it was there', muttered Mr Hayward, at which Fr O'Connor smiled. The old Priest was most interested in the Fortescue tomb and monument 'Erected 50 years after his death I note'. He turned decisively to the Inspector and to the Anglican.

'I need a couple of hours, gentlemen. Your permission—and your company, please, Inspector, to visit this William Stokes, whom Mr Hayward says is his former Sexton; and I need to look at your Parish Records Mr Hayward; I only hope they are not elsewhere? Oh, good, you have them here in the Vestry; excellent. Well, gentlemen, you priests have much to do; I suggest we meet at the police station this afternoon, eh?'

Such was the determination and conviction of the old priest, that his proposal was accepted. Rev Hayward saying, 'Yes, yes; anything to clear up this awful business before Christmas.'

'If this was a fictional story,' said Fr O'Connor, when they were all ensconced in the Inspector's office, 'I could hope to round everything off and to give a convincing explanation; but we have a real situation here, and much of it is my conjecture and a lot of loose ends. I'm no occultist, just an old, doddery parish priest who has had some odd experiences, that have made me study these matters a little more than most; that's all.

'The Inspector and I have seen Mr Stokes, and we think we understand his involvement, even if its effects are hard to believe.' (The Inspector nodded vigorously in agreement).

'I can tell you that we are dealing here with at least two things. Firstly a species of 'little devil', or whatever it might be. Spengle called them flibbertigibbets, whereas I believe Latimer had them docketed as relatives of Puck! And, yes, Inspector, I see your smile! It was also a term of our parents for flighty young girls of easy virtue! Whatever they are, their character is malignant and requires fresh blood to activate them. There was a degree of malice in the attempts to oust old William from the Choir; and if I dare suggest it, some feeling that music and ritual are as important as prayer, which plays right into the hands of such—er—'infestations'. That awakened the dormant evil with which old Bill had truckled before in his youth. His rage made it easier—but what complicated things most was the 'presence'—if so I may call it!—of old Squire Fortescue.

'I commend your parish records, Mr Hayward, they are excellently kept and the story is there for anyone to read. Squire Fortescue made his fortune with preserves, but he also made an evil reputation for himself for offences against young children. I don't wish to particularise further; but after one particularly outrageous attempt on a young girl, her father and uncle—who worked in the preserve factory—took their revenge and attempted to stop the evil for once and all. They almost succeeded. It seems they may have tampered with the gantry around the fruit vats, and pushed—or in some other way caused the fall of—the Squire into the boiling jam mixture! He died instantly of

[337]

course, and I suspect the apparition seen by Fr Denis and the Carter family is linked with his last living moment and condition at death.

'There was no direct evidence to prosecute the avengers, and to be fair, the Fortescue family were anxious to hush the matter up. Although Jasper was interred in the family tomb in the chancel, it was without benefit of service and there was no memorial. That was carried out from his son's will, some 50 years later.

'Now the luring of old William to the church at night served two ends, as I see it; it gave the little devils the substance to wreak their malicious pranks, and it brought a use-able victim within reach of Jasper's latent evil, waiting a source of energy to aid his "purpose"— whatever that may have been! I confess I do not understand the "choice" of Sarah Carter to torment; though it may be that there is some connection with the past of which we—and they—are ignorant.' He paused.

'So long as Mr Stokes retained good health there was no particular threat to his life; in fact Jasper Fortescue would have every reason— assuming that word applies to his actions—to prolong William's existence: he supplied the energy needed to materialise and work. But if Stokes weakened (and he was in his mid-80s remember) then Fortescue could drain his resource like a vampire or parasite, and kill him.

'From my experience, I am confident that the return of old Mr Stokes to the proper communion of your church, and an especial prayer for the rest and forgiveness of Jasper Fortescue, will solve the problem. Without the malice the "little devils" are useless; they need hatred as well as blood, and a simple blessing will remove them.

'Since the Fortescues were Anglican and St Osyth's is in Anglican hands' (his eyes twinkled), 'I suggest not a special mass, but that as part of your Christmas Eve communion tonight, you move to the tomb and say a special prayer for Jasper Fortescue's peace, and give him your blessing, Mr Hayward. At a time when we recall the birth of Hope for Man, it should prove particularly effective!'

The Inspector intervened: 'This is all beyond me, gentlemen, though you all seem to be nodding agreement; and if Mr Haywood is not pressing any charges—and I can see there are none—I can leave it to you to settle; but many years ago I *was* involved in a strange case where they "cleaned up" afterwards, as it were, with an Exorcism: Bishop, bell, book and candle, sort of thing. Yet here you are saying a little prayer will undo all this evil? I find that incredible!'

Father O'Connor smiled. 'Prayer is not little, nor trivial. It is the absolute essence of the church. The papers today make much of the falling-off in church attendance, and it is (sadly) true. But those "falling off" have been they who viewed "church" as a custom, a habit, "something done", but not *lived*. The congregations of today are regrettably smaller, but they are much more committed in Faith, and their prayer is particularly efficacious, whatever the creed. It is one reason why malignant hauntings are dying out! Believe me, Inspector, it *will* suffice.' He sighed.

'It is Christmas Eve, and we are united in our wish to celebrate the authentic miracle of Christ. Happily we have that in common. I suggest that I come to your Midnight Communion with Mr Stokes and share your celebration. Father Denis will include a prayer for all Christian souls in his service at the Catholic church, and our united Faith will end this unpleasant episode.

It was snowing again as Christmas morning began and the midnight congregation issued from St. Osyth's. The Rev Hayward shaking hands with his congregation at the West door, detained Old William and Fr O'Connor.

'Bill, you must let me see you safely home, and wish you a Happy Christmas', he said. 'Later on, perhaps you will join us for dinner at the Vicarage, where we are hoping to entertain Father O'Connor, Father Denis and the Carter family. We have decided to "pool" our resources this year. We have much to be thankful for.'

It needs, perhaps, to be added that no further disturbances of the sort were experienced in the village community. Mr Stokes lived to be 93 and until his death carried the title of Churchwarden *Emeritus* in recognition of his services to St. Osyth's.

ACKNOWLEDGEMENTS

The Publisher has made every effort to contact the Copyright holders, but wishes to apologise to those he has been unable to trace. Grateful acknowledgement is made for permission to reprint the following:

'The Kit-Bag' (1908) and 'Transition' (1917) by Algernon Blackwood. Copyright © A.P. Watt on behalf of Sheila Reeves.

'The Irtonwood Ghost' by Elinor Glyn (1911). Copyright © Estate of Elinor Glyn, courtesy of Mrs George

'Bone of his Bone' by E.G. Swain (1912). Copyright © Estate of E.G. Swain, courtesy of Mrs Bertha Turner.

'The Snow' by Hugh Walpole (1929). Copyright © Estate of Hugh Walpole, courtesy of Mrs Eva Reichmann.

'Smee' by A.M. Burrage, courtesy J.S.F. Burrage.

'The Prescription' by Marjorie Bowen (1933). Copyright © Marjorie Bowen, courtesy Hilary Long.

'The Demon King' by J.B. Priestley (1934). Copyright © Estate of J.B. Priestley, reproduced by permission of the Late J.B. Priestley Estate.

'Lucky's Grove' by H. Russell Wakefield (1940). Copyright © H. Russell Wakefield, reproduced by permission of Curtis Brown Ltd.

'Christmas Meeting' by Rosemary Timperley (1952). Copyright © Rosemary Timperley by kind permission.

'Someone in the Lift' by L.P. Hartley (1955). Copyright © 1973 Executors of the Estate of L.P. Hartley, by permission of Hamish Hamilton Ltd.

an apple. The voices massed toward the door of the flat. 'Don't offer them money,' Jill choked. 'Give them that present.'

I lunged for the mantelpiece, thrusting bodies aside. Everyone seemed determined to ignore what was happening, to leave the decision to me; I waded through entangled conversations and clusters of faces like blank bubbles. I threw out my hand and caught up the cardboard box, and the student pinioned my arm. 'Don't touch it, you fool!' he cried. 'Not now!'

The voices were at the door, roaring a single note or a million, a sound which could never have emerged from throats but might have burst forth from a tunnel. I struggled with him. 'One moment more,' he pleaded. 'Just to see.'

And Jill shrieked and snatched the cardboard box from me and threw it into the fire.

For a moment the trembling flames were crushed, struggling, helpless. The bell crashed like tons of drowned iron; the voices squealed in triumph. Then the flames sprang up, swarmed up the corners of the box, and a minute later it puffed like rotten wood and collapsed into shapeless ash. The bell swung up into an aching silence; a draught muttered where the voices had been.

We waited until Bill knocked on the flat door. 'Why on earth did I go downstairs?' he wondered.

'So much for your myths,' Jill said to the student. 'Damn you.'

I controlled myself. 'There's one thing I want to know,' I said. 'What did you put in that box?'

'Surely you can see that that doesn't matter,' the student said. 'Just something to give form to a belief, that's all. It was a sort of anti-Christmas present, actually. The antithesis of a Christmas present. An experiment, mate, you know. Or do you mean the actual contents of the box?'

'We don't need to know that,' I told him. 'In fact, I think Jill would rather not.' I hit him only once, but he fell.

'Here, hang on,' Bill protested. The others looked away. That I expected; but Jill clutched my shoulders and cried: 'Bring him round! Bring him round, for God's sake! How do we know where he was before he met us? How do we know he didn't give someone else a present?'

And now we can't bring him round.

CHRISTMAS ENTERTAINMENT

by Daphne Froome

Daphne Froome's Christmas tale, based on the
nineteenth century stage experiments by
Professor Pepper to conjure up 'ghosts' in cunningly
placed mirrors, originally appeared in
The Fifteenth Fontana Book of Great Ghosts
Stories (1979).

P rofessor Conway, the well-known scientist, opened the door of his study, which, with its leather armchairs, green velvet cushions, and its parchment-shaped lamp in one corner, was his favourite room in the house.

There was almost half an hour to spare before the children were due to arrive for the Christmas party, just time to make a note of an idea which had been running through his mind all day. The Professor hated writing, particularly when he was working under the influence of some sudden inspiration. He hated the expression of his thoughts to be delayed even by the time it took to form the letters with a pen, so now, padding rather heavily across the shabbily carpeted floor, he bent and lifted the black plastic cover of his tape-recorder, set the reel spinning, and dictated his idea at considerable length into the microphone. Having used the tape to the end, he removed it, numbered it and filed it away in the appropriate cabinet with all the others. Then he stood gazing complacently round at the walls, crowded on every side with shelves and cupboards, each crammed

with data concerning every conceivable kind of psychical pheno-
menon, from vampires, via poltergeists, down to the mere unresolved
echo in an empty, modern flatlet.

For years he had spent his spare time happily ghost-hunting. His
hobby had given him an excellent excuse to travel to places all over
the world, and to meet all kinds of people, different from and far more
interesting than the academics who were normally his associates.
What was more, as not one of the apparently mysterious incidents
reported to him had withstood a properly organized scientific scrutiny,
he had convinced himself absolutely that ghosts did not exist. Now he
was ready to begin writing the book that would dispel for ever the
mists of superstition and probably make him a substantial sum in
royalties as well.

Plugging in the electric typewriter he sat down at his desk and
tapped out the title page:

THE FINAL DISAPPEARANCE
by
Harold E. Conway

There was no time for any more now. What a nuisance this party was
proving to be! Mrs Barker, the wife of his closest colleague, had
established some years ago the tradition of holding a Christmas party
for the children of the College staff. This year, however, she had
taken it into her head to go away and foist the whole thing on to him.
He had not liked, either, the acid way she had remarked that for once
he could give up his solitary, self-centred existence and put his large
house to good use.

He went thoughtfully over to the window and stood looking up at
the darkening sky. It had been raining, and the recently lighted
antique lamps, in keeping with the architecture of the small square in
which the house was situated, shone peacefully as inverted mirror
images in the limpid water of the puddles. Suddenly the reflections
were disturbed by a crowd of small boys as they came splashing along.

His guests were beginning to arrive.

Mrs Megan Dent, the Professor's cleaner and cook, a tall, smart,
energetic young woman, lifted a tray of hot mince pies from the oven
and began to arrange them on a large dish, chattering all the while to

her husband, Tim, who, blowing up the last of the balloons, was for once unable to stem her flow of words.

'There's the first child arriving now. Oh I do hope the party will go all right, everyone's bound to blame me if it doesn't! I must say it's not at all like it was last Christmas in Mrs Barker's house when everywhere was bright and seasonal-looking. The Professor would only let me put up a few bits of holly—not that any amount of decoration would make this place look cheerful. Then again, instead of you dressed up nicely as Father Christmas, doling out presents (and what generous presents they were!), there's to be a demonstration of some queer optical illusion in his old lecture room that's full of cobwebs and cold as charity because it's been out of use for years!'

Mr Dent, deciding the balloon had reached a satisfactory size, stopped blowing, tied it securely with string and said, 'Actually the Professor's going to conjure up a ghost. It's an old trick but I don't expect the kids will have seen it before. I reckon they'll love it; it's far more exciting than Father Christmas.'

'You only say that because you've spent every evening this week helping him to get it ready.'

'You'll see later on. I bet it will give you the creeps!'

After tea Mr and Mrs Dent escorted the children, still consuming the remains of the cakes and sweets, into the small lecture theatre for the entertainment.

Professor Conway, twitching slightly, was beckoning Mr Dent. 'I think we ought to check everything's all right before we begin.'

Mr Dent pursued him on to the stage and disappeared behind the curtain. His wife, after hesitating for a moment, followed curiously behind.

'How's it done?' she asked.

'Quite simply really,' the Professor answered in a patronizing tone. 'You just have this large sheet of plate glass'—he gave the glass a loud resounding tap—'and by setting it up at an angle of forty-five degrees to your audience the light rays are reflected in such a way that it looks as if the spectators are seeing a transparent ghost behind the glass instead of an illuminated dummy placed out of sight at the side of the stage.'

Mrs Dent glanced at the dummy. 'It's very cleverly constructed. Who made it?'

'The Professor,' Tim Dent replied, then added more quietly, 'being a bachelor he's a dab hand with a needle and thread!'

'They mustn't realize the glass is there, of course,' the Professor continued. 'I hope you like the way your husband has camouflaged the edges with his paintings of witches and dragons.'

'You get a better idea of them from a distance of course,' Mr Dent put in rather diffidently.

The Professor coughed impatiently at the interruption. 'The illusion is very convincing. When it was first demonstrated by one Professor Pepper in the nineteenth century, people came flocking to see it. Plays with his ghosts in were all the rage. They were better staged, of course, than ours will be, with real actors playing the ghosts, but the principle was the same.'

Glancing at the dummy once more, Meg noticed that the Professor had neglected to fasten one of the shoes. As she was a neat, tidy person, the sight of the trailing lace worried her. She walked across, bent down, and knotted it in a secure double bow.

Standing up, she clutched at one of the arms to steady herself. It felt soft, almost human to the touch. As she moved, the grotesquely featured head rolled forward towards her.

'Hey, be careful!' shouted Tim. 'What are you trying to do, wreck the show? You'd better be getting back to your seat. The Professor will be waiting to make his introductory speech.'

'Before I came to live in this house,' the Professor began, 'it was occupied by a man named Sir Arthur Stanbrook. Now, there is no doubt that Sir Arthur was a very clever scientist—he was an expert in electronics, like me. We often helped each other with our work; in fact, we soon became friends. We shared the same hobby, too. We were both fascinated by anything supernatural. I've always found it an absorbing subject—investigating ghostly happenings and proving that they don't exist. But Sir Arthur spent his time going round saying they did. Can you imagine someone as intelligent as that considering it possible that ghosts exist?'

The Professor paused for effect, then went on.

'I thought it was dreadful that so clever a man should believe in such superstitious nonsense, so I challenged him to produce for me one of his ghosts. Of course he was unable to do so, and I am afraid we quarrelled violently. It is now over twenty years since Sir Arthur died, but when I decided to conjure up an apparition for your entertainment today I couldn't resist the temptation to make it like Sir Arthur. Later on I will try to explain how the trick is done, and perhaps one or two of you might be prepared to come up on to the stage and be turned into temporary spectres yourselves. Now, if someone will kindly put out the lights. . . .'

During the rather apprehensive whispering and shuffling that followed, Tim Dent switched on the arc lamps and then, drawing back the curtains, revealed the ghostly image. After about a minute he switched the lamps off, then on, so that the apparition disappeared and reappeared again. Then he walked round behind the sheet of glass and stood in the circle of chalk he had carefully positioned so that the body of the ghost seemed to be superimposed on to his own. A nice touch this, Tim thought. The children had suddenly become very quiet, he noticed. Perhaps they were beginning to get bored. He sauntered over to the edge of the stage and stood there, rather self-consciously, bowing.

His wife sat watching him quite proudly. She had seated herself at the back of the room, as far away as possible from the illusion on the stage. She was glad to see the image flicker and become blurred— perhaps the demonstration would go wrong and they could all spend the rest of the time playing games and singing a few songs. But the spectre gradually began to appear again; only now the general shape had taken on more realistic contours, the mitten-like hands possessed fingers, and the mask-like face was transformed into something distinctly human. She opened her mouth to shout a warning to Tim, but for once the power of speech utterly deserted her and she could only gasp, fishlike.

Professor Conway had descended from the stage and was walking between the rows of children, studying their obviously delighted reaction with smug satisfaction. Then he turned to survey the shadowy reflection he had created. It was certainly very realistic, but there was something odd about it when seen from this angle, he thought, a distortion that gave the impression that the sagging limbs were straightened and the lolling head had reared upright above shoulders suddenly squared. Then, as Tim extinguished the arc lamps, the spectre vanished and there was a roar of appreciative applause from the audience.

The Professor turned to Meg, huddled pale and mute in her chair. 'What a success! Look at them now, all pestering Tim to let them take a turn at being a ghost!—I say, are you all right?'

[321]

'I feel rather faint,' Meg whispered. 'I think I'll go outside for a bit.'

Professor Conway smiled condescendingly down at her. 'Good heavens, Megan, it was only a trick!'

He elbowed his way back up on to the stage, among the crowd of excited children, and shifted the dummy in order that they could stand, one by one, in its place. Controlling so many energetic youngsters was certainly absorbing work, but he still found time to worry about the strangeness of that final image. He found it impossible to concentrate on the problem with all these children enjoying themselves so enthusiastically around him. It was extraordinary how long it took them to get tired. The party seemed to continue for an almost interminable time, but when it had eventually dragged to a close he turned to Tim and said, 'Really, the ghost looked most peculiar the last time you showed it. Could we see it again, do you think? Your wife seemed quite upset by it, too.'

'You don't mean you were scared, Meg?' Tim laughed.

'You just sit here with me, Mrs Dent, and we'll soon solve all this with a simple, scientific explanation,' the Professor added.

'I'd rather not—there's all the clearing up to be done.'

'Oh do stop fussing, we can clear up tomorrow—it's Saturday.' Tim sounded impatient as he rather wearily began to demonstrate the spectral effect yet again. 'I can't see anything wrong,' he called. 'Everything seems to be working perfectly to me.'

'I agree. Your wife and I were mistaken, of course.' Professor Conway beamed at Meg. 'Let me give you a drink before you go— you've certainly earned it.'

He rose, and ushering them into his study, he happily dispensed generous quantities of whisky to them both.

The house seemed very silent after Megan and Tim's departure. It was just the contrast, the Professor decided, after the pandemonium of the afternoon. Thank goodness it was over. The cost of the food had been quite excessive, not to mention all the extra electricity they had used. Megan was certainly not the most economical of housekeepers; there were electric fires and lights still burning in all the downstairs rooms. Wandering round switching them off, he came to the lecture room, where the image was still distinctly visible on the screen.

He stood just inside the door, surveying it gloatingly. It really had amused the children—they would not think very highly of Mrs

Barker's parties after this! The effect really was extraordinarily good. The arc lamps seemed to be giving a far more powerful image than he had anticipated, too, and from here they almost produced the odd impression that the spectre was lit by some inward source of its own. It also looked disconcertingly like Sir Arthur. He thought he saw the momentary gleam of white teeth as the mouth opened and closed again . . . The Professor blinked, then fixed the apparition with a coldly questioning scientific stare. He wished he hadn't given the thing eyes—even from this distance they seemed to be glowering back at him. And now the tall figure, swaying slightly, appearing to become more solid every moment, moved with slow deliberation out of the circle of chalk, straight through the glass, down from the stage and along the aisle between the rows of chairs. Professor Conway suddenly realized that he could even hear the man's heavy gold watch chain clinking with a small rhythmic jingle. Still illuminated in the darkness by an eerie glow, its bald head gleaming, its loosely knotted tie flapping, the ghost turned and inclined its head, in a supercilious fashion, towards him, before disappearing into the corridor.

Professor Conway hesitated only momentarily before giving chase. He caught a vague glimpse of it making its way across the darkened hall before it disappeared from sight. Glancing into each of the rooms as he passed, he reached and flung open the front door, and stood surveying the scene outside. The rain clouds had given way to a clear sky and the moon irradiated the area with almost daylight brightness. The cutting wind had cleared the square of people; it was quite deserted.

Very thoughtfully he went back into the house. The whole thing must be a hoax perpetrated by Tim, he decided. This was the only possible explanation. And Meg, of course, had pretended to feel faint at the appearance of the ghost during the party, just to add to the effect. Tim had probably by now crept into the house by the back door and they were no doubt waiting together in the lecture room to plague him with further stupid, infantile pranks. Well, they would not be given the opportunity to fool him a second time. He went into his study, and filling a large glass with the remainder of the whisky from the decanter, he stamped upstairs with it into his bedroom.

Stumbling into the kitchen the following morning, Professor Conway set the left-over coffee from the day before re-heating on the stove, then turned to address Tim.

[323]

'I did not think much of your idea of a walking ghost,' he stated acidly.

Tim looked confused. 'Walking ghost? What walking ghost?'

The Professor brooded wearily over the pungent liquid full of grounds in the saucepan. 'You didn't return then, after the party?'

Meg looked at the Professor sharply. 'Hardly! We'd had quite a long enough day of it, as it was.'

'Well, someone played a ridiculous prank on me.' The Professor's red-rimmed brown eyes glared blearily into Meg's wide grey ones. 'Those loose slates rattling on the roof disturbed me, too. It was a very stormy night. I hope you haven't forgotten that I've asked you once or twice to climb up and deal with them, Mr Dent.'

Tim, with the air of a man fighting to retain the final vestiges of his patience, washed the last of the mugs, handed it to his wife to dry, squeezed the suds from the dishmop, pulled the plug out of the sink and waited while the water bubbled slowly down the drain before replying, 'You sometimes seem to forget, Professor, that I do have my own work to do, and if there's anything to be dealt with today it had better be the vacuum cleaner. It blew up when my wife plugged it in this morning—why, she might very easily have been killed!'

The Professor, haughtily ignoring Tim completely, turned out the gas beneath the saucepan and stepped across to the refrigerator for milk. As he opened the door a small stream of water dribbled out and spread into a pool on the floor. 'Why, look at this! The thing's defrosted. Everything's swimming in water.' He looked up. 'The blasted plug's in pieces!'

'Those children!' Tim laughed weakly. 'Little demons! They must have done it. Last year at Mrs Barker's we had hunt the thimble and it took us days to sweep up, the horsehair stuffing they'd torn out of the chaise-longue.'

'Nonsense, it was perfectly all right when I went to bed.'

'Then perhaps you and Tim really did conjure up a ghost,' Meg cried. 'Perhaps it was that you saw walking. Perhaps it did for the vacuum cleaner, too. Who knows what it might not get up to next?'

The Professor swore loudly. 'Of course there isn't a ghost! If that dummy is giving you hysterics I'll go and burn the thing now, right away!'

Rushing from the kitchen, Professor Conway arrived, breathless, in the lecture room.

The apparition that once more stared down from the sheet of plate glass seemed to be standing watching him, the face creased in the frown of malignant concentration which the late Sir Arthur Stanbrook always wore when wrestling with some particularly taxing problem. The figure was already beginning to move.

'I'll soon put paid to you!' the Professor shouted. 'I'll turn the lamps off!'

Running forward he mounted the steps on to the stage and hurled himself towards the switch.

Tim and Meg reached the doorway just in time to see a brilliant flash reflected in the glass, as the body of the Professor slumped on to the stage.

The ghost of Sir Arthur Stanbrook had disappeared, and, perfectly distinct behind the glass, that of Professor Conway had taken its place.